Buried Lives

Buried Lives

Incarcerated in Early America

edited by

MICHELE LISE TARTER

and

RICHARD BELL

THE UNIVERSITY OF GEORGIA PRESS
Athens & London

© 2012 by the University of Georgia Press
Athens, Georgia 30602
www.ugapress.org
All rights reserved
Designed by Walton Harris
Set in 10/13 New Baskerville
Printed and bound by Thomson-Shore

The paper in this book meets the guidelines for
permanence and durability of the Committee on
Production Guidelines for Book Longevity of the
Council on Library Resources.

Printed in the United States of America

16   15   14   13   12   P   5   4   3   2   1

Library of Congress Cataloging-in-Publication Data

Buried lives : incarcerated in early America /
edited by Michele Lise Tarter and Richard Bell.
        p.   cm.
Includes index.
ISBN-13: 978-0-8203-4119-4 (cloth : alk. paper)
ISBN-10: 0-8203-4119-3 (cloth : alk. paper)
ISBN-13: 978-0-8203-4120-0 (pbk. : alk. paper)
ISBN-10: 0-8203-4120-7 (pbk. : alk. paper)
1. Prisoners–United States–History. 2. Prisons–United
States–History. 3. Inmates of institutions–United
States–History. 4. Punishment–United States–History.
I. Tarter, Michele Lise, 1960– II. Bell, Richard, 1978–
HV9466.B847 2012
365'.97309033–dc23   2011030205

British Library Cataloging-in-Publication Data available

For our families.

CONTENTS

Foreword

MICHAEL MERANZE

SYSTEMS OF INCARCERATION HAUNT American society and the American imagination. Whether it involves the approximately two million men and women held in jails and prisons, the youths held in juvenile halls and lockups, the growing number of imperial lockups from Guantanamo to Bagram and numberless other secret locations, it is difficult to grasp the contours of the American present without considering the costs, effects, and reasons for our commitment to incarceration. Although it is clear that the United States' commitment to systems of incarceration has expanded dramatically since the 1970s, the importance of incarceration to American society—as the essays in *Buried Lives* make clear—has a much longer history.

Buried Lives saw its conception during a conference at the McNeil Center for Early American Studies in Philadelphia in 2009. Over two days, scholars drawn from early American history and literature considered the provenance of America's identity as an "incarceration nation." This theme proved somewhat controversial, for what emerged out of the papers was something less than a "nation." Instead, the scholars—eight of whom are represented in this collection of ten essays—illuminated a constellation of incarcerative institutions and experiences spread out in time and place. These scholars presented a series of discrete histories that shared common practices of incarceration but little (at least before the nineteenth century) common reflection or purpose. Still, as Leslie Patrick pointed out in her comments at the conference, the notion of an "incarceration nation" did point us to one very significant issue — the connection in the Atlantic social and political imagination between the early American republic and the establishment of modern systems of imprisonment. If for no other reason, the history of the United States and the history of incarceration have been joined in a fundamental way ever since.

I stress both the timing and the theme of the conference because they are important for grasping the historiographical and intellectual significance of the essays in *Buried Lives*. This volume contributes to what we may think of as the third wave of histories of incarceration since the field was rejuvenated in the 1970s. The first wave comprised the seminal works of the 1970s: David Rothman's *The Discovery of the Asylum*, Michael Ignatieff's *A Just Measure of Pain*, and towering above both, Michel Foucault's *Discipline and Punish*. These were followed, with some delay, by a group of works that included my own *Laboratories of Virtue*, Adam Hirsch's *The Rise of the Penitentiary*, and Patricia O'Brien's *The Promise of Punishment*. *Buried Lives*, in turn, joins Rebecca McLennan's recent *The Crisis of Imprisonment* and Robert Perkinson's *Texas Tough* in their efforts to break incarceration free of its historiographical roots in the rise of the penitentiary.

Indeed, while the history of the penitentiary remains a fundamental reference point among the essays in *Buried Lives*, it is not the only one. One of the important accomplishments of the authors — and here I think especially of Billy G. Smith, Simon P. Newman, and Jacqueline Cahif on the ways that inmates could use almshouses and workhouses for their own purposes; Jennifer Lawrence Janofsky on the irregularity of prison discipline; and Jodi Schorb and Daniel E. Williams on the reversibility of memoirs of confinement — is their capacity to show the many nodes and uses of incarceration. Reading these essays makes it impossible not to recognize that inmates as well as authorities made use of these institutions and that the boundaries between incarcerative institutions and the wider society were often remarkably porous. In part, these essays take up the themes of another historiographical milestone of the 1970s, the essays collected in *Albion's Fatal Tree*. Compared to Foucault,

Ignatieff, and Rothman, the authors of that volume—Peter Linebaugh and Douglas Hay prominent among them—were more concerned with the everyday imbrications between crime, punishment, and social relations in communities beyond institutional walls. It is this second line of investigation that has allowed a greater appreciation of the uses to which incarceration has been put—and not simply by the authorities.

In their emphasis on the mediations surrounding incarceration—and the possibilities of reversals within incarcerative settings—the essays of *Buried Lives* also highlight a historiographical paradox. There has been a reversal in the stability and status of both the prison specifically and incarceration more generally since the 1970s. Foucault, Ignatieff, and Rothman wrote in a moment when it seemed possible that the age of the penitentiary was coming to an end. Although criticized (somewhat unfairly, to my mind) for understating resistance to power, they constructed their narratives to highlight systems that were then vulnerable. In other words, their works provided a historical context for movements in society that were then denaturalizing the prison.

In the decades since, scholars have placed still greater emphasis on resistance to institutions of incarceration, but all the while these institutions have become even more deeply embedded within society and the state. The authors of the 1970s wrote to help bury a set of institutions; the authors of *Buried Lives* are struggling to prevent the memories of inmates from being buried by those institutions. Indeed, they write in a moment when these institutions are more powerful than ever. Prophecies of the last days of the penitentiary have proved to be wide of the mark. On the contrary, it now seems impossible to imagine America without them.

Part of the reason that the United States has become an "incarceration nation" is the historical combination of slavery and expansion. While many scholars have demonstrated the connections between race and imprisonment, and while some current commentators draw upon the legacies of slavery to explain the contemporary explosion of incarceration, the authors of *Buried Lives* take a different and quite provocative tack. Instead of seeing slavery and the penitentiary as parallel institutions—or arguing that after the Civil War imprisonment took over the functions previously fulfilled by the plantation and the slave code—Jason T. Sharples, Susan Eva O'Donovan, and Matthew J. Clavin demonstrate the ways in which jails were the servants of the slave regime even as they became loci for challenges to slavery's power. Rather than relying on the tired dichotomies of south versus north and premodern versus modern, *Buried Lives* reveals that imprisonment and slavery were intertwined both in British imperial expansion and then in the continental expansion of the nineteenth-century United States.

This unexpected intersection between imperial expansion and incarceration brings us to the final theme that I would like to highlight: the relationship between incarceration and national identity. This relationship is highlighted most clearly by Judith I. Madera on floating prison-hulks and Caleb Smith's consideration of Harry Hawser's prison poetry. While separated by time and context—Madera focusing on a Revolutionary War experience, Smith on a debate in the 1840s on prison reform—each highlights the ways that prison narratives and prison experience became, through acts of authorship and dissemination, symbols of national character. In the one case, Americans used the "cruelty" of the British army to differentiate American from British; in the other, the poetry of Hawser was deployed to protect the American experiment in separate confinement from charges of cruelty. In this complex war of words about the national nature of incarceration, the linkages between the penitentiary and the American republic took shape.

As a whole, then, the essays in *Buried Lives* force us to think anew about the nature of the incarceration nation that is the United States. In fact, they offer new ways to think about the relationship between incarceration's past and the ways we narrate that history. They reveal that what was at stake in the nineteenth century was less the birth of incarcerative institutions than their increasing and systematic importance. Colonials used incarceration in a range of places and for a variety of purposes. What they did not do was begin to think about those institutions in a systematic way or to insist that they were central to the nature of the state. These were largely nineteenth-century developments. Moreover, these developments were not simply an intensification of practice; rather, they marked an intensification of the imagination. The United States *became* an incarceration nation in the nineteenth century because incarceration grew so crucial to an internal and international debate about the nature of the United States. *Buried Lives* has done more than preserve the image of those otherwise forgotten. Indeed, it enables us to see more clearly the work that has gone into the persistence of American imprisonment both in the past and in the present.

Buried Lives

"He is a man buried alive; to be dug out
in the slow round of years."
    —CHARLES DICKENS, *American Notes* (1842)

Introduction

MICHELE LISE TARTER AND RICHARD BELL

HENRY MILLS WAS EXECUTED at half past two in the afternoon on July 15, 1816. He had been sentenced to die for murdering his wife, a woman he had long suspected of faithlessness, and their five young children. Angry, exultant, and thoroughly unrepentant when first apprehended, Mills's demeanor had changed dramatically ever since the judge had passed down the capital verdict and set the date of his execution. According to visitors to the jail in Galesboro, Pennsylvania, the prospect of his own impending death wrought a complete change of character in the prisoner. Now Mills spent his days hunched over in prayer or absorbed in religious reading, looking for all the world like the very model of a "person truly penitent." In conversations with the earnest clergymen who visited him in the jail, Mills quickly began to acknowledge the depths of his prior depravity and paranoia. He could soon be heard explaining to anyone who would listen that "Sabbath breaking and his disobedience to his parents, were the first inlets to the great sin, for which he was to suffer an ignominious death."[1]

Brought to the scaffold in chains, Mills used his last words to express his sincere hope that everyone assembled to watch him swing that July

1

day would learn from his own "dreadful example" (see figure 1). Then, "with a firm step," the condemned man took his final position, launching himself into eternity. He would hang there for three-quarters of an hour, the crowd watching in awed silence, before the sheriff cut down his body and delivered it to Galesboro's sexton for interment.[2]

The proceedings of the day had unfolded precisely as planned. Everyone—the sheriff, the jailer, the local ministers, the townspeople, and even the prisoner himself—acted their parts perfectly. Justice had been served; power had been displayed; forgiveness had been begged; and lessons had been learned. In the weeks to come, a pamphlet distilling the affecting moral messages this execution had summoned for all those gathered in Galesboro would make the rounds, dramatizing Mills's journey toward judgment for readers farther afield.

There was only one problem: Henry Mills did not exist. He was a fictional character—a phantom. Anyone who had attended a real execution, or read about others in newspapers or in one of the many moralizing pamphlets this account subtly parodied, knew that execution days rarely went off so smoothly. Mills's idealized performance had never happened; it was too good to be true. In fact, Mills had been dreamed up by an anonymous author to help parents in Massachusetts—not a make-believe town in Pennsylvania—teach their sons and daughters "to regard their future welfare" and develop the proper respect for state power and socially sanctioned codes of conduct. Although the pamphlet telling the story of Mills's life and death may have fooled some children, savvy parents were surely in on the hoax and recognized the tale for the didactic fantasy it was.[3]

In reality, messages about obedience to parents, to God, and to the law were easily obscured or overlooked during these grisly justice rituals. Gathered in town squares and city commons across colonial and early national America, spectators were rarely so reverent or easily awed. On the contrary, they often found something in the condemned man's history or demeanor to arouse their sympathy, causing them to boo as the hangman did his work or to jeer at him if the rope snapped unexpectedly. Even ministers were unreliable: despite the polish of the execution sermons they often corrected, revised, and published after the fact, in person they often lost their train of thought or mumbled their words. Some ministers bored spectators with their tedious scolding, while others infuriated their audiences with their puffed-up sanctimony.

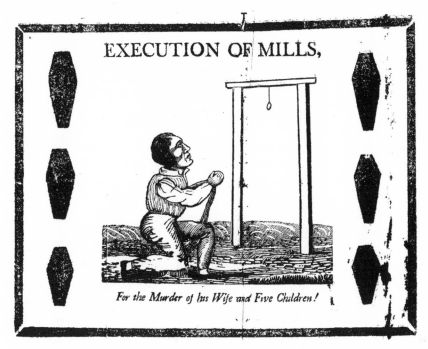

FIGURE 1. Anon., *Narrative of the Pious Death of the Penitent Henry Mills* (Boston: H. Trumbull, 1817). Courtesy of Historical & Special Collections, Harvard Law School Library.

Most commonly of all, it was the prisoners themselves who disrupted these highly scripted morality plays. In jail awaiting execution, many refused visitors and hurled abuse at clergymen who ventured in to counsel them. Others tried to escape or to commit suicide at some point during their desperate final weeks. What's more, on execution day itself, confessions and sincere pledges of repentance like those offered up by Henry Mills were actually quite rare; more likely, the condemned prisoner would weep with terror at the sight of the scaffold or beg in vain for mercy. Others were defiant to the last, using their final breath to spit into the crowd or to curse God, the sheriff, and all the people gathered to gawk at them.

Nor was execution day the only early American penal ritual to be compromised by its central actors. Wherever one looked, the practice of punishment was messy, contested, and thoroughly unpredictable. Take Eastern State Penitentiary, a purpose-built, genuinely state-of-the-art reformatory opened on the outskirts of Philadelphia on October 23,

1829. Boosters had secured state funding for this massive project on the promise that its pioneering system of "separate confinement" and surveillance would replace public executions, prevent the contaminating mingling of inmates common in other early national prisons, and transform the city's most recalcitrant criminals into docile bodies and malleable souls. In a deluge of promotional literature, reformers had trumpeted the penitentiary's tomblike cell design, assuring skeptics that its architecture would prevent convicts from even "the least association" with one another. The prisoner would instead be "abandoned to that salutary anguish and remorse which his reflections in solitude must inevitably produce."[4]

The power of this vision bore little resemblance to the clamor and chaos that consumed Eastern State soon after its opening. According to Jennifer Lawrence Janofsky, whose examination of the penitentiary's internal records is included in this collection, prisoners routinely ignored work assignments; rejected religious counseling; defaced and eviscerated moralistic reading material; tapped out messages to one another through heating ducts; sent packages and gifts through watercourses; drove wedges between penitentiary personnel; and gossiped with, complained about, and often attacked their keepers.

Across America, prisoners rarely behaved as justice officials and reformers anticipated. Indeed, their often insistent resistance to the penal regimes that tried to control and subdue them belies doctrinaire rhetoric about the totalizing power of the death penalty, the penitentiary, and allied disciplinary institutions like the almshouse and the workhouse.

Despite this essential tension, scholars who have examined the history of the American penal state have tended to ignore the behavior and minimize the testimony of prisoners, preferring instead to focus almost exclusively on the political and ideological underpinnings of power. In large measure, this is due to the outsize influence of three seminal texts first published in America in the 1970s — David J. Rothman's *The Discovery of the Asylum: Social Order and Disorder in the New Republic* (1971), Michel Foucault's *Discipline and Punish: The Birth of the Prison* (1977, trans. Alan Sheridan), and Michael Ignatieff's *A Just Measure of Pain: The Penitentiary in the Industrial Revolution, 1750–1850* (1978). Each of these vigorously argued books took the techniques of domination as its subject, a decision that rendered inmates as powerless figures caught within a matrix designed to carefully manage and control them. In Michel Foucault's analysis, for instance, the prisoner's body is trapped in a nexus of power relations that "invest it, mark it, train it, torture it, force it to carry out tasks, to perform ceremonies, to emit signs."[5]

This tendency to focus on the machinery of control has had a blinkering effect, obscuring the widespread, various, and often creative means by which those confined in America's carceral institutions have contested, compromised, and transformed the workings of penal power. The traces that their lives leave in historical and literary records are, to be sure, often difficult to access or interpret. Texts authored by condemned men or incarcerated women are necessarily vexed and mediated ones, complicated by the dialectic between the body and the state. However, careful work can pay great dividends. As the ten essays collected here demonstrate, studying the history of penal practice can illuminate infrapolitical struggles that require us to rethink the hegemonic nature of early American disciplinary regimes.

Buried Lives: Incarcerated in Early America examines the rise of the American penal state from this unfamiliar vantage point. The essays in this volume explore the many aspects of the carceral experience from the perspectives of those confined at its center. Interdisciplinary in nature, this collection investigates several carceral institutions in order to interrogate the dynamic relationships between confinement and identity, politics, and imagination in early America. Together, the scholars of this volume expand the conventional understanding of incarceration, considering not only prisons and penitentiaries as carceral settings but also scaffolds, almshouses, workhouses, family-run jailhouses adjoining slave plantations, and floating prison-ships.

The sources for this endeavor thus veer far from the familiar treatises of Italian jurist Cesare Beccaria and Philadelphia physician Benjamin Rush. Instead, they encompass warden logs, petitions, execution sermons, physicians' clinical notes, poetry, memoirs, confessions, private letters, newspaper articles, runaway slave advertisements, and legal documents. In their pages, we find the many voices of the captive and imprisoned in early America: vicious men, calculating women, diffident drunks, runaway slaves, immigrant workers, homeless children, victims of domestic abuse and sexual assault, and, above all, the vagrant, the poor, and the enslaved.[6]

Discipline and Punish

In *Discipline and Punish*, Michel Foucault describes the redistribution of the economy of punishment that took place in Europe and the United States between 1760 and 1840. Over the course of eighty years, the penitentiary displaced the scaffold as the preeminent institution of penal power. Accordingly, detention and surveillance replaced pain and spectacle as the instruments of punishment; the soul displaced the body as the target of punishment; keepers and wardens replaced executioners as the technicians of punishment; and reformation replaced vengeance as the purpose of punishment.[7]

For Foucault, the birth of the modern penitentiary did not reflect any diminishment of the power of the state to punish citizen-subjects, or any loss of appetite to exercise that power. On the contrary, Foucault understood the rise of the penitentiary as an impulse "not to punish less, but to punish better . . . to insert the power to punish more deeply into the social body." In his view, the spread of cellular technology and disciplinary correction marked an important change in penological grammar, but it did not alter the fundamental function of the penal system. "It remained," writes literary scholar Caleb Smith, "a ritual practice of performing the myths of submission on which the political order was founded."[8]

Historians have largely validated the basic outline of this broad and suggestive conceptualization of change over time. However, several have taken issue with Foucault's decision to emphasize the ways in which disciplinary ideology pervaded every corner of the social system, a decision that led him to refuse to identify the active agents in this dramatic transformation and to adopt the passive voice. Monographs by his contemporaries—notably David J. Rothman and Michael Ignatieff—sought greater specificity. In *The Discovery of the Asylum*, a wide-ranging account of the rise of several corrective institutions in the northern states of antebellum America that anticipated many of Foucault's broad conclusions, Rothman told a story in which anxious patriarchs, alarmed by rising immigration and urbanization, crumbling social deference and the spread of market capitalism, took on the mantle of philanthropic reformers. In *A Just Measure of Pain*, Ignatieff told a similar tale, identifying the influence of a shifting coalition of politically powerful, propertied men in England who were eager to recalibrate the criminal justice system to the task of disciplining a new breed of "masterless" men produced by the first stirrings of industrialization. Indeed, while Foucault had explained the move away from sanguinary punishments as merely a ruse of power, Rothman and Ignatieff offered a more nuanced portrait. Both authors noted the religious convictions of many of the proponents of penal reform and argued that the institutions they devised reflected the mutually constitutive properties of benevolence and social control.[9]

Despite such differences of emphasis, Foucault, Rothman, and Ignatieff agreed on a great deal. They each took what legal scholar David Garland has termed "the ideological genesis of modern punishment" as their focus and sought to relate the origins of carceral correction to the rise of liberal democracy, industrial capitalism, and the concomitant development of other coercive instruments of social reform, notably the asylum, the almshouse, and the workhouse. Most strikingly of all—given the number of high-profile prison riots in America and Europe throughout the early 1970s and the outspoken activism of political prisoners such as Angela Davis and George Jackson—these scholars banished matters of penal practice and inmate resistance to dependent clauses and footnotes. It is testimony to the length of their combined shadow cast within the academy that the same priorities and preoccupations have shaped the work of subsequent scholars, notably Thomas L. Dumm (1987), John Bender (1987), Adam J. Hirsch (1992), and Mark E. Kann (2005).[10]

While many scholars continue to conflate design with implementation and idea with practice, the last two decades have witnessed a long-overdue surge of interest in the apparently quotidian struggles between officials and prisoners that went on behind bars. In part, this realignment reflects the degree to which social history has come to permeate academic research agendas. Marginalized at the edges of the profession in the 1960s and 1970s, scholars interested in the political lives of long-silenced subjects, such as slaves, beggars, and working women, captured the center during the 1980s. Beyond the ivory tower, the 1990s saw the dramatic escalation of the "War on Drugs" and the passage of "three-strikes" laws in twenty-three states—developments that together drove the number of incarcerated Americans above one million for the first time. This unwelcome milestone served to focus media attention on the conditions within grossly overcrowded state prisons and, encouraged by shifting priorities within the academy, seems to have spurred a number of scholars to examine the historical experience of incarceration with unprecedented interest and enthusiasm.[11]

In July 1994, in the midst of these events, the Philadelphia Historical Commission published a two-volume *Historic Structures Report* intended to guide ongoing preservation efforts at Eastern State Penitentiary, which had been closed and abandoned since 1971. Alongside assessments of the complex's architectural significance and its signature role in the realization of competing penal theories in nineteenth-century America, a section of the report authored by Leslie C. Patrick-Stamp turned to the question of penal practice at Eastern State prior to the Civil War. Assessing the historiography, Patrick-Stamp noted that "none of the otherwise excellent secondary literature on Eastern State . . . acknowledges the presence and perspectives of people who lived (and sometimes died) behind those massive walls." Using a small sampling of institutional records, Patrick-Stamp set out a research agenda for future scholars of penal practice to pursue, an agenda centered upon the study of interactions among inmates as well as between inmates, their keepers, and the world beyond their walls.[12]

The same agenda informed the work of Michael Meranze, whose *Laboratories of Virtue: Punishment, Revolution and Authority in Philadelphia, 1760–1835* (1996) should be regarded as a landmark book in the penological history of the United States. *Laboratories of Virtue* marks the first attempt by a historian working in the intellectual tradition of Foucault, Rothman, and Ignatieff to integrate the practice and performance of power within carceral institutions into an investigation of penal ideology. By taking the opening of Eastern in 1829 as its endpoint and limiting itself to a single city and a narrow time frame, Meranze's study of early national Philadelphia succeeded in demonstrating how inmate action consistently shaped and reshaped the transformation of punishment in the unsettling aftermath of the American Revolution.

More recently, Rebecca M. McLennan's *Crisis of Imprisonment* (2008) has extended the study of penal practice—and the role of prisoner labor, in particular—over a much longer period, linking the founding of early national penitentiaries like Auburn (1816) and Sing-Sing (1826) in New York State to the development of the prison-industrial complex in the twentieth century. Placing prisoners' traditions of protest and evasion at the center of her analysis, McLennan argues that "a long continuum of episodic instability, conflict, and political crisis has characterized prison-based punishment in the United States," and that "prisoners and their keepers were often at the forefront of these various struggles to remake and control the prison and the penal arm of the state."[13]

Buried Lives exhibits a deep debt to the path-breaking work of Patrick-Stamp, Meranze, and McLennan. Indeed, the following brief history of the early American penal state rejects the Foucauldian focus on penal institutions as totalizing forms of social control. Building upon the most recent scholarship, this new outline embraces the study of penal practice and examines the shaping, destabilizing, and oppositional influence of inmates on the exercise of disciplinary power in early America. In this retelling, we hope to refocus the familiar story of the transition from scaffold to penitentiary upon the incarcerated Americans whose patterned defiance provided an important impetus for each successive wave of penal reform and innovation.

Toward a History of Penal Practice

Throughout the colonial period, the scaffold reigned supreme. Forceful and spectacular, it served as a powerful, theatrical tool to display state power and to try to exert social control. Whether in England, in its mainland American colonies, or in the Caribbean, the rituals of execution day were remarkably consistent and changed little between the early seventeenth century and the first decades of the nineteenth century. The day began with a procession from the jail through the streets toward a market square or well-trafficked crossroads. Hundreds of people usually gathered to watch along the route, while thousands more sometimes waited at the place of execution (see figure 2). At the scaffold, the condemned was allowed a final opportunity to voice his repentance to the assembled multitude, and to the legal and religious officials ceremoniously grouped before him, or to have a clergyman speak on his behalf. Soon enough, the hangman—sometimes a fellow convict—would fasten the noose around the criminal's neck and make the rope take his weight.[14]

Until the late eighteenth century, statutes compelled judges to hand down death sentences for a broad range of crimes, ensuring that execution day maintained its status as a regular feature of the secular calendar. In Georgia and South Carolina, for example, murder was one of more than 160 crimes punishable by death. In Pennsylvania, eighteen crimes were capital offenses, with assaults on persons (rape, sodomy) and property (arson, counterfeiting, burglary) accounting for a large share of all death sentences. In New England, New York, and New Jersey, laws similar to those in Pennsylvania led to the execution of 402 people between

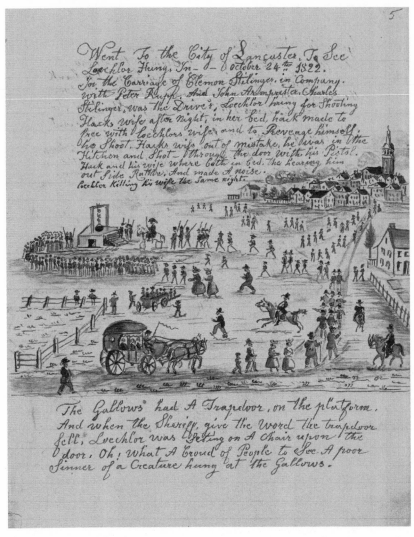

FIGURE 2. Lewis Miller, *The Hanging of John Lochlor at Lancaster, 1822.* Courtesy of the York County Heritage Trust.

1700 and 1773, more than half of whom (234) were convicted of crimes other than murder.[15]

Lesser offences warranted other types of ignoble public punishment. In Philadelphia, the pillory and the whipping post shared a prominent site at the corner of Third and Market streets. They were pressed into service several times a year, usually on Wednesdays and Saturdays when the city's busy market provided a ready crowd of spectators, many of whom thought nothing of hurling abuse at the humiliated criminals on display there before continuing with their shopping. In the South, where planters favored painful, shaming deterrents that did not impair a slave's ability to work for very long, whipping (thirty-nine lashes was the scriptural limit), branding (H for hog-stealers, T for thieves), and even ducking ponds served secondary functions in the penal system.[16]

Despite their obvious differences, these brutal and humiliating punishments shared much in common with the scaffold. Whether the outcome was death or disfigurement, the colonial justice system exerted its will by attacking the integrity of the criminal body. It did so in carefully staged rituals designed to display to the public the rude power of the law. "Visibility and corporality were the true coin of that penal realm," writes Michael Meranze.[17]

The dramas of transgression and punishment these symbolic inflictions enacted typically unfolded in and around the colonial jail. The jail housed the suspected felon while he or she awaited trial or interrogation. If found guilty of a capital crime, the prisoner would remain confined there until the date of execution. Jails also housed witnesses, debtors, drunks, ne'er-do-wells, prisoners of war, and runaway slaves who had been captured by slave patrols but were not yet returned to their masters. Debtors, Indian war captives, and a few fugitive slaves aside, most stays were short, lasting only a few days or weeks. Indeed, imprisonment for the purpose of punishment was rare in the colonial period. It was typically limited to those convicted of social offenses such as vagrancy and disturbing the peace; indeed, the names of the same men and women often stud the intake records of mid-century almshouses.[18]

Whether in the North or the South, colonial jails were understaffed, family-run affairs. Often housed in rundown buildings converted on the cheap, seventeenth- and eighteenth-century lockups typically comprised little more than a single room in which up to thirty inmates mixed freely (see figure 3). Only the most dangerous were shackled. These confined spaces were foul, fetid, loud, and overcrowded, usually without heating or ventilation. In one Georgia jail, the only conveniences consisted of a straw bed and a chamber pot. Walls were thin, sometimes wooden. Escapes were common and visitors frequent. Jailers' fees were paid by the inmates themselves, and many keepers and their families developed an easy familiarity with their charges. As essayists Jason T. Sharples and Jodi Schorb demonstrate in their contributions to this volume, signs of authority and penitence were hard to find.[19]

The chaotic conditions inside colonial jails mirrored the conflicts, crises, and general instability that plagued the exercise of public punishment. Far from being the orderly, awesome spectacle imagined for Henry Mills, public executions were, by the late eighteenth century, more commonly associated with disorder and disarray. Prisoners regularly acted out, taking the scaffold in ways that manifested their contempt or indifference. The more willful and defiant the condemned, the more likely it was that the crowd too would refuse to play the part assigned to it. Indeed, in some corners of the colonies, mid-century authorities were growing increasingly concerned that rather than drawing spectators closer to the rule of law, the severity and finality of public executions often seemed to set the two at odds with one another.[20]

Concern about sanguinary punishments only intensified after the outbreak of the American Revolution. After all, the war had kept hangmen very busy: sedition, mutiny, treason, espionage, desertion, marauding, looting, and counterfeiting accounted for the lion's share (152 of 232) of the legal executions carried out in New England, New York, New Jersey, and Pennsylvania between 1775 and 1781. In its aftermath, as patriots and lawmakers struggled to define the principles that the citizens of the new republic should live by, the use of the death penalty to deter such a dazzling array of crimes became the subject of sustained scrutiny. Embracing elements of a larger transatlantic conversation about the purpose of punishment in enlightened society, many revolutionaries now passionately condemned the scaffold as a barbaric relic of monarchical rule entirely unsuited to the task of deterring crime. "It lessens the horror of taking away human life, and thereby tends to multiply murders," Philadelphia doctor and activist Benjamin Rush wrote when he tried to make the case for its total abolition.[21]

Determining an appropriate and effective alternative to capital punishment proved more difficult. With no working model of effective

FIGURE 3. Benjamin Evans, *Stone Prison S.W. Cor. 3rd & Market St., 1723*. Built in 1718, this building, situated at the corner of Third and Market streets, combined the functions of both jail and workhouse before its inmates were removed to the new Walnut Street Jail in 1775. Courtesy of the Historical Society of Pennsylvania.

republican government to draw upon, northeastern legislators were forced to experiment. In the region's largest city, Philadelphia, reformers found inspiration in a recent scheme to extract productive labor from recipients of welfare. The opening of a workhouse—or "bettering-house," as its boosters tellingly referred to it—in this bustling port city in 1766 had marked an important shift in the way urban elites perceived connections between poverty, degeneracy, and crime. Agitated by evidence of crumbling deference, surging unemployment, and widespread indigency coincident with the arrival of waves of runaway slaves and poor European migrants, city leaders had recently set about criminalizing poverty, herding the "idle" poor into this new workhouse where they might be compelled to cobble shoes, weave cloth, pick oakum, or fashion nails.[22]

As essays by Jacqueline Cahif, Simon P. Newman, and Billy G. Smith illustrate, by the 1780s, Philadelphia public officials were forcing vagrants off of the streets in ever-greater numbers, restraining and regulating them in the workhouse and also, increasingly, in the city's almshouse and jail. Indeed, a man who had known the inside of all of these carceral institutions—each of which enforced codes of conduct, lock-in times, and constant surveillance—was often dubbed a "gentleman of three inns."

It was this same paternalistic belief in the rehabilitative virtue of discipline, surveillance, and labor productivity that guided the course of penal reform in this period. In Philadelphia, a deluge of petitions from Benjamin Rush and his allies persuaded state legislators to institute a more moderate, proportional system of punishments than that afforded by public hanging. In 1786, officials passed what came to be known as the "wheelbarrow" law. This new provision spared the lives of convicted felons but sentenced them instead to humiliating terms of hard labor on public works projects intended to transform their habits and, in time, mend their morals. Shaven-haired prisoners in brightly colored uniforms would now be set to work on highly visible sanitation projects throughout the city, all the while remaining under close supervision. Curtailing freedom and constraining movement rather than degrading the body directly, the wheelbarrow law marked a significant step away from sanguinary punishment and indicated a recognition of the revulsion the scaffold now commonly inspired. Indeed, related legislation passed by the Pennsylvania General Assembly in 1786 eliminated the death penalty as punishment for robbery, burglary, and sodomy, a precedent emulated in several other northeastern states over the following years.[23]

Of course, in practice, enforcement of the new public labor law unfolded quite differently than boosters like Rush had expected. While small crowds gathered daily in Philadelphia to watch the wheelbarrow men, it was not, newspapers quickly noted, in order to soak up respect for state power or to be reminded of the grinding ignominy that might await those convicted of serious crimes. Instead, many spectators taunted and jeered at the prisoners as they worked; others tossed them coins in unanticipated exhibitions of solidarity. Nor did many convicts show any sign of contrition or reformation. On the contrary, their keepers faced a daily struggle to keep order as wheelbarrow men acted out in violent and often drunken displays of insolence and noncooperation. Escapes were common—thirty-three on a single day in 1788—leading newspapers to warn that marauding thieves and thugs stalked city streets after dark. "Far from embodying the rational, humane, deterrent workings of the law," writes historian Rebecca M. McLennan, "the wheelbarrow men quickly came to signify a weak and failing criminal legal system, and all that was unrepublican, lawless and ugly."[24]

Casting around for an alternative that would not spur unwarranted sympathy (or vicious contempt) for the criminal, Rush and other members of the newly founded Philadelphia Society for Alleviating the Miseries of Public Prisons (Philadelphia Prison Society) went back to the drawing board. Despite mounting evidence that other coerced labor schemes were running aground—in the workhouse, managers now complained that most of its indigent residents worked too slowly and unprofitably, while others "are entirely dead Weight"—they eventually settled upon a scheme that would preserve the use of labor while removing the exercise of punishment from the public gaze. In an influential pamphlet published in 1787, Rush recommended that convicted offenders should, in future, endure an extended period of confinement in a "house of repentance," inside which the prisoner could be carefully supervised and habituated to a routine of daily labor. "Within its confines all inmates could be made subjects of the same diagnostic and curative processes," explains political theorist Thomas L. Dumm. "The environment would be controlled, the inmates would be controlled, and reform would follow from control." In Rush's latest vision, punishment would now be privatized; any direct links between prisoners and the public would be cut. Citizens beyond the walls of these new reformatories would know little about what went on inside; it would be left to their imaginations.[25]

As reports that crime was rising continued to proliferate, in 1790 the Pennsylvania General Assembly took up the petitions put forward by Rush and the members of the Philadelphia Prison Society. While murderers would continue to take the scaffold, those found guilty of offenses such as robbery, burglary, sodomy, horse-stealing, bigamy, or receiving stolen goods would, the assembly decreed, now be committed for a fixed term of years to a new facility built inside the perimeter of a jail on Walnut Street. This new "penitentiary house" promised higher standards of hygiene and diet than those found in a typical jail. Following in the footsteps of urban almshouses and workhouses—institutions that increasingly treated indigents as if poverty was their crime and discipline and labor their punishment—the complex would also include workshops where convicts would be set to work in manufacturing industry, as well as a number of large common rooms in which they would sleep for the duration of their sentences (see figure 4). A block of six-by-eight-foot cells intended for solitary confinement was added later, but only as an occasional tool with which to punish "the more hardened and atrocious offenders."[26]

Like the wheelbarrow law, this experiment with penitentiary confinement did not run smoothly or as planned. The first inmates of the Jail and Penitentiary House at Walnut Street, as it was officially named after 1790, refused to cooperate, making it clear that they would not submit to being treated like slaves. On the very first night it opened, the new building almost suffered a massive prison break. Over the next few years, the convicts incarcerated there engineered a never-ending series of riots, mutinies, disobediences, and property damages that made a mockery of attempts to institutionalize a daily routine conducive to moral reform. And, like apprentices and journeymen on the other side of the prison's walls, the inmates laid down tools each Monday, refusing to work. On Sundays, they ignored attempts to focus their minds on the state of their souls and instead shouted lewd songs, gambled, and fought.[27]

Similar disciplinary problems proved to be endemic to other experiments with penitentiary punishment across the northern states over the

FIGURE 4. "Proposed Treadmill for the Baltimore Almshouse," in Stephen Allen, *Reports on the Stepping or Discipline Mill, at the New York Penitentiary* (New York: Van Pelt and Spear, 1823). Entering almshouses and workhouses required inmates to forfeit various freedoms and submit to disciplinary regimes similar to those of the new penitentiaries. Courtesy of the Library of Congress.

next three decades. At Newgate Prison in New York, inmates often sabo-taged machinery and slept at work. In 1799, several dozen convicts there even took their keepers hostage — an act of resistance they repeated a few months later. Within twenty years, disciplinary problems had esca-lated dramatically and mass breakouts were increasingly common. The more overcrowded these early penitentiaries became, the more strength inmates seemed to draw from their growing numbers. Between 1817 and 1821, Walnut Street suffered through four crippling riots and the murder of a black inmate by other prisoners, while in 1823 prisoners in Charlestown, Massachusetts, threatened violence to keepers there who tried to flog one of their number.[28]

As early as 1820, the overcrowded and patently dysfunctional peniten-tiaries at Walnut Street, Newgate, and Charlestown had become symbols of the failure to keep order behind bars. Many newspapers now described them as incubators of vice, places where hardened criminals initiated novices into the habits of law-breaking. Prisoners had thoroughly un-dermined the labor requirement; standards of diet and hygiene had fallen precipitously; prisons were understaffed; and keepers lived in fear. "For the duration of its existence," writes Rebecca M. McLennan, "the penitentiary house remained an unstable, crisis-prone institution — one that resembled the orderly repentance house of Benjamin Rush's fertile imagination in name more than in fact."[29]

By this time, Rush and many other Revolutionary-era activists had long since passed from the scene. Thus it fell to a new generation of penal reformers and northeastern lawmakers to decide how to proceed. The experience of the past few years had thoroughly eroded confidence in public labor schemes, and with use of the death penalty now limited only to murder in the first degree in most northern states, there was no turning back to the widespread use of sanguinary punishments. So in-stead, reformers sought to reform the penitentiary itself, focusing their energies on designing new institutions that could amplify the authority of keepers and make inmates' experience of confinement more isolat-ing, more uniform, and more exacting.[30]

In New York State, authorities attempted to achieve isolation by im-posing a regime of silent labor upon the prisoners. The plans for Auburn Penitentiary, to be constructed on the banks of the Hudson River just north of Manhattan, called for small solitary cells in which prisoners would sleep. During the days, prisoners would be corralled into large industrial workshops where they would eat and work in utter silence under the watchful eye of guards trained to intercept even the subtlest attempts at communication. "While confined here," the Auburn warden, Gershom Powers, informed his charges in 1826, "you are to be literally buried from the world." Even a whisper might elicit a whipping or an iron gag. Yet, despite its monastic routines, the Auburn model took no interest in the state of the convict's soul. On the contrary, it emphasized embodied authority and strict hierarchy and, like the workhouse model it was based upon, placed its hopes in the habits of hard, productive labor and the threat of corporal punishment as the basis of correction.[31]

In Pennsylvania, authorities set out to establish corrective isolation by alternate means: by investing in architecture and the promise of spatial control. In the plans for Eastern State Penitentiary at Cherry Hill on the outskirts of Philadelphia, the English-born architect John Haviland envisaged a radial arrangement of 252 solitary cells (see figure 5). Much larger than the sleeping cells at Auburn, each twelve-by-eight-foot cell would be equipped with its own heating, plumbing, and exercise yard so that prisoners need never leave its confines or find opportunity to mix, conspire, or riot with other criminals. Instead, prisoners would be left alone in perpetual seclusion so that they could confront the memory of their crimes and examine their consciences, all the while living under a circular skylight intended to represent "the eye of God." They were to be distracted from the task of penitence only by light labor tasks that could be accomplished from within their cells, such as spinning, shoe-making, or weaving, and by occasional visits from religious instructors. Here, then, was a plan to train prisoners in more than the habits of obedience. Vastly more optimistic (and idealistic) than the silent system practiced in New York, the solitary system developed in Pennsylvania embodied a bold, uncompromising Quaker vision in which even the most heinous sinners could be reformed and reborn. "Auburn was society itself reduced to its bare essentials," Foucault concluded after reviewing the promotional literature. "Cherry Hill was life annihilated and begun again."[32]

The inhabitants of early American penitentiaries, of course, had visions of their own. While there is much that historians do not yet understand about penal practice behind the hulking Gothic façade of Eastern State, this much is clear: within a few years of its 1829 opening it was in crisis and disarray. A report commissioned by the Pennsylvania General Assembly and published in 1835 reproduced a torrent of prisoner testimony to the brazen corruption in the warden's office and among the

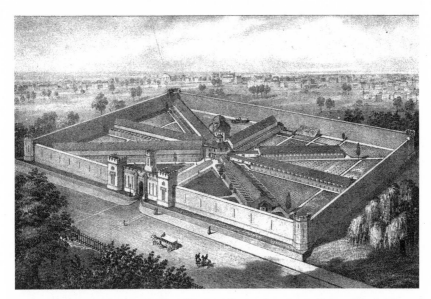

FIGURE 5. Samuel Cowperthwaite, *The State Penitentiary, for the Eastern District of Pennsylvania* (Philadelphia: P. S. Duval, 1855). Courtesy of the Library Company of Philadelphia.

guards (or "overseers" as they were known). Guards stole building materials and tools, threw parties, entertained friends, and pulled convicts from their cells to serve as waiters and cooks for their guests. Inmates also claimed that their keepers indulged in all sorts of extralegal penalties. They cut food rations arbitrarily and banned use of the exercise yards Haviland had ingeniously attached to each cell. Some inmates were apparently forced to wear straitjackets; others were beaten repeatedly and sometimes at random. One prisoner, Mathias Maccumsey, asphyxiated after being made to wear a gag.[33]

The warden and his men defended their conduct as necessary responses to the deficiencies of Haviland's design and the naïveté of the Christian vision that had guided it. Indeed, while many European visitors to Eastern State had cautioned that the long-term effects of penal isolation upon inmates might be counterproductive—"There really is no torture more severe, even to a virtuous mind, than absolute solitude," Basil Hall, a Scottish naval officer, protested after inspecting the construction site in December 1827—they need not have worried. As it turned out, thick walls and solitary cells were not sufficient to prevent inmates from communicating. Nor were convicts content to dwell calmly and peacefully on the state of their souls from dawn to dusk, seven days a week. On the contrary, many grew agitated and violent, and overseers who abided by the prison's rule banning the carrying of clubs or weapons into cells did so at their peril.[34]

In New York, things weren't much better. Enforcing the silent system was a daily struggle and hugely labor intensive. Though Gustave de Beaumont and Alexis de Tocqueville would claim after a visit to Auburn in 1831 that "the cases of infraction are so rare that they are of little danger," others observed structural frailties at every turn. W. A. Coffey, an ex-prisoner, published *Inside Out; or, an Interior View of the New-York State Prison . . . by One Who Knows* in 1826 (see figure 6). The daily regime he described to readers of this pungent exposé was structured not only by the factory-style routines of lock-smithing and comb-making, but also by the noise of convicts "conversing unrestrainedly" during "intervals of leisure." By way of proof, he recalled a prolonged, shouted exchange between a Scotsman and a Vermonter about which of their native lands was superior. Nor, Coffey claimed, were offenders at Auburn set apart from distracting and potentially corrupting external influences. He described all manner of visitors, even children, and noted that the keepers, often drunk and abusive, set a terrible example. "The prison has failed to promote the object of its institution," this ex-inmate concluded. It is a "sink of corruption."[35]

Coffey's warnings—much like the warnings of other inmates analyzed in essays by Daniel E. Williams and Caleb Smith—were widely ignored. Throughout the antebellum period, jurisdictions across the country and throughout the Atlantic world embraced the prospect of carceral punishment and began to experiment with their own variations of Pennsylvania's separate system or New York's silent system. Several European nations rushed to build penitentiaries modeled after Eastern State, as did legislatures in Maine, Rhode Island, and New Jersey. Yet, the great expense associated with Haviland's radial design and the necessity of building capacious solitary cells and adjoining individual exercise yards persuaded many penurious states to reject the Pennsylvania system in favor of the cheaper congregate-labor model pioneered at Auburn. Between 1825 and 1850, impoverished legislatures in New Hampshire, Vermont, Massachusetts, Connecticut, Maryland, Virginia, Tennessee, Missouri, Illinois, Ohio, and the District of Columbia each approved congregate-labor designs in which poor, predominantly white convicts

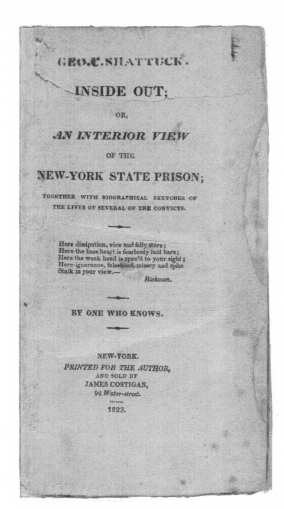

FIGURE 6. *W. A. Coffey, Inside Out; or, An Interior View of the New-York State Prison* (New York: J. Costigen, 1823). Courtesy of the Harvard College Library.

would work to offset the cost of their incarceration by engaging in larger-scale industrial manufacturing. Of course, the rise of the industrial penitentiary did not spell the end of the local jail. As essayists Matthew J. Clavin and Susan Eva O'Donovan remind us, in the Deep South town and county jails persisted in serving as sites of corporal punishment for chattel slaves throughout the antebellum era. Nonetheless, in the ever-expanding prison-industrial complex, an important shift was underway. By the eve of the Civil War, contractual penal servitude had eclipsed reformative isolation almost completely within the greater United States.[36]

Although state after state embraced the Auburn model in hopes that their own personnel could prevent recurrence of the disciplinary problems experienced in New York, inmates had other ideas. Silent system penitentiaries across America were daily violated by "the shrieks, and groans and pleadings," as one Missouri prisoner recorded in his 1847 diary. Whether in Missouri, Ohio, or Alabama, the incarcerated found ways to protest three-to-a-cell overcrowding and to retaliate against guards who continued to play favorites, to steal the clothes and money of their charges, and to brawl at all times of the day and night. In response, antebellum penitentiary inmates—the vast majority of whom were poor whites—tricked some keepers into bending the rules, belted out obscene songs on Sundays, and, in the words of a report to the Georgia Senate, "embezzl[ed] the goods committed to their charge."[37]

The most determined among them went much further, staging riots and setting fires designed to facilitate escape attempts and damage the buildings and capital upon which many self-financing congregate-labor prisons depended. In Mississippi, convicts tore to pieces the textile factory in one prison, wielding loom-weights as weapons and fighting their way to the gate before guards opened fire. In Georgia, the Milledgeville penitentiary suffered one breakdown after another—in 1826, 1831, and 1837—as inmates set fire to wooden buildings, somehow secured weapons and ammunition, and mounted the walls. As a direct result, the state legislature passed an act closing the twenty-year-old penitentiary until it could be properly rebuilt with fireproof structures and also entertained debate about returning to a system based exclusively on corporal punishment.[38]

Buried Lives

In the midst of a vicious pamphlet war between ideologues advocating for the supremacy of one or the other of these two competing penitentiary systems, Charles Dickens paid a visit to Eastern State. In his famous account of that depressing experience, *American Notes for General Circulation* (1842), Dickens searched for an image to convey his compassion for the inmates he had met—prisoners whose vitality, individuality, and near-constant battles with wardens and guards seemed to have been concealed or overlooked by boosters eager to convince skeptics of the perfection of one carcerative model or the other. "He is a man buried alive; to be dug out in the slow round of years," Dickens wrote.[39]

Many decades later, much digging remains to be done. The ten essays that comprise this collection, eight of which began life at a conference held in Philadelphia to mark the 180th anniversary of the opening of Eastern State in 1829, endeavor to advance this excavation. While Philadelphia's several carceral institutions thus loom appropriately large—the city, after all, is a pivotal site in America's penal history—the ten essays gathered here encompass numerous jurisdictions in mainland Anglo-America and the British Caribbean from the earliest years of the seventeenth century to the eventual triumph of the Auburn system in the 1850s.

The essays have been divided into two groups. Part One, "Brokering Power behind Bars," comprises five essays, arranged in broad chronological order, that introduce the research methods of historians of penal practice. Using an array of often neglected or misunderstood social history texts, these authors interrogate the ways by which confined men and women asserted themselves amid regimes of subjection within the jails, almshouses, workhouses, and penitentiaries of early America. Taken together, they offer a corrective to scholarship that has too long dismissed the agency of those punished, supervised, surveilled, corrected, and controlled by systems of power.

We begin at the heart of the eighteenth-century British Empire, on the sugar island of Antigua. This first essay reconstructs the ways in which the shared experience of congregate incarceration gave shape to the testimony elicited from black suspects implicated in an island-wide slave revolt in 1736. According to its author, Jason T. Sharples, the slaves thrown together in a makeshift lockup in St. John's turned their common confinement to their advantage by colluding to concoct and disseminate faulty knowledge about the alleged conspiracy that they hoped would trick informants, satisfy investigators, and save their lives.

The next two essays examine movements in and out of several carceral institutions in early national America. Using Philadelphia as a case study, Simon P. Newman and Billy G. Smith examine the consequences of municipal efforts to get rising numbers of the impudent poor off the streets at the turn of the century. Once inside the city's almshouse, workhouse, or jail, assertive inmates steadfastly resisted efforts to forcibly instill in them the values of hard work and self-control, and instead set about appropriating institutional resources to help them survive harsh winters, provide for loved ones, and, on occasion, turn the expense of their incarceration into a bargaining chip by which they might be released from bondage and servitude.

Some inmates had entered these often-punitive institutions voluntarily. The venereal sex workers who talked their way into the city's almshouse in search of medical treatment during the 1790s were, Jacqueline Cahif reports, a self-confident lot. Brash and sometimes brazen, this remarkable group of women exploited the resources of the almshouse as if it was designed to cater to their wants and needs, brushing off efforts to render them submissive and industrious, and then absconding before the almshouse officials could exact any work from them in lieu of payment.

Thirty years later, in 1829, Eastern State received its first inmates, providing authorities with an important new tool in the management of urban disorder. Yet, prisoners soon challenged the code of silence and segregation envisioned by proponents of the Philadelphia system. As Jennifer Lawrence Janofsky argues, isolation was continually compromised, and suicide and self-mutilation were as frequent as reformation. Despite the limits placed upon them by Haviland's architecture, inmates at Eastern State found unusually creative means to contest the nature of power, affect the corrective regime, and define the texture of daily life.

In contrast to institutions such as Eastern State, in the Lower South, most penitentiary prisoners tended to be poor whites. According to political leaders there, black slaves had no place behind their bars because, as chattel, they had no character worthy of reformation and no freedom to be curtailed. Instead, planters kept order by perpetuating the use of vicious corporal punishments, often co-opting local jailers to do their dirty work. In consequence, Susan Eva O'Donovan writes, the South's shabby county jails were bustling places in which blacks enjoyed unfettered contact and communication with one another and with the many itinerant northern abolitionists who ran afoul of local laws from time to time. These interactions often proved formative, providing conduits for the brokering of advice, information, and encouragement that contributed to some of the most notorious acts of black empowerment in American history.

Part Two, "Writing the Carceral Experience," returns to the questions posed by Henry Mills's narrative. Specifically, what special burdens do incarcerated authors bear? How should scholars treat oral testimony solicited from prisoners and transcribed and edited by ministers or justice officials? What is the nature of the relationship between the pen and the penal state? In answer, the five essays presented here probe prisoners' attempts to develop their literacy skills, their acts of self-fashioning and representation, their graphic and disturbing descriptions of confinement, and their newly evolved "rhetoric of authenticity."

Surveying the confessional literature produced by condemned prisoners between 1693 and 1770, Jodi Schorb argues that prisoner literacy was fundamental to the theatrics of public execution throughout the eighteenth century. Yet, in practice, authorities such as Cotton Mather found that controlling and directing prisoner literacy toward suitable reading and appropriate writing created unforeseen problems that only served to deepen doubts about the use of the death penalty and heighten broader anxieties about the expansion of print literacy throughout the colonies.

The prisoners of war at the heart of Judith I. Madera's essay engaged in their own collective acts of self-determination. Holed up in the fetid prison hulks moored in New York Harbor for the duration of the Revolutionary War, American privateers captured by the British later authored a cohort of memoirs that reveal how this beleaguered population elaborated a system of by-laws and disciplinary mechanisms to maintain community healthfulness and integrity in the face of pervasive squalor, disease, and repeated efforts to impress them into the British Navy.

As the last of these veterans laid down their pens, Ann Carson was taking up her own. By the early 1820s, Carson—a convicted accessory to murder, a bigamist, an adulterer, and a would-be bomber and kidnapper—was the most notorious female inmate in America. Yet, in his analysis of her 1822 autobiography, Daniel E. Williams finds Carson playing the victim, recasting her reckless and defiant conduct behind bars at Philadelphia's Walnut Street Prison as a series of misunderstood struggles against a ruthless, arbitrary power.

Twenty years later, in 1844, the voice of another Philadelphia prisoner found its way into print. George Ryno, an inmate at Eastern State, published a book of poetry ostensibly dedicated to rebutting Charles Dickens's recent attacks on the provocative and peculiar Pennsylvania system of prison discipline. Yet, as Caleb Smith explains, beyond a gushing preface in which Ryno, writing under the pen name Harry Hawser, describes his incarceration as "the happiest moment of my life," the verses themselves speak more candidly and liken the experience of solitary confinement to being buried alive—"fated to a living tomb."[40]

While Ryno engaged in a transatlantic dispute about prison conditions at Eastern State, one thousand miles further south, in Pensacola, Florida, an incarcerated abolitionist was taking careful notes of the violence perpetrated by a jailer against slaves brought in for correction. After his release in 1844, Jonathan Walker authored a whistle-blowing memoir in which he describes the Pensacola jail as a brutal extension of plantation power. Walker framed his observations, Matthew J. Clavin demonstrates, as further proof of the Slave Power's control over every aspect of southern society, using his own carceral experience to propel northern readers to outrage and action.

Together, the ten essays that comprise *Buried Lives* evidence the range of strategies inmates developed to defend against external control of their bodies and souls. No matter the setting, inmates' defiance—prompted by a variety of motives—often thwarted the purpose of punishment. At times, their behavior served to exacerbate existing structural weaknesses, exposing fault lines that could bring penal institutions to the verge of collapse. On other occasions, inmates imposed their own disciplinary imperatives to contrast and compete with those forced upon them by their keepers. Time and again, their acts of resistance—whether small victories or great disturbances—proved sufficiently challenging enough to regimes of power that they reset the course of American penal history.

Indeed, the essays gathered here recover such urgent connectivity and sustained vitality among the incarcerated that the equivalence scholars once assumed between civil death and social death requires revision. In common with recent scholarship on the experience of enslaved people in America, we find no evidence of social death behind bars. On the contrary, inmates formed new social bonds both within carceral institutions and beyond them, giving the lie to notions that early American jails and prisons formed impermeable barriers between society and its discontents.

By placing these long-buried lives at the center of analysis, *Buried Lives* argues for a new history of penal practice that is vastly more complex and multifaceted than that implied by the eventual triumph of the New York penitentiary model. Indeed, we hope that this volume will suggest new opportunities to apply historical and literary perspectives to the task of understanding America's continuing obsession with incarceration.

NOTES

1. *Narrative of the Pious Death of the Penitent Henry Mills, Who Was Executed at Galesboro's, Penn, on the 15th of July Last, for the Murder of His Wife and Five Children* . . . (Boston: H. Trumbull, 1817), 3–4.

2. Ibid., 6, 8.

3. Ibid., 3–4. No record of Mills's life, crimes, or execution appear in the tens of thousands of papers indexed in the Readex database of America's Historic Newspapers or in the catalog of legal public executions compiled by Negley K. Teeters. Negley K. Teeters, *Scaffold and Chair: A Compilation of Their Use in Pennsylvania, 1682–1962* (Philadelphia: Philadelphia Prison Society, 1963), 44–67; Louis P. Masur, *Rites of Execution: Capital Punishment and the Transformation of American Culture, 1776–1865* (New York: Oxford University Press, 1989), 105. Other deceptive fictions include *A Faithful Account of the Massacre of the Family of Gerald Watson* (Boston: N. Coverly, 1819).

4. Roberts Vaux, *Letter on the Penitentiary System of Pennsylvania. Addressed to William Roscoe, Esquire, of Toxteth Park, near Liverpool* (Philadelphia: Jesper Harding, 1827), 2; George Washington Smith, *Description of the Eastern State Penitentiary* (Philadelphia: C. G. Childs, 1829), 7. For similar claims as to the transformative effects upon prisons of the "Pennsylvania system," see Roberts Vaux, *Notices of the Original, and Successive Efforts, to Improve the Discipline of the Prison at Philadelphia, and to Reform the Criminal Code of Pennsylvania: With a Few Observations on the Penal System* (Philadelphia: Kimber and Sharpless, 1826).

5. David J. Rothman, *The Discovery of the Asylum: Social Order and Disorder in the New Republic* (Boston: Little, Brown, 1971); Michel Foucault, *Discipline and Punish: The Birth of the Prison*, trans. Alan Sheridan (New York: Vintage, 1995); and Michael Ignatieff, *A Just Measure of Pain: The Penitentiary in the Industrial Revolution, 1750–1850* (New York: Columbia University Press, 1978). Quote is taken from Foucault, *Discipline and Punish*, 25.

6. This inclusive definition of incarceration owes a debt to David Rothman's work on the concomitant rise of various institutions engaged in confinement and reformation in Jacksonian America. See Rothman, *Discovery of the Asylum.*

7. Foucault, *Discipline and Punish*, passim. For an astute summation of Foucault's thesis, see David Garland, *Punishment and Modern Society: A Study in Social Theory* (Chicago: University of Chicago Press, 1990), 133–36.

8. Foucault, *Discipline and Punish*, 82; Caleb Smith, *The Prison and the American Imagination* (New Haven: Yale University Press, 2009), 14.

9. Ignatieff, *Just Measure of Pain*, 11; Michael Meranze, *Laboratories of Virtue: Punishment, Revolution and Authority in Philadelphia, 1760–1835* (Chapel Hill: University of North Carolina Press, 1996), 14; Michael Ignatieff, "The State, Civil Society and Total Institutions: A Critique of Recent Social Histories of

Punishment," in *Social Control and the State*, ed. Stanley Cohen and Andrew Scull (New York: St. Martins, 1983); David Garland, "Foucault's 'Discipline and Punish'—an Exposition and Critique," *American Bar Foundation Research Journal* 11, no. 4 (1986): 870. These three works were in dialogue not only with one another but also with earlier work that had drawn connections between capitalism and the rise of the penal state in the West, notably George Rusche and Otto Kirchheimer, *Punishment and Social Structure* (1939; reprint, New York: Russell and Russell, 1968); Douglas Hay et al., *Albion's Fatal Tree: Crime and Society in Eighteenth-Century England* (New York: Pantheon, 1975).

10. Garland, *Punishment and Modern Society*, 144; Thomas L. Dumm, *Democracy and Punishment: Disciplinary Origins of the United States* (Madison: University of Wisconsin Press, 1987); John Bender, *Imagining the Penitentiary: Fiction and the Architecture of Mind in Eighteenth-Century England* (Chicago: University of Chicago Press, 1987); Adam J. Hirsch, *The Rise of the Penitentiary: Prisons and Punishment in Early America* (New Haven: Yale University Press, 1992); Mark E. Kann, *Punishment, Prisons and Patriarchy: Liberty and Power in the Early American Republic* (New York: New York University Press, 2005). For commentary on the evolving meaning of "social control," see David J. Rothman, "Social Control: The Uses and Abuses of the Concept in the History of Incarceration," in *Social Control and the State*, ed. Stanley Cohen and Andrew Scull (New York: St. Martins, 1983), 106–17. On the impact of *Discipline and Punish*, see Garland, "Foucault's 'Discipline and Punish,'" 865–68. Foucault, Ignatieff, and Rothman each gestured briefly toward matters of penal practice: Foucault acknowledged that penitentiaries produce delinquents, Ignatieff admitted the opposition penal reformers encountered from "the lower sort," and Rothman called for subsequent scholars to recover prisoners' social history. While each author thus displayed healthy skepticism about the efficacy of successive reform efforts, they eschewed concerted engagement with the questions of agency, identity, and negotiation provoked by the daily workings of power behind bars. Foucault, *Discipline and Punish*, 266–67; Garland, *Punishment and Modern Society*, 157–75; Rothman, "Social Control," 116–17.

Prison riots at Long Island City Prison, in New York, and Folsom, San Quentin, Soledad, and the Men's Colony at San Luis Obispo, all in California, made front-page news in 1970. At Folsom, prisoners wrote and distributed a political manifesto condemning American prisons as "fascist concentration camps" and demanding an "end to the injustices suffered by all prisoners, regardless of race, creed or color." Phil Scraton, "Protests and 'Riots' in the Violent Institution," in *The Violence of Incarceration*, ed. Phil Scraton and Jude McCulloch (New York: Routledge, 2009), 63; Angela Y. Davis, *If They Come in the Morning: Voices of Resistance* (New York: Third Press, 1971), 22, 144. In his preface, Michael Ignatieff acknowledged that "nearly a decade of hostage-takings, demonstrations, and full-scale uprisings" had, in combination with other factors, "broken the fragile order inside the [contemporary] prison." Ignatieff, *Just Measure of Pain*, xi–xii.

11. Landmark scholarship on the lives of unwelcome and unfortunate Americans prior to the Civil War includes Billy G. Smith, *The "Lower Sort": Philadelphia's Laboring People, 1750–1800* (Ithaca, N.Y.: Cornell University Press, 1990); Billy G. Smith, ed., *Down and Out in Early America* (University Park: Pennsylvania State University Press, 2005); Billy G. Smith and Susan E. Klepp, eds., *The Infortunate: The Voyage and Adventures of William Moraley, an Indentured Servant* (University Park: Pennsylvania State University Press, 1992); Ruth Wallis Herndon and John E. Murray, eds., *Children Bound to Labor: The Pauper Apprentice System in Early America* (Ithaca, N.Y.: Cornell University Press, 2009); Ruth Wallis Herndon, *Unwelcome Americans: Living on the Margin in Early New England* (Philadelphia: University of Pennsylvania Press, 2001); Seth Rockman, *Scraping By: Wage Labor, Slavery, and Survival in Early Baltimore* (Baltimore: Johns Hopkins University Press, 2009); Alfred F. Young, *The Shoemaker and the Tea Party: Memory and the American Revolution* (Boston: Beacon, 1999); Myra C. Glenn, *Campaigns against Corporal Punishment: Prisoners, Sailors, Women, and Children in Antebellum America* (Albany: State University of New York Press, 1984), 85–101.

12. Marianna Thomas, ed., *Eastern State Penitentiary: Historic Structures Report* (Philadelphia: Philadelphia Historical Commission, 1994), Sections 1-E, 6-H, 6-I, 7. See also Leslie C. Patrick-Stamp, "Numbers That Are Not New: African Americans in the Country's First Prison, 1790–1835," *Pennsylvania Magazine of History and Biography* 119, nos. 1/2 (1995): 95–128.

13. Rebecca M. McLennan, *The Crisis of Imprisonment: Protest, Politics, and the Making of the American Penal State, 1776–1941* (New York: Cambridge University Press, 2008), 2, 3. For a recent study of penal practice in Gilded Age Philadelphia, see Kali N. Gross, *Colored Amazons: Crime, Violence, and Black Women in the City of Brotherly Love, 1880–1910* (Durham, N.C.: Duke University Press, 2006), 125–49.

14. Meranze, *Laboratories of Virtue*, 21; Masur, *Rites of Execution*, 25–49; Hay et al., *Albion's Fatal Tree*, 65–117.

15. Meranze, *Laboratories of Virtue*, 21; Daniel Allen Hearn, *Legal Executions in New York State: A Comprehensive Reference, 1639–1963* (Jefferson, N.C.: McFarland, 1997), 5–18; Hearn, *Legal Executions in New England: A Comprehensive Reference, 1623–1960* (Jefferson, N.C.: McFarland, 1999), 1–160; Hearn, *Legal Executions in New Jersey: A Comprehensive Registry, 1691–1963* (Jefferson, N.C.: McFarland, 2005), 5–34. On the expansion of capital offenses to cover a greater share of property crimes in Anglo-American criminal law after 1688, see Hay et al., *Albion's Fatal Tree*, 17–63.

16. Meranze, *Laboratories of Virtue*, 21, 45–6; Michael S. Hindus, *Prison and Plantation: Crime, Justice, and Authority in Massachusetts and South Carolina, 1767–1878* (Chapel Hill: University of North Carolina, 1980), 38, 99–102, 45; Raphael Semmes, *Crime and Punishment in Early Maryland* (Montclair, N.J.:

Patterson Smith, 1970), 35; Donna Spindel, *Crime and Society in North Carolina, 1663–1776* (Baton Rouge: Louisiana State University Press, 1989), 122–25.

17. Meranze, *Laboratories of Virtue*, 24, 53–54; Foucault, *Discipline and Punish*, 45.

18. Meranze, *Laboratories of Virtue*, 175; Hirsch, *Rise of the Penitentiary*, 6–11; Sally E. Hadden, *Slave Patrols: Law and Violence in Virginia and the Carolinas* (Cambridge, Mass.: Harvard University Press, 2001), 60.

19. Bender, *Imagining the Penitentiary*, 13–16; Hirsch, *Rise of the Penitentiary*, 9; Pieter Spierenburg, "The Body and the State: Early Modern Europe," in *The Oxford History of the Prison: The Practice of Punishment in Western Society*, ed. Norval Morris and David J. Rothman (New York: Oxford University Press, 1998); Spindel, *Crime and Society*, 120–21; Semmes, *Crime and Punishment*, 33–37; James C. Bonner, "The Georgia Penitentiary at Milledgeville, 1817–1874," *Georgia Historical Quarterly* 55 (1971): 305.

20. Meranze, *Laboratories of Virtue*, 38, 54. For demonstrations of the bond between the prisoner and the public in England at this time, see Hay et al., *Albion's Fatal Tree*, 65–117.

21. Benjamin Rush, *Essays Moral, Literary, and Philosophical* (Philadelphia: Thomas and F. Bradford, 1798), 164; Hearn, *Legal Executions in New York State*, 18–23; Hearn, *Legal Executions in New England*, 1–160; Hearn, *Legal Executions in New Jersey*, 35–53; McLennan, *Crisis of Imprisonment*, 18–23; Masur, *Rites of Execution*, 50–70.

22. Gary B. Nash, "Poverty and Poor Relief in Pre-Revolutionary Philadelphia," *William and Mary Quarterly* 33, no. 1 (January 1976): 20. Also see John K. Alexander, *Render Them Submissive: Responses to Poverty in Philadelphia, 1760–1800* (Amherst: University of Massachusetts Press, 1980); Rothman, *Discovery of the Asylum*; Simon P. Newman, *Embodied History: The Lives of the Poor in Early Philadelphia* (Philadelphia: University of Pennsylvania Press, 2003); Smith, *"Lower Sort"*; and Bruce Dorsey, *Reforming Men and Women: Gender in the Antebellum City* (Ithaca, N.Y.: Cornell University Press, 2002). On the limited scope and slow pace of reform in the South, see Edward L. Ayers, *Vengeance and Justice: Crime and Punishment in the 19th Century American South* (New York: Oxford University Press, 1984), 42–43; Hindus, *Prison and Plantation*, 101–2.

23. McLennan, *Crisis of Imprisonment*, 32–33; Negley K. Teeters, *The Cradle of the Penitentiary: The Walnut Street Jail at Philadelphia, 1773–1835* (Philadelphia: n.p., 1955), 28; Masur, *Rites of Execution*, 71–92; Meranze, *Laboratories of Virtue*, 55, 69, 71–72, 84.

24. McLennan, *Crisis of Imprisonment*, 33–35, quote on 35; Masur, *Rites of Execution*, 76–79; Meranze, *Laboratories of Virtue*, 87–90, 126–27.

25. Almshouse Managers' Minutes, Nov. 3, 1775, quoted in Nash, "Poverty and Poor Relief in Pre-Revolutionary Philadelphia," 28; Benjamin Rush, *An Enquiry into the Effects of Public Punishments upon Criminals, and upon Society*

(Philadelphia: Joseph James, 1787), 12; Dumm, *Democracy and Punishment*, 94; McLennan, *Crisis of Imprisonment*, 35–37; Meranze, *Laboratories of Virtue*, 131–33.

26. J. T. Mitchell and Henry Flanders, eds., *The Statutes at Large of Pennsylvania from 1682 to 1801* (Harrisburg, Pa.: Harrisburg Publishing, 1896–1908), 13:515; McLennan, *Crisis of Imprisonment*, 37; Meranze, *Laboratories of Virtue*, 167–68; Dumm, *Democracy and Punishment*, 97, 104; Smith, *Prison and the American Imagination*, 99. For scholarship that highlights the punitive and disciplinary aspects of confinement within the growing numbers of almshouses and work-houses to be found in urban centers, see Rothman, *Discovery of the Asylum*, 180–205; Rockman, *Scraping By*, 194–230; Monique Bourque, "Poor Relief 'without Violating the Rights of Humanity': Almshouse Administration in the Philadelphia Region, 1790–1860," in Smith, *Down and Out in Early America*, 198; Alexander, *Render Them Submissive*, 61–85; Michael B. Katz, *In the Shadow of the Poorhouse: A Social History of Welfare in America* (New York: Basic, 1986), 15–23; Smith, *"Lower Sort"*; Dorsey, *Reforming Men and Women*; and Newman, *Embodied History*.

27. McLennan, *Crisis of Imprisonment*, 44–46. On the comparisons between penal confinement and slavery, see Hirsch, *Rise of the Penitentiary*, 71–111.

28. McLennan, *Crisis of Imprisonment*, 44–46. By 1804, similar institutions had opened in Trenton, New Jersey, and Baltimore, Maryland. Dumm, *Democracy and Punishment*, 106–7.

29. McLennan, *Crisis of Imprisonment*, 49; Howard O. Sprogle, *The Philadelphia Police: Past and Present. Illustrated with Portraits and Etchings* (Philadelphia: Printed for the Author, 1887), 62–63; Meranze, *Laboratories of Virtue*, 219; Dumm, *Democracy and Punishment*, 105. By 1828, Philadelphia officials had also dismantled what was left of the colonial poor relief system and had moved the alms-house out of sight, to the outskirts of the city.

30. McLennan, *Crisis of Imprisonment*, 48; Smith, *Prison and the American Imagination*, 83; Gustave de Beaumont and Alexis de Tocqueville, *On the Penitentiary System in the United States, and Its Application in France; with an Appendix on Penal Colonies, and also Statistic Notes* (Philadelphia: Carey, Lea & Blanchard, 1833), 22.

31. De Beaumont and de Tocqueville, *On the Penitentiary System*, quote on 32; Foucault, *Discipline and Punish*, 238; Dumm, *Democracy and Punishment*, 119; Gershom Powers, *A Brief Account of the Construction, Management, & Discipline of the New York State Prison at Auburn* (Auburn, N.Y.: U. F. Doubleday, 1826); W. David Lewis, *From Newgate to Dannemora: The Rise of the Penitentiary in New York, 1796–1848* (Ithaca, N.Y.: Cornell University Press, 1965).

32. Foucault, *Discipline and Punish*, 239, 47–48; de Beaumont and de Tocqueville, *On the Penitentiary System*, 23–24; Meranze, *Laboratories of Virtue*, 217, 28; Dumm, *Democracy and Punishment*, 108, 22; Norman Johnston, Kenneth Finkel, and Jeffrey A. Cohen, *Eastern State Penitentiary: Crucible of Good Intentions*

(Philadelphia: Philadelphia Museum of Art, 1994), 31–45; G. W. Smith, *A View and Description of the Eastern Penitentiary of Pennsylvania* (Philadelphia: Philadelphia Society for Alleviating the Miseries of Public Prisons, 1830).

33. Meranze, *Laboratories of Virtue*, 305–11; Thomas B. McElwee, *A Concise History of the Eastern Penitentiary of Pennsylvania, Together with a Detailed Statement of the Proceedings of the Committee, Appointed by the Legislature, December 6th, 1834* (Philadelphia: Neal & Massey, 1835).

34. Basil Hall, *Travels in North America in the Years 1827 and 1828*, 3 vols. (Edinburgh: Andrew Shortreed, 1830), 2:352; Meranze, *Laboratories of Virtue*, 312–13.

35. De Beaumont and de Tocqueville, *On the Penitentiary System*, 2; W. A. Coffey, *Inside Out; or, An Interior View of the New-York State Prison: Together with Biographical Sketches of the Lives of Several of the Convicts* (New York: J. Costigan, 1823), ix–xi, 19, 52, 70–74, 93, 134.

36. McLennan, *Crisis of Imprisonment*, 4, 53–86; Dumm, *Democracy and Punishment*, 127; Smith, *Prison and the American Imagination*, 106; Ayers, *Vengeance and Justice*, 34–35.

37. George Thompson, *Prison Life and Reflections* (Hartford, Conn.: A. Work, 1857), 119–20, 29–32, 51, 56, 96, quote on 19; Martha A. Myers, *Race, Labor, and Punishment in the New South* (Columbus: Ohio State University Press, 1998), 14; Bonner, "Georgia Penitentiary," 307.

38. Ayers, *Vengeance and Justice*, 59–61; Bonner, "Georgia Penitentiary," 309; Thompson, *Prison Life*, 155; Myers, *Punishment in the New South*, 14.

39. Charles Dickens, *American Notes for General Circulation* (New York: Harper and Brothers, 1842), 40.

40. Harry Hawser, *Buds and Flowers, of Leisure Hours* (Philadelphia: G. W. Johnson, 1844), 70.

PART ONE

Brokering Power behind Bars

Hearing Whispers, Casting Shadows

Jailhouse Conversation and the
Production of Knowledge during
the Antigua Slave Conspiracy
Investigation of 1736

JASON T. SHARPLES

IN THE COURTROOM IN JANUARY 1737 during a trial for a slave conspiracy, Parham Attaw gave a solemn and dramatic performance for
the judges. Before this moment, the thirty-three-year-old enslaved man
had been living and working as a driver of other slaves at the sprawl-
ing Parham plantation on the Caribbean island of Antigua. When he
was accused of participating in an alleged insurrection conspiracy, he
gained some degree of control over his situation by becoming an informant. But the possibility of reprieve or reward depended, precariously,
on how the investigating judges regarded his effectiveness as a court
witness in bringing convictions. On this day, Attaw came face to face
with a suspected conspirator named Cudjoe and testified that he saw

him participate in forming the conspiracy at particular meetings. When Cudjoe denied some of the details of these accusations, Attaw "laid his hand upon his heart[,] looking Cudjoe in the face, and wish'd that God might Eternally Damn him, if what he said of Cudjoe was not true." As he locked eyes with the suspect, the other four informants in the room must have studied the court's response. The second witness, Dick, took his cue from Attaw and after giving his evidence against Cudjoe "laid his hand upon his heart[,] looking upon Cudjoe, and wish'd that he might never Enter into the Kingdom of Heaven, if all that he had said of Cudjoe was not true." The judges marveled at his demonstration of sincerity and scribbled down the drama into their trial minutes. Cudjoe was burned at the stake. Attaw and Dick were pardoned and reenslaved.[1]

In a series of moments like this, white magistrates and enslaved blacks forged the understood "truth" of the conspiracy. This particular truth held more consequence for the people of Antigua than the narrow question of whether anyone really intended to revolt. Recent scholarship that has debated the so-called authenticity of particular rebellion conspiracies has missed the more significant point that white settlers at times believed these conspiracies to be real. By acting on their fears, they destroyed the lives of many enslaved people and undermined the formation of Afro-Caribbean communities, regardless of alleged rebellious intent. Therefore, the crucial intellectual problem is to unravel how, exactly, accusations of conspiracy became credible and coherent in the eyes of Antigua's magistrates.[2]

The understood truth of the Antigua conspiracy began forming in jail. At one level, much of what came to light as evidence of a conspiracy resulted from the physical restraint of so many suspects in an already overcrowded makeshift jail. The investigating judges also enforced a sort of incarceration in the courtroom. During the trials, they assembled a suspect and several witnesses in a confined and guarded space before the court. There they attempted to limit the participants' autonomy by directing their behavior, and they deliberately secluded them from a public audience while forcing them to watch one another.

These interlocking incarcerations encouraged prisoners to cultivate faulty knowledge that they passed on to magistrates. Shared physical imprisonment enabled suspects to exchange information (and often misinformation) that helped them make decisions and craft performances that they believed would preserve their lives. Some suspects became informants on promises of reprieve or reward, producing information that fashioned their indispensability to the magistrates in power. They developed their testimony based on information they gathered in jail. Group confinement also allowed informants to note the names of jailed suspects and assemble a roster of alleged conspirators to include in their testimony, enhancing their own credibility and indispensability. Stripped of familiar support networks, individuals in these incarcerations tried to regain some power by reaching out to a range of other participants: some tried to help one another, others combined against each other, and a devastating few formed an alliance with the investigators.

Together, magistrates, informants, and suspects produced knowledge of a conspiracy that had not existed before incarceration. That plot came into existence only when investigators arrested disparate strangers, confined them in close proximity, and invited them to discuss what little they knew of their shared predicament. In this crucible, terrified prisoners melded together fragments of information and forged the truth of the Antigua conspiracy. Almost everything we know about slave conspiracies in early America came to light in this way. As colonial magistrates produced knowledge of the plot in the course of the investigation, they not only "discovered" a story that they had already outlined but also, through the ceremony of court proceedings, manufactured apparent proof that their longstanding fears and assumptions were accurate.

The Panic

As with other conspiracy panics in early America, scholars have long viewed the discoveries produced in Antigua as the portrait of a failed attempt at organized rebellion. Yet, if we focus on the cultivation of evidence through incarceration, the events in Antigua appear to be a group panic, fueled by fear and official inquisition, rather than an actual rebellion conspiracy. Magistrates crystallized aspects of these investigative processes in a report that reflected a devastating scene painted by enslaved informants. Conspirators supposedly planned to begin the rebellion by striking the colony's populous government seat of St. John's Town. They would explode hidden gunpowder at an upcoming ball in order to wipe out the leading planters, as one resident put it, "in the height of their mirth." Rebel units styled after an English militia would then descend on the town from three or four directions, slaughter the survivors, take over their households, erect a new government, and install an African king.[3]

Informants produced these revelations during an investigation and a series of trials that began in October 1736 and continued until March 1737, during which several hundred suspects were arrested and questioned. At first, justice of the peace Robert Arbuthnot, by himself, indulged a hunch and made informal inquiries beginning October 11. Based on his preliminary findings, on October 19 the assembly appointed a four-man tribunal (including Arbuthnot) and authorized it to arrest and try anyone whom the original suspects impeached.[4] When the members of this first court became fatigued in late December by the cascading accusations, arrests, and trials, the assembly relieved them with a five-man board that served for the remainder of the investigation.[5] Both panels of judges applied judicial, psychological, and physical coercions to extract information. As a result, over time, at least 32 of the suspects confessed and agreed to become informants in exchange for a sliding scale of reduced punishment or material reward. All told, this process brought convictions against 132 of the suspects (including 8 underperforming informants), 88 of whom were executed and 44 transported. (See Table 1 for summary.)

What made magistrates and slaveholders in Antigua susceptible to a conspiracy panic at the end of 1736? In a way, the view from Antigua at the time was that of a slave system under siege. In the 1730s, numerous revolts and imagined plots occurred throughout the Caribbean. Antigua had already faced down a conspiracy panic in 1729, while on the Danish island of St. John, slaves had staged a five-month-long insurrection as

TABLE 1. Summary of number of suspected conspirators in the Antigua investigation, October 1736 to March 1737.

JUDICIAL FATE	NUMBER OF ENSLAVED MEN
Arrested	250 to 400 (estimate)
Released or Acquitted	100 to 250 (estimate)
Deemed Guilty	156
Trial Witnesses	24
Convicts	132
Transported	44
Executed	88

Source: Judges' Report, 25 Jan. 1737, and Conspiracy Trials, Nov. 1736–Jan. 1737, in Antigua Council Minutes, TNA: PRO CO 9/10, fols. 49–91 (trials), 116, 119 (report); 9/11, fols. 35–44 (trials).

recently as 1733. In 1734, a conspiracy panic gripped the island of New Providence in the Bahamas. Meanwhile, as newspapers and magazines reported amply, the maroon polities in rural Jamaica were garnering unprecedented success in guerrilla warfare against the colonial government.

Antigua's particular vulnerabilities contributed to its susceptibility to panic. It is a small island of only 108 square miles, situated among the Leeward Islands (near Guadeloupe, Montserrat, St. Christopher, and Nevis). The economic downturn of the 1730s disrupted a small colony heavily oriented toward sugar production. War seemed more and more likely as Spanish guarda costas seized British shipping in an effort to curb smuggling. Demographic shifts in the years before the 1729 and 1736 conspiracy panics also made the colony increasingly difficult to defend. The white population had diminished from a peak of 5,200 in 1724 to only 3,772 in 1734. More than half lived in either the political center, St. John's Town on the northeast coast, or the nascent naval post of English Harbor in the south, which was also home to a garrison of 150 soldiers. Dense urban settlement, although normally an assurance of safety, could trap townspeople if conspirators planned to use arson or a gunpowder explosion to draw inhabitants into a coordinated ambush.

Meanwhile, the black population grew, surging from 19,800 in 1724 to 24,408 in 1734, as sugar planters purchased newly enslaved Africans. The island's black population was also becoming more visible and mobile. Town slaves, comprising perhaps less than a third of the island's black workforce, labored in occupations that afforded them considerable mobility. Therefore, as magistrates worried, they had the opportunity to coordinate a network of conspirators capable of simultaneous insurrection. At plantations, skilled tradesmen and gang drivers also had greater opportunity to leave the estate than did field hands who needed to evade stricter pass laws. On Saturday nights and Sundays, black town dwellers often went to weekend gatherings in the countryside, and hundreds of enslaved plantation dwellers went to the Sunday market at St. John's Town. During the 1736 investigation, magistrates came to believe that these social gatherings provided venues for conspiracy. The ensuing investigation, in turn, riddled these fragile Afro-Caribbean communities with suspicion and distrust, making them even more brittle.[6]

Despite the alarm, the evidence indicates that—whatever violence had been planned—no conspiracy existed on the scale imagined by investigators. For one thing, several "discoveries" about the means and scope of the Antigua plot reflected a number of conventional elements commonly imagined by American slaveholders to constitute slave conspiracies. The Antigua plan to massacre the gentry during the confusion of a gunpowder explosion was a local adaptation of the arson plots familiar to anyone who read or heard about alleged slave conspiracies elsewhere in the British Atlantic world. During an arson plot, conspirators who intended to massacre white residents supposedly would set fire to a central location to distract settlers, draw them into the open, and ambush them at a moment of vulnerability. Magistrates knew that their predecessors had discovered plots such as this in Antigua in 1687 and Barbados in 1675 and 1692.

Despite such precedents, when slaves did engage in collective violence, the aims and scope of their revolts rarely resembled the elaborate doomsday scenarios imagined by masters. Usually the slaves of only one or two estates revolted at a time. Rebels aimed their efforts not at massacre but escape; they often established or joined maroon communities outside the reach of the colonial state, rather than fixating on vengeance against their former masters. When insurrections occasionally did take on larger proportions, such as during the Stono Rebellion in South Carolina (1739), they gained strength by spreading in viral fashion from one estate to the next. Throughout the seventeenth and eighteenth centuries, no one orchestrated any colony-wide massacres.

The white fantasy and black confirmation of a widespread conspiracy became unmoored from slaves' actual intentions because of the coercions inherent in inquisition and incarceration. The initial investigator, justice of the peace Robert Arbuthnot, polluted his findings from the start. From his initial report, it was clear that he relied heavily on circumstantial evidence. When he reached a dead end and was "Casting about" for a new lead, it suddenly "Occurr'd to him" to interview a "Sensible" town slave who had a Christian background. He asked leading questions such as "Whether [the slave] thought the Negro's were not arrived to a much Greater highth of Insolence than he had Ever Observed?" The man's careful responses appeared to Arbuthnot to confirm his hunch. When Arbuthnot again ran out of suspects a few days later, he arrested two slaves based on his impression of their reputation: "if any thing Criminal was going forwards," he reasoned, "they were Probably Concern'd in it."[7] After five days of investigation, Arbuthnot presented the assembly with a report filled with circumstantial evidence and hearsay. Based on these preliminary findings, the assembly appointed a formal investigative board that was empowered to arrest new suspects, torture them for the names of others, and conduct trials using enslaved witnesses.

Elevating the investigation from one man's hunch to an institution's duty added irreversible coercive pressure and quickly raised questions about the reliability of slave testimony. Some of Arbuthnot's initial suspects now turned informant by accusing other slaves of conspiring and serving as witnesses at the trials that began in earnest on October 19. As more and more suspects turned king's evidence, they accused a wider network of enslaved men and caused a cascading series of arrests. As this witch-hunt proceeded, one of the newly jailed suspects confided to his guard that he "was afraid that Fellows to Save their own lives would Say any thing against him." More publicly—outside of the jail—slaveholders whose property was at stake confronted the board of judges with an "Outcry about false Evidence and Combination." In response, the judges issued a statement arguing that the informants could not have lied because, categorically, slaves held deep loyalties to one another and engaged in few rivalries. The judges also claimed—incorrectly as it turned out—that jail guards would overhear any collusion.[8]

During the five months of official investigation, the judges received the bulk of information about the conspiracy from just 24 informants rather than the other 134 men who were found guilty. Historians have tended to focus on the sensational discoveries of the few, rather than the routine denials of the many.[9] Several suspects defended themselves at trial by making "Obstinate Denyals of Every thing." Others refuted key details in the testimony against them: at least eight denied attending one particular weekend social gathering at Colonel Francis Carlile's plantation that was thought to be a major conspiracy meeting. Some of them said they had not visited the estate in question "since Mr. Carlile's Death [in 1734]," others said "these 4 or 5 Years," and in a few cases "in his [the speaker's] life time." Even up to the moment of execution, the judges observed, more than three dozen convicted conspirators stoically refused to confess.[10] One should also note that the Antigua investigation failed repeatedly to find material evidence of an intended insurrection, even though suspects accused each other of hoarding weapons and powder. As early as the first day, searches of suspects' dwellings did not yield any weapons cache. After one such raid, Arbuthnot surmised that the resident had "Received Notice [and] . . . had just time to Strip his House and Put Every thing Out of the way." The judges persistently asked about the location of the powder. One informant tried to placate them by saying he saw a covered package "which by the Shape he took to be a bottle & imagined but Do's not know it was Powder." Months later, when judges believed they had finally tracked down the fabled ten-gallon keg, they went to seize it "but the Powder was Gone." They were chasing shadows cast by coerced confessions.[11]

The Investigation

Torture was not part of the common law tradition in the British Atlantic world. Nevertheless, during panics such as this one, desperate investigators occasionally forgot themselves. The Antigua justices congratulated themselves on their restraint in only torturing suspects three times after receiving formal authorization from the assembly. They "Declined further use of it," they explained, because the results were "Fruitles[s]."[12] But the investigating judges needed to widen their net by gathering fresh names from reluctant informants. Despite their avowed restraint, the judges became dissatisfied with the paucity of impeachments coming from men who burned at the stake and therefore demanded that the next group undergo a more prolonged and agonizing death "in Order to produce Discovery's." They gibbeted these convicts alive, killing them over days, not hours, by thirst, starvation, and exposure in iron cages that towered over the public market in St. John's Town. The cages faced each other "in a Quadrangle, so that [the victims] cou'd see and speak to one another."[13] Although the judges sentenced only ten slaves to hang in these gibbets, they received a staggering windfall of information. They took down at least two dying confessions and fifty new names. They also used the gibbets to recruit three loquacious informants who became star witnesses for the next several months. One of these men endured twelve hours in the iron cage before finally agreeing to turn king's evidence and inform against his brother.[14]

Yet, the investigators did not rely exclusively on physical coercion. The psychology of interrogation between a white magistrate and a legally powerless slave, and in the shadow of the gallows, could also serve as a startlingly effective prompt. Questioning under such conditions built up massive cognitive pressure until it forced some suspects to break their silence. In these coerced confessions, suspects did not necessarily convey accurate information. Instead, a speaker pursued a purpose unrelated to accuracy: he was attempting to alleviate the physical and mental stress.

The confession became less informational and more instrumental; the speaker no longer valued accuracy so much as he valued any action that promised to allay the pain.[15]

Judicial incentives also motivated informants who seized this opportunity to parlay imaginative testimony into a sliding scale of rewards. They hoped to receive lighter punishment (banishment instead of execution), pardon, freedom, or even a monetary prize. The Antigua justices waited until the conclusion of the trials, when they evaluated witnesses' performances to revise earlier promises upward or downward, before informing the assembly about rewards that each compliant informant had earned. Ultimately, ten witnesses were officially pardoned and allowed to continue living in Antigua, but only two of them garnered freedom and a stipend (a third man received just the stipend). Someone else won a sum of £14 but was still banished from the island. Other informants did not fare so well: four were executed as convicted conspirators, one was sold to slave traders in a Spanish colony with the other banished convicts, and nine were sold to slaveholders in British North America.[16]

The panel of investigators worked simultaneously as a tribunal of prosecutors and judges who governed suspects' trials and orchestrated witnesses' testimony.[17] They made the unusual decision to keep the conspiracy trials closed from public viewing, prohibiting the presence of anyone but jailers and constables in an effort to control the flow of information. During each trial, the suspect and relevant witnesses attended all together in the courtroom. The witnesses were usually "Produced Joyntly" or, if one's name unexpectedly came up, "Call'd in" as needed. This allowed the judges to check, in the event of a dispute, that "all the Witnesses do agree."[18] A witness always gave evidence in the presence of the suspect on trial, while the accused frequently disputed his testimony. Often, suspects and witnesses interjected comments to impugn one another's credibility, for example, by tarring the adversary as "a great Stealer of Goats" or having "a Mind to [the suspect's] Wife." The judges recorded the enslaved participants' accusations and recriminations as if they were the unvarnished truth, even though each man drew on information that he had developed, colluded about, and accumulated during group incarceration.[19]

Judges convicted suspects on the basis of stunningly slight evidence. It took only two witnesses to send an enslaved man to the flames; they had to provide "positive evidence," meaning an eyewitness account of a specific conspiratorial oath or material support for the plot. Circumstantial evidence and hearsay could strengthen the case, but—contrary to the low threshold of evidence for beginning the inquiry—the court now insisted on procuring two pieces of positive evidence before sending any man to his death. On weaker evidence, the court sent a man into banishment by arranging for his sale in Spanish America—a fate owners preferred because the forced sale mitigated their financial losses. This single-witness standard for establishing a slave's guilt and double-witness requirement for ordering his death reflected juridical practices in other colonies where one witness also sufficed to bring a conviction.[20]

The Jail

Whether the judges knew it or not, incarceration structured their understanding of the alleged slave conspiracy by producing, tautologically, incriminating evidence. Prisoners easily exchanged all kinds of information in jail because the building was constructed for other uses instead of conspiracy investigations. In lieu of a dedicated prison and courthouse, the assembly utilized buildings in St. John's Town leased from Philip Darby, a merchant. Darby's "tenements adjoining the Guard-house," as far as we can tell, became the jail. The house was better suited for short-term imprisonment of debtors and runaway slaves than for a conspiracy investigation that required the isolation of suspects and witnesses.[21]

The physical circumstances of this makeshift holding pen provided witnesses and suspects many opportunities to collude and to draw inferences that structured their stories in the courtroom. Jailers kept the prisoners in five rooms, split between the upper and lower levels of the building, with a total capacity of about fifty people. One prisoner in "an upper Room in Goal" communicated to another in "the Room under him," through "a large hole in the Floor, which he Could run his hand through." Three of the five rooms held the main trial witnesses, who numbered around fifteen at any given time. One of the rooms for witnesses was "a very long One" that allowed distance between the prisoners, who could not move because of irons on "both hands and feet." The witnesses remained there for weeks and months at a time while waiting to serve at the trials of newly jailed suspects. Two other rooms held the bulk of suspects and minor informants, usually numbering around thirty-five prisoners.[22]

Even the prison guards—the human instruments of incarceration—proved to be a permeable boundary and an ineffective barrier to communication. From outward appearances, a formidable combination of militiamen and professional soldiers guarded the jail and its prisoners. Members of the militia kept watch at "the Common Goal Door." At least one constable, James Hanson, and "two Gentlemen who are Officers of the Guard" took up stations at the two rooms holding the prisoners awaiting trial or already convicted. In the other three rooms, according to an officer's report from February 1737, "Sentrys" kept guard over the trial witnesses "night and Day," and "Several Soldiers" stayed "between every two Evidences."[23] Despite this policing—or perhaps because of prisoners' daily, mundane encounters with their guards—inmates turned to jailers for help and found that they entertained their requests. A newly arrested suspect asked guard Thomas Collins "to Stoop Down, that he might Speak with him . . . not to be overheard." When the suspect confided that he believed other prisoners would concoct lies about him to win reprieve, Collins misguidedly advised him "by no means, to Say any thing that was false to Save his life." Two weeks later, the suspect was burned at the stake.[24]

Suspects and witnesses had opportunity to collect and create information as they rubbed shoulders in this overcrowded and underguarded space. Newly arrested suspects stayed in confinement for as long as it took to discover and marshal evidence against them, while convicted slaves returned to jail to await the execution of their sentence. During the busiest weeks of the investigation, convicts who were sentenced for execution usually waited less than a week before they were sent to the stake as a group. Toward the end of the panic, several waited up to a month for execution as their cases were reviewed. Other convicts, awaiting their banishment, remained in confinement for several months so that the entire group could be transferred at one time to a single slave trader. All the while, new suspects continued to arrive as informants made fresh impeachments.

Although the judges did not worry that close confinement would taint the evidence, they did believe that the jail could become vulnerable to revolt if it held more than fifty prisoners. Even after the jail reached its capacity, investigators continued to become aware of new suspects whom they believed they needed to arrest but did not have space to accommodate. Rather than lease another expensive building in St. John's Town, they turned to the Antigua Council for access to the *Fleuron*, a French vessel recently seized for smuggling. At the end of November 1736, the judges transferred to the harbor ship several convicted suspects who awaited banishment. Through December, the judges shifted convicted conspirators back and forth between the jail and the ship, as executions and new arrests ebbed and flowed. In January 1737, the judges expected a new influx of arrested slaves and looked for a second prison ship, "to make Room in the Prison for more that were to be taken up." They contracted with a Captain Sutcliffe to hold at least forty convicts on his vessel for the next two months.[25]

As Judith I. Madera demonstrates elsewhere in this collection, jailing men onboard ship presented peculiar difficulties. The twelve-man guard on Sutcliffe's ship came from the pool of sailors serving on other vessels in the harbor. The sailors "very much neglected" the duty by denying that the king's authority extended to them, even though the royal governor's council observed that His Majesty's colony and ships in its harbor shared a mutual obligation to preserve each other's safety. In order to achieve enforcement and strengthen the position of settlers' representatives in this constitutional debate, the assembly intervened to pass a law ordering captains to keep the twelve-man guard, "only from Sun Set to until Sun Rise," recruited from the 200 sailors estimated to be in the harbor. After all of this wrangling, the shipboard jail ceased its service at the end of February 1737, as the investigation slowed.[26]

Whether on land or at sea, neither of these makeshift jails had been designed to accommodate a mushrooming conspiracy investigation. Insurrection panics occurred only periodically, and no other use of the jail in colonial America required the same expansive capacity and isolation of prisoners from each other. The deficiencies of the jail in Antigua allowed prisoners to communicate unbeknownst to their jailers. Even without whispering through holes, those suspects who chose to become trial witnesses carried information with them that they had gathered as prisoners in the holding pens.

Perils and Opportunities for Prisoners

Despite its physical inadequacies, the jail environment was nonetheless a technology of coercion that helped to pressure suspects to confess and provide information.[27] Almost daily, prisoners saw suspects return from trial as convicts, and then watched as convicts were led away to burn at the stake. In this setting, prisoners looked for a way to come up with some kind of valuable information that could save their lives. Some inmates told their jailers that they had key information for understanding the plot. Often this backfired. Although a prisoner intended for his limited confession to be a sign of good faith, judges often viewed it simply as confirmation of involvement in the plot, announcing that a suspect "Confessed his Guilt in Goal" or "Own'd his Guilt in Goal."[28]

In Antigua, as in other conspiracy investigations, some prisoners successfully preserved themselves by producing incriminating information about other people with whom they were incarcerated. The jail furnished precisely the information that informants needed because it enforced close proximity among dozens of desperate suspects. The close quarters encouraged prisoners to speak to each other. Aspiring informants listened in as some suspects confided in each other, and they engaged in sympathetic conversations to draw confessions out of others. When men were squeezed together in jail, they soon gushed with speech and speculation. Informants tapped into this flow of tainted information because they knew judges would find it useful in the courtroom.

The investigating judges knew that jailing suspects in close proximity would encourage them to discuss their crimes, thus generating evidence. They harnessed this effect of incarceration by recruiting several men to serve as spies in jail. Godsell's Ionian, Byam's Quou, and Weatherill's Booty began spying soon after their confessions and convictions. Chester's Frank, upon conviction, attempted to spy in exchange for a pardon. Within three days, however, the judges found his results unsatisfactory and burned him at the stake. Three other men may also have served as spies, although the judges did not label them as such: Parham Attaw, Parham George, and Hanson's Quash each gave evidence describing jailhouse conversations, but each also provided information about earlier social gatherings at plantations.[29]

As suspects turned to each other, the jail reverberated with information and misinformation about the apparent conspiracy. Some jailed men, wary of eavesdroppers, took precautions in their conversation. One was overheard to reprimand two others that "they were turn'd Fools or Children to Confess their Guilt in a place where they Did not know their friends from their foes." Yet, prisoners still shared information with each other, and informants frequently found advantage in repeating those jailhouse conversations to judges.[30]

Spies and informants twisted words to sound incriminating, especially when suspects filled each other in about a conspiracy to which they had not been privy but about which they now needed a primer in order to maneuver their way out of jeopardy. At one of the trials, an informant claimed overhearing a prisoner say that he would have fled from justice if given the chance. At someone else's trial, an informant relayed a rumor from jail that a suspect had taken the conspiracy oath at a certain feast, meeting the judges' standard of positive evidence. Another informant claimed that a third jailed suspect had confided in him that he was in fact guilty. Even a tasteless joke became evidence against a flippant suspect who chortled one day, when several men went to the stake, "that they had done all the Roast Meat already." He was sentenced to banishment.[31]

Savvy suspects knowingly played to eavesdropping spies and jailers. Three men loudly complained to one another that certain other persons from their plantation "ought to have been brought to Town, instead of them, for that they [the persons still at large] were more guilty than they [the jailed suspects] were." Someone else in jail mentioned a person from his plantation who "was as Guilty as he . . . himself." Their ruminations caught the ears of a spy and the attention of the judges, who then took up the new suspects and eventually found them guilty (one banished, one burned).[32]

The judges clearly hoped that prisoners would implicate themselves in jail by discussing the details of how they had formed the alleged conspiracy and what, precisely, it entailed. Instead—because no such rebellion had been planned—suspects mostly talked about the investigation and how to survive it. Judges believed that any such conniving signaled a cover-up because only guilty parties would have anything to hide. Ironically, suspects' incarceration encouraged them to commit another version of the very crime of which they were falsely accused. Although these men probably had not plotted a grand rebellion, once they arrived in jail they began to conspire (in a more limited legal sense) about how to perform in the courtroom. Suspects' conversations about the investigation satisfied the judges' need for incriminating evidence.

Despite these dangers of being overheard, prisoners attempted to help each other by sharing information about the judicial process. They consulted about "what Signifies Confessing to the Justices" and reassured one another that "Two Witnesses are not Sufficient to take away a Negro's Life, nor three, Nor hardly four." In reality, the judges required only two positive evidences to sentence a man to death. The faulty information may have originated with two spies in jail who tried to elicit confessions by telling prisoners that "two or th[re]e Witnesses would hardly Convict a Negro of being in the Plot."[33]

Some prisoners consulted one another about who had accused them and caused their arrest, while others shared impressions of the temperament of the judges. One newly arrested man, "as Soone as [he] came into Goal," asked two cell mates "if they had been tried" and what exactly had happened in the courtroom. Although those two men had little information of value because they still awaited trial, the next day another inmate returned to the cell from a trial at which he had just been convicted. He related "what the Justices said to him" and observed that "the other Justices were easier with him than Colonel [Valentine] Morris." The convicted man lamented that, were it not for Morris's zeal, "the rest of the Negro's would all get Clear."[34]

In these whispered conversations, tactical planning slipped into outright collusion. Some of the Antigua suspects attempted to coordinate their stories to protect one another. "When you go before the Justices, keep one Tongue, and don't Confess any thing against the Johnson's, but Die like Men," one suspect reportedly said to two of his cellmates. According to informants, he went on to threaten two witnesses that if they "Should Say any thing of Driver Cuffey, the Johnsons or himself, they would ruin them all." Although informants may have embroidered the statement to ensure this man's conviction (burned at the stake), three witnesses corroborated the incident.[35] Another newly arrested man apparently tried to get his story straight with others upon his arrival by speaking with someone in the room above through a hole in the ceiling. From above, he received instructions to deny several specific allegations: that the other suspect contributed to a certain feast, that a particular witness attended it, that anyone performed the oath there, and that the suspect went to a ringleader's house afterward ("but Say," his adviser instructed, "that he came directly to Town"). At trial, the suspect attempted to defuse the spies' charge of collusion by insisting that he rejected the instructions, responding through the hole that "he Could not Deny" certain details, "for that it was true." His efforts failed; he was soon executed.[36]

In a particularly bold collaboration, eight convicts authored a grand story while jailed together on the *Fleuron* in an attempt to earn a reprieve from banishment. They claimed that one of the sailors guarding the ship had offered to "Rescue them and Carry them" to another island, perhaps wrongly assuming that the judges appreciated the possibility that such an alliance might form. The group told the judges that they had refused the offer, "Cho[o]sing Rather to Die to Shew their Innocence," but their effort was wasted. The group remained scheduled for banishment from the British colonies.[37]

Through all of these discussions and collaborations, prisoners learned many things from each other. Other scholarship on incarceration has emphasized jails as venues where criminals became acquainted and instructed each other in illicit activity. In Antigua, prisoners might have picked up a few ideas regarding how to form a conspiracy undetected, but they actually learned much more about how to survive an investigation than how to rebel.

Take Langford's Billy, a prisoner and trial witness who escaped with his life by furnishing evidence against at least fourteen suspects (three executed, eleven banished). In an attempt to protect Billy from island slaves who "intended to kill me," the judges sold him to a slave trader bound for Britain's mainland colonies. In New York five years later, during the conspiracy panic of 1741, Billy's reputation for being "very expert at Plots" landed him in jail once again. In prison, he immediately drew on his experience from Antigua. He confided to a fellow prisoner, Pedro, that he "understood these Affairs very well" and that "unless he . . . did confess and bring in two or three, he would either be hanged or burnt." He even prompted Pedro with likely names "as proper ones to be accused."[38]

Billy pleaded guilty at his New York trial and attempted, while burning at the stake, to save himself by performing a stunning confession. He implicated two white soldiers, "reputed to be Papists," and nine slaves. He protected only his friend from jail, saying that "Pedro . . . is innocent for what he knows," not realizing that his confidant had betrayed him. Pedro had informed the judges of Billy's efforts to coach him in jail. Although Billy learned a great deal about manipulating testimony when jailed in Antigua in 1736, in New York his student surpassed him in applying what should have been a principal lesson: when jailed for a conspiracy investigation, one could not so easily distinguish between friends and foes.[39]

Populating Testimony with Prisoners

During the Antigua investigation, slave witnesses drew on all of these experiences during group incarceration to construct their testimony around the names of people they saw in jail, whether or not they had known them prior to arrest. When testifying against any suspect, witnesses bolstered their credibility in the eyes of the judges by populating their stories with prisoners who had already drawn suspicion. For example, a witness at one trial named a long list of guests at a plotters' supper, in what seemed to be a single breath: "Targut[,] . . . Court, Tomboy, Hercules, Hoskin's Quashee, Wilkinson's Quashee, Morgan's Ned and Jack," as well as "Maria," "Mulatto Ned, & many of Chester's Negros, many of Doctor Haddons, & some from the Town."[40] All together, witnesses mentioned third parties in this manner 269 times throughout the extant trial record, excluding references to other witnesses and the main ringleaders. Most of these instances involved men who became known to informants when passing through the jail. (See Table 2 for summary.)

The most effective testimony invoked the names of prisoners who had already been found guilty at trial, whether they were recently executed or still languishing in jail. At least seventy-eight times, witnesses mentioned

TABLE 2. Identification and judicial status of third parties whose names were mentioned by witnesses during trials of suspected conspirators in Antigua, 1736–1737.

STATUS OF THIRD PARTY AT THE TIME HIS OR HER NAME WAS MENTIONED	NUMBER OF INSTANCES
Convicted Slaves	109
Deceased	78
Awaiting Execution or Transportation	31
Prisoners Awaiting Trial	103
Slaves Ultimately Convicted	25
Slaves Ultimately Released	61
Free Blacks (held and tried separately)	17
At Large	30
Enslaved Men	6
Enslaved Women (never arrested)	24
Unknowable	27
TOTAL	269

Source: Antigua Slave Conspiracy Trials, in Antigua Council Minutes, TNA: PRO CO 9/10, 49–91; CO 9/11, 35–44. This data is drawn from the 56 extant trial records only, and does not account for the totality of names mentioned at all 132 trials that resulted in conviction.

the names of suspects who had already been executed. They invoked the deceased to populate their stories with conspirators of incontrovertible involvement in the plot. What's more, witnesses could also make claims about the speech or actions of dead conspirators with less danger of denials or contradictions. At least thirty-one times, witnesses named living conspirators, already convicted, who still sat in jail awaiting their fate of banishment or execution. Unlike dead conspirators, living convicts could still try to refute the details of a witness' evidence against another suspect. However, a determined witness could usually overpower the protests of a convicted conspirator whose credibility already suffered in the eyes of the judges.

In addition to fingering convicted men, witnesses also found power in mentioning the names of prisoners who still awaited trial. They used the names of jailed suspects at least 103 times. They incorporated newly jailed men into their testimony perhaps to avoid describing stale scenarios with familiar dead conspirators. Although witnesses correctly noted the cloud of suspicion hovering over these new inmates, they may have regretted their decisions when, later, only some of the men were deemed guilty at trial. Many were released or acquitted, including "at least one hundred" in a six-week period.[41]

Although it may appear that witnesses tried to limit new arrests by overwhelmingly naming suspects already in jail, in fact their decisions were far from heroic and did not resemble the racial solidarity that judges projected onto the enslaved population. Witnesses named dead, convicted, and jailed men in order to help prosecuting judges achieve convictions at trial. If these witnesses wanted to gum up the investigation, they had missed their chance during the pretrial examinations when inquisitors demanded fresh impeachments. In fact, it was precisely their early compliance that qualified them to serve as trial witnesses. At the trial stage, witnesses' indispensability to judges rested on their avoidance of patent falsehoods and their achievement of convictions. They knew that the judges valued a witness who gave plenty of detail yet seemed never to perjure himself. The tactic of naming dead, convicted, and jailed "conspirators" in trial testimony helped witnesses accomplish that standard, rendering them worthy of reprieve and reward. Coerced by their multiple incarcerations to contribute to the investigation, witnesses also relied on their physical imprisonment to produce useful testimony.

Convictions slowed in February 1737 when the magistrates noted the diminishing returns of their increasingly costly investigation. They eliminated the extra guards and patrols that drained the government coffers. Concerned about the expense of holding so many men in jail, the island's government pushed for a speedy contract with merchant Arthur Wilkinson to transport the convicts to the Spanish colonies. The last of the executions occurred in March 1737.[42]

Final Condemnation

Incarceration, and close confinement in particular, created an environment that perpetuated the Antigua conspiracy investigation and crystallized faulty knowledge about it. Incarceration—an instrument of coercion—encouraged confessions and recriminations. It brought together suspects into a physical prison where they exchanged information about the "findings" of the investigation. In this artificially intimate social setting, informants produced evidence they would not have otherwise known, including the identities of the likeliest suspects. In this makeshift jail under these coercive conditions, suspects overcame their social isolation to form alliances with one another, and informants secretly joined with investigators.

The pressures and processes of incarceration would not have produced the same abundance of knowledge for crimes other than conspiracy. Conspiracy, a crime of speech and intended violence, relied heavily upon social interconnection and hushed conversations; it was a crime predicated on community. When investigators demanded that suspects implicate their acquaintances, they pulled at threads and caused a social unraveling that began in the courthouse and affected most of the island's plantation communities. With mushrooming accusations and cascading arrests, trusting one's neighbor in a slave quarter could be as dangerous as relying on anyone encountered in prison. Conspiracy investigations severely undermined Afro-Caribbean communities that already struggled to cohere within the confines of slavery.

Colonial officials incompletely understood the social nature of the crime of conspiracy and especially the interpersonal aspect of the crime's investigation. In everyday life, to be sure, magistrates who anticipated attempted insurrections fretted endlessly about communication among slaves from far-flung plantations: they worried about unregulated visiting, group gatherings at funerals, and communication through drums and horns. And yet during conspiracy panics, ironically, the same magistrates who tried to prevent slaves from communicating also brought them together from disparate plantations into a confined space as jailed suspects. Not only did these prisoners experience the coercive pressure of their multiple incarcerations, they also assembled together in precisely the configuration officials feared. Whether or not these suspects had preexisting social connections, upon imprisonment they came to know each other through their common involvement with the investigation. Collective incarceration allowed suspects—encouraged them, even—to discuss what was happening to them and whatever they knew about the purported crime that had brought them together. Conversations that necessarily centered on their predicament also tended to sound to the judges like evidence of the conspiracy's authenticity. Through coercion and confinement, investigators asked the incarcerated to produce knowledge about an imagined conspiracy. The judges believed that the resulting "discoveries" confirmed their hunches, but they failed to comprehend that by incarcerating the powerless they did not face down their fears so much as they enacted a fantasy of mastery.

NOTES

The author would like to acknowledge the support of the American Academy of Arts and Sciences, the McNeil Center for Early American Studies (MCEAS), the John Carter Brown Library, the Princeton Institute for International and Regional Studies, and the Department of History at Princeton University at various stages in producing this essay. I am grateful to Sir Francis Ogilvy for permission to use the Walter Tullideph Letter Book in the Ogilvy of Inverquharity Papers at the National Archives of Scotland. Helpful critiques of earlier versions came from Linda Colley, Philip D. Morgan, Peter Silver, Brian Connolly, Natalie Zacek, Gergely Baics, Hannah Weiss Muller, Elena Schneider, the members of the Johns Hopkins seminar in Atlantic History, and the participants of the Incarceration Nation Conference sponsored by the MCEAS and the Library Company of Philadelphia. Thanks also to David Barry Gaspar for lending his expertise.

1. As late as 1750, Attaw's name and occupation still appeared on a list of people enslaved at the Parham plantation. Parham Attaw and Stephens's Dick, Trial of Vernon's Cudjoe, Jan. 26, 1737, The National Archives of the UK (TNA): Public Record Office (PRO) CO 9/11, fols. 13, 15; David Barry Gaspar, *Bondmen*

and Rebels: A Study of Master-Slave Relations in Antigua (Durham: Duke University Press, 1985), 103 (inventory information).

2. Herbert Aptheker, responding to sanguine portrayals of master-slave relations, presented an exhaustive catalog of revolts, plots, and rumors of unrest in mainland North America to argue for blacks' perpetual collective resistance against their enslavement. Subsequent scholars such as Michael Craton, Monica Schuler, David Barry Gaspar, Thomas J. Davis, and Douglas Egerton have contributed to Aptheker's argument by fleshing out the string of averted conspiracies, especially in the Caribbean, that would have been racial revolutions. Michael P. Johnson and Richard C. Wade have raised questions about the extent of revolutionary activity by iconic figures like Denmark Vesey and Gabriel Prosser. Peter Charles Hoffer has contributed to this revisionist school by framing the New York conspiracy (1741) as a legal event best understood from the vantage of the courthouse. Similarly, Winthrop Jordan emphasized the process, not findings, of the investigation when he pieced together an alleged plot in nineteenth-century Mississippi. Aptheker, *American Negro Slave Revolts* (New York: Columbia University Press, 1944); Wade, "The Vesey Plot: A Reconsideration," *Journal of Southern History* 30 (1964): 143–61; Schuler, "Akan Slave Rebellions in the British Caribbean," *Savacou* 1 (1970): 8–31; Schuler, "Ethnic Slave Rebellions in the Caribbean and the Guianas," *Journal of Social History* 3 (1970): 374–85; Craton, *Testing the Chains: Resistance to Slavery in the British West Indies* (Ithaca, N.Y.: Cornell University Press, 1982); Gaspar, *Bondmen and Rebels*; Davis, *A Rumor of Revolt: The "Great Negro Plot" in Colonial New York* (New York: Free Press, 1985); Egerton, *Gabriel's Rebellion: The Virginia Slave Conspiracies of 1800 and 1802* (Chapel Hill: University of North Carolina Press, 1993); Jordan, *Tumult and Silence at Second Creek: An Inquiry into a Civil War Slave Conspiracy* (Baton Rouge: Louisiana State University Press, 1993); Egerton, *He Shall Go Out Free: The Lives of Denmark Vesey* (Madison, Wis.: Madison House, 1999); Johnson et al., "*Forum:* The Making of a Slave Conspiracy," parts 1 and 2, *William and Mary Quarterly*, 3rd Series, 58 (2001): 913–76, and 59 (2002): 135–268; Hoffer, *The Great New York Conspiracy of 1741: Slavery, Crime, and Colonial Law* (Lawrence: University Press of Kansas, 2003).

3. Judges' Report, Dec. 30, 1736, in Antigua Council Minutes for Jan. 25, 1737, TNA: PRO CO 9/10, fols. 97–114; Walter Tullideph to David Tullideph, Jan. 15, 1737, Walter Tullideph Letter Book, Ogilvy of Inverquharity Papers, National Archives of Scotland (NAS), GD 205/53/8, 52–54.

4. For routine trials of lesser crimes, if enough justices of the peace assembled, they could convene a slave trial on the spot. One or two JPS sufficed at Antigua slave trials for most of the eighteenth century, depending on the seriousness of the crime. Slave trials in colonies other than Antigua required varying numbers of JPS, but they too were usually impromptu hearings at houses or taverns. Elsa V.

Goveia, *Slave Society in the British Leeward Islands at the End of the Eighteenth Century* (New Haven: Yale University Press, 1965), 169, 176, 182–84; Alan Watson, "North Carolina Slave Courts, 1715–1785," *North Carolina Historical Review* 60 (1983): 24–36; Philip J. Schwarz, *Twice Condemned: Slaves and the Criminal Laws of Virginia, 1705–1865* (Baton Rouge: Louisiana State University Press, 1988), 30; Thomas L. Morris, *Southern Slavery and the Law, 1619–1860* (Chapel Hill: University of North Carolina Press, 1996), 211–15; Robert Olwell, *Masters, Slaves and Subjects: The Culture of Power in the South Carolina Low Country* (Ithaca, N.Y.: Cornell University Press, 1998), 63, 75–76.

5. Ashton Warner (attorney general), Nathaniel Gilbert, John Vernon, and Robert Arbuthnot formed the first court; Benjamin King, Henry Douglas, Thomas Watkins, Valentine Morris, and Josiah Martin formed the second court.

6. Gaspar, *Bondmen and Rebels*, 83, 97–105 (population numbers); *Voyages: The Trans-Atlantic Slave Trade Database*, http://slavevoyages.org/tast/assessment /estimates.faces?yearFrom=1690&yearTo=1750&disembarkation=203.202 (accessed Feb. 2, 2009) (quickening pace of arrivals); Brian Dyde, *A History of Antigua: The Unsuspected Isle* (London: Macmillan Caribbean, 2000), 79–83; Goveia, *Slave Society in the British Leeward Islands*, 230–42; Vincent Brown, "Social Death and Political Life in the Study of Slavery," *American Historical Review* 114, no. 5 (Dec. 2009): 1231–49.

7. Robert Arbuthnot, Report on Discovery of a Conspiracy, [Oct. 15, 1736], in Antigua Council Minutes for Jan. 8, 1737, TNA: PRO CO 9/10, 41–50.

8. Deposition of Thomas Collins, Trial of Vernon's Cudjoe, Jan. 26, 1737; Judges' Report on Possibility of False Testimony, [Feb. 1737], Antigua Council Minutes. TNA: PRO CO 9/11, 16, 21–34.

9. For example, Gaspar, *Bondmen and Rebels*; Craton, *Testing the Chains*, chap. 10; Mindie Lazarus-Black, *Legitimate Acts and Illegal Encounters: Law and Society in Barbuda and Antigua* (Washington, D.C.: Smithsonian Institution Press, 1994); John Thornton, "The Coromantees: An African Cultural Group in Colonial North America and the Caribbean," *Journal of Caribbean History* 32, nos. 1–2 (1998): 161–78. See also other works cited in n. 2. The 134 guilty men included two free black men.

10. Judges' Note, Trial of Langford's Robin, Nov. 13, 1736; JN, Trial of Monk's Mingo, Nov. 15, 1736; Trial of Tom, Dec. 8, 1736; JN, Trial of Ocoo, Dec. 11, 1736; JN and Information of Elliott's Jemmy, Evidence against Johnno, Jan. 21, 1737; JN, Evidence against Royal's Hector, Jan. 26, 1737. TNA: PRO CO 9/10, 57, 59, 60, 83, 88; CO 9/11, 11, 19; Vere Langford Oliver, *History of the Island of Antigua*, 3 vols. (London: Mitchell and Hughes, 1894–99), 1:118.

11. Arbuthnot, Report on Discovery of a Conspiracy, [Oct. 15, 1736]; Langford's Billy, Trial of Morgan's Newport, Nov. 9, 1736. TNA: PRO CO 9/10, 41–47 (initial searches), 55 (ten gallons of powder).

12. Judges' Report, Dec. 30, 1736, Antigua Council Minutes; Antigua

Assembly Minutes, Oct. 22 and 23, 1736. TNA: PRO CO 9/10, 112; CO 9/12, fols. 14v–17. Morris, *Southern Slavery and the Law*, 238; Hoffer, *Great New York Conspiracy*, 28; Jill Lepore, *New York Burning: Liberty, Slavery, and Conspiracy in Eighteenth-Century Manhattan* (New York: Knopf, 2005), 91–92.

13. Judges' Messages to Governor, Nov. 6 and 11, 1736, Antigua Council Minutes. TNA: PRO CO 9/10, 2–3, 10; Letter from Boston, Mar. 15, 1737, *Virginia Gazette*, May 20, 1737 (quadrangle).

14. Judges' Note, Trial of Budinot's Dick, Nov. 19, 1736, TNA: PRO CO 9/10, 64, 65 (brother); Walter Tullideph to David Tullideph, Jan. 15, 1737, Tullideph Letter Book, Ogilvy Papers, NAS. For a rare recorded example of a dying confession, that of Codrington's Jacko (gibbeted), see Evidence against Billy Sabby, n.d. [after Jan. 20, 1737], CO 9/11, 41.

15. Jordan, *Tumult and Silence at Second Creek*, 90–94; James L. Given, *Inquisition and Medieval Society: Power, Discipline, and Resistance in Languedoc* (Ithaca, N.Y.: Cornell University Press, 1997), esp. 54; Peter Brooks, *Troubling Confessions: Speaking Guilt in Law and Literature* (Chicago: University of Chicago Press, 2000), esp. 20–21, 23–25; Lisa Silverman, *Tortured Subjects: Pain, Truth, and the Body in Early Modern France* (Chicago: University of Chicago Press, 2001), esp. 11, 86–88.

16. Judges' Message to Governor, Nov. 6, 1736, Judges' Note, and Messages of Council, Assembly, and Justices, Jan. 20, Mar. 9–10, 1737, Mar. 16, 1738, in Antigua Council Minutes. TNA: PRO CO 9/10, 2–3; CO 9/11, 39–40, 51, 56–59, 103–4; Gaspar, *Bondmen and Rebels*, 37–38.

17. For the use of unsworn slave testimony into the courtroom, see Morris, *Southern Slavery and the Law*, 229–35; Roger N. Buckley, "Slave Testimony at British Military Courts," in *A Turbulent Time: The French Revolution and the Greater Caribbean*, ed. David Barry Gaspar and David Patrick Geggus (Bloomington: Indiana University Press, 1997), 232.

18. For joint production, see Judges' Report on Possibility of False Testimony, [Feb. 1737], TNA: PRO CO 9/11, 23–24. For call backs, see Judges' Note, Trial of Vigo, Dec. 10, 1736, CO 9/10, 86. For group agreement, see JN, Trial of Ned Chester, Nov. 26, 1736, CO 9/10, 68–69. See also JN, Stephens's Dick, Trial of Cromwell, Nov. 30, 1736, and JN, Trial of Sydserf's Robin, Nov. 15, 1736, CO 9/10, 58, 75. A few of the earliest trials were open to the public, but the judges found that spectators gummed up the proceedings by asking too many questions of the suspects and the witnesses.

19. Trial of Cuffey, Dec. 13, 1736; Trial of Primus, Dec. 13, 1736; Chester's Frank (a spy), Evidence against Parham Watty, Jan. 14, 1737. TNA: PRO CO 9/10, 90 (wife), 90a (goats); CO 9/11, 9 (in presence of suspect).

20. Hoffer, *Great New York Conspiracy*, 27. For the assembly's extraordinary maneuvers to try the free black suspects Benjamin and Billy Johnson by bill of attainder, and for the brothers' robust defense, see Gaspar, *Bondmen and Rebels*, 43–62.

21. Deputy provost marshal Robert Delap, the eighteen-year-old son of grandee Francis Delap, oversaw the jail's day-to-day operation while provost marshal George Ford was away in England. By the end of the investigation, he spent £1,764 on provisions for guards and prisoners and on firewood for burning convicts. Robert Delap, petition to assembly, Nov. 29, 1736; Philip Darby, petition for one year's rent ending Dec. 27, 1736, Antigua Council Minutes, Jan. 31, 1737. TNA: PRO CO 9/10, 18, 132; Oliver, *History of the Island of Antigua*, 1:xcix, cii, 195–97; 2:305–8; 3:404, 419.

22. Chester's Frank (spy), Evidence against Parham Watty, Jan. 14, 1737; Judges' Report on Possibility of False Testimony, [Feb. 1737]. TNA: PRO CO 9/11, 9, 29–30.

23. Antigua Assembly Minutes, Oct. 22, 1736; Judges' Report on Possibility of False Testimony, [Feb. 1737]; Antigua Council Minutes, Mar. 10, 1737 and Mar. 16, 1738. TNA: PRO CO 9/11, 23–24, 29–30, 55, 104; CO 9/12, 15v–16.

24. Thomas Collins (guard), Trial of Vernon's Cudjoe, Jan. 26, 1737, TNA: PRO CO 9/11, 16.

25. Antigua Council Minutes for Nov. 29, Dec. 9, 20, 30, 1736, Jan. 3, Feb. 24, 1737. TNA: PRO CO 9/10, 16, 23, 28–29, 33, 37; CO 9/11, 45. Walter Tullideph to David Tullideph, Jan. 15, 1737, Tullideph Letter Book, Ogilvy Papers, NAS; Newcastle to BT, Nov. 3, 1736; Agents of the Leewards Islands to BT, [Nov. 23, 1736]; Memorial of West Indian Merchants to BT, Dec. 1, 1736. *Calendar of State Papers: Colonial Series* CD-ROM, ed. Karen Ordahl Kupperman, John C. Appleby, and Mandy Banton (Routledge and Public Record Office, 2000), Items 435, 460, 474, vol. 42 (1735–1736): 319, 336–38, 355–57.

26. Antigua Council Minutes and Governor's Message to Assembly, Jan. 3, 1737; Antigua Assembly Minutes, Jan. 24, 1737. TNA: PRO CO 9/10, 35–37; CO 9/12, 61v.

27. During the conspiracy panic in New York in 1741, the famously unbearable jail in the basement of the stone-built City Hall was crucial to the progress of the investigation. The New York jail was notorious for exposing prisoners to the elements and bringing them to the brink of starvation if they did not pay the jailer for food or receive it from friends outside. At the beginning of the conspiracy panic, the star witness Mary Burton testified only after she was threatened with the prospect of being jailed. The information she gave to avoid incarceration was crucial to expanding the inquiry. When more suspects had been corralled, the investigating justices leveraged the unpleasant jail once again by holding prisoners five extra days, delaying trial, in order to inspire confessions or accusations (Hoffer, *Great New York Conspiracy*, 54, 76, 80).

28. Trial of Skerret's Billy, Nov. 19, 1736; Trial of Delap's Tom, Dec. 8, 1736; Trial of Delap's Robin, Dec. 8, 1736; Judges' Note, Trial of John Sabby, Dec. 10, 1736; JN, Trial of Caesar alias Geddon, Dec. 10, 1736; JN, Trial of Troilus, Dec. 10, 1736. TNA: PRO CO 9/10, 63, 83, 85–88.

29. The investigators in New York in 1741 also relied on a spy in jail. Arthur Price, a white servant imprisoned for stealing goods, chatted up prisoners and loosened their tongues with rum punch bankrolled by the judges. He informed the jailer of any evidence he produced for the judges (Hoffer, *Great New York Conspiracy*, 85–86; Lepore, *New York Burning*, 86–89).

30. Judges' Note, Trial of Vigo, Dec. 10, 1736, TNA: PRO CO 9/10, 86.

31. Chester's Frank (spy), Trial of Budinot's Dick, Nov. 19, 1736; Godsell's Ionian, Evidence against Oliver's Quou, n.d.; Godsell's Ionian, Evidence against Cusack's Yorke, Dec. 12, 1736; Martin's Jemmy, Evidence against Parham Watty, Jan. 14, 1737; Hanson's Quash, Evidence against Barton's Joe, Jan. 20, 1737. TNA: PRO CO 9/10, 64–65 (Frank); CO 9/11, 9 (Jemmy), 13 (Ionian), 36 (Ionian, on Yorke saying "roast meat"), 38 (Quash).

32. Godsell's Ionian, Evidence against Parham Cuffey, Dec. 15, 1736; Godsell's Ionian, Evidence against Parham Watty, Jan. 14, 1737. TNA: PRO CO 9/11, 9, 37.

33. Chester's Frank (a spy), Trial of Budinot's Dick, Nov. 19, 1736; Judges' Note, Trial of George, Dec. 11, 1736. TNA: PRO CO 9/10, 65, 88–89. George received the faulty instruction from the spies Chester's Frank and Byam's Quaw.

34. Weatherill's Booty (spy), Evidence against Barton's Joe, Jan. 20, 1737; Weatherill's Booty, Langford's Cuffey, and Parham George, Trial of Vernon's Cudjoe, Jan. 26, 1737. TNA: PRO CO 9/11, 17, 40.

35. Weatherill's Booty, Langford's Cuffey, and Parham George, Trial of Vernon's Cudjoe, Jan. 26, 1737, TNA: PRO CO 9/11, 17.

36. Chester's Frank (a spy), Evidence against Parham Watty, Jan. 14, 1737, TNA: PRO CO 9/11, 9.

37. Judges' Note, Trial of Morgan's Newport, Nov. 9, 1736; JN, Trial of Monk's Mingo, Nov. 15, 1736; JN, Trial of Lavington's Sampson, Nov. 17, 1736. TNA: PRO CO 9/10, 55, 60, 61.

38. Antigua Council Minutes, Mar. 16 and Apr. 12, 1737, TNA: PRO CO 9/11, 77, 104; Daniel Horsmanden, *A Journal of the Proceedings in the Detection of the Conspiracy Formed by Some White People, in Conjunction with Negro and Other Slaves, for Burning the City of New-York* (New York: James Parker, 1744), 118–19 (coaching Pedro), 119–20 (trial), 147 (expert at plots).

39. Horsmanden, *Journal of the Proceedings*, 125.

40. Martin's Jemmy, Trial of Tilgarth Penezar alias Targut, Nov. 26, 1736, TNA: PRO CO 9/10, 71.

41. Judges' Reports, Antigua Council Minutes, Jan. 25 and 31, 1737; Judges' Report on Possibility of False Testimony, [Feb. 1737]. TNA: PRO CO 9/10, 116, 119; CO 9/11, 28 (quote).

42. Antigua Council Minutes, Apr. 12, 1737 and Mar. 16, 1738, TNA: PRO CO 9/11, 77, 104.

"There is no scandal like rags nor any crime
so shameful as poverty."
    — GEORGE FARQUHAR

"Wherever there is a man who exercises authority,
there is a man who resists authority!"
    — OSCAR WILDE

Incarcerated Innocents

Inmates, Conditions, and Survival Strategies in Philadelphia's Almshouse and Jail

SIMON P. NEWMAN AND BILLY G. SMITH

ON JUNE 17, 1787, SEVERAL PEOPLE hung through the windows of the Walnut Street Jail "angling for farthings," in the parlance of the time. Lowering their caps on long poles, they begged for quarter pennies from passersby. The inmates shouted, cursed, and "loaded" citizens who did not give them money "with the most foul and horrid imprecations." Throughout that hot summer, the prisoners hassled people, even taunting the likes of John Adams, Alexander Hamilton, and George Washington as they walked to and from the Constitutional Convention at the statehouse, just across the street from the Walnut Street Jail. The imprisoned "vagrants" broke both the institution's rules and state laws by begging, using vulgarity, and causing a public disturbance, but so what?

These were minor infractions compared to selling liquor and opium, squeezing new convicts for garnish (money), or stealing clothes and bedding—activities already common within the gaol. Colonial Philadelphia had rarely been a quiet, easy city for authorities; and it grew only more turbulent in the decades following the Revolution.[1]

Most of the farthing anglers were not criminals; they were merely poor. During the late eighteenth century, the single greatest cause of incarceration in the City of Brotherly Love was poverty. For every person incarcerated in jail for committing a criminal offense (usually a crime against property), fifteen Philadelphians were confined to either the jail or the almshouse because they were destitute, vagrant, sick, old, abandoned, or escaping slavery or servitude. Regardless of the causes, whether related to individual character or simply due to the vagaries of fortune, blameless people were locked up behind brick walls and sturdy doors far more often for being indigent than for any other reason. At the very same time that Philadelphians earned a reputation for their humanitarian treatment of lawbreakers, they imprisoned innocents in record numbers.[2]

City officials wanted to get the poor off the streets and into institutions that could refashion their morals and bring them into accord with strengthening middle-class values in the new nation. To authorities, the almshouse constituted an "asylum of beneficence," where the interred were "customers" rather than "inmates" or "prisoners." They planned the workhouse section of the jail to operate in a similar, if considerably more punitive fashion, hiring a "corrector of vagrants" to manage the place. These two institutions, as scholars from Michel Foucault to Michael Meranze have recognized, were intended to control, "correct," and discipline the bodies and minds of the poor and instruct them in the values of hard work, dependability, and self-control.[3]

After the Revolution, a growing population of poor people forced officials to respond. Thousands of people—black, white, and the Irish—flooded Philadelphia, frightening city residents and local authorities. The number of black Philadelphians doubled in the 1780s, then tripled again during the next decade. Free African Americans and escaped slaves born on American soil accounted for most of this flood of migrants, and a thousand black refugees from the revolution in Saint Domingue (Haiti) added another stream in the 1790s. The economic dislocation following the American Revolution likewise produced a tributary of white Americans to the city, while a cascade of Irish passengers disembarked at the port at the turn of the century. "By the resort of people, both by sea and land, to this metropolis, many become burdensome," complained almshouse managers. "In addition . . . the city and environs are greatly oppressed by numbers of beggars and vagrants, not only from various parts of this State, but from many others of the United States."[4]

These "vagabonds of all nations" posed acute challenges to the social order because of their growing assertiveness. Inspired by the American Revolution's ideology of equality and liberty as well as by the circumstances of their daily lives, the urban lower classes became more insolent and impudent. Laboring people frequently and freely articulated their own sense of morality without the cloak of deference. Black slaves from Saint Domingue and their migrant counterparts from the United States introduced a new militancy into the city's race and class relations: with racial slaughter devastating the Caribbean island, the boldness of Philadelphia's enslaved and free blacks alarmed many of the city's white residents. Accordingly, authorities responded by redefining and strictly enforcing "vagrancy" as a crime, by hardening rules in the almshouse and jail, and by tightening residency requirements allowing indigents to receive public assistance.[5]

Forcing vagrants into these two carceral institutions did not resolve these social conflicts; doing so merely relocated them behind the walls of the almshouse and the gaol. Interactions among managers and inmates involved complex, nuanced negotiations. Historians have theorized about the infrapolitics and microresistance involved in these types of confrontations and compromises, but they have been considerably less successful in specifying the day-to-day reality of those relationships.[6] The interactions inside these two institutions, especially the ways in which inmates devised ways to accept, accommodate, manipulate, bargain, resist, and challenge the turnkeys and the almshouse stewards, is the focus of this essay. Their daily engagement in infrapolitics allowed many of these men and women to achieve a range of goals, including making financial ends meet, improving the chances of their physical survival, enhancing the quality of their existence, expressing their resentment against the organization of society, expanding control over their own lives, and even, on occasion, gaining their personal freedom from racial bondage and indentured servitude.

Inmates

When the runaway Benjamin Franklin arrived in 1723, Philadelphia was little bigger than an English market town. In common with most residents and new arrivals, Franklin did not seek out or require public relief.[7] Rarely during the first half of the eighteenth century did more than 1 percent of Philadelphians depend upon public relief. This changed dramatically during the second half of the eighteenth century, as the city expanded spectacularly, its population buoyed by natural increase, in-migration of new arrivals from other colonies, and immigration from Europe and the Caribbean. A quickly growing immigrant population, business cycles, and the inequalities inherent to commercial capitalism encouraged the intensification of wealth disparities. The Seven Years' War and then the War for Independence compounded the difficulties faced by a growing number of impoverished Philadelphians who found themselves unable to feed, clothe, and house themselves and their families.

Philadelphia endured several economic downturns during the late eighteenth century, which battered the lower sort in particular. The interruptions in trade occasioned by the War for Independence and the Napoleonic Wars exacerbated unemployment. These dislocations meant that poverty increased among previously "respectable" working folk, and the city's system of poor relief was forced to accommodate ordinary laboring people who simply could not make ends meet. When Mary McNeal broke her thigh, she had no recourse but the almshouse because her husband, "a poor labouring man," was unable "to support himself and her." Ignatius Waterman's illness made it impossible for him to continue working, with the result that he and his entire family were forced into the almshouse.[8]

During the final quarter of the eighteenth century, approximately 5 percent of the population of the rapidly growing city was on poor relief, a massive increase in both numerical and proportional terms. The number of Philadelphians receiving support was likely much larger, however, since private organizations and charities provided further relief to impoverished workers and to many who were ineligible for public support, including sailors, slaves, servants, and free blacks. The absence of records makes it impossible to gain an accurate sense of the scale of poor relief in the late eighteenth century, but historians have calculated that one-third—and during hard times, as many as one-half—of Philadelphians received some form of aid. What is clear is that destitute Philadelphians applied to or were confined to the almshouse, or to the adjacent house of employment, only as a last resort.

One of the largest buildings constructed in the colonies in the decade before the Revolution, the joint almshouse and house of employment was both a refuge and a prison. Its two buildings were intended to function quite differently: the east wing (almshouse) housed the supposed "deserving poor" who were incapable of working; the west wing (house of employment) incarcerated those who could work. Before authorities turned over a portion of the city jail to function as a workhouse in 1789, the house of employment also accommodated vagrants. Yet, despite such investments in infrastructure, the annual cost of poor relief remained expensive. To balance their budgets, civic authorities raised taxes to support assistance and devised ever-more-stringent residency requirements, forcing many nonresident paupers to leave Philadelphia and treating those vagrants admitted to the almshouse to a regime so severe it seemed almost penal.

In theory, only legal residents of Philadelphia (including Southwark and the Northern Liberties) were entitled to enter the almshouse. Those who sought admission required signed documentation from one of the official Guardians of the Poor, attesting to their good character and straitened circumstances. Both those who sought admission and those who were involuntarily incarcerated had details of their residence recorded by an almshouse clerk, so that the appropriate section of the city could be billed for the cost of incarceration. These records reveal, however, that a number of people sought admission without proper documentation, pleading their cases and attesting to their place of origin within the city.[9]

Admission records reveal that the inhabitants of the Philadelphia almshouse were a diverse yet vulnerable group. Almshouse officials in 1800 and 1801, for example, recorded that among the 895 men, women, and children admitted, 6 percent were elderly, like eighty-five-year-old William Wooten, "feeble and unable to contribute towards his support." Many more, a total of 53 percent, were incapacitated by sickness and disease, especially venereal infections: John Morris was an elderly German who had arrived in Philadelphia as a servant many years before, and had served in the army during the Revolution, but was currently "poor, sick and palsied" and unable to work.

The most pressing reason for people to apply voluntarily for admission to the almshouse was desperation. The Daily Occurrence Docket is filled with the names and descriptions of new inmates who lacked the basics of life: food, clothing, fuel, and shelter. Many had been employed, but some had been sleeping in stables and wagons, others were frostbitten, some were emaciated from starvation, and a few were paralyzed by disease (see figure 7).

Children and women comprised significant portions of the almshouse population. Children entered when their parents were no longer able to provide for them, when their parents died, or, as was the case for both Margaret Dillmore and Frederick Robertson, when their mothers and fathers deserted them.[10] White women, rarely able to earn more than about half as much as men, often found themselves at the almshouse gate when their husbands died, left, or fell ill. Mariah Rawling and her three children were forced to seek refuge in the almshouse after they were abandoned by her husband, as did Sarah Hamilton whose husband

FIGURE 7. William Birch, *Alms House in Spruce Street* (Philadelphia: W. Birch & Son, 1799). Courtesy of the Library Company of Philadelphia.

eloped upon learning that Sarah was expecting their child.[11] For pregnant and physically abused women, the almshouse was a very different kind of refuge.

While almshouse authorities were generally sympathetic to abandoned wives and children, unmarried women and prostitutes often received a less favorable reception. Those who entered the almshouse while pregnant were pressured and strenuously interrogated, even during labor itself, to reveal the identity of the father so that he might be held financially accountable for the cost of the care and upkeep of both mother and child. When frightened and vulnerable young expectant mothers refused to reveal the identity of the father, they were questioned closely and intensely during the actual delivery: Sophia Watson finally "Declared in the Extremity of her labour, That one Cornelius Hyatt, a young lad of Allen Town in New Jersey is the Father of her said Child." Sophia's daughter died within a month. The almshouse authorities were surely surprised when Mary Berry revealed that "the Father of the Child that she now bears is Named Matthias Clay, a Member of [the U.S.] Congress."[12] Perhaps because of the ways in which they were treated as being guilty of a crime, and knowing that their children would quite likely be taken and bound out, some women sought to escape the almshouse. Such was the case with Rachel Davis and Sarah Smith, "Two pregnant women who last night both Eloped." Somewhat bemused at this action by two heavily pregnant women, the clerk noted that "It is strange how they got away."[13]

Prostitutes were deemed to be the most undeserving of the poor, ranked lowest in the estimation of civic and almshouse authorities, and judged most worthy of incarceration. These women were often suffering from the venereal diseases that would deform and kill many of them, and they received medical care and treatment in the almshouse, leading authorities to complain that prostitutes "repeatedly Burthen & incommode this Institution with this Filthy Disease, & Still with Impunity."[14]

African American inmates of the almshouse confronted similar attitudes. With the largest free black community in the nation, and the first free black church, the City of Brotherly Love became a beacon for free blacks and for runaway slaves after the war. Yet, while many found work, others faced limited opportunities in a society that restricted employment by race as well as gender. Consequently, former slaves like Cato, James Breahere, and Sarah Bordley were forced by poverty, illness, and injury to enter the almshouse.[15]

The increasing number of newcomers in the city, together with the dramatic rise in the number of paupers, encouraged a significant change in elite attitudes toward the poor. Many of those who were incarcerated in the almshouse were innocent of anything other than hunger, homelessness, and poverty. However, Pennsylvania and Philadelphia state officials decided that those who could not support themselves in respectable employment should be removed from the streets and committed to an institution in which they were required to work. Homelessness and joblessness were redefined as vagrancy, a crime that might be punished by expulsion or by incarceration and forced labor. Such attitudes and policies had long been common in England, but it was only in the later eighteenth century that civic authorities in American cities began to regard symptoms of poverty as evidence of personal moral degeneracy and criminality rather than as the result of larger social circumstances. The rising number of impoverished immigrants from Europe, especially Ireland, as well as of black migrants from the middle states and upper South (and during the 1790s from Haiti) contributed to an increasing sense that a rapidly growing class of masterless men and women threatened property, proper social order, and good republican government.[16]

While many impoverished folk voluntarily sought refuge in the almshouse during the 1780s, the number of poor people arrested and incarcerated for vagrancy increased dramatically during the 1780s and 1790s. A new law in the spring of 1790 gave officials the legal right to sweep vulgar riffraff off the streets and into the gaol. The newly hired High Constable responded vigorously, confining 455 vagrants in the first year. Within five years, constables escorted more than 900 people to the jail annually.[17] The number of vagrants and indigents committed to the almshouse or jail thus far eclipsed the number of convicted lawbreakers in the 1790s (see table 3).

To middling and elite Philadelphians, vagrancy was not only criminal in itself, but it also offered suggestive evidence of a criminal disposition and a disinclination to industrious behavior—an offense to a middle-class morality that emphasized the value of hard work. Articles from Philadelphia's newspapers reveal that the meaning of "vagrancy" itself assumed a new viciousness in the decades after the American Revolution. Vagrants were not just "idle" but also had "depraved morals" and no "principles." In the 1780s and 1790s, the term *vagrancy* evolved to describe a host of "disorderly" people, including not only the "wandering poor" but also Indians, ex-slaves, apprentices, protestors,

TABLE 3. Incarcerations in Philadelphia.

YEAR	ALMSHOUSE ADMISSIONS	"VAGRANTS" (JAIL)	CONVICTS (JAIL)
1790	888	455	112
1791	—	435	78
1792	754	376	65
1793	727	272	45
1794	825	304	92
1795	939	924	116
1796	1039	924	145
1797	1050	924	114
1798	1159	924	122
1799	821	—	145
1800	1091	—	—
MEAN ANNUAL AVERAGE	929	615	103

Sources: Almshouse admissions are from the Daily Occurrence Docket and the Treasurer, General Ledger, Guardians of the Poor, Philadelphia City Archives. The number of vagrants between 1790 and 1794 are from the Vagrancy Dockets, Philadelphia City Archives. In *The Cradle of the Penitentiary: The Walnut Street Jail at Philadelphia 1773–1785* (Philadelphia: Temple University Press, 1955), 138, Negley K. Teeters found that 3,698 vagrants were confined to prison from 1795 through 1798; this table includes the average for each of those four years. The number of convicts is from Rex A. Skidmore, "Penological Pioneering in the Walnut Street Jail, 1789–1799," *Journal of Criminal Law and Criminology* 39, no. 2 (July–August 1948): 172.

prostitutes, political radicals, the lower classes in general, a few pesky Canadians, and, of course, the Irish. This motley crew, possessed of "neither property nor principle," was well known (at least by nonvagrants) to be burglars and horse thieves.[18] According to officials, they required institutionalization and constant supervision (see table 4).

The language of admission records for the institutions likewise reflected changing attitudes toward vagrants: Daniel Murphy, his wife and their two children were "Noted Vagrants & beggars & infamous former Customers," Mary Allen was admitted as "a naked Distressed Rambler swarming with vermin," while James Willis appears in the docket as a "Vagrant Pockey Negro" who died a month following his incarceration in the almshouse.[19] A growing number of men and women accused of vagrancy were apparently well known to city authorities, having cycled through multiple civic institutions. For instance, in 1799, Rebecca Jones was incarcerated for disturbing the peace, completing her circuit through the almshouse, the workhouse section of the jail, and the

TABLE 4. Alleged crimes of people recorded in the Vagrancy Docket for Philadelphia County.

CRIME	PEOPLE IN VAGRANCY DOCKET %
Assault	2
Begging	1
Runaway slaves, servants, apprentices, or mariners	16
Misbehaved slaves, servants, apprentices, or mariners	8
Disorderly or drunken conduct	27
Miscellaneous	3
Prostitution	4
Vagrancy	40
TOTAL	101

Source: Vagrancy Docket, 1790–1932, Philadelphia City Archives. Based on a sample of 533 people in the Vagrancy Docket for 1791, 1792, and 1804. When a person was accused of multiple crimes, only the initial one noted by the clerk was counted in the tabulations. The proportion of inmates who were prostitutes is a minimum, since they often were charged with other crimes instead.

jail itself.[20] Similarly, Robert Nesbit Jr. passed between the Pennsylvania Hospital and the almshouse. Upon his admission into the latter institution, he was recorded as

> a notorious, worthless chap. . . . a common nuisance to the institution, [who] has been here repeatedly and has often eloped; not long since he was discharged from the Pennsylvania Hospital where he had been some considerable time a burthensome charge to this House.[21]

In case after case, the records obliquely suggest that many people incarcerated as vagrants were innocent of any actual lawbreaking. Their real crime was unemployment and poverty. Sarah Ann Boardley had been manumitted by her Maryland master Robert Thompson. Denied legal residence anywhere close to her family, she, like many freed blacks, had migrated to Philadelphia. For two long years she had struggled to support herself and her five-year-old daughter Ann "in the line or business of a Washerwoman." Yet, no matter how hard she worked, her wages could not support an adult and a child. She finally entered the alms-house so "much afflicted with pains through all her limbs that she cannot labour for her support." Mother and child were "in a perishing condition," having avoided incarceration for as long as possible, but to no avail. In December 1800, Ann was taken from her mother and bound out for thirteen years, so that when Sarah was released in March 1801 she had been somewhat restored to good health and freedom but had lost her small family.[22]

Conditions

However innocent of crime many may have been, those confined to the late-eighteenth-century almshouse entered a kind of low-security gaol or house of correction. A prison is often defined as a place of incarceration into which inmates are legally committed, effectively depriving such people of their personal liberty in an environment wherein all of their activities are strictly regulated. As such, jails have much in common with the almshouses of late-eighteenth-century America. Surrounded by a tall fence and secured by locked gates and a doorkeeper, the Philadelphia almshouse required inmates to rise and retire at fixed times, prescribed institutional clothing, regulated mealtimes, and proscribed items like alcohol. Able-bodied inmates were forced to work in order to help pay the cost of their own incarceration. Lesser-skilled men, women, and children engaged in such mind- and finger-numbing work as picking oakum, while those with appropriate skills spun, sewed, made clothes and shoes, gardened, or pursued such trades as were of benefit to the almshouse. Punishment awaited anyone who, according to the almshouse rules, "neglect to repair to their proper places for work, or being there, shall refuse to work or shall tatter, be idle, or shall not well perform the task of work set them."[23]

To civic authorities and numerous reformers, the almshouse/house of employment combination was intended to function as a "bettering-house" or reformatory. Within its walls, the indigent and helpless poor would be confined and cared for, with many prepared for a productive and socially useful existence upon their release. However, to the urban and transient poor, the almshouse more often seemed like a prison, a place to avoid when possible, since within its walls they would be controlled, their behavior modified, and their morals "improved." Removed from the relative freedom of Philadelphia's markets, streets, and docks, almshouse residents were expected to "behave soberly, decently, and Courteously to each other," and they were required to act "submissively to their superiors & Governors."[24] Those who disobeyed the almshouse rules were disciplined, as in the cases of such men and women as Richard Crosby, Ann Wallace, and James McGroty, all of whom had disobeyed the prohibition on alcohol. The more serious the transgression, the greater the punishment. When Anthony Muff, "an Old Gardener and very worthless former Customer," was drunk and impudent, the almshouse steward sent him to the "black hole."[25] The fact that almshouse officials referred to the penal cell as a "black hole"—the familiar term for a military prison—shows that even authorities who proclaimed the virtues of the bettering-house were all too aware of its dual role as a place of incarceration.[26]

Almshouse authorities also took undue liberties that undermined the integrity of the family unit. While 23 percent of the children admitted into the almshouse had been orphaned or deserted by their parents, almost three times that number were incarcerated with one or both parents, or they belonged to parents who were unable to support them.[27] Once admitted, almshouse authorities regularly usurped parental authority and set about apprenticing such children out, compelling them to labor as indentured servants and apprentices in exchange for their bed, board, and training.

Recognizing the dangers facing their children, and desperate to keep their families together, married couples and single parents often struggled to prevent the almshouse authorities from binding out their children. Isabella Johnson's child, who was not even named by the almshouse record-keepers, was bound out to Philadelphian John Schneeds. Upon her release from the almshouse, "the Mother of said Child, finding to who it was bound, went and took her away by force." For this crime, Johnson was confined to the jail and her child returned to the almshouse; as punishment, Johnson was herself bound out for fourteen years to a farmer in Delaware. While the records make no further mention of the child, it is likely that he or she was returned to Schneeds. Mary Ann Landram's escape from the almshouse was facilitated by her brother, who was determined to prevent his sister from being bound out. However, such examples of successful resistance to the binding out of children were rare.[28]

Conditions were no better in the jail (see figure 8). The 1790 law specified that inmates there were to be "clothed in habits of coarse material." They were "sustained upon bread, Indian meal [cornmeal], or other inferior food" and "allowed one meal of coarse meat in each week." The notations in the Vagrancy Docket that Henry was to receive "no Bread" and that Billy was "to be fed upon Bread & Water only for the space of 36 Hours" indicates that jailkeepers sometimes cut rations even more, in this case for two African Americans identified only by their first names. As in the almshouse, labor was the prescribed cure for their moral failings. According to the rules, inmates must "work every day in the year, except Sundays" for between eight and ten hours daily, not counting "an interval of half an hour for breakfast, and an hour for dinner." Spinning, cabinet making, and cutting of nails and stone did, however, make the occupational possibilities more varied than in the almshouse, at least for men.[29]

Resistance

In response to the various humiliations associated with their incarceration, inmates found various ways to resist: passively, actively, subversively, and directly. The most defiant and obvious act of resistance was to escape

FIGURE 8. William Birch, *Goal [sic] in Walnut Street* (Philadelphia: R. Campbell, 1799). Courtesy of the Library Company of Philadelphia.

incarceration, and many poor folk absconded from the almshouse, even though they could not leave legally without the consent of the steward. For some inmates, running away surely was a political act, an expression of personal rebellion. For others, it was a coping mechanism, a response to their incarceration for the crime of being poor. For some alcoholics, taking flight was necessary to obtain liquor. Thus, "notwithstanding his being seventy years of age," Matthew Richards "scaled the fence" one morning, presumably in search of rum. Later that day, after being "brought back in a Cart," he climbed the barrier again. "He has been here often," the clerk noted dryly, "and always took this method in getting out." Robert Nesbit and James Loddo, like many others, were frequent "customers" of the institution who ran away nearly every time. Hugh O'Hara, after being "cured and cloathed and now very Hearty—is according to Custom run off."[30]

For many, escape was a strategy to preserve their survival. Some female inmates in jail, according to one official, performed extra spinning "for a short space only, to obtain clothing, then generally run off." Authorities experienced even greater problems keeping the inmates in their cells. In the late 1780s, nearly 30 percent of the prisoners fled, some in mass escapes. Jack, incarcerated on suspicion of being a runaway slave, promptly scaled the prison's wall; he may have confirmed the jailer's fears that he would sneak onto a ship bound for anywhere outside of North America.[31]

Insolence, rule breaking, refusal to work—all were additional forms of noncompliance and passive resistance practiced by the institutional poor. Instances of this behavior tumble from the pages of the dockets of the almshouse and jail. Anthony Muff, the old gardener mentioned previously, "made use of very impertinent language" in the almshouse, thereby challenging the rules about deferential conduct; the steward punished him with detention in "the black hole." Judith Boyd, "past all description impudent," and Daniel Boyd, "as impudent as possible," likewise suffered the steward's chastisement. John Howell, nicknamed the "singing sailor," not only was rude to almshouse bureaucrats but also spent forty days in jail for, in his words, "having a brush with the Mayor in the public Market."[32]

Others took the opposite approach, manipulating authorities with their verbal eloquence. As novelist Charles Brockden Brown noted about the Philadelphia protagonist in *Arthur Mervyn*, "He had always been cautious of giving countenance to vagrants, that came from nobody knew where, and worked their way with a plausible tongue." Then, as now, an artfulness of speech could fool authorities, achieve personal goals, ease the burdens of living on the margins, and perhaps provide a sense of satisfaction for having outsmarted the powerful. Almshouse admission records regularly include such terms as "artful" and "imposter," demonstrating that the authorities were inclined to disbelieve much of what they were told by those who were admitted.[33]

Liquor, often a comfort to those in distress, was omnipresent in both the jail and the almshouse in the years following the Revolution. In 1787, according to a Grand Jury report, debtors and criminals gathered in the main corridor of the gaol, where the jailer peddled liquor "at the door, by small measure, or by his permission, contrary . . . to the law of this commonwealth." At the same time, the smuggling of rum into the almshouse was so widespread that managers complained about "the Generality" of the house being "devoted" to the beverage. Both institutions cracked down on these activities, in part because they had gotten out of control, but also because officials in the new nation grew increasingly concerned about transforming the morals of criminals and indigents. In the early 1790s, almshouse overseers stopped distributing the traditional daily allowance of rum to inmates who worked. They even prohibited the possession or consumption of any liquor in the institution. Ann Wallace and James McGroty were but two of the numerous inmates who violated that policy. Harry Musgrove made it a "Practice of going over the fence for Rum in the night, with which he got intoxicated & behaved very riotous & disorderly, greatly to the disturbance of the other People." Richard Crosby "introduced spirituous liquor among some of the women . . . the consequence of which was, disorderly and quarrelsome behavior." The steward sent Crosby to jail.[34]

Some inmates focused their energies on gaming the system, devising ingenious tactics to make ends meet, including using the city's welfare system to their own advantage. Retreating to the almshouse for a few weeks in the colder months when work was scarce was such a common strategy that it earned its own nickname: "burning the ken."[35] Like numerous other indigents, Philip and Sarah Haines entered "as usual to be fed and kept warm during the Winter and jump the fence in the Spring." Sarah, complained the clerk, is "as good at fence jumping as [Philip] is." The winds of "cold Boreas" blew John Douglass into the institution nearly every winter. "Poor and ragged," according to the Docket, Douglass "is come in at this time as usual for Winter quarter to be clothed and kept Warm, and in the Spring go out and continue till autumn."

James Barry, a "frequent Autumnal Customer," entered the almshouse with the common complaint of "sore legs," to "be nursed, doctored and kept warm all Winter, and when cured, he will procure a discharge and go out in the spring as usual." Barry initially applied to the almshouse in October 1789; he was admitted at least sixteen more times during the next decade and a half. An invalid soldier from the Revolutionary War, Barry drew an annual pension from the federal government, part of which he paid to the almshouse to help defray the cost of his maintenance. When he left the institution in 1790, Elizabeth McGee, a "Noted Strumpet," according to the clerk, went with him as his wife. They and their three children entered again in November 1793. The Managers bound one child in 1793 and another in 1796. Arrested for larceny and burglary in 1798, James landed in the jail the next year as a vagrant. He had achieved the status of a "gentleman of three inns," having been an inmate of the workhouse portion of the gaol and the almshouse.[36]

African Americans were among the almshouse residents who resisted incarceration, with occasionally remarkable success. As the moral and legal power of slaveowners in Pennsylvania declined after the Revolution, some bondspeople seized the initiative: they challenged their masters by refusing to obey them. With fewer disciplinary options (like whipping or selling their slaves out of state), frustrated slaveowners more frequently paid to incarcerate their slaves in jail. Between 1793 and 1797, whites imprisoned nearly 700 black people in Philadelphia's jail at a time when the entire state contained fewer than 2,000 slaves. Even President George Washington's power was stretched thin in his Philadelphia household: Wilhelmina Tyser and Martin Cline were both confined to the jail, Tyser for "being a disorderly Servant," and Cline for "being frequently Drunk, neglecting his duty, and otherwise misbehaving." As long as they paid for their upkeep, masters could confine their human property to the city's jail indefinitely.[37]

However, slaves who refused to toil either in the institution or for their owners created a conundrum for their titleholders: either pay for the maintenance of workers who did not work, or come to some accommodation with them. Slaves who behaved in this fashion had pushed the issue, adopting a pattern of disobedient, disrespectful, unruly, and even violent behavior once incarcerated, and refusing to submit and return to obediently work for their masters afterward. Jean Baptiste (likely a slave from Saint Domingue) refused to go back to his owner or "consent to do his duty."[38] Faramong likewise "refused to be removed from the Work House and be employed in his Masters Service," while Frank "*positively* refused to return to his Masters house or to serve him." Laurencine declined "in a *peremptory* manner to return to the Service of her Master." Fortune was "charged with *peremptorily* refusing to serve her master."[39]

"Peremptorily," of course, means aggressively, assertively, forcefully, demandingly, or, by Samuel Johnson's eighteenth-century definition, *absolutely* and *positively*. The white clerk who kept the Vagrancy Dockets used these words, although we might make an educated guess about the gist if not the precise language employed by the slaves themselves. If they adopted lower-class slang common in the Atlantic world, they may have called their master or their jailer a "bloody mutton-headed cacafue-ogo" (translation: a damned stupid shit-fire tyrant). Alternatively, they may have drawn on a rich West African and Caribbean vocabulary to express similar strongly held feelings. Fortune, unfortunately, endured the consequences of such risky behavior, spending four months in the workhouse portion of the jail, on a diet of bread and water, but refusing *peremptorily* at the end of each month to return to her master. Officials eventually transferred her from the almshouse to the jail, where she disappeared from the historical records.[40]

On rare but precious occasions, these strategies of defiance succeeded in gaining slaves their liberty. Harry, described as "mild," "slow spoken," and with scars on his hand and cheek, was born seven years before Pennsylvania's 1780 gradual emancipation law, meaning that he was condemned to bondage for life. When he turned seventeen, Harry ran away, making it as far as Chester (south of Philadelphia) before he was caught and incarcerated. He broke out of the Chester institution but then was recaptured and returned to his master. Six months later, in February 1791, Harry's owner confined him in the Philadelphia jail for "disorderly behavior, getting drunk, and absenting himself day and Night from the service of his master." A month of hard labor clearly did not break Harry's spirit. Just one day after being released to his owner, he absconded again, landing in jail for another thirty days. In May, Harry fled his master for the third time, for which he was imprisoned eight days. He ran once again just a single day after his discharge, followed by one more week behind bars, where this time he was forced to dine on a diet of bread and water. Harry appears in the Vagrancy Docket in August, with the same limited cuisine, for—what else?—running away. Harry apparently was not very good at eluding the authorities; or, maybe he was. Perhaps he may have had a grander plan in mind. After spending another week in the jail in September, Harry refused either to leave the institution or to promise better behavior. Harry had pushed his master to the limit. Wanting "to avoid trouble," his owner finally caved in. He signed a contract drawn up by the Pennsylvania Abolition Society, which promised Harry freedom in six years. Harry, in turn, agreed to serve his master "faithfully" as an indentured servant during that entire time. The Abolition Society, which regularly visited black prisoners in jail, drafted dozens of similar contracts during the 1790s as slaves learned that resistance and a willingness to endure months in the jail sometimes resulted in the incredible reward of freedom.[41]

While some of those in both the jail and the almshouse resisted their incarceration, others feigned sickness and injury in order to enter the almshouse, since officials usually did not accept lack of employment as sufficient grounds for admission. When work was slow, the vague excuse of "sore legs" reached near epidemic proportions among able-bodied people struggling to make ends meet. While "sore legs" referred to dermatological symptoms or inflammation occasioned by malnutrition, in its early stages the condition was often not visible to the naked eye. Thus "sore legs" provided a justification for both infirm and able people who sought refuge or relief in the almshouse. Yet, even those who sought entry were not slow to negotiate the terms of their stay, taking full advantage of their situation and stealing large items or pilfering smaller ones. Walking off with clothing, food, furniture, and bedding from the almshouse was a popular enterprise in the 1780s, and these activities were part of the justification for building a brick wall around the institution in 1789. By pawning clothes acquired in the almshouse to buy liquor, a good many people became "Master of the Wardrobe," a slang parody of the official position in the British Royal Household. Archibald McCowan "comes here for Maintenance [and] Clothing," then "robs the House of blankets," "runs off," and "then returns and so keeps up a Regular Round of Villainy." Hugh O'Hara followed a similar strategy: he "Winter'd here, got cured & clothed, and went off in the Spring . . . and immediately sold most of his Clothing and soon drank the whole they produced." Not everyone imbibed their illegally gotten gains; some spent it on necessities like food and firewood, attempting to reassert their independence and exercise control over their own lives.[42]

Some pregnant women challenged authorities directly. When pressured to identify the father-to-be, Charlotte Britton declared that "she will suffer death sooner than she will expose the Man who is father of the Child she now bears." The almshouse steward sent Margaret Saffern to jail for "obstinately persisting" in not naming the father. After two weeks in jail, Saffern still refused to disclose his identity. While being returned to the almshouse, she fled to a friend's home, where she gave birth. Saffern apparently never revealed the name. Sarah Lackey misidentified the father of her child, claiming that Samuel Hanson, a white man who worked in the institution's bakery, had impregnated her. The almshouse clerk could not resist demeaning Sarah and Samuel with a smutty joke, writing that if Hanson "had heated one Oven only, it would have been better for him." When Lackey gave birth to "a Mulatto Child whom she calls Charlotte Marborough," suspicion fell on Thomas Marborough, a "Black Man who eloped" from the almshouse six months earlier, as "the real Father of the Child." Many pregnant women, regardless of their vulnerable position, simply refused to bow to power.[43]

Of course, not every act of defiance qualified as conscious, planned resistance to the institution and the power behind it. Like all humans, inmates were sometimes simply cranky, obdurate, tired, or in need of a tankard of grog (rum and water), and they responded accordingly. From the perspective of officials, though, resistance was resistance, no matter what the motivation. And it did have its effects. One important impact of daily defiance was that the almshouse managers found it harder than ever to make the institution financially solvent. Too many detainees worked at a slow pace or refused to work at all. Even in the best of economic times, shoemaking, oakum picking, tailoring, sewing, and clothes-washing barely permitted free people to earn a living, regardless of how hard they labored.[44] The capitalist system usually rewarded these lesser-skilled, if still arduous, tasks with wages below subsistence. When institutionalized people worked with considerably less diligence, the chances of making a profit for the almshouse were nonexistent. Oliver Lynch, for example, dismayed officials by being "too lazy to work out doors, or in doors." They jailed him for a few days, and then actually discharged him from the almshouse for his recalcitrance. Like many others, Lynch challenged and rejected the bourgeois values that emphasized hard, continual toil, which ennobled labor for its own sake.[45]

The Crime of Being Poor

"There is no scandal like rags," wrote George Farquhar in 1707, "nor any crime so shameful as poverty."[46] During the late eighteenth and early nineteenth centuries, Philadelphia experienced the kind of dramatic increase in the ranks of the rootless poor that had so terrified English authorities in Farquhar's day. The English playwright's sentiments were echoed by elite and civic authorities of late-eighteenth-century Philadelphia, who were both shocked and frightened by the increasing number of poor Philadelphians, and they held their impoverished neighbors morally and legally responsible for their own condition. There were indeed many more poor Philadelphians, for between 1760 and 1800 the population of their city had almost tripled while population density had nearly doubled.[47] The small market town of the late-colonial era seemed a distant memory to early national Philadelphians, whose rulers sought to control the problems posed by the rapidly growing number of poor people. William Birch's engravings of street scenes at the turn of the nineteenth century show Philadelphia not as it really looked but rather as the city's elite and middling sorts desired it to appear, with a series of bucolic urban scenes of wide and nearly empty streets. Only a handful of honest, independent working men and women populated these engravings. Even Birch's images of the almshouse and the jail were all but devoid of depictions of any of the city's many thousands of impoverished residents.[48] This was Philadelphia as the better sort hoped and imagined it, a city in which vagrants, criminals, and the dependent poor were invisible — incarcerated within the almshouse and the jail.

For lower-sort white and black Philadelphians, poverty was nothing new, but economic dislocations, urban expansion, and, above all, changing attitudes and policies among the city's rulers meant that many more of them now faced the effective criminalization of their situation. Injury, unemployment or underemployment, and an inability to command wages sufficient to meet the cost of living all meant that some Philadelphians found themselves, through no fault of their own, unable to survive without assistance. Such help came at a high price, for in numerous cases it meant incarceration in the almshouse and prison. The jail, too, housed vagrants as well as slaves and servants who resisted the authority of their masters; standing a block from Independence Hall, the Walnut Street Jail provided the foundation of a system of social control designed to control the dependent poor. Together, the jail and almshouse were organized "to construct a more regulated form of working-class subjectivity and individuality."[49]

These institutions had an enormous impact on many impoverished Philadelphians. Incarcerated, often against their will, men, women, and children were forced to conform to a harsh regimen and work to support the cost of their own imprisonment. Families were torn apart with children bound out to work for masters until they were adults; both blacks and whites found their freedoms curtailed. Yet, many resisted not just the terms and conditions of their incarceration and the rule of the almshouse authorities, but more profoundly the very idea that poverty was a crime. The prison and almshouse records are full of the stories of Philadelphians who sought to make use of the almshouse or the gaol for their own purposes and to retain and exercise a degree of personal independence. A significant number of residents were people whose lives were already defined by a struggle for liberty and independence, from Irish, English, and Haitian immigrants seeking better lives to runaway or recalcitrant servants and slaves who believed that they too might aspire to enjoy life, liberty, and the pursuit of happiness. Even prostitutes, many ill or disfigured by diseases that would cut short their lives, refused to bow to almshouse authorities who condemned them. On the contrary, as Jacqueline Cahif shows elsewhere in this volume, they took advantage of basic medical services, controlled the "venereal ward" of the almshouse, and came and went as they pleased.[50]

Early national Philadelphia's almshouse and jail did not function as urban authorities hoped, nor were the poor always able to control the conditions of their incarceration. These were negotiated and contested spaces, and the institutions ultimately failed. As the city continued expanding, with a consequent increase in the ranks of unemployed, underemployed, and impoverished residents, the almshouse and jail could not reform residents into self-sufficient citizens, since harsh social and economic realities rendered such self-improvement all but impossible for many. Increasingly, incarceration in the almshouse became part of an all but unbreakable cycle of poverty and dependence, an end in itself rather than the desired means to a better end. Yet, in the institutional records, the bleak lives and harsh existence of many Philadelphians is matched by the incorrigible spirit and resistance of the many incarcerated innocents who refused to submit to the idea that poverty was shameful and criminal.

NOTES

1. The slang is from Captain Grose, Hell-Fire Dick, and James Gordon, *1811 Dictionary of the Vulgar Tongue* (Cambridge, U.K.: n.p., 1811); the quote is from the July 14, 1787 diary entry in William Parker Cutler, Julia Perkins Cutler, Ephraim Cutler Dawes, and Peter Force, eds., *Life, Journals and Correspondence of Rev. Manasseh Cutler*, 2 vols. (Cincinnati: Clark, 1888), 1:263. On the harassment of the founding fathers, see also Negley K. Teeters, *The Cradle of the Penitentiary: The Walnut Street Jail at Philadelphia 1773–1785* (Philadelphia: Temple University Press, 1955), frontispiece.

2. Statistics about the incarcerated and the poor are in table 3; and in Billy G. Smith, "Poverty and Economic Marginality in Eighteenth-Century America," *Proceedings of the American Philosophical Society* 132, no. 1 (March 1988): 97.

3. Quotes from J. P. Brissot de Warville, *New Travels in the United States of America, Performed in 1788* (New York: T. and J. Swords, 1792), 112; Michel Foucault, *Discipline and Punish: The Birth of the Prison*, trans. Alan Sheridan (New York: Pantheon Books, 1977); Michael Meranze, *Laboratories of Virtue: Punishment, Revolution, and Authority in Philadelphia, 1760–1835* (Chapel Hill: University of North Carolina Press, 1996).

4. On migration to the city, see Gary B. Nash, "Reverberations of Haiti in the American North: Black Saint Dominiguans in Philadelphia," *Pennsylvania History* 65, no. 5 (Special Supplemental Issue, 1998): 49–50, 62; Simon P. Newman, *Parades and the Politics of the Street: Festive Culture in the Early American Republic* (Philadelphia: University of Pennsylvania Press, 2000); and Billy G. Smith, *The "Lower Sort": Philadelphia's Laboring People, 1750–1800* (Ithaca, N.Y.: Cornell University Press, 1990), chap. 6. Quote by Board of Managers of the Almshouse cited in Charles Lawrence, *History of Philadelphia Almshouses and Hospitals* (Philadelphia: Gaylord, 1905), 31–32. Quotes from newspaper reports: Dec. 14, 1785 and July 28, 1790, *Pennsylvania Gazette* (Philadelphia).

5. Gary B. Nash discusses the new militancy in "Reverberations of Haiti in the American North," 56–59. On changes in deferential behavior after the Revolution, see all of the essays in Billy G. Smith and Simon Middleton, eds., "Deference in Early North America: The Life and/or Death of an Historiographical Concept," *Early American Studies: An Interdisciplinary Journal* 3, no. 2 (Fall 2005).

6. See, for example, Robin D. G. Kelley, *Race Rebels: Culture, Politics, and the Black Working Class* (New York: Free Press, 1996); and James C. Scott, *Domination and the Arts of Resistance: Hidden Transcripts* (New Haven: Yale University Press, 1992).

7. Benjamin Franklin, *The Autobiography of Benjamin Franklin* (New York: Dover, 1996).

8. Daily Occurrences, 1800: McNeal, June 29; Waterman, July 12.

9. See John K. Alexander, *Render Them Submissive: Responses to Poverty in*

Philadelphia, 1760–1800 (Amherst: University of Massachusetts Press, 1980), 86–91; Jacqueline Cahif, "'She Supposes Herself Cured': Philadelphia Almshouse Women and Venereal Disease, c.1790–1820," PhD diss., University of Glasgow, 2010, 98–103; and Smith, *"Lower Sort,"* 166–70.

10. Daily Occurrences Docket (hereafter Daily Occurrences), Philadelphia City Archives, 1800: Wooten, July 17; Morris, Sept. 29; Dillmore, Oct. 3; Robertson, Dec. 9.

11. Daily Occurrences, 1800: Rawling, Dec. 26; Hamilton, Aug. 31.

12. Daily Occurrences, 1800: Sophia Watson, Dec. 20; Mary Berry, Oct. 6.

13. Davis and Smith, October 16, 1790, Daily Occurrences.

14. Note at the end of the entry for Jeremia Cronen, Dec. 6, 1790, Daily Occurrences.

15. Daily Occurrences, 1800: Cato, July 11; Breahere, Nov. 6; Bordley, Dec. 2.

16. Heath, Nov. 27, 1793, Daily Occurrences.

17. Philadelphia was legally reincorporated in 1789, after which the city passed a series of laws regulating everything from the incarceration of vagrants to driving carriages on the right side (rather than the British side) of the street; *The Ordinances of the City of Philadelphia* (Philadelphia: Poulson, 1798), 23, 95, 128–32. See also Alexander, *Render Them Submissive*, 81; Smith, "Poverty and Economic Marginality," 97.

18. A keyword search of the digitized *Pennsylvania Gazette* (Philadelphia) indicates how the meaning of "vagrancy" changed over time. Indeed, the term was rarely even used before mid-century. The following issues contain a sampling of the most important post-Revolutionary articles: Dec. 14, 1785; Feb. 28, 1787; July 1, 1789; Nov. 28, 1792; Jan. 30, 1793; and April 1, 1795.

19. Daily Occurrences, 1787: Murphy, Nov. 7; Allen, Nov. 24; Willis, Dec. 11.

20. Jones, Nov. 3, 1800, Daily Occurrences; Prisoners for Trial Docket, 1799.

21. Nesbit, Nov. 18, 1800, Daily Occurrences.

22. Boardley, Dec. 2, 1800, Daily Occurrences.

23. On the rules of the almshouse, see Alexander, *Render Them Submissive*, 85–95.

24. As quoted in ibid., 128.

25. Daily Occurrences, 1800: Crosby, June 25; Wallace, July 15; McGroty, October 5; Muff, Oct. 21.

26. The online *Oxford English Dictionary* notes that "black hole" was, until 1868, the official military designation for the "punishment cell or lock-up in a barracks." This usage gained notoriety in 1756 when more than 100 Europeans perished in one night while incarcerated in the black hole of the barracks in Fort William, Calcutta. Harry Flashman, of course, was among the most famous of the surviving occupants of that episode.

27. The figure of 65 percent includes 33 percent of children who were committed with their parents, 17 percent with parents incarcerated in the jail,

and 15 percent whose parents were unable to support them; Admissions to Philadelphia's Almshouse, 1800–1801, Philadelphia City Archives.

28. Daily Occurrences, 1800: Johnson, Aug. 16 and Nov. 17; Landram, Jan. 2.

29. Rules of the prison are from *Collection of the Penal Laws of the Commonwealth of Pennsylvania* [1790–1794] (Philadelphia, 1794), 10–12. Henry and Billy, June 14, 1790, Vagrancy Docket.

30. Daily Occurrences, 1800: Richards, July 3; Nesbit, Nov. 18; Loddo, July 6; and O'Hara, Dec. 13, 1789.

31. Seventy-eight of 290 convicts escaped between 1787 and 1789, according to Thorstein Sellin, "Philadelphia Prisons of the Eighteenth Century," *Transactions of the American Philosophical Society* 43, no. 1 (1953): 327. The advertisement for Jack is in the *Pennsylvania Gazette*, Oct. 18, 1786.

32. Daily Occurrences: Muff, Oct. 21, 1800; Judith Boyd, Nov. 1, 1787; Daniel Boyd, Nov. 18, 1793; Howell, July 14, 1800.

33. Charles Brockden Brown, *Arthur Mervyn, or Memoirs of the Year 1793* (New York: Holt, Rinehart, Winston, 1965), 288.

34. The 1787 report is cited in Sellin, "Philadelphia Prisons of the Eighteenth Century," 327; conditions in the almshouse are reported in Alexander, *Render Them Submissive*, 117. Daily Occurrences: Wallace, July 15, 1800; McGroty, Oct. 5, 1800; Musgrove, Nov. 8, 1793; Crosby, June 25, 1800.

35. "Burning the ken": Grose et al., *Dictionary of the Vulgar Tongue*.

36. Daily Occurrences, 1800: Philip and Sarah Haines, Nov. 24 and 27; Douglass, Nov. 29; Barry, Nov. 15 and numerous other times. "Gentleman of three inns": Grose et al., *Dictionary of the Vulgar Tongue*.

37. The number of incarcerated black people is from the Vagrancy Docket; the estimated number of slaves in Philadelphia and Pennsylvania during the 1790s are based on the 1790 and 1800 federal censuses. Tyser, July 2, 1794; Cline, August 6, 1794, Vagrancy Docket.

38. Vagrancy Docket: Baptiste, Sept. 16, 1796.

39. Emphases ours. Vagrancy Docket: Faramong, June 1, 1790; Frank, April 9, 1796; Laurencine, Jan. 20 and Feb. 22, 1797; Fortune, Nov. 4 and Dec. 4, 1797.

40. Johnson's dictionary is available at http://johnsonsdictionaryonline.com/, accessed May 17, 2011; the slang is from Grose et al., *Dictionary of the Vulgar Tongue*.

41. Vagrancy Docket: Harry, Feb. 28, May 3, May 9, May 17, May 24, Aug. 19, Sept. 26, 1791. Box 4A: Manumissions, Indentures and Other Legal Papers, Oct. 4, 1791, Papers of the Pennsylvania Abolition Society, Historical Society of Pennsylvania. See also the advertisements for the escaped slave Harry in the *Pennsylvania Gazette*, May 17, June 30, and Aug. 4, 1790.

42. Grose et al., *Dictionary of the Vulgar Tongue*. Daily Occurrences: McCowan, Jan. 4 and Oct. 22, 1790; O'Hara, Nov. 21 and Dec. 13, 1789. For a discussion of

the symptoms of malnutrition, as observed in black patients in the Pennsylvania Hospital between 1751 and 1775, see Susan E. Klepp, "Seasoning and Society: Racial Differences in Mortality in Eighteenth-Century Philadelphia," *William and Mary Quarterly*, 3rd ser., 51 (1994): 492–93.

43. Daily Occurrences: Britton, Dec. 31, 1800, and Jan. 5, 1801; Saffern, Nov. 1 and Nov. 14, 1797; Lackey, Sept. 18 and Nov. 9, 1800.

44. On the difficulty of poorer urban citizens to earn a living, see Billy G. Smith, "The Material Lives of Laboring Philadelphians, 1750–1800," *William and Mary Quarterly*, 3rd ser., 38 (April 1981): 163–202.

45. Lynch, July 1, 1800, Daily Occurrences. On the rules of the almshouse, see Alexander, *Render Them Submissive*, 85–95.

46. George Farquhar, *The Beaux-Stratagem* (1707) (London: J. M. Dent, 1898), 11.

47. Carole Shammas, "The Space Problem in Early American Cities," *William and Mary Quarterly*, 3rd ser., 57 (2000): 509.

48. Shammas, "Space Problem," 505–8; Simon P. Newman, *Embodied History: The Lives of the Poor in Early Philadelphia* (Philadelphia: University of Pennsylvania Press, 2003), 1–7.

49. Meranze, *Laboratories of Virtue*, 289.

50. Cahif, "She Supposes Herself Cured."

"Those Insolent Hardened Husseys Go on Dispensing All Rule & Order Here"

Women with Venereal Disease in the Philadelphia Almshouse

JACQUELINE CAHIF

IN JUNE 1800, RACHEL WARD LEFT the Philadelphia Almshouse for the last time. Known to the managers as "one of our polishing room gang," and a "frequent . . . infamous venereal customer," Rachel sought medical treatment in the city's almshouse repeatedly throughout the 1790s. Leaving, it seems, was her speciality. As notes taken by almshouse steward John Cummings attest, Rachel escaped the almshouse at least five times, usually by "scaling and jumping the fence." On one occasion she "ran off half cured," only to return a month later. She is a "hussy [who] returns at pleasure," Cummings fumed. Following a further spell of medical treatment, Rachel, brought to near total blindness by the extent of her infection, absconded with fellow inmate Catherine Hayes, and "ran [off] in the night." Only the jail seemed able to contain her.

"After being caught in the house for fornicating" in June 1800, Ward was "committed" to Philadelphia's Walnut Street Jail (the workhouse) for thirty days. After her release a month later, Rachel Ward disappeared entirely from city records.[1]

This essay recovers the voices, behaviors, and attitudes of diseased almshouse women like Rachel in order to explore the ways they experienced and responded to incarceration in early national Philadelphia. Whether held against their will or voluntarily admitted, many diseased pauper-women found means to exploit their incarceration. Prostitutes like Rachel Ward proved so adept at taking only what they needed from their term of confinement that they behaved more like customers than inmates. In order to avoid reimbursing the city for their care, almshouse women employed a range of strategies that took advantage of lax enforcement of almshouse rules; in effect, these women negotiated incarceration on their own terms. With no real precedent for indoor poor relief on this scale, city and almshouse officials expressed confusion over new ideas of reform in the early republic, and continuous bickering and uncertainty over the true purpose of the almshouse left a vacuum in which inmates were able to influence the conditions of their captivity.[2]

As the nation's capital, Philadelphia greeted foreign ambassadors and America's most distinguished politicians, as well as hosting a booming port that welcomed migrants from Europe, the Caribbean, and elsewhere in the United States. However, as the city's population escalated in the late eighteenth century, so too did poverty. As the impoverished grew in number and became more visible, anxieties about the lower sort and social disorder increased among middling and elite Philadelphians. Thus, as Billy Smith and Simon Newman demonstrate elsewhere in this collection, institutions were created or expanded in order to contain and control those perceived to threaten the moral fabric of society. Despite disagreements about the nature of this confinement, historians accept that American almshouses functioned to a certain extent as instruments of social control and moral reform and served as receptacles for the containment and surveillance of the indigent poor and unruly rabble.[3]

Prostitutes were one of many groups who appeared to threaten the social order, and Rachel Ward was just one of a growing number of prostitutes working in early national Philadelphia. Moreau de St. Mery, a French aristocrat living in Philadelphia during the 1790s, noted "the frequent houses of ill fame, which have multiplied [here]."[4] As the number of prostitutes working in the city rose, so too did the numbers of venereal patients entering the almshouse infirmary. Every week the doors of the Philadelphia Almshouse were opened by the gatekeepers, letting a constant stream of venereal sufferers into their wards. By 1798, the numbers of venereal patients entering the almshouse infirmary had swollen to the extent that "it has become absolutely necessary to erect a new Building for the accommodation of venereal patients."[5]

Access to medical treatment in early national Philadelphia varied. For the most part it was dependent on a sick person's social standing. Diseased women could self-treat or seek counsel from one of the many healers who made it their business to offer "specialist" services.[6] While wealthier citizens preferred home treatment and a personal visit from a physician, only a relatively small number of the laboring "virtuous" (deserving) poor were able to afford hospital care in the Pennsylvania Hospital. Poorer patients might also seek out dispensary care, though; as Charles Rosenberg reminds us, dispensaries were intended to provide relief to the "worthy" poor, rather than the "prostitute, the drunkard, the lunatic and the cripple."[7] While a fraction of the city's venereal sufferers were no doubt able to procure medicines from the dispensary, for many of Philadelphia's poorest residents the almshouse was their only hope.[8]

A large number of unlicensed medical practitioners who swamped the medical marketplace were mercurialists; that is, they claimed mercury was a specific remedy or antidote for venereal disease. Yet, prostitutes more than any other group—beside much of the medical profession itself—were fully aware that the mercury "cure" could be worse, or at least as bad, as the disease itself. For a number of women, a crucial factor determining the decision to submit to incarceration in the infirmary wing of the almshouse was based on an understanding of the nature of treatment provided there. While a handful of scholars have examined the medical understanding of venereal disease and its links to prostitution in this period, there is much work to be done to recover the social history of the people who experienced treatment regimens within institutional settings. Historians have insinuated that venereal therapeutics reflected the punitive nature and sinister side of poorhouse or workhouse institutions.[9] This interpretation claims that prostitutes were served with a harsh dose of rough justice in the form of abrasive medical treatment, always with the dreaded and poisonous mercury.[10] However, an examination of almshouse venereal-ward medicines and physicians' modes of practice illustrates that treatments for both gonorrhea and syphilis were often nonmercurial. Philadelphia Almshouse patients were supported by gentler therapeutic regimens than has been realized, mostly involving plant-based remedies with limited or simply no mercury.[11] This was the result of financial expediency, and also wider transformations in ideas of disease causation, therapeutic approaches, medical education, and doctor-patient relationships. Importantly, such therapy involved copious amounts of alcohol and heavy doses of opiates. To this end, women suffering from venereal disease often selected incarceration in the almshouse infirmary as a first choice, despite the range of alternatives in the medical marketplace.

The almshouse infirmary was hardly a retreat for advanced healthcare, its conditions being rudimentary and, as Rosenberg claims, "brutal."[12] Nevertheless, it provided Philadelphia's indigents with a healthcare system that was clinically superior to many of its counterparts. For the prostitute who witnessed firsthand the effects of mercury on her companions, a short stay in the almshouse, which provided food and personal medical attention with a short course of treatment, no doubt served as an attractive option. This may have motivated a woman's decision to seek admission into the almshouse in the first instance.

Negotiating Incarceration

The original intentions of Philadelphia's almshouse managers was that the institution would control, condition, and heal the poor or sick, who would work to help pay for their own incarceration. While most venereal inmates certainly surrendered some aspects of their own independence to avail themselves of the treatment regimes available inside, almshouse records nonetheless reveal a broad range of behaviors, ranging from submissive deference to subtle resistance to outright subversion. The data demonstrate that female venereal inmates, more than any other almshouse group, found means and opportunity to shape and even control the conditions of their confinement. This was achieved through individual acts of assertion and defiance, as well as by more extreme measures of collective resistance and riotous confrontation. While almshouse administrators sought to instill codes of behavior, they were inconsistent and ineffective in their methods, allowing inmates room to manipulate the institution and, importantly, to assume public welfare as their just and legitimate right.[13]

A diseased woman's admission into the almshouse reveals a great deal about how she regarded her role as a welfare recipient. To obtain entry, she first had to produce a letter of recommendation from an upstanding citizen. For the diseased prostitute seeking treatment for venereal disease, this required some measure of deference, submission, and perhaps even contrition. Only a few women gained entry without an order, and that behavior typically drew notice. When Hannah Levy was first admitted in 1793, John Cummings complained she was sent "by one of the overseers from the N[orthern] L[iberties]" district of the city "without an order contrary to Law, order or custom." Sarah Clark was admitted "without [an] order or invitation," but once inside, she was ordered "into the dark room until the further discretion of the managers."[14] After the turn of the century, as rising poverty forced a tightening of almshouse admissions policies, the chances of being admitted without a letter diminished further. The only way to get inside at this juncture of the almshouse experience was to show sufficient respect toward those in positions of authority to win their recommendation.

For many, however, this first hurdle in the almshouse experience was where the show of respect ended. When a woman arrived at the doors of the almshouse, she effectively stood in the dock awaiting trial. And unfortunately for many of these women, John Cummings—the human face of the institution—was their judge. Cummings, who kept a careful record of all paupers he admitted, found diseased and destitute venereal inmates a constant source of exasperation, in part because members of this group appeared to slip in and out of the almshouse whenever they pleased and with relative ease. In December 1790, Cummings complained that "some examples are not made . . . of those numerous Dirty Fellows & Hussys who so repeatedly Burthen [*sic*] . . . this Institution with this filthy disease and still with impunity." Moreover, that many sick inmates were labeled by the steward as "customers" implied that economic considerations were never far from his mind and those who seemingly siphoned almshouse resources at their own convenience and with "impunity" only added to his frustration.[15]

Cummings had little patience or sympathy for the dozens of women who lied to him about the cause of their distress. Given the stigmatizing nature of venereal disease, it is understandable that many women hoped to conceal the true nature of their illness, instead preferring to allege a more socially acceptable ailment that would merit admission. For instance, Cath Hayes declared that she was "afflicted with Fitts," though

Cummings recorded his belief that she was, in fact, venereal. Many such women complained of "sore limbs." Jane Dolly claimed to be "inflicted with the Rh[e]umatism," though she later "owned up . . . that she hath the Venereal Disease." Likewise, when Jane Brady was admitted in 1794, she complained of having "pains in her limbs," and the clerk noted that this was "commonly the first complaint made here by most of the dirty venereal hussys." Susanna Doyle, a known prostitute, is a case in point. In 1791, Susannah acted as nurse in the venereal ward, in order to pay for her own treatment. She was discharged in November of that year and "sent to service," only to be readmitted the following month. On her admission, despite being known as a prostitute, she was admitted "on pretence of being Rh[e]umatic," much to Cummings's vexation.[16] But the steward knew he would have little choice but to let them enter the wards for treatment.[17]

Some women embellished their stories by emphasizing their helplessness and innocence, in hopes of currying sympathy from cynical managers. Pregnant and venereal, Catherine Seaman told John Cummings that she was married and that her seafaring husband was at sea. When Cummings questioned her on his exact whereabouts, she "*supposed . . .* it was about 8 months ago that the Ship sailed" and "it was reported the said Ship was cast away, but [was] not yet confirmed." Yet, when asked about the details of her marriage, Catherine was unable to produce a marriage certificate, "having left it in town." The steward was in no doubt that "by all appearances her story is very dubious and equivocal."[18] Catherine's account reveals much about how inmates endeavored to negotiate as best they could in order to secure a place in the almshouse. By playing down her independence, she was visibly stripping herself of agency and portraying herself as a victim of circumstances beyond her control. By recounting a fictional illness or adding a dramatic, tragic dimension such as abandonment, Catherine garbed herself in a gown of tattered respectability.

An unspecified number of women chose a different form of pretense to gain admission. Adopting an alias was a common trick of the trade for prostitutes (and still is). Rachel Ward, whom we encountered earlier, used several variations on her surname during multiple admissions interviews. Hannah Levy, a "noted and infamous" prostitute well known to administrators by this name, occasionally went by the name Hannah Orr, clearly in an attempt to fool the different Overseers of the Poor who might authorize her recommendation for admission. It seemed to work:

every application she made was successful. Likewise, Hannah Sharp was admitted under this name in 1790 and 1797, yet in 1798 was admitted under the alias Mary Smith.[19] The steward was well aware of such ploys. In June 1794, a woman who named herself Hannah Virgin turned up at the almshouse. Cummings, a man with his wits about him, quipped, "Maybe she was a long while ago."[20]

Refusing to stoop to the indignities required by the recommendation system and admission interviews, a few venereal women came up with even more ingenious plans to gain access to the hospital wards. Under the pretense of being a visitor, Jane Shiever "procured admittance to see her mother." According to Cummings, once inside the almshouse, she had the audacity to "introduce herself into the Polishing Room expecting she might remain there until she was a little polished over." When Jane's deception was uncovered, Cummings had her removed from the almshouse, "but she again soon returned," this time clutching a legal order of admission. Similar deceptions are scattered throughout the almshouse records. In December 1801, Cummings complained that a frequent patient, Mary Carlisle, had turned up again, this time without having been interviewed or formally admitted: "By what means she came in again is not known . . . but she has been in the House for some time past . . . employed in Spinning." Over a period of eleven years, Mary Carlisle was admitted as a venereal patient on twelve separate occasions, until she finally died from the effects of her disease.[21] Other women had no time or inclination for pretense and readily owned up to the fact that they were suffering the effects of venereal disease. For Elizabeth Halden, her frank admission was a means of avoiding harsher confinement in the neighboring house of employment and guaranteeing a bed in the hospital wing. According to the steward, "[She is] a very disorderly girl who for several years past has been confined to the Work House, but has always . . . ret[urne]d to her former lewd & disorderly conduct, and now complains of being Infected with the Venereal Disease, which renders her an Improper Object for the Work House."[22]

There seems to have been an unspoken agreement between officials and venereal patients, one that involved initial compliance whether real or feigned. Some women humbly submitted to those in charge in order to obtain admission. Others, comfortable in the knowledge they would not be refused admittance, believed they held a fundamental right to relief and thus made a more brazen appearance at the doors of the almshouse.

"The Whoars march": Collective Discipline among the Incarcerated Sisterhood

Once inside the venereal ward, diseased women formed friendships. It was within these networks that prostitutes learned strategies for survival, including how to deal with unwanted pregnancy and venereal disease and how best to access, use, and escape the almshouse. In the ward, diseased women learned how to shirk their work duties and ultimately secure medical care for free.

After a diseased woman was admitted, she would be kept in the venereal ward until deemed "cured" by a physician. Thereafter, she would be "discharged from the Sick List . . . on a Diet of Bread and Water . . . and kept at work according to her ability."[23] It was commonly at this stage of the almshouse experience that such women escaped, and an overwhelming number left with relative ease after receiving sufficient healthcare to allow them to return to their livelihoods. By shirking work duties assigned to them to defray the cost of their medical care to the city, staggering numbers escaped the confines of the almshouse.[24] Indeed, venereal inmates were more likely to elope than any other group of sick patients. Between 1790 and 1799, an average 54.5 percent of female venereal admissions absconded without waiting for an official discharge.[25]

While most women escaped alone, some slipped away in pairs or occasionally in larger groups. Mary Golden and Jane Bigely, for example, waited until the rest of the inmates were dining in the communal area before sneaking out unnoticed.[26] Time and again, women were arrested by the city watch along with the same companions who acted with them in the almshouse. Indeed, many diseased women from the same districts of Philadelphia appeared to consort together inside the almshouse. In 1796, Margaret Powers jumped the fence along with Sarah Evans. A year later, Cummings reported that Sarah had eloped along with two others from the "polishing room" and all were from the same area of Philadelphia. In 1798, Evans joined Mary Allen, a "companion and consort," and together they ran off into the night. Evans and Allen hailed from the Northern Liberties area of Philadelphia, a particularly disorderly part of the city that was home to many prostitutes. It is also possible that the women already knew each other from the streets, taverns, or brothel households of that district prior to almshouse admission. Often, they were arrested for being "drunk and disorderly . . . lewd girls" and "abandoned prostitutes." Mary Carlisle was another of Sarah Evans's companions. Mary was, in fact, from Southwark, the part of Philadelphia that was farthest from the Northern Liberties. However, Mary was often arrested with companions from the Northern Liberties district. It is possible that Sarah Evans introduced Mary Carlisle to this neighborhood after the two first met in the almshouse. A similar relationship was apparent between almshouse women Phoebe Lewis and Mary Watson, who were arrested together for being "idle vagrants" in 1805. Although it is not clear where in the city they were arrested, Phoebe originally came from the Northern Liberties while Mary was from the city proper. It would appear that they established a connection inside the almshouse five years prior to their arrest.[27]

Perhaps the best example of community, or a subculture of incarcerated prostitutes, can be found in 1789, when "Insolent & Disorderly behaviour" was reported amongst the "polishing room gang" in the venereal ward. Jane Bickerdite was a former venereal patient who had become a nurse of the ward and thus a representative of the almshouse authorities. She was "discharged at her own desire" after the venereal patients "quarrelled with and abused her very much." Cummings later recalled their encounter: "they mob'd her severely and raised a Bawling Clamerous noise & Clanger with . . . Rattling Frying pans after her, all of which together, they called the Whoars march, and of which Doubtless they are competent judges . . . as every step they have taken for several years have been in line and true to the Beat."[28]

Clearly those involved in the riot held their own beliefs about customary procedure, and although we will never know what happened to unleash such a backlash, almshouse prostitutes refused to accept Bickerdite's position as legitimate. They stigmatized Bickerdite with her newfound autonomy in the almshouse, which she had perhaps exercised to an extent deemed unnecessary by the venereal ward patients. This was an almost conservative way of thinking that their low-ranking status was immutable. Such shared behaviors and concepts fit with the classic model proposed by E. P. Thompson, in which "the conservative culture of the plebs as often as not resists, in the name of custom . . . innovations . . . which rulers, dealers or employers seek to impose. . . . Hence the plebeian culture is rebellious . . . but in defence of custom."[29]

This breaks down when relationships are complicated by change, as was the case with the "Whore's March." For Jane Bickerdite, the punishment for transgressing her given role as inmate was public humiliation in a form that resembled the popular early modern European custom of charivari (rough music). This involved "noisy, mocking demonstrations" generally instigated toward a member of the community who had upset the locals by an "infraction of community norms."[30] In the venereal ward riot, the prostitutes' anger was not directed toward their managers or steward, or indeed their incarceration, but rather against one of their own who appeared to be abandoning the community and identifying herself too closely with the authorities. Moreover, as Barry Reay has noted, "charivari will only be effective when the target is sufficiently integrated into the community."[31] Until Bickerdite became nurse of the ward, she was indeed perceived to be one of them—an almshouse patient; yet, she abandoned her given role as inmate and was targeted as a corrupting influence who threatened the status quo. The nurse had overstepped her mark by collaborating with the almshouse authorities, and the "polishing room gang" attempted to put a check on this.

At the same time, those involved in the riot were administering their own rules, and perhaps setting their own precedents. In a fit of exasperation, Cummings noted that "those insolent hardened Husseys go on dispensing all Rule & Order here."[32] Prostitutes—like other members of the lower classes—attempted to defy and undermine those who sought to use the almshouse as a coercive tool. As Gary Nash reminds us, the poor had their own rules, which were often used to frustrate their betters.[33] Resorting to public assistance in the first place signified a loss of autonomy, and the prostitutes' response was to retain whatever power they could and direct it as best they could to improve their conditions and environment inside the almshouse. Until male pimps dominated prostitution from the early twentieth century, it was women who controlled the trade—in brothels and on the street—on their own terms. This relative independence was carried into and reenacted in the almshouse.

The Revolving Door of the Polishing Room

Nothing infuriated John Cummings more than those women who treated the almshouse as their private clinic. The steward waxed vehemently about diseased prostitutes coming and going at their apparent pleasure, having received only the minimum of treatment. For example, Patty O'Craft "sailed forth only a little mended" while Nancy McCollister brazenly "appear[ed] for polishing." Mary Carlisle, a "common prostitute," was a particular irritation to the steward. In February 1794, she was discharged by the almshouse doctor, and, according to Cummings, she was "somewhat relieved thinking herself fit for business again." Mary was admitted again in June in the "foulest . . . diseased" condition, yet, after medical aid, eloped a few weeks later "well bottomed but not thoroughly repaired."[34]

Evidently, women like Mary understood the almshouse to be a resource they could use periodically for recuperation, with little in the way of respect for administrative procedure, particularly when it was time to pay for their care. When Ann Barber escaped, Cummings noted that the "vile little dirty hussy has absconded again . . . but will soon be back so need not be counted gone."[35] These women took full advantage of lax organization, and however much they abused the system by escaping on a regular basis, they normally managed to acquire a fresh order for admission.[36] With money to be made on the streets, many were most likely seeking a quick-fix solution to their afflictions in the hope of making a speedy return to the job.

The almshouse was also an alternative to destitution during a slump in business. As such, almshouse admissions were also highly seasonal, particularly for women whose disease had forced them into extreme poverty. Like many other able-bodied and sick inmates, prostitutes too sought food, clothing, and shelter in the almshouse during the winter months. When custom for prostitutes declined at the end of each fall, there was an exceptionally rapid increase in women seeking relief, with a rise from 3 percent of the almshouse population in October to 16 percent in November.[37] This figure remained consistent throughout the winter period until springtime, when the weather improved and the ships sailed again. By contrast, the women who sought treatment during the profitable summer months tended to be those suffering the most advanced stages of the disease. In the months of June and July 1794, for instance, seven women arrived at the almshouse for medical assistance. Of those women, five were noted as either "very far advanced in the venereal disease," "highly diseased," or in the "foulest venereal condition." One of those women, simply known as Grace a "negro woman," was entered as "highly venereal and far past all medical aid and died this evening."[38] None of the remaining women took to their heels, which suggests they were too ill to even contemplate navigating their way out of the building and over the fence.

English historians have argued that elopement from workhouse infirmaries was in light of the abrasive nature of medical treatment offered.[39]

In the Philadelphia Almshouse, it is more likely that once diseased alms-house women accessed the necessary medicine, clothing, and food, they escaped without paying, often returning to their lives restored to health. This was clearly applicable to varying degrees, with many women either homeless or too sick to even contemplate life in the outside world again. Elopement was therefore not merely the consequence of a woman's dis-taste for her medicine. She may not have held much say in what drugs she would be prescribed, but there was a fair idea from previous experi-ence and hearsay.

The Steward and the Prostitute

Taken together, the almshouse records bear witness to a group of women who exploited resources controlled by some officials who perceived these women as the lowest of the low, and their actions may indeed have been in response to what was in all probability visible resentment displayed by the steward. Indeed, John Cummings's harsh misogyny of-ten seemed to get the better of his humanity. His notes are filled with a whole host of derogatory terms depicting women seeking medical relief. Catherine Bachus was a "saucy black wench"; Elizabeth Bradley, "another pockey trull"; Ann Hoffner, a "vile Strumpet"; and Mary Stroud was simply a "strap[p]ing Prostitute." Mary Allen was "choice stuff" and Martha Peters, although broken down and "very far advanced in the venereal disease," was a "one eyed Bruiser."[40]

To Cummings, the fact that these women were infected by a debilitat-ing disease was secondary to the fact that they had come by their condi-tion through prostitution. The steward often made a distinction between those women he perceived to be victims of syphilis—namely innocent wives such as twenty-year-old Sarah Yates whose husband "deserted her, but took care before he went off to give her the Venereal Disease"—and those he blamed for their own condition and for spreading infection. On Mary Killgallant's admission note, his remarks were scathing: "I am real[l]y glad that I never was a *gallant* of yours, tho [*sic*] probably a good fellow has been, and that you kill[e]d them all *dead, dead, dead*, over and over *again* and *again*."[41]

Cummings's unbridled antipathy for prostitutes likely sprang from a dark and personal place. Yet, his remarks are also indicative of the ways that a man in his position was conditioned to perceive bold and assertive women who threatened social order on the streets and within the almshouse. His tone and vocabulary together suggest that he was made uneasy by loud, confident, and forceful women. Prostitution was the most powerful symbol of female economic and sexual independence, and such social and gender disorder offended polite male society in the virtuous new republic.[42] Accordingly, men like Cummings viewed independent women with suspicion. Thus, when single woman Mary Vandlike was admitted with a more "socially respectable" illness, Cummings was perturbed that she was "neither maid widow nor wife But a single woman."[43] Many lower-class women were not disconcerted by their independent status or, if they were, showed little sign of it. The tone of Cummings's records suggests that he was intimidated by such explicit working-class sexuality.

Despite his caustic rhetoric, there is no evidence that Cummings ever turned a venereal patient away, and his authority was regularly undermined by the assertiveness of a group of women who clearly intimidated him. In a sense, the dockets had functioned for years as a diary for Cummings's private sentiments, which he clearly did not intend for public viewing. His colorful metaphors and use of nicknames added a dramatic dimension and depth to the sad lives of those he admitted. On occasion, Cummings appears to have found difficulty reconciling some of his feelings toward diseased women, and his notes reveal glimmers of compassion for those whose indigence resulted in circumstances beyond their control and, consequently, almshouse incarceration. For example, when known prostitute Ann Holland sought relief without a recommendation, he bent almshouse rules on account of "her being destitute and having no shelter or place to go."[44] When Elizabeth Saunders died after a painful and protracted illness, Cummings noted that "one of our unhappy venereal Ladies of long standing here Expired this evening." On another occasion, Rachel Ward's plight elicited some uncharacteristic concern from the steward, and he went so far as to nominate her as being worthy to "receive compensation for her services according to her merit or behaviour" in the "polishing or venereal ward."[45] By doing so, he was effectively allowing negotiation and compromise between himself and his charges.

At a management meeting in May 1800, Cummings was made to account for his dereliction of duty and the rampant misogyny evident in his recordkeeping. Prior to this, the steward had been ordered to "lay before the board every Monday a list of all persons admitted the previous week." Such information could not be produced by the steward to the satisfaction of the managers, who exclaimed that "the great increase of duties by the Steward makes it impossible for him to attend to the Records of the institution." This was not the end of the matter, however. It would appear that for the first time in many years the managers had actually read Cummings's annotated records, rather than relying upon the statistical summaries that he customarily provided. The steward's subjective and gratuitous notations embedded within his admission and discharge notes alarmed the managers: "the board observing with Concern, the many Improper . . . expressions in the Minutes of the Daily Occurrences . . . [which] are filled with irrelevant matters." As a result, the board "resolved that the steward be directed in future to have the daily Minutes kept in a plain and decent style, recording only such facts and circumstances as are necessary for the information of the managers." Furthermore, Cummings was ordered to destroy some of his records.[46]

Relations between the steward and the managers could often prove antagonistic. He played a huge role in almshouse administration, and although he held a degree of power, he was aware of its limitations and was clearly protective of a role that in theory was subject to the managers. The steward was overworked in his supervision of the daily operation of the house and matters relating to inmates, and he frequently complained that his wages did not compensate the burdens of service adequately. We often see glimpses of his resentment toward the managers. Many of these gentlemen who sat on the board were members of Philadelphia's elite, and they came and went every six months with little knowledge and less personal involvement with the inmates. Cummings was rarely consulted by the managers on his opinion over the running of the institution, and as a middle man between civic authorities and inmates, he often struggled to exert control and retain as much influence as possible. Moreover, the steward was essentially unsupervised in his position, which would have profoundly affected how a pauper would experience his or her stay.

The Buried Lives of Public Women

John Cummings contributed significantly to the texture of almshouse life. Although he recorded what he saw in the most unbureaucratic style, his story is crucial for providing a framework into understanding how diseased women experienced the almshouse. The face-to-face admission interviews with the steward provided women like Rachel Ward with a platform to negotiate medical care through the public poor relief system. The narratives contained within the steward's Daily Occurrence Dockets and the Managers' Minutes illuminate the various power struggles within the Philadelphia Almshouse, as new forms of incarceration and social discipline triggered acceptance, deception, and resistance among the prostitutes who sought admission and medical treatment. Historians might expect that prostitutes like Rachel Ward, blighted by a cruel and disfiguring disease, and curtailed by a society that sometimes condemned indigent, "public" women, would have displayed passivity and compliance when facing almshouse officials. Yet, this study of diseased almshouse women instead finds such women resilient, relentless, and resourceful in their use of public charity. When women applied for admission, they encountered a steward who found them repugnant, yet who also cowed in the face of a sometimes brazen group of women. Once familiar with the almshouse routine, they developed a range of techniques to deal with such resentment and condemnation. While prostitutes and those diseased women associated with them recognized that they had to adhere to some of the rules and expectations of almshouse officials, the records reveal a vociferous and confident group of women undaunted by the judgments made about them by those in positions of power.

Venereal inmates displayed a strong belief in their customary right to public welfare in the form of free medical treatment. Although they engaged in acts of resistance, they held their own ideas about how the almshouse and its officials should function, and ultimately had their own codes of behavior, as illustrated in their "Whore's March." This confrontation highlighted how inmates set certain precedents and standards for all almshouse actors to adhere to, including themselves.

That their strategies were effective is clear; there are only rare instances when women suffering from venereal diseases were denied relief and turned away from the wards of the almshouse infirmary.[47] Venereal patients held their own expectations and ideas about incarceration. They consistently manipulated almshouse procedure, and were able to mold and recast almshouse tradition to continually negotiate medical care, if and when they wanted it. By doing so, they in effect helped to shape the later development of the infirmary through their continual readmissions and general abuse of the system. This undermined the original intentions and stipulations of the institution's governors, who did not envision their institution to act primarily as a hospital, and instead sought to provide temporary relief in the form of clothing and shelter to the worthy poor.[48] Yet, as a response to the overwhelming numbers of Philadelphia's sick poor (especially venereal paupers) who were driven to seek medical aid, officials unintentionally endorsed the ad hoc development of a sophisticated healthcare system, and the almshouse evolved into the Philadelphia General Hospital. The Overseers of the Poor simply could not turn away ill paupers with a legal residence, and, as Billy G. Smith notes, the almshouse was "ostensibly designed to serve the needs of the elderly, widowed, orphaned and infirm"; these types of inmates accounted for relatively few of those incarcerated by the turn of the century.[49] Diseased women's role here is of paramount importance; the number of women using the institution kept rising, and officials had to continually reconstruct and enlarge space behind the institution's walls to accommodate them.

In October 1803, the *Philadelphia Repository* recorded the death "on the 15th of an Apoplectic fit, Mr. John Cummings, late superintendent of the Bettering House."[50] Cummings's wife, who acted as matron, died in 1793 during the yellow fever epidemic, and it is possible the steward began sexual liaisons with some of the almshouses inmates after this time. His most scathing remarks against diseased women occurred in the years following her death. Cummings, then, may have contracted some form of disease through sexual relations with an infected woman, perhaps a prostitute at the almshouse, which would certainly help explain his disproportionate bitterness toward the venereal women of the almshouse. Six months after the disgrace brought upon Cummings for his methods of record-keeping, the steward retired from his job after more than thirty years of service. The details of his retirement are hazy, although there is evidence to suggest his retirement was forced. Unfortunately, we will never know the exact details, or if his death a couple of years later was the result of venereal infection.[51]

NOTES

1. Rachel Ward, Oct. 7, 1789, Dec. 14, 1789, March 22, 1790, Aug. 6, 1794, March 1796, Nov. 1797, Dec. 1797, June 1798, May 1799, June 16, 1799, May 27, 1800, June 27, 1800, Daily Occurrence Docket, Guardians of the Poor,

Philadelphia City Archives, hereafter cited as Dockets; Vagrancy Docket, August 18, 1790, Philadelphia City Archives, hereafter cited as Vagrancy. Many women entered the almshouse suffering from venereal disease, and although some were categorized by almshouse authorities as helpless victims, many more were held responsible for their condition. Not all members of this latter group were career or even casual prostitutes, although much of the anecdotal evidence of this essay focuses largely (but not exclusively) on those who appear to have been prostitutes.

2. Historians have reached different conclusions over the aims of almshouse confinement, in particular whether desires to control the poor superseded genuine philanthropy. See John K. Alexander, *Render Them Submissive: Responses to Poverty in Philadelphia, 1760–1800* (Amherst: University of Massachusetts Press, 1980); Priscilla Ferguson Clement, *Welfare and the Poor in the Nineteenth Century City: Philadelphia 1800–1854* (London: Rutherford, 1985); David J. Rothman, *The Discovery of the Asylum: Social Order and Disorder in the New Republic* (Boston: Little Brown, 1971).

3. Billy G. Smith, *Life in Early Philadelphia: Documents from the Revolutionary and Early National Periods* (State College: Pennsylvania State University Press, 1995), 3–5.

4. Kenneth Roberts and Anna M. Roberts, eds. and trans., *Moreau de St. Mery's American Journey, 1793–1798* (Garden City, N.Y.: n.p., 1947). Despite previously living in the sexually liberal communities of Paris and Saint Domingue, the Frenchman was quite taken aback by Philadelphia's permissive climate. For a discussion on the geography of brothels, and the apparent high incidence of nonmarital sex in Philadelphia, see Clare A. Lyons, *Sex among the Rabble: An Intimate History of Gender and Power in the Age of Revolution, 1730–1830* (Chapel Hill: University of North Carolina Press, 2006), 189. Also see Marcia Carlisle, "Prostitutes and Their Reformers in Nineteenth Century Philadelphia," PhD dissertation, Rutgers University, 1982; Steven Ruggles, "Fallen Women: The Inmates of the Magdalen Society of Philadelphia, 1836–1908," *Journal of Social History* 16 (Summer 1983): 65–81.

5. May 15, 1798, Managers Minutes, Philadelphia Almshouse, Philadelphia City Archives. Hereafter cited as MM.

6. For an overview of both orthodox and irregular medical services offered in Philadelphia's medical marketplace, see Lisa Rosner, "Thistle on the Delaware: Edinburgh Medical Education and Philadelphia Practice, 1800–1825," *Social History of Medicine* 5, no. 1 (1992): 19–42.

7. Charles E. Rosenberg, "Social Class and Medical Care in Nineteenth Century America: the Rise and Fall of the Dispensary," *Journal of the History of Medicine and Allied Sciences* 29 (1974): 43.

8. Northern Dispensary of Philadelphia for the Medical Relief of the Poor, Register of Patients, 1816–1826, Historical Society of Pennsylvania, Philadelphia.

9. For the classic interpretation, see Judith Walkowitz, *Prostitution and Victorian*

102 JACQUELINE CAHIF

Society: Women, Class and the State (Cambridge, U.K.: Cambridge University Press, 1980), 55. According to Walkowitz, "Repressive moralist views still influenced the treatment of syphilis and gonorrhoea . . . Because mercury application was very painful, it remained an appropriately punitive method of treating syphilitics."

10. According to Marcia Carlisle, in Philadelphia, "the only treatment men and women received was mercury." Carlisle, "Prostitutes and Their Reformers", 49. Richard Godbeer states that venereal treatment in the Philadelphia Almshouse was "gruelling and ghastly . . . the prominence of abrasive therapy meted out by almshouse physicians is underlined by the official record's repeated description of the ward set aside for that purpose as the polishing room." This he attributes to the "clerk's" frequent use of "nautical metaphors to characterize prostitutes and their medical treatment." Yet, the sole source for this contention is the use of anecdotal evidence left by the "clerk" (who was in fact the steward John Cummings). Godbeer's assertion is also based on a reading of Scottish doctor John Hunter's 1786 *Treatise on Venereal Disease*. From these sources, he suggests that medical experts "were virtually unanimous in arguing that mercury based therapies were by far the most effective in combating both 'local' and 'constitutional' manifestations of the disease." Richard Godbeer, *Sexual Revolution in Early America* (Baltimore: Johns Hopkins University Press, 2002), 320. However, Hunter's thesis provoked controversy, and in Philadelphia, medical opinion dictated otherwise. In the almshouse infirmary, doctors differentiated between various manifestations of venereal diseases and treated each accordingly, often locally. Moreover, one should be hesitant at taking this nautical labeling of prostitutes and the venereal ward at face value. The managers rarely used the term "polishing room," and the physicians never did so. The use of nautical metaphors to depict prostitutes was in fact commonplace from the early eighteenth century, particularly among seafarers in the port towns of England.

11. As I argue elsewhere, venereal diagnoses in the almshouse were more nuanced and treatments more measured than has been realized. Broadly speaking, almshouse doctors did not sanction drastic depletion with the use of mercurial compounds unless deemed absolutely necessary. Many women (who were in a financial and physical position to do so) selected the almshouse infirmary based on their knowledge and understanding of therapeutics carried out there. See Jacqueline Cahif, "'She Supposes Herself Cured': Almshouse Venereal Women in Late-Eighteenth and Early Nineteenth Century Philadelphia," unpublished PhD thesis, University of Glasgow, 2010, especially chaps. 4, 5, and 6.

12. Charles Rosenberg, *Explaining Epidemics and Other Studies in the History of Medicine* (Cambridge, U.K.: Cambridge University Press, 1992), 179–80.

13. For similar conclusions of venereal paupers in eighteenth-century London workhouses, see Kevin Siena, *Venereal Disease, Hospitals and the Urban Poor* (New York: University of Rochester Press, 2004), 1, 258. On inmates' institutional resistance and manipulation of almshouse resources in Philadelphia's

outlying regions, see Monique Bourque, "Poor Relief 'Without Violating the Rights of Humanity': Almshouse Administration in the Philadelphia Region, 1790–1860," in *Down and Out in Early America*, ed. Billy G. Smith (University Park: Pennsylvania State University Press, 2004).

14. Hannah Levy, Aug. 12, 1793; Sarah Clark, March 26, 1801, Dockets.

15. Jeremiah Cronin, Dec. 6, 1790, Dockets. It was a rare instance when a venereal male inmate came under Cummings's cutting remarks. The most caustic labels a male syphilitic generally received were "worthless" or "troublesome."

16. Cath Hayes, April 21, 1790; Jane Dolly, March 6, 1790; Jane Brady, March 6, 1794; Susannah Doyle, Nov. 29, 1791, Dec. 9, 1791, Dockets.

17. Almshouse authorities had a civic obligation to admit all paupers with a legal residency status. Moreover, while the early national period preceded an era when the spread of venereal disease would constitute a very real and significant public health concern, contemporaries nevertheless held an understanding and concern of the basic communicable nature of the infection and its threat to the health and moral fiber of Philadelphia's citizens. By the 1860s, diseased almshouse women were recorded on a separate Prostitutes' Register.

18. Catherine Seaman, Feb. 20, 1798, Dockets.

19. Hannah Levy as Hannah Orr, March and Oct. 1800, July 1801, Dockets; as Mary Smith, March 1798; Hannah Sharp, March 1790, June 1797.

20. Hannah Virgin, June 4, 1794, Dockets.

21. Jane Shiever, March 5, 1793; Mary Carlisle, Dec. 1801, Dockets. For other references to Mary Carlisle, see Jan. 19, 1791, Jan. 17, 1792, Nov. 22, 1792, April 1793, Feb. 1794, July 1794, Dec. 19, 1800, March 5, 1801, May 1801, Dec. 16, 1801, Jan. 6, 1803, Dec. 1803, April 8, 1804, April 10, 1804, Dockets; Oct. 30, 1790, June 6, 1791, April 19, 1792, Oct. 13, 1792, July 22, 1792, March 24, 1794, May 11, 1795, Aug. 1795, Sep. 7, 1795, Dec. 7, 1795, Vagrancy.

22. Elizabeth Halden, Jan. 1798, Dockets.

23. Dec. 1788, MM.

24. The almshouse registers and cost account books confirm that habitual elopers were continually readmitted with the cost of their care from a prior spell of treatment carried over. Often, the inmate would simply abscond again.

25. This figure is derived from a database of 493 female venereal patients. See Guardians of the Poor, Daily Occurrence Dockets 1790–1840; Admission Register 1800–1806; Female Register 1803–1820; Almshouse Admission Book 1785–1827; Almshouse Hospital Apothecary's Register of Sick and Surgical Ward Patients, 1800–1803; Almshouse Hospital Weekly Return of Patients in Sick and Surgical Wards, 1805, 1807, and 1808; Guardians of the Poor Almshouse Hospital Weekly Census and Admissions, 1812–1828. Philadelphia City Archives.

26. Jane Bigley, May 13, 1798, Dockets.

27. Sarah Evans, Margaret Powers, March 13, 1796, April 6, 1797, Dockets;

Sarah Evans and Mary Allen, March 23, 1798, Dockets, Aug. 4, 1795, Vagrancy; Pheobe Lewis and Mary Watson, Jan., March, Aug., 1800, Dockets; Aug. 30, 1805, Vagrancy.

28. Jane Bickerdite, Dec. 22, 1789, Dockets. Cummings's reference to "whore's march" may have held a double meaning: the military used a version of the whore's march to drum prostitutes out of their camps. The clerk hints that Jane Bickerdite had formerly acted as a prostitute, and the venereal ward display saw her being drummed out of the ward in an analogous fashion to camp prostitutes.

29. E. P. Thompson, *Customs in Common: Studies in Traditional Popular Culture* (London: Merlin Press, 1991), 9.

30. Martine Ingram, "Judicial Folklore in England Illustrated by Rough Music," in *Communities and Courts in Britain, 1150–1900*, ed. Christopher Brookes and Michael Lobban (London: Hambledon Press, 1997), 62.

31. Barry Reay, *Popular Cultures in England, 1550–1750* (London: Longman, 1998), 160.

32. Dec. 22, 1789, Dockets.

33. Gary Nash, "Poverty and Politics in Early American History," in Smith, *Down and Out in Early America*, 19–20.

34. Patty O'Craft, March 1796; Mary Carlisle, Feb., June 1794, Dockets.

35. Ann Barber, April 19, 1790, Dockets. Guardians of the Poor, Philadelphia Almshouse Hospital Apothecary's Register, Sick and Surgical Ward Patients, 1800–1803, May 23, 1803.

36. Alexander, *Render Them Submissive*, 97.

37. Seasonal use of the almshouse is derived from the years 1790 to 1810.

38. Mary Carlisle, June 6, 1794; Hannah Levy, July 1, 1794; Priscilla Wilson, July 1794; Martha Peters, July 23, 1794; Isabella Donnahoe, July 30, 1794; Grace, July 21, 1794, Dockets.

39. Kevin Siena argues that in London workhouses, elopement was a response to mercury treatment, and when patients could no longer endure the pain of mercurial salivation, they took matters into their own hands and fled. Siena, *Venereal Disease*, 131. This interpretation may be in light of different therapeutic practices in England.

40. Catherine Bachus, June 1796; Elizabeth Bradley, Dec. 1789; Ann Hoffner, Dec. 1789; Mary Stroud, Jan. 1789; Mary Allen, Jan. 1792; Martha Peters, July 23, 1794, Dockets.

41. Sarah Yates, June 15, 1801; Mary Killgallant, Feb. 10, 1796, Dockets.

42. Lyons, *Sex among the Rabble*, 320.

43. Mary Vandlike, Dec. 27, 1793, Dockets.

44. Ann Holland, March 16, 1798, Dockets.

45. Elizabeth Saunders, May 4, 1794, Dockets; Rachel Ward, Aug. 13, 1797, MM.

46. May 12, 1800, MM.

47. This was usually when a pauper was not a legal resident.

48. John Duffy, *From Humors to Medical Science: A History of American Medicine* (Urbana: University of Illinois Press, 1993), 36.

49. Billy G. Smith, *The Lower Sort: Philadelphia's Laboring People, 1750–1800* (Ithaca, N.Y.: Cornell University Press, 1994), 168–69. For the year 1800 to 1801, Smith has calculated that around 60 percent of the almshouse population were admitted as medical-related cases.

50. Herbert M. Sheldon, *Syphilis, Is It a Mischievous Myth or a Malignant Monster* (Mokelumne Hill, Calif.: Health Research, 1962), chap. 3.

51. Very little has been written about Cummings, although there appears to have been a scandal surrounding his retirement, which involved lawyers, and the ex-steward handing back his pension. For a short reference, see Robert J. Hunter, "The Origin of the Philadelphia General Hospital," *Pennsylvania Magazine of History and Biography* 7 (1933): 33. During his appointment as almshouse steward, it appears Cummings had been trying his hand at a horticulture business in order to supplement his income. A number of advertisements appeared in local newspapers, publicizing his flower seeds and plants. See, for instance, *Philadelphia Gazette and Universal Daily Advertiser*, March 14, 1794. In October 1801, six months after his departure from the almshouse, Cummings placed a notice in Poulson's *American Daily Advertiser* announcing his new business premises on "the corner of Walnut and Eleventh Streets," where the buyer would be supplied with a variety of flowers and plants. Thus, if old age was behind his retirement, it is unlikely he would have commenced a new entrepreneurial adventure.

"Hopelessly Hardened"

The Complexities of Penitentiary Discipline at Philadelphia's Eastern State Penitentiary

JENNIFER LAWRENCE JANOFSKY

IN 1835, PHILADELPHIA'S EASTERN STATE PENITENTIARY received prisoner number 145. Samuel Brewster was forty years old and had worked as a cabinetmaker in the city. He was married and the father of three children. Brewster's crime goes unrecorded, but state records reveal that he received a five-year sentence in the new prison that sat on a hill just outside of the city. It was not the first time Brewster had had a run-in with the law. He had served time on at least one prior occasion, though when, where, and for what, we do not know. Brewster proved to be a challenging inmate. In his first month, he produced only four pairs of shoes—well below the production target—and informed Eastern's warden that "he never would make another pair." Brewster was not alone in his distaste for work. Eastern's inmates routinely refused work assignments, rejected religious counseling, and took out their anger and frustration on their overseers. While Eastern's promoters publicly touted the benefits of separate confinement, privately the institution struggled to discipline its uncooperative prison population.[1]

For decades, our understanding of penitentiary life has been driven by a "top-down" approach, with reformers and their interests dominating our understanding of these complex institutions. Indeed, scholars such as Michel Foucault and David J. Rothman have directed very little attention to the prisoners' own experiences. Doing so gives the lie to Foucault's characterization of prisoners as "docile bodies."

This study of the dynamics of power at Eastern State places inmates like Samuel Brewster at the center of analysis. From this vantage, it is readily apparent that institutional life was far from the reality envisioned by reformers and assumed by several subsequent scholars. Disciplinary records, wardens' daily journals, and ministers' writings reveal a complicated history—a history in which prisoners exerted considerable influence over penitentiary life by denying work, damaging work supplies, destroying cell furniture, rebuffing and manipulating religious counselors, and attacking overseers. Through their denial of silence, industry, and counseling, inmates at Eastern rejected the bourgeois, middle-class value system so important for effective penitentiary management.[2]

"This mode of punishment . . . is eminently calculated to break down his obdurate spirit"

Opened in 1829 and operated under the Pennsylvania system of separate confinement, Eastern State Penitentiary served as the flagship of the antebellum prison reform movement—a purpose-built response to some of the problems endemic to earlier penal schemes. Reformers had complained to the state for decades about the miserable conditions of its dilapidated, colonial-era prisons. Capable of little more than temporary detention, these early institutions were an embarrassment to early national sensibilities that valued cleanliness, structure, and order. Their reputation as "schools of vice" and "dens of debauchery" rested on a host of depredations: large common rooms warehoused seasoned criminals alongside vulnerable and impressionable youths; prostitutes thought nothing of plying their trade; disease and filth proliferated everywhere. Pennsylvania's reformers, led by Benjamin Rush and the Philadelphia Society for Alleviating the Miseries of Public Prisons, lobbied for a new system of incarceration commensurate with the values of the new nation. Eastern State would embody this vision. Inside John

Haviland's massive gothic compound, prisoners were expected to spend the duration of their sentences alone in their cell, the intensity of their isolation mitigated only by the Bible, some small-craft labor, and visits from the occasional minister or manager. Thick stone walls enclosed individual cells, intended to provide prisoners an environment for contemplation and reform.[3]

Haviland's design placed a great premium on the reformative effects of isolation in particular. Without it, prisoners would be distracted from the task at hand: contemplation. Reformers intended the system to function as a series of processes, each one inextricably linked to the others. First, isolation and silence would break the prisoner's spirit. For the first few days of an inmate's incarceration, penitentiary staff had instructions to leave him alone in his cell with nothing to puncture the solitude. This provided prisoners with a taste of the true horror of isolation—an experience intended to force prisoners to beg for work and confess their guilt. Second, having expressed contrition, prisoners would receive materials to allow them to work in their cell or read the Bible. Each day, officials expected prisoners to perform essentially the same tasks: rise when instructed, eat when instructed, labor when instructed, and rest when instructed. Intense religious counseling and small-craft training would work hand-in-hand with enforced isolation to promote a regimen intended to reform the soul of the wayward criminal. Reformers believed if prisoners accepted their moral failure and embraced a life of religion and labor, they could effectively be reintegrated into society.[4]

Lest there be any confusion regarding expectations for appropriate behavior, officials equipped each cell with a list of eight rules that reflected the middle-class value system that reformers embraced and promoted. The rules emphasized cleanliness and orderliness and instructed prisoners to routinely wash themselves and neatly store plates, utensils, and food until a guard removed them. They were to be "industrious" at their trade and, when not working, were to read approved religious materials or develop their literacy skills. The rules directed prisoners to be respectful and courteous to staff and to never allow feelings of revenge or anger to color those relationships.[5]

"The picture is ideal. It is like Plato's Republic, rather what it ought to be than what it is."

The international penal community hailed John Haviland's plan as an architectural wonder, while Eastern's local supporters championed the

Pennsylvania system as an effective and humane response to man's failings. The reality of penitentiary management, however, was quite different. Penitentiary managers struggled to maintain control over their charges while prisoners quickly determined how best to exploit the new building's architectural deficiencies to fashion illicit communication networks. Officials instructed prisoners to "not make any unnecessary noise, either by singing, whistling, or in any other manner," yet with little success. Burrowing holes between cells took considerable time, but for prisoners who had nothing but time, the opportunity for human interaction was worth the risk. Nails, hammers, and pieces of iron, intended for shoemaking, became the tools of resistance as prisoners tenaciously attacked the walls, determined to communicate with their neighbors. Some, like William Grenage and George Geney, used their tools to burrow holes between cell walls to engage in conversation. Karl Goffin used his work tools to tap messages to another prisoner, and it was only when officials restrained him with manacles to stop him from reaching the pipes that he was finally thwarted. Although Haviland had designed extraordinarily thick cell walls to prevent this kind of interaction, neither he nor Eastern's backers anticipated the extent of prisoners' fortitude in forging interpersonal relationships.

It did not take prisoners long to realize that they were not closely monitored throughout the day. Guards, or "overseers," bore the responsibility of observing almost forty prisoners each, thus making constant observation of every individual impractical. Inmates realized they possessed some degree of autonomy during the day and used this time to their advantage. Some, like David Anderson, used their shoemaking and weaving tools to help them speak with their neighbors. Despite the almost twelve-foot-tall ceilings, Anderson used his weaver's loom to hoist himself closer to the "Eye of God" skylight where it was easier to be heard. Without close surveillance of the goings-on within individual cells, inmates communicating this way were difficult to detect. Anderson's innovative scheme was only discovered after he fell and broke his leg.[6]

Other prisoners pioneered less physically dangerous means to converse. To prevent prisoner interaction, Haviland had equipped each cell with a commode and with central heating. Each system was, in its own way, an engineering marvel and the source of much envy among prison administrators elsewhere. The inmates themselves treasured both systems, not only for the comforts they provided but also because the plumbing and heating pipes located underneath each prisoner's cell offered another conduit for exchanging messages. Inmate Jesse Quantrill revealed to a visiting member of the Pennsylvania Prison Society that he could hear the "signal taps on the heating pipes" between prisoners and that it was possible to shout into the plumbing pipes and be heard, so long as the system had been recently flushed. In 1836, Warden Samuel Wood disappointedly reported in his daily log book, "Discovered that 6 prisoners had been talking through holes made along side of their hot water pipes." On another occasion, officials moved five prisoners to darkened cells to punish them for speaking to one another through the plumbing lines. Short of ripping out the entire apparatus, overseers could do little to prevent prisoners from exploiting these signature design features.[7]

Pipes not only served as conduits for conversation but also as highways for goods. A prisoner could drop a note or other goods through the toilet and use one of his work tools to push it along to the next cell. After one inspection, Prison Society members reported that prisoners were "passing bottles, boxes, &c., along the water courses." So extensive had these communication networks become that by the 1850s the Prison Society worried that any semblance of inmate isolation was little more than fantasy. In 1852, a report on Eastern declared: "One of the committee observes the injurious influence on the mind of many prisoners in consequence of their having too much knowledge of the affairs of other prisoners." The prisoners, they continued, "have some knowledge of the recent commitments and know by name the occupant of most of the neighborly cells." The idea that prisoners would be totally isolated from the criminal community had obviously failed as administrators struggled to maintain any semblance of contemplative isolation.[8]

How to maintain order and discipline at an institution that prided itself on its rejection of corporal punishment remained a challenge. In contrast to routine violence inflicted by wardens at the factory-like prisons of Auburn and Sing Sing in New York State, Eastern's managers faced limits on how much punishment they could administer. In public, at least, the managers of Eastern professed that corporal punishment was entirely antithetical to their reform objectives. Privately, however, Eastern's managers bemoaned their failure to conjure a system of incentives to encourage steady work, good behavior, and meaningful isolation. In 1833, managers set their ideals aside and punished a prisoner named Mathias MacCumsey for his repeated attempts to communicate with neighbors by making him wear an "iron gag." When he choked and died in the gag, an embarrassing public investigation ensued in which state authorities advised shame-faced wardens to devise alternative punishments. The results were decidedly uneven. If a prisoner was caught violating the rules, officials were now expected to respond by removing work materials and reading matter from the cell. For continued infractions, officials could limit the offender to a diet of bread and water. If that proved ineffective, they moved the inmate to a completely dark cell.[9]

In practice, isolation in a darkened cell proved a wholly inadequate means to discipline individuals whose prior experience as free workingmen had steeped them in the tactics of labor protest. A survey of Eastern's intake records demonstrates the vast majority of inmates came from the laboring classes. Before arriving at Eastern, prisoners had worked as shoemakers, tailors, chair makers, and carpenters. Within these trades, workers had created a unique work culture that drove the pace of production, governed the hours one worked in a day, and even determined which days they would work. Work slowdowns, "Blue Mondays," and sabotaging of tools and machines all characterized the labor movement of the early nineteenth century and, for many, became the tools of resistance at Eastern State. Administration officials, drawn from the middle classes, struggled to understand this culture and proved singularly ineffective at managing semiskilled craftsmen accustomed to exercising their prerogative over what constituted a fair work environment.[10]

By 1836, Samuel Wood, the institution's first warden, had begun to complain to the state legislature that prisoners' production typically declined dramatically after their first year of incarceration. This pattern was especially pronounced among inmates whose prior work experience consisted solely of unskilled manual labor. "Up to this period," he explained, "the novelty of their learning a trade and the desire to perfect themselves in it, prompts them to exertion." Unfortunately, he continued, "after this novelty ceases, and they think they understand as much as they care for, the great majority appear content to do as little as they can and thus play at their work." It did not take long, apparently, for inmates to conclude that the only rewards for hard work were existential. Work for the sake of work was not a concept prisoners eagerly embraced. Some pushed back by not keeping the pace. Others engaged in more overt displays of dissatisfaction. In 1835, prisoner John Levrow informed Warden Wood that "he had knocked off weaving," and would

"never weave another day." Likewise, in 1841, Ambrose Payne exasper-
ated officials when he broke his loom and destroyed his yarn, while in
1842 inmate Henry Browser destroyed his shoe leather. One prisoner
even attempted to influence the work habits of the future inhabitant
of his cell. In 1856, guards discovered George Race had "scratched on
a slate words designed to prevent whoever might succeed him therein
from working at the labor at which he had been employed."[11]

"Hopelessly Hardened"

Inmates at Eastern found a number of ways to demonstrate to authorities their lack of enthusiasm for the reformers' agenda. In addition to
dismissing work projects and compromising their own isolation, prisoners frequently rejected the program of moral counseling established for
their benefit. Boosters of the Pennsylvania system earnestly believed that
religious reading and private counseling would provide the foundation
to rehabilitate prisoner character. Yet, authorities seemed singularly un-
prepared to address the degree of reading illiteracy evidenced among
many early inmates. Warden Samuel Wood noted in 1833 that "of the
142 prisoners which have been received here from the commencement,
only four have been well educated, and only about six more who could
read and write tolerably." In this context, the activities of visitors who
pressed Bibles and religious tracts into the hands of prisoners during
these early years seem hopelessly misguided or naive. Indeed, officials
were surprised to find out that inmates preferred to deface or eviscerate
the moralistic titles stocked in the prison library rather than read them.
In 1837, members of the Pennsylvania Prison Society (who maintained
the library) complained that "about forty books belonging to the library
had been lost or destroyed by the prisoners and many other volumes
injured." A few years later that total had risen to three hundred.[12]

Inmates also expressed their frustration and anger at attempts to offer them religious instruction by endlessly provoking the institution's
newly appointed "moral instructor." In 1838, Eastern hired Baptist minister Thomas Larcombe. In the role of "moral instructor," Larcombe was
charged to meet with prisoners, evaluate their character, offer counseling to those he deemed in need, and provide them rudimentary school-
ing. He soon realized that he had his work cut out for him. "Prisoners,"
he complained, "seem to have given an appetite for whatever may amuse
the mind, rather than a true relish for moral improvement." After

examining the library's holdings, he found that the titles most likely to induce moral reform were almost entirely "unused" and soon resolved that "all future additions of religious books should be of a modern style, attractive, and adapted to the common mind." Nevertheless, library records from the Pennsylvania Prison Society suggest that most inmates continued to shun religious books, no matter how attractive or contemporary. "Religious books," Pennsylvania Prison Society member William Foulke observed, "are not liked." Indeed, prisoners vastly preferred secular genres. "Histories, voyages & novels/biographies & any magazines of a light character" are appreciated, Foulke reported.[13]

Prisoners' rejection of "religious books" did not prove promising for the newly hired educator. Larcombe was a Baptist minister from Philadelphia who likely envisioned Eastern's inmates as a sea of lost souls in need of redemption. Prisoners, however, made it perfectly clear that they had little to no interest in his proselytizing. Inmates certainly craved personal contact, but they would not indulge a preachy minister to ease that suffering. A survey of Larcombe's journals documents the trouble they gave him. Some outright refused to meet with him. Indeed, deciding who could or could not enter their cell was a powerful expression of prisoner autonomy—and there was nothing penitentiary managers could do to persuade prisoners to engage with the instructor. Such was the case of prisoner John Day, who made Larcombe bristle when he had "no wish to have intercourse with me on religious subjects." Likewise, Larcombe discovered prisoner William Clerk, who was "exceedingly rough & uncourteous. Not disposed to hear on the subject of religion." Similarly, Nathan Adams "rejects the gospel, will not converse of religion," while prisoner George Thomas "does not read the scriptures, has no wish to repent."[14]

Catholic prisoners posed other challenges. Throughout the 1840s and 1850s, Eastern State Penitentiary became home to a growing population of Catholic inmates from Cork, Dublin, and Donnegal. Many of these immigrants had already faced discrimination and occasional violence at the hands of Pennsylvania's Protestants—confrontations that had often led, directly or indirectly, to their imprisonment at Eastern. The same religious tensions continued behind bars. Tired of defending themselves against Pennsylvania Protestants, Eastern's Catholic prisoners were not about to submit to the ministrations of a bombastic Baptist who seemed congenitally predisposed to dislike the Irish people. Having interviewed John Hannegan, an inmate serving time for sexual assault,

Larcombe recorded his belief that Hannegan's victim was "Irish too & would no doubt like to be raped." With an attitude that embraced all the popular stereotypes of the day, it is no surprise so many Irish dismissed Larcombe almost out of hand.[15]

In 1841, Catholic prisoners secured a small victory when their constant protests against Larcombe's visits to their cells won them the privilege of a series of appointments with local priests. Yet, Larcombe continued to pester. Perhaps out of frustration with Larcombe's incessant visits, Irish prisoner Thomas Coyne made it perfectly clear that he had already embraced Catholicism and had no wish to embrace Larcombe's Protestant faith. In his journal, Larcombe noted that Coyne had hung crosses all around his cell, an action that led the minister to conclude Coyne was "superstitious." Other inmates expressed their resentment less subtly. According to Larcombe, Hugh Miller had a "Very bad temper [and was] exceedingly irritated as soon as he saw me approach him to converse on the subject of religion, said he had his bible to direct him interprets for himself & wishes none to interfere with him." Pig-headed as ever, Larcombe concluded that Miller was "hopelessly hardened" to the comforts of any religion, despite Miller's assertion that he already had faith and was fluent in the Bible. Larcombe's attitude in this episode reveals why prisoners constantly pushed back against his ministry. He saw prisoners as ignorant, incapable of interpreting the Bible or issues of faith, and regarded those that disagreed with him as beyond the reach of reformation.[16]

The only prisoners Larcombe found more frustrating than those who denied him an audience were those who feigned interest in his religious instruction. One such tormentor was James Stewart, a fifty-year-old man serving an eight-year sentence for counterfeiting. Eight years in isolation likely seemed an eternity for this practiced dissembler. Perhaps to pass the time or to amuse himself, Stewart attempted to dupe Larcombe into believing that he had embraced religion. He would welcome Larcombe into his cell and converse readily with him on religious topics. Stewart's actions kept Larcombe coming back for months. Then one day those visits came to a sudden, abrupt end. In his journal, Larcombe recorded that Stewart's protestations of faith were "false." He did not elaborate further, but the sense of shock and disillusionment was palpable. James Stewart was not the only inmate who tried to dupe Larcombe during his long tenure at Eastern. George Hark made almost identical overtures to Larcombe in 1835, only to later confess that he was only "pretending."

In 1836, Larcombe discovered prisoner Robert Wilson had also been deceiving him. "Have evidence of his hypocrisy and can therefore have no further confidence in him," he wrote with obvious frustration and disappointment. Two years later, it happened again. Archibald McClarity, a forty-year-old convicted murderer from Ireland, professed "to be a Protestant," Larcombe remarked in 1838, "but is evidently a Catholic."[17]

Sources produced by other personnel at Eastern confirm the frequency with which inmates resorted to deception to gain privileges or to mitigate the agony of isolation. In 1856, a disgruntled former employee penned an exposé of life within the penitentiary that ran in Philadelphia's *Sunday Dispatch.* The author, Thomas Roe, informed the public that he had been an overseer for five years, qualifying him "to give the public a correct idea of the working of the system of solitary confinement." Unlike Thomas Larcombe who, at least initially, had been seduced into believing that many of the prisoners he worked with had found salvation, Roe knew better. "Prison-piety," Roe explained, "always carries suspicion with it and bears watching — there are so many motives besides a 'godly sorrow for sin' for being religious; it sometimes secures a relaxation of discipline . . . it brings him books, it brings him company." To illustrate, Roe shared the story of two prisoners — one seasoned, the other a first-time offender — who, on their way to begin their sentences at Eastern, discussed how they might manipulate the system to their advantage. "Now if you want to get along well down there," the veteran criminal explained to his companion, "be religious — not all at once at first, but after a while." Once settled inside, this cunning recidivist set about acting on his own advice, making increasingly vociferous claims about his healed soul and "[throwing] dust in the eyes of some" who alleged that he was putting it on.[18]

As this savvy veteran was acutely aware, feigning interest in moral counseling had numerous benefits. A visit from Larcombe, however unproductive, could ease the monotony of physical isolation and provide one outlet for conversation. For some inmates, such human contact likely made all the difference. For others, its absence could prove costly. Physician reports from the era document many cases of prisoners suffering from mental illness. Suicides, self-mutilations, and hallucinations plagued many inmates.

Playing the good prisoner could also bring more tangible rewards. While Haviland's design had not anticipated that prisoners would be removed from their cells for any length of time, Eastern's managers frequently did so on health grounds and for the purposes of maintaining disciplinary control. Now and again they would reward individual inmates with the opportunity to do shift work in the library or the gardens. These positions were reserved for prisoners who demonstrated exemplary behavior. Faking a conversion or feigning interest in Larcombe's Baptist books seemed worth the time and effort if it meant access to a life outside of their cell.

Some prisoners believed that this kind of exemplary behavior might also lead to their early release. Having somehow heard that some of their fellow inmates had received state pardons, several convicts became anxious to prove that they had mended their ways and turned a corner. A report from the Prison Society in 1852 noted that "many of the prisoners are in a very unsettled state of mind, owing to the numerous pardons lately granted; and hoping the same might soon be extended to them." Several among them soon availed themselves of moral counseling, presumably in hopes that it would demonstrate their reformed character and secure them an early release.[19]

Eventually, even Larcombe realized how often he was being played. Indeed, by 1853, after a decade of working with prisoners, he appeared to have given up any hope for prisoner reformation. In the institution's annual report he complained that "the character of a prison population is unlike that of any other class of persons whatsoever. In all others the varied shades of good and evil intermingle, but in these almost all is dark. Generally ignorant, and frequently the offspring of the profligate and licentious, with some cases of unmitigated depravity, the whole mass as it lies before you presents a cheerless aspect."

Prisoners' deceit and manipulation seem to have affected Larcombe deeply. Over time he became, much like the prisoners he now regularly condemned, "hopelessly hardened." Confronted by a sly and stubborn population, Larcombe's early, idealistic expectations that isolated inmates could be rescued and reborn by the force of his will had given way to deep cynicism about the prospects of carceral correction.[20]

"Strict vigilance is our only safeguard"

Prisoners may have seen a fair amount of Thomas Larcombe, but their time with him paled in comparison to the time they spent with the institution's guards, known as "overseers." Unlike Larcombe, overseers came from the same working-class backgrounds as the inmates themselves. In many instances, inmates and overseers shared the same neighborhoods, acquaintances, previous employers, and favorite taverns. Once confined, inmates had daily opportunities to build relationships with overseers. Together, they commiserated over long workdays, and perhaps found occasional common ground in an institution that pitted middle-class values against working-class culture. Indeed, prisoners were well aware that their guards shared little in common with men like Larcombe or the members of the board of visitors.

This was not entirely unexpected. Having learned of the problems several administrators at Walnut Street had experienced with corrupt guards, Eastern's managers had anticipated that inmates and overseers might forge alliances. Officials put considerable effort into identifying appropriate individuals to monitor prisoners. According to the board, overseers were to be "master" workmen in the "trades they respectively superintend." They looked for men who avoided "indulgences in low vices . . . impure conversation, gossiping" or those who expressed too much "familiarity with prisoners." In Boston, the prison society there followed similar guidelines, decreeing that recruiters should only hire "temperate men" of "inveterate sobriety." Keepers ought to possess "great benevolence" and strong moral character. Explaining its reasoning, the Boston Prison Society argued that if overseers "are profane and obscene; if they revile religion, or even do not speak respectfully of it; if they feel themselves at home, when conversing with convicts in perfect accordance with the taste and habits of the convict; what is to be expected, but an amalgamation of officers and keepers in one corrupt mass?"[21]

Essentially, prison reformers wanted to hire men similar to themselves — working men who embraced middle-class values of industry, sobriety, and discipline. The rules — to which all overseers were subject — read like a concentrated formula for modeling middle-class identity, not all that dissimilar to the rules that governed inmates. At Eastern, officials advised overseers to "preserve [a] mild and conciliatory conduct toward them [prisoners]; to suppress every passion or resentment, and at all times and on all occasions, show entire self-possession, but resolutely, and with unflinching firmness of purpose, enforce the discipline of the Penitentiary." In training prisoners to work, monitoring exercise yard time, delivering meals, and conducting disciplinary observation, Eastern's administrators expected that overseers would embody, project, and instill middle-class values.[22]

It was rarely so simple. During the 1840s, inmates found numerous opportunities to exploit the cultural and socioeconomic differences between overseers and the administration. While inmates may have been isolated in their cells, they were not ignorant of the battles being waged between Larcombe and the guards. In 1841, for example, overseer James Tweed was fired for "improper conduct" after physically assaulting the minister. Tweed had just disciplined a prisoner by removing all reading materials from the cell, only to watch dumbfounded as Larcombe marched into the cell to present the prisoner with a Bible. For prisoners listening as this scenario unfolded, the episode revealed a seam of division that might be turned to their future advantage. Indeed, over the following few years, Larcombe found himself competing with overseers for inmates' favor. In his journal for the period 1845–1850, he reflected on the fix he now found himself in: "Overseers conceive hostility against him for trivial causes or for none at all—sometimes for the obvious discharge of duty. They either speak to their prisoners against him or insinuate something to his disadvantage . . . misrepresent him or having their imagination imperfect they watch him closely and often wrongfully interpret his language." Larcombe and the officers may have seen prisoners as pawns in their power struggle, yet the inmates appreciated the vacuum created in these situations and adeptly played the two parties against each other.[23]

Whether putting up a united front against Thomas Larcombe or against other administrators, inmates and overseers often found common cause. Like inmates, Eastern's guards were subject to an unrelenting routine. They awoke inmates in the morning, delivered their food and set work orders, released them for exercise, issued clean uniforms, maintained the pace of work, and (in theory) insured each prisoner's isolation from one another. Given this regime, it is not surprising that a review of the Warden's Daily Journal from the period 1830–1850 reveals the firing of overseers almost every month for failure to satisfactorily complete their duties. Frequent complaints included low pay, long hours, and a lack of autonomy over their daily routine. In May 1855, warden John Halloway changed guards' start time from 6:00 a.m. to 5:00 a.m., a time, he later observed, "distasteful to some of the overseers." Prisoners, too, complained of the time change, as overseer Michael Cassidy recorded in his journal: "Prisoner 3292 refused to come down on account he says the days are too long. He thinks that going to work at 6 o'clock early enough." Here, guards and prisoners found common ground. Indeed, guards likely found receptive listeners in prisoners, who well understood the toll this encompassing regime took on those it ensnared.[24]

Inmates and guards shared other mutual resentments. Both groups hated being the subjects of constant observation. In the penitentiary hierarchy, guards ranked only above prisoners and endured practically the same level of scrutiny as that of the inmates. A variety of authorities monitored overseers' itinerations, including the warden, the moral instructor, the penitentiary doctor, and members of the Prison Society. Standing in the central "hub" of the prison's iconic hub-and-spoke design, one could not see within a prisoner's cell. However, one could see clearly if an officer was walking the halls regularly and properly monitoring his charges. Indeed, on rare occasions, prisoners might abandon their attempts to build alliances with overseers and complain to administrators or visitors that certain guards were shirking their duties. In 1846, one inmate informed a Prison Society member that if the keepers were more "vigilant," communication between prisoners could be reduced or perhaps even prevented. "The warden ought to be careful to visit the cells," the prisoner advised the astonished visitor, "for the keepers have *partialities* & that there may be great inequality of treatment." Such observations led to frequent crackdowns upon lax officers. In 1845, penitentiary inspector Thomas Bradford directed warden Thomas Scattergood "to inform the overseers that an increased watchfulness over each & every prisoner, by day & by night, is required to be observed by them."[25]

As such episodes suggest, prisoners frequently found cause to overlook their natural kinship with guards from familiar backgrounds, and instead they expressed their resistance to penitentiary discipline by drawing their overseers into open conflict. Aggravated to the point of violence by the monotony of solitary confinement, inmates sometimes lashed out at overseers, their most frequent visitors. Throughout the 1830s, 1840s, and 1850s, prisoners targeted overseers in a series of brutal attacks often triggered when an inmate refused to be transferred to special punishment cells. Desperate to avoid a darkened cell and reduced diet, they armed themselves with makeshift weapons fashioned from tools, work supplies, and even pieces of furniture and lashed out at their unarmed guards. On one occasion, prisoner David Pledge refused to be moved from his cell and threatened guards with a slingshot he had made. On another occasion, George Dark stopped up his toilet and when officers attempted to move him to another cell, they found that he had armed himself with stones, a knife, and a piece of bed-iron.[26]

Sabotaging toilets appears to have been a popular means to draw guards into a fight: when John Billman complained to overseer James Merrill "that his privy was running over," and beckoned him to enter his cell, Merrill quickly observed the prisoner "holding the end of a rope in his hands made out of his blanket, and much to his alarm the other part fix'd with a slip knot & nicely adjusted." As Warden George Thompson later remarked, "It would have been an easy manner to have noosed him & strangled him without anyone knowing it. But the wariness of the officer & the timely discovery of the trap I fully believed saved his life." Prisoner Michael Trusty, a "violent" and "abusive" charge at the best of times, used his shoemaker's knife to attack overseer William Wray in 1836. Several years later, in 1853, prisoner George Clifford stabbed overseer Joshua Dickerson in the chest, abdomen, and groin when he tried to move him to another cell. Other assaults were apparently more impulsive. Overseer William Blundel was lucky to survive after being stabbed in the throat by prisoner Eli Smith in 1842.[27]

As these examples make clear, the threat of violence remained a part of institutional life, and while some guards and prisoners formed significant relationships, suspicion and anxiety persisted on all sides. Eastern's managers had gone to great lengths to hire men of good, moral character. But managers had failed to consider the plethora of opportunities for common ground between the two parties. Drawn primarily from the working classes, guards were more likely to identify with prisoners who shared common values. Yet, the relationship between the two remained complicated and uneasy. While many prisoners sought relationships with guards, others discovered an outlet for their anger and frustration. Consequently, alliances were frequently short-lived or marked by suspicion. The historical record does not offer one instance of moral instructor Thomas Larcombe or any other middle-class manager being assaulted by a prisoner. Guards were the primary targets of prisoners' violent actions, demonstrating the precariousness of interpersonal relationships behind bars.

This analysis of Eastern State's daily operation reveals a world very different from the theoretical model of penitentiary reform. From its opening in 1829, prisoners worked to exploit architectural deficiencies to forge interpersonal relationships. Administrative punishments, ranging from dark cells to reduced diets, frequently proved ineffective as time and again prisoners were caught speaking through plumbing lines, carving holes between cells, shouting out through skylights, and passing notes to one another. The frequency with which these episodes occurred demonstrates the prisoners' determination to maintain human contact at all costs. Isolation—so crucial to the Pennsylvania system's recipe for reform—remained unattainable as inmates devised numerous strategies to subvert the system designed to separate and surveil them. Eastern State never functioned as a silent reformatory. Rather, the institution served as a site of negotiated space where prisoners frequently exercised considerable influence over the course of penitentiary management.

The same impulses explain inmates' repeated rejection of moral instruction and the duplicity some demonstrated by feigning religious conversion. Prisoners' denial of Thomas Larcombe and their several false conversions demonstrate the difficult task penitentiary reformers faced in putting inmates on the path to a "contrite heart." Irish prisoners, in particular, frequently found themselves at odds with Larcombe and his Protestant mission, and their resistance eventually secured them the services of a Catholic priest. Other inmates pressed in other directions, seizing opportunities created by the tension between Larcombe and the overseers in order to secure access to reading materials or a relaxation of the rules. On other occasions, prisoners realized they could turn the tables by complaining to higher-ups about lax overseers. Inmates correctly realized that power within the penitentiary was never absolute; it shifted between parties on a seemingly daily basis.

The shifting nature of power can most clearly be seen in the complex relationships between prisoners and guards. At one level, the two groups shared much in common. Despite penitentiary officials' attempts to hire men of respectable character, inmates accurately surmised their keepers had more in common with men like them than with the middle-class reformers who had hired them. Consequently, inmates and officers frequently found common cause and grievance against the administration.

Prisoners' acts of resistance complicated reformers' vision of silence, reflection, and deterrence, as they reminded officials of the complexity of power relations behind bars. Ultimately, the inmates' relentless attempts to contest authority and subvert institutional order demonstrate the capacity of the human spirit to persevere, endure, and survive.

NOTES

1. Eastern State Penitentiary, Intake Register, R.G. 15, Pennsylvania Historical and Museum Commission (hereafter PHMC). Warden's Daily Journal, Jan. 1, 1835, R.G. 15, PHMC.

2. David J. Rothman, *The Discovery of the Asylum: Social Order and Disorder in the New Republic* (1971; rev. ed., New York: Little Brown, 1990); Michel Foucault, *Discipline and Punish: The Birth of the Prison*, trans. Alan Sheridan (New York: Vintage Books, 1977).

3. *First and Second Annual Reports of the Inspectors of the Eastern State Penitentiary Made to the Legislature at the Sessions of 1829–30, and 1830–31* (Philadelphia: n.p., 1831), 10; Negley K. Teeters, *The Cradle of the Penitentiary: The Walnut Street Jail at Philadelphia, 1773–1835* (Philadelphia: Temple University Press, 1955); Michael Meranze, *Laboratories of Virtue: Punishment, Revolution, and Authority in Philadelphia, 1760–1835* (Chapel Hill: University of North Carolina Press, 1996).

4. *First and Second Annual Reports*, 9–10; *Fourth Annual Report of the Inspectors of the Eastern State Penitentiary*, 10.

5. Eastern State Penitentiary, Board of Inspectors (hereafter Brd. of Insp.), Minutes, Dec. 5, 1840, R.G. 15, PHMC; Bruce Dorsey, *Reforming Men and Women: Gender in the Antebellum City* (Ithaca, N.Y.: Cornell University Press, 2002); Christine Stansell, *City of Women: Sex and Class in New York, 1789–1860* (Chicago: University of Illinois Press, 1987); Rodney Hessinger, *Seduced, Abandoned, and Depraved: Visions of Youth in Middle-Class America, 1790–1850* (Philadelphia: University of Pennsylvania Press, 2005).

6. Thomas McElwee, *A Concise History of the Eastern Penitentiary of Pennsylvania, Together with a Detailed Statement of the Proceedings of the Committee, Appointed by the Legislature, December 6, 1834, for the Purpose of Examining into the Economy and Management of That Institution, Embracing the Testimony Taken on That Occasion, and Legislative Proceedings Connected Therewith* (Philadelphia: n.p., 1835), 1:20; Brd. of Insp., Minutes, June 4, 1836, Dec. 3, 1836, Jan. 7, 1837, June 17, 1840, Nov. 7, 1840, Dec. 5, 1840; Warden's Daily Journal, May 14, 1837.

7. Warden's Daily Journal, Jan. 27, 1835; Punishment Log, PHMC; Minutes of the Philadelphia Society for Alleviating the Miseries of Public Prisons (hereafter, PSAMPP), Nov. 11, 1859, Historical Society of Pennsylvania; William Parker Foulke Papers, "Notebooks Concerning Prisons and Prisoners," American Philosophical Society, May 14, 1847.

8. Minutes of the PSAMPP, May 11, 1852, Nov. 11, 1859.

9. McElwee, *A Concise History*; Punishment Log, Nov. 25, 1843, May 1, 1844, May 22, 1844, Aug. 6, 1845; W. David Lewis, *From Newgate to Dannemora: The Rise of the Penitentiary in New York* (Ithaca, N.Y.: Cornell University Press, 1965).

10. Bruce Laurie, *Working People of Philadelphia, 1800–1850* (Philadelphia: Temple University Press, 1980), 53–55.

11. Warden's Daily Journal, Jan. 1, 1835, Aug. 11, 1835, Aug. 11, 1836, Feb. 12, 1841, Jan. 17, 1842, Jan. 28, 1856; Intake Register; Brd. of Insp., Minutes, May 17, 1836; Punishment Log, Dec. 1, 1852, Dec. 4, 1852.

12. *Fourth Annual Report*, 9; Foulke Papers, Nov. 15, 1846; Minutes of the PSAMPP, Feb. 10, 1852. A prisoner, alone in his cell, reviewing the library catalogue, might have found selections such as: *Stories from Ancient History, The Hive and Its Wonders, First Book of History* and *Second Book of History, Beecher's Lectures to Young Men,* and *Think Before You Act* (no doubt a highly unpopular selection).

13. *Twenty-Fifth Annual Report of the Inspectors of the Eastern State Penitentiary Made to the Legislature at the Sessions of 1853–54* (Philadelphia: n.p., 1854), 36; State Penitentiary for the Eastern District of Pennsylvania Records, American Philosophical Society, Thomas Larcombe Papers, volume 2 ("B"), 1839–1843; Foulke Papers, Nov. 15, 1846.

14. Larcombe Papers.

15. Ibid.; Warden's Daily Journal, Oct. 22, 1841. On prejudicial attitudes toward the Irish and their capacity for superstition and obduracy, see Dale T. Knobel, *Paddy and the Republic: Ethnicity and Nationality in Antebellum America* (Middletown, Conn.: Wesleyan University Press, 1986), 39–68. See also Stansell, *City of Women,* 67.

16. Larcombe Papers.

17. Ibid.

18. "Eastern State Penitentiary," *Sunday Dispatch* (Philadelphia), March 16, 1856; Warden's Daily Journal, March 17, 1856.

19. Minutes of the PSAMPP, April 13, 1852; Negley K. Teeters, *The Prison at Philadelphia, Cherry Hill: The Separate System of Penal Discipline: 1828–1913* (New York: Columbia University Press, 1957), 191–95.

20. Larcombe Papers; *Twenty-Fourth Annual Report,* 31.

21. Brd. of Insp., Minutes, June 3, 1829, Sept. 5, 1829; *Second Annual Report of the Boston Prison Discipline Society* (Boston: n.p., 1827), 31–32; *First and Second Annual Reports,* 9; *Sixth Annual Report of the Inspectors of the Eastern State Penitentiary Made to the Legislature at the Sessions of 1833–34* (Philadelphia: n.p., 1834), 5.

22. Brd. of Insp., Minutes, Dec. 5, 1840.

23. Warden's Daily Journal, Dec. 5, 1855.

24. Warden's Daily Journal, April 5, May 21, May 24, 1855; Michael Cassidy, *Journal Relating to the Third Block,* R.G. 15, PHMC, May 27, 1856.

25. Foulke Papers, Oct. 6, 1849; Brd. of Insp., Minutes, Jan. (n.d.) 1846.

26. Warden's Daily Journal, April 9, 1850.

27. Warden's Daily Journal, May 10, 1842.

Universities of Social and Political Change

Slaves in Jail in Antebellum America

SUSAN EVA O'DONOVAN

IN THE LAST DAYS OF SEPTEMBER 1854, a number of the enslaved workers on George Noble Jones's El Destino estate, a massive cotton plantation in west Florida, schemed their way into jail. Precisely what the details of the plot were and how many people were involved is not altogether clear from the record. What is clear is that at least four, maybe more, of the El Destino slaves, all "runaway [and] went rit Strait to Tallahassee and was put in jail." "I have been with Negroes for Somtime," the bemused overseer, D. M. Moxley, reminded the absentee owner, George Noble Jones. Yet "I never have knowe nor heard tell of thar running away to be put in Jail befor." "[T]har is Somthing rong about it but I am not able to See it yet, but I think that I have got on the rit track."[1]

In reporting the events that had disrupted production on the El Destino plantation just as cotton harvest was reaching its peak, D. M. Moxley offered more than a puzzling and idiosyncratic story about slaves who had deliberately plotted their way into jail. He revealed something about jails too, and about the ways in which enslaved Americans understood and occasionally exploited public and private jails in the slaveholding states. While slaveholders and many subsequent scholars have generally represented such institutions as one of the more visible symbols of state power, many enslaved Americans saw something different. To be sure, jails were loathsome and often deadly places that most enslaved people appropriately feared. Jails were, after all, closely associated with some of the worst horrors that visited black people's lives while in bondage: sale, forced migration, family rupture, and brutal punishment. But at the same time and in one of those ironic twists that define so much of slavery's history, detention behind bars could sometimes be used by the enslaved to advance their own interests in a world in which power was otherwise stacked steeply against them.

The bondswomen and -men who so frustrated D. M. Moxley were not alone in this knowledge. Harriet Jacobs, for example, saw in jails sanctuaries of a sort from the horrors daily visited on her by a lewd and lecherous owner.[2] Likewise, the enslaved men who shared a crowded jail cell with a young abolitionist, George Thompson, used their time behind bars to develop their religious knowledge. They pressed white inmates to read aloud from the Bible, transforming first the jail in Palmyra, Missouri, and later the state penitentiary at Jefferson City into what one of the enslaved inmates described as "a House of God and a gate[way] to heaven."[3] Most significantly, these communal cells (see figure 9) returned to the enslaved precisely what owners wanted desperately to deny them: opportunities for the kind of comings and goings, contacts, and conversations that had, as Donna Haraway noted of a later revolution in technologies of knowledge, "serious potential for changing the rules of the game."[4]

Jails in the Antebellum South

Common jails, as northern penal reformers were quick to observe, were notoriously insecure and porous places. Meant to serve as little more than temporary warehouses for miscreants, murderers, and misfits, jails were, in the words of historian Lawrence M. Friedman, "dirty, undisciplined, unisex" places in which authorities rarely made any attempt to isolate inmates from each other, never mind from the external world.[5] Contacts and conversations of the sort that were purportedly the goal behind the El Destino slaves' plot to land themselves in jail, and which George Thompson described at length in his memoir, were

FIGURE 9. "The Interior of the Jail in Palmyra, Missouri," in George Thompson, *Prison Life and Reflections* (Hartford, Conn.: A. Work, 1857). Courtesy of the University of Tennessee Libraries, Knoxville, Special Collections.

an everyday part of an inmate's life. Walls and bars did little to slow the flow of information and individuals into, out of, and through local jails. Shoved willy-nilly into what were usually one or two common cells, inmates freely consorted, conversed, and traded with each other and with anyone who ventured to visit. When the windows of a cell opened outward and no fence stood in the way, which seemed to be a fairly universal condition, those exchanges could and often did include people who passed by on the street.[6] Despite the best efforts of a growing legion of penal reformers, the result was a swirl of words over which authorities repeatedly failed to exert effective control.[7] Jails, decried critics throughout much of the antebellum era, remained little more than "seminaries of vice," "nurser[ies] of crime," and schools of "hideous depravity."[8]

Jails in the southern states were judged by reform-minded contemporaries to be particularly bad. Although jails were among the first public structures built in the wake of a massive migration that washed across the Appalachians, down the Tombigbee, Tennessee, and Mississippi rivers, and eventually to Texas, the citizens who paid for their construction were usually more interested in the state of their crops than the state of their public facilities.[9] Chronically underfunded and frequently constructed of whatever material came most readily to hand—usually lumber and logs, infrequently stone—the jails that sprouted in slaveholding states between settlement and secession were small and crowded spaces in which as many as a dozen or more inmates mixed freely (see figure 10).

Congestion was a major problem. While a few communities, generally cities, kept jails large enough to separate at least a part of the inmate population by sex, status, or crime, the vast majority made do with "small log pens" too cramped and tiny to permit any sort of segregation.[10] The jail that served as abolitionist Jonathan Walker's home for the better part of a year spent in custody in Pensacola, Florida, is a good case in point. Measuring just fifteen feet square, and ventilated by a single small

FIGURE 10. "Jail at Williamsburg, Tennessee, near Fort Blount, ca. 1803–1820." In a state of near ruin when this photograph was taken, the jail in Williamsburg, Tennessee, built in 1803 and operated until at least 1820, was a small, uncomplicated wooden structure that would have struggled to accommodate more than a handful of inmates. Courtesy of the Tennessee State Library and Archives.

window, the Pensacola jail bulged at the seams, as it played host to a constantly revolving population of free and slave, men and women.[11] Many other southern jails were equally overcrowded. A visitor to the Louisville, Kentucky, jail in 1830 counted "*nine* prisoners: three runaway slaves" thronged together in a single cell. In another there were "*eleven*, I think, in all": a white man confined for debt, three fugitive female slaves, and "several colored men" of indeterminate status.[12] Even those facilities that were designed to minimize internal crowding seldom did so in practice. On a visit made in the late 1820s to the jail that served the nation's capital, a Mr. Thompson of Pennsylvania found that of sixteen available cells, one was a complete ruin, three were in use for storage, and "forty-four persons, among whom were five women and four children," were lodged in the remainder.[13]

From time to time, grand jurors and earnest government inspectors would try to goad southern citizens into investing attention and money in their local and common jails. In some instances, constituencies listened, diverting public funds to strengthen walls and windows, or sloshing some paint on exterior walls.[14] More often, citizens did nothing (see

FIGURE 11. Milton Elijah Warthen and his family at the Warthen jail, Washington County, Georgia, ca. 1867–1869. The jail, which, according to local legend, once confined Aaron Burr, is the small structure on the right. Consisting of a single room of rough-cut lumber and topped with a simple, gabled roof, it nevertheless survived at least one war and Reconstruction. Courtesy of Georgia Archives, Vanishing Georgia Collection.

figure 11). Apparently unimpressed by reports about the crime, unrest, and frequent escapes that were an artifact of poorly maintained structures, most communities stumbled along with ramshackle and deteriorating jails. Distinguished by loose boards, broken locks, and slack supervision, buildings such as the one that served Darlington District, South Carolina, came in for repeated condemnation from those who feared the dangerously "free intercourse" that rotting walls and unsecured windows encouraged between inmates and others.[15] According to a correspondent to a New Orleans newspaper, the jail in Mobile, Alabama, was "an old wreck of an affair."[16] In South Carolina, the decrepitude of the state's jails was such that during an 1820 inspection, the superintendent of public works noted places where prisoners had gouged holes through the walls—damage that not only for years went unrepaired but also, he explained, obliged the jailer to "confine persons in the same apartment from which others have escaped."[17] South Carolina was hardly alone. Jails across the South were in similarly sad shape, and in Bibb County, Georgia, broken locks and door latches permitted inmates of that community's jail to "ru[n] at large."[18]

Porous walls, windows, and doors did not necessarily make jails healthy places. In fact, as penal reformers, government officials, and concerned visitors repeatedly observed, southern jails were typically dirty, unlit, and unheated. Beset by overcrowding and poor ventilation, they were fetid and infectious environments. At Edgefield District, South Carolina, the state's inspector surveyed the interior from the doorway, where the stench he met proved too awful for further admission. "Any confinement in this gaol," he concluded (presumably with one hand holding the pen and the other his nose), was equivalent to a death sentence for it "must prove fatal to the unfortunate persons subject[ed] to it."[19] French investigators Gustave de Beaumont and Alexis de Tocqueville shuddered when they discovered pigs and prisoners jostling for space in the noisome confines of a New Orleans jail.[20]

The situation worsened in jails where jailors whipped, paddled, and otherwise punished slaves for owners who were too squeamish to do the work of keeping their enslaved workers in line.[21] Shortly after her arrival in Savannah, northerner Emily Burke confided of a practice that put extra cash in jailers' pockets: "It was easy enough to know when the hour of flagellation in jail had arrived, from the dreadful groans and shrieks that poured forth from the iron grated windows."[22]

Slaves in Jail

Picked up on the lam, arrested for crime, sent in by owners for punishment, or simply locked behind bars for security purposes, slaves represented an ever-present and ever-more-predominant part of the South's
inmate population. While judges sentenced increasing numbers of
white people to reformative terms in the region's slowly growing penitentiary system, slaves typically endured stints in town and county jails.
Mindful that long prison sentences would remove much-needed black
labor from circulation, most southern lawmakers accepted and acted
upon Georgian jurist Thomas R. R. Cobb's claim that the only way for
the law (or, for that matter, a slaveowner) to reach a recalcitrant slave
was "through his body." Though slaves appeared occasionally within the
confines of southern prisons and penitentiaries, they dominated southern jails.[23] Thus by the time Robert Everest visited New Orleans in the
mid-1850s, he found the city's four police lockups filled with what he
estimated were at least 240 enslaved inmates, all of whom he suspected
had been sent in by their owners "for correction."[24]

In many cases, the time slaves spent behind bars was fairly short. Slave
traders, for instance, often locked their human wares into local jails for
safekeeping during overnight stops.[25] Tyre Glen, a North Carolinian
who traded in slaves before he shifted his entrepreneurial attention to
dry goods and groceries, would stash newly purchased slaves in local
jails until he had accumulated a large enough number to make it worth
his while to drive them further south for sale.[26] Owners, too, occasionally tucked their slaves into jail for safekeeping. Fearful that their cook,
Marie, might have become intoxicated by thoughts of freedom after having accompanied her owners to Europe, the Doussans of Baton Rouge
made it a practice to consign Marie to that city's jail every night for
eight years. Indeed, Marie's nocturnal incarcerations only came to an
end when she petitioned successfully for manumission, basing her case,
as a matter of fact, on the nine months she had spent with the Doussans
in France.[27] Alexander Farnsley of Kentucky briefly considered remand-
ing one of his father's slaves to jail overnight so that Alexander might
attend a dance with the woman who would soon be his wife. "Early this
morning I had to go over on Clark Plank Road, to attend to some business for pa, and when I returned, I found a negro man drunk, who
is really dangerous when he is so [and] Pa is afraid for me to leave
the place," Alexander wrote as he explained why he had to miss the

evening's entertainment. "It is true," he admitted, "I could put [the slave man] in gaol, and just avoid the necessity of my staying home to-night; but I though[t] if I were to put him in gaol, and let him out again, that it would only make him worse, because he might infer from it, that I was afraid of him too."[28]

Given the value attached by free people to slaves' labor, those who were confined on suspicion of crime moved into and out of jail at an especially speedy rate. Most stayed in jail just long enough for their cases to be considered and, if so ordered, punishment inflicted. Thus while an enslaved North Carolinian named Isaac remained in the sheriff's custody for 306 days before the court dropped the murder charge against him, and a Kentucky slave named Frank waited "many months" behind bars before he received a gubernatorial pardon, most of those who landed in jail on criminal charges came and went in a matter of hours.[29] More typical were those like ten-year-old Julia Ann of Delaware or William, who was arrested for "drinking rum" in one of New Orleans' cabarets. In the first case, not wanting to retain a person of "so dangerous a character" in the bosom of their community, the justices of the New Castle County court held Julia Ann three days before granting her owner permission to carry the child out of state for sale.[30] In the second case, William remained in custody just long enough for the New Orleans court to hear his case and for the jailer to lay on a sentence of twenty lashes.[31] An enslaved Mississippian named Jim did not stay behind bars for long, either. Arrested on February 17, 1838, for larceny, he was back on his owner's plantation five days later. Washington was in and out of jail just as quickly. Like Jim, he was arrested on a larceny charge, and like Jim, he was released into his owner's custody after just five days in jail.[32]

While large numbers of slaves passed through jails at considerable speed, others lingered much longer behind bars. This was especially true of fugitives, who, depending on the state in which they were captured, could be held from four to twelve months while jailers advertised for owners to come forward to claim them. Even then, there was no guarantee that immediate release would follow. If the owner failed to appear in the allotted time, the same legislation usually directed local officials to dispose of the slave at "public outcry," a process that could add considerably to an inmate's stay.[33] A fugitive named Henry, who made his way from west Mississippi to southern Alabama before being caught, spent at least seven months in confinement while the sheriff advertised for Henry's owner. When no one came forward, the sheriff arranged to sell the slave at auction "for cash."[34] A man named Charles spent even more time behind bars. Arrested as a fugitive on September 23, 1847, he remained in jail at least through August of the following year, waiting for someone to claim him or buy him.[35] Long stays were not necessarily reserved for black men, either; women and children who had managed by some means to give owners the slip also endured long periods of public confinement. Laura, a black woman who was picked up on suspicion of being a fugitive on July 1, 1854, remained behind bars a year and a half later, with no release in sight.[36] Another Henry, this one just fifteen years old when arrested on May 11, 1848, by Habersham County, Georgia, officials, was still in that county's jail on October 30, 1849. He had gone unclaimed and unsold perhaps because of the scars that marked his hands: grisly reminders of self-inflicted wounds.[37]

It was those who landed in jail for no other reason than being the property of quarreling slaveholders who often endured the longest stints in one squalid jail cell or another (see figure 12). Incarceration for this category of slaves could often be measured in years. Take Edmund, for example. The subject of a long and complicated pair of suits brought by two different parties against his owner, Edmund spent 591 days in jail in Russell County, Alabama. As the sheriff later reported to the court, he had taken custody of the slave "on the 22 day of November [1856] and Kept him until the 5th day of July 1858."[38] Swedish reformer Fredrika Bremer stumbled onto a similar situation while touring a jail in Louisville, Kentucky. Perplexed at finding among the female part of the population two young enslaved women who "bore so evidently the stamp of innocence" on their faces, Bremer could not help but ask what evil deed they had committed. None, replied her guide, who explained that the women had been lodged behind bars to prevent them from being seized and sold to cover their owner's debts. "How long will they remain here?" Bremer inquired. "Oh, at furthest, two or three weeks—quite a short time," came the reply. On hearing that, one of the young women "smiled, half sadly, half bitterly": "Two weeks!" "We have already been here two years!"[39]

Subversive Spaces

As terrible as they were, the conditions that brought the South's jails to reformers' and inspectors' attention imperiled the very control on which slavery and slaveowners depended. In a world in which social,

FIGURE 12. Arthur Lumley, "Secrets of the Prison-House—a Cell in the Female Department of the Washington Jail," *Frank Leslie's Illustrated Newspaper*, December 28, 1861. Courtesy of the Library of Congress.

political, and productive success hinged on a master's or mistress's ability to distance their laborers from competing—and almost by definition, subversive—influences, the custom of lumping miscreants with murderers, thugs with thieves, the innocent with the depraved, and above all slaves with each other seemed more than a little paradoxical. For as crowded as they were with all manner of people from all manner of places, the dreary, dank, and sometimes deadly cells contained within them the potential to destabilize what was always an unstable balance of power. "The prison," Marcus Rediker and Peter Linebaugh observe of an earlier age, "was something of a leveler."[40] It was a truism that even slaveholders occasionally admitted. Fully aware that no inmate—male or female, enslaved or free, innocent or depraved—could be made to check their eyes, ears, minds, or mouths at the jailhouse door, an antebellum Natchez correspondent described the social and political potentials of his state's jails in language that could just as easily have come from a Boston reformer. They were, the writer groaned, nothing more than "school[s] of experimental villainy, in which each [inmate] is taught new lessons by the other."[41]

Subverting what were meant to be frontline defenses against public disorder, jails promoted precisely what slaveholders by the late 1820s had come to fear most: free and unfettered conversation among and between slaves and all those with whom they might share a cell.[42] Thus at the same historical moment that state lawmakers across the South were enacting increasingly draconian measures—quarantining black sailors, evicting enslaved workers from print shops, and prohibiting the unsupervised gatherings of slaves—in order to insulate slaves from outside influences and isolate them from each other, a steady stream of chatter emanated from southern jails as enslaved inmates struck up conversations with all manner of people. Cacophony, in fact, was what fugitive Henry Bibb remembered most about the day he was ordered by authorities to the workhouse in Louisville, Kentucky. Stepping through the door, it was not what he saw so much as what greeted his ears—inmates who filled the air with their prayers, their cries, and their curses—that made the deepest impression on a man who experienced some of slavery's most heinous abuses.[43]

As Bibb soon came to learn, cacophony was a constant condition of the inmate experience. Words swirled freely and sometimes fiercely behind bars. But as was commonly the case among slaves—a people for whom talk was key to social survival—many of those words and the messages they conveyed were relatively innocuous, touching on the problems of slavery only lightly, if they touched on slavery at all.[44] The enslaved inmates who circulated through Jonathan Walker's account of the months he spent in police custody in Pensacola, Florida, spoke, for example, about their homes, their families, and the distances that kept them apart.[45] Benny, Harriet Jacobs's young son, talked with an inmate who would go on to be the boy's tutor. Before his two months were out, Benny had learned to count.[46] Others talked about their criminal exploits and the deeds they had committed that had put them behind bars. The "gamblers, drunkards . . . [and] harlots" with whom Henry Bibb shared his jail space took delight, for instance, in boasting about how they had "robbed houses, and persons on the highway, by knocking [their victims] down."[47] Israel Campbell, his cellmate Barry, and a woman named Lucinda turned their eleven-day stay into a reunion of sorts. "We all had quite a lively time in prison," Israel later recalled, "laughing, talking and singing."[48] In Mecklenburg, North Carolina, a slave named Jeff also spoke, but in his case, he chose both topic and audience imprudently. Arrested on suspicion of rape, Jeff allowed himself to be led by a stranger he met while in jail into admitting his guilt. The judge in Jeff's case later agreed, and ordered Jeff's reckless words about having "had his will" of a white woman to be entered into the records as a lawful confession. It was a decision that would cost Jeff his life, for the court eventually sentenced him to death.[49]

Sooner or later, however, the words that swirled behind bars would gravitate toward slavery and its grave injustices. Indeed, cells provided an especially fertile environment for this kind of talk, for while much of the more innocuous thoughts could be safely released by speakers out in the open, the South's dimly lit, loosely supervised, and internally open jails invited a distinctly dissident brand of exchange.[50] It was a phenomenon with which fugitive slave Anthony Burns was deeply familiar. Apprehended in Boston in 1854 and then sent by his owner to Richmond, Virginia, Burns was first secured in the city's public jail before being removed to a slave trader's pen. Distinguished primarily by its scale (it was not unusual for the larger of the privately owned slave pens to contain several hundred enslaved inmates at any one time), Burns settled into Robert Lumpkin's filthy dungeon to await his turn on the auction block.[51] As was the case with countless other inmates across space and through time, Burns refused to settle silently. Using a spoon, he soon dug a hole in the floor that allowed him to open a channel of verbal "intercourse" with those confined in the cell directly below. According to his biographer, Burns then proceeded to occupy otherwise idle time by "fill[ing] their eager and wondering ears with the story of his escape from bondage, his free and happy life at the North, his capture, and the mighty effort that it cost the Government to restore him to Virginia." With his lips close to the floor, Burns relayed accounts of the places he had seen to the inmates below. He told his audience of the people he had met. He warned them of perils that must be avoided. He suggested the size of the prize that might even be won. He may even have told his listeners about the five hundred free black men who had staged a protest on his behalf after his capture in Boston. Burns performed, in short, as the slaves' "Columbus," the explorer home from foreign shores, eager to share what he had heard and learned and observed while living beyond the horizon.[52]

Burns's relation was hardly unique. People who fulfilled similar roles could be found scattered throughout the commons that were the South's local jails, ready to expand the epistemological boundaries of enslaved inmates' minds and lives. In the process, these impromptu leaders, teachers, and guides helped transform the southern jail—one of the most ubiquitous and visible symbols of slaveholders' power—into what Stokely Carmichael would later describe as "university[ies] of social struggle and moral" change: sites that in the turbulence of the mid-twentieth century would give rise to a black power movement. "For us," Carmichael explained, the carceral experience "would be life altering, a rite of passage, a turning point."[53]

The time slaves spent in jail could change their lives, sometimes in profoundly political ways and sometimes in ways that could change the rules of the game. Powerful and potentially leveling ideas and dreams circulated throughout antebellum sites of confinement, carried along by inmates who talked. Thus just as George Thompson came to know something about the people he met during his imprisonment at Palmyra and later in Jefferson City, Missouri, so his enslaved cellmates came to know something about Thompson, a young theologian from Illinois who in 1841 launched his own assault on human bondage.[54] Announcing themselves "eager for conversation" that would "enlighten their minds," the slaves who shared the white abolitionist's cells took advantage of the shabby and crowded surroundings to expand on their own bodies of knowledge. According to Thompson's later account, the slaves who occupied those Missouri jails learned, for example, about antislavery activities both near to home and further abroad. One of them, a man named Albert, learned how to write; someone else asked for and obtained a counterfeit pass while still in jail. On receiving much prized "directions to liberty" from Thompson, yet another enslaved inmate assured his abolitionist-adviser that "one word from you is better than gold."[55]

And so it went in other jails and in other sites of confinement. John Parker recalled using his time behind bars in New Orleans to learn how to effectively "outwit men and [their] combinations," while Henry Bibb, though shocked by the depravity of the crooks and thieves with whom he was forced to share cells, appreciated the practical knowledge about the lay of the land and fugitive tactics that they freely shared with those around them.[56] In Richmond, slaves confined in the same facility that would later contain Anthony Burns likewise took impromptu and informal instruction in geopolitical knowledge. But rather than teach one another about how to get out of the South and into the North—a topic that figured prominently in Bibb's recollections of jailhouse talk—the slaves who preceded Burns through the Richmond slave-trader's pen heard and learned about abolitionists' Atlantic outposts, about maritime life, and about how to take command of a ship from a hostile crew. In a demonstration of the tectonic forces that simmered inside the South's common and usually crowded jails, these were lessons that a cohort of those Richmond inmates would later put to good use when in November 1841 they hijacked the slave ship *Creole* and sailed her away to freedom in the British Bahamas.[57]

Nor did the lessons stop there. Because of the practice of lumping inmates together regardless of age, sex, color, or crime, inmates frequently learned from and sometimes cooperated across racial and class lines. In the process, they challenged categories of control that had long been mainstays of American slavery. Much to the consternation of local authorities, this is what matured within the close confines of the Scott County, Mississippi, jail. Sneaking in an auger (a long flexible metal tool used for boring holes through wood), one black inmate, apprehended on suspicion of being a fugitive slave, used it to destroy the locks on the jail doors. He and two white inmates escaped to freedom, forging in the process a spontaneous and pragmatic bridge across a racialized gulf that slaveholders had opened centuries before in an effort to preempt precisely this kind of action: a class-based alliance against privilege and power.[58] Strikingly similar jail breaks shocked other southern communities. In early 1855, for instance, a Savannah newspaper reported that four black men—one of whom "belongs in New Orleans"—had opened a hole in a wall and then returned to release the lone white man with whom they had shared their confinement, a convicted murderer named Charles Griffith.[59] Not a month later, a slave named Bill slipped from the irons that held him in the Bibb County, Georgia, jail; freed six of his fellow inmates (at least two of whom were white men); and together they descended to the ground through a hole in a second-floor wall using their blankets as rope.[60]

It is likely that the majority of slaves did not benefit immediately or even personally from what they heard and learned behind bars. For some, it was enough, or perhaps all they could do, to share the content of carceral conversations with others, taking "great pleasure," as Henry Bibb once did, in relaying to family, friends, and occasionally strangers the knowledge they had obtained while in jail.[61] Many more alert and attentive inmates simply stored what they had heard and learned for future use, building a library of ideas, information, and inspiration that could be drawn on as conditions permitted. The enslaved who passed through Rebecca Crouch's cell during the three (or perhaps four) years she spent in jail in Warren County, Mississippi, probably fell into the latter category, committing to memory accounts about how Rebecca had been freed in Mobile, Alabama; about her subsequent life in Ohio; and about how a person who dreamed of freedom might purchase passage as Rebecca did, aboard one of the northbound vessels that plied the South's largest river.[62] Likewise, those slaves who crossed paths with the suspected slave rebel John during his stint in a Louisiana jail may have tucked away images of a world upturned: one in which white Europeans allied themselves with enslaved black men and who, together, dared to mount an armed challenge to the South's masters.[63] And who knows what John Pedro and Richard Coleman spoke of—or to whom—during the months they overlapped in the Vicksburg jail. One was a free-born black sailor from Venezuela who knew his way around the Caribbean and Atlantic littoral, and the other was a free man of color from Westmoreland County, Virginia, who had moved west to work on a railroad. Both had been wrongly arrested as fugitive slaves, and both were founts of geopolitical—and in Pedro's case for sure, transnational—knowledge.[64]

The Politics of Talk

Denied the right to read and write by both custom and law, enslaved women and men evidently vested special importance in talk.[65] It was in meeting and conversing with others, Henry "Box" Brown would freely admit, that he and his brother came to know something about "whatever was going on in the world." The Brown brothers received much of that instruction while shuttling between their owner's plantation and a local gristmill, a twenty-mile excursion the boys were ordered to take on a regular basis.[66] Hundreds of thousands of other enslaved people received their news while traipsing along behind migrating slaveholders, waiting tables for gregarious white diners, or talking to one of the many northern or foreign visitors who frequented Deep South plantations. Moses came to understand something about the world around him while chalking up as he did close to 4,000 miles on the road every year while driving a wagon for his owner. So did Ben, who sometimes accompanied Moses, as well as Daniel, who went with his owner from Georgia to California and back again in the early 1850s.[67] Still other slaves, particularly personal servants and nurses, claimed a share of their enlightenment by traveling to Philadelphia, New York, Boston, and occasionally abroad, bearing witness on their return to the sounds as well as the sights of full freedom.[68]

But as we have seen, large numbers of enslaved Americans took at least some of their lessons while biding their time behind bars. As critics of the antebellum penal system kept pointing out, common jails and the unsupervised contacts and conversations that they fostered were indeed universities of a dank and fetid sort. Bearing more than a passing resemblance to the encampments of slaves who built the South's railroads, dug its canals, and mined its precious minerals, jails made possible precisely what the South's lawmakers had been desperately attempting to preempt ever since Nat Turner's 1831 insurrection had sent shock waves through the slaveholding states. Lapsing into language that accorded a striking degree of political power to slaves, Richard Lyon, a Georgia slaveholder, likened unsupervised gatherings such as those that unfolded in the South's county jails to "regular conventions" at which all slaves would be "abley represented." Fretting about exchanges of the kind that took place between an enslaved man named J. H. Banks and the six other inmates with whom he shared a Deep South cell, conversations that in this particular instance culminated in a mass escape, Richard Lyon warned that any slave who returned to his owner's estate after such an experience, if not rebellious himself, would surely "inform those who are of what he has seen & heard—and incalculable mischief . . . [would] follow."[69]

The vast majority of the meetings that Lyon granted the status of political convention yielded little of the mischief that made him so nervous. Only infrequently did enslaved inmates translate what they had learned while behind bars into immediate freedom. John Brown, who acquired his "useful and practical hints" about routes out of the South while penned up in New Orleans, was the exception, not the rule. So too were King and Jack, a pair of slaves who "came to the dungeon grates about the dead hour of night" to have a conversation with Henry Bibb "about Canada, and the facilities for getting there" and who, Bibb proudly remembered, successfully applied what they had heard and learned. Within a week of their conversation with Bibb, Jack and King had arrived at their Canadian destination.[70] Nor did jailhouse talk always arrive at a *Creole* conclusion: such dramatic outcomes were the exception, not the rule, following on prisoners' shared conversations. Yet, in a nation that by the 1850s was splitting along sectional and ideological seams, for slaves to know who was a friend, who was a foe, and something of the world in which they existed was no mean or futile achievement.

Thus while the years leading up to Abraham Lincoln's election stand out for the absence of large-scale revolts, America's bound workers nonetheless spent much of those years accumulating a potent body of knowledge: about their surroundings, about their owners, and about a nation that was hurtling toward war. It was information that some were able to use to escape slavery altogether, actions that in calling northerners' attention to the horrors of human bondage helped to intensify sectional tensions.[71] It was information that gave many more the means to deflect some of slavery's abuses — by introducing them to allies in unlikely places, by giving rise to new social connections, and by opening slaves' eyes and minds to a much larger political terrain. It was information that many of the nation's slaves accumulated in whole or in part while locked in a cell.

Most of all, it was information that slaves would draw on in the weeks and months following the Confederate secession. For it was then that the meetings Lyon so graphically imagined bore their most radical fruit. Acting under the cover of war, America's slaves were at last able to put into practice lessons that many had heard while confined to a cell, laying aside their tools, taking to their feet, and launching what has been recently described as the largest of New World rebellions.[72] In the process, those four million people would accomplish a whole lot more. Perhaps Henry Bibb was right when, in reflecting back on his experience as a prisoner in southern jails, he noted that if slaveholders had understood what unfolded on a daily basis behind the bars, "they would never [have] let their slaves" do time.[73]

NOTES

I would like to thank Christina Adkins, Richard J. Blackett, Richard Brown, Vincent Brown, Daniel Rasmussen, Joshua Piker, and Calvin Schermerhorn for reading earlier drafts of this essay; I would also like to thank David Blight and the Gilder Lehrman Center for the Study of Slavery, Resistance, and Abolition for making possible the initial research on which this essay rests.

1. Ulrich Bonnell Phillips and James David Glunt, eds., *Florida Plantation Records: From the Papers of George Noble Jones* (Gainesville: University Press of Florida, 2006), xii–xiii, 106–8, 113.

2. Harriet Ann Jacobs, *Incidents in the Life of a Slave Girl*, ed. L. Maria Child (Boston: Published for the Author, 1861), 62.

3. George Thompson, *Prison Life and Reflections; or, A Narrative of the Arrest, Trial, Conviction, Imprisonment, Treatment, Observations, Reflections, and Deliverance of Work, Burr, and Thompson who Suffered an Unjust and Cruel Imprisonment in Missouri Penitentiary, for Attempting to Aid Some Slaves to Liberty* (Hartford, Conn.: A. Work, 1857), 21.

4. Donna Haraway, "A Manifesto for Cyborgs: Science, Technology, and Socialist Feminism in the 1980s," in *Feminism/Postmodernism*, ed. Linda J. Nicholson (New York: Routledge, 1990), 191.

5. Lawrence M. Friedman, *Crime and Punishment in American History* (New York: Basic Books, 1993), 77; Michael Stephen Hindus, *Prison and Plantation: Crime, Justice, and Authority in Massachusetts and South Carolina, 1767–1878* (Chapel Hill: University of North Carolina Press, 1980), 202–3; Dorthea Dix, *Memorial Soliciting a State Hospital for the Protection and Cure of the Insane, Submitted to the General Assembly of North Carolina* (Raleigh, N.C.: Seaton Gales, 1848), 6.

6. Among many examples, see Timothy J. Gilfoyle, *A Pickpocket's Tale: The Underworld of Nineteenth-Century New York* (New York: W. W. Norton, 2006), 132–33.

7. For a recent contribution to a large scholarly literature on antebellum penal reform and its limits, see Rebecca M. McClennan, *The Crisis of Imprisonment: Protest, Politics, and the Making of the American Penal State, 1776–1941* (Cambridge, U.K.: Cambridge University Press, 2008), chaps. 1–2.

8. *Reports of the Prison Discipline Society, Boston, 1826–1835* (Boston: Press of T. R. Marvin, 1855), 1:26, 30.

9. See, for example, "Extracts from an Act to establish certain Counties, therein named, and for other purposes," passed Dec. 13, 1816, in Harry Toulmin, comp., *Digest of the Laws of the State of Alabama: Containing the Statutes and Resolutions in Force at the end of the General Assembly in January, 1823* (Cahawba, Ala.: Ginn & Curtis, 1823), 114–15; and "An Act for the Building and Keeping in Repair the Court-Houses and Jails in the Respective Counties within This State, and for the Support of the Poor," approved Feb. 21, 1796, in Oliver H. Prince, comp., *A Digest of the Laws of the State of Georgia: Containing all Statutes and the Substance of all Resolution of a General and Public Nature, and Now in Force, Which Have been Passed by This State, Previous to the Session of the General Assembly of Dec. 1837*, 2nd ed. (Athens, Ga.: Oliver H. Prince, 1837), 169–70; Montgomery, Ala., *Daily Journal*, Nov. 14, 1851; Houston, Tex., *Telegraph and Texas Register*, Nov. 25, 1837; D. Clayton James, *Antebellum Natchez* (Baton Rouge: Louisiana State University Press, 1968), 77–81.

10. Robert David Ward and William Warren Rogers, *Alabama's Response to the Penitentiary Movement, 1829–1865* (Gainesville: University Press of Florida, 2003), 16–17. In New Orleans, for example, the second municipality jail that was built in the late 1830s consisted of "four apartments, one for white male prisoners and another for white female prisoners. . . . The other two rooms are for the colored prisoners and chain gang of either sex" (*The* [New Orleans] *Daily Picayune,* Aug. 15, 1839).

11. Jonathan Walker, *Trial and Imprisonment of Jonathan Walker, at Pensacola, Florida, for Aiding Slaves to Escape from Bondage* (Boston: Anti-Slavery Office, 1846); see 38 for a physical description of the jail.

12. *Reports of the Prison Discipline Society,* 796–97.

13. Ibid., 796.

14. David Kohn, comp., *Internal Improvement in South Carolina, 1817–1828* (Washington D.C.: private printer, 1938), 4; Ward and Rogers, *Alabama's Response to the Penitentiary Movement,* 17.

15. Montgomery, *Daily Alabama Journal,* Nov. 14, 1851; Tuscaloosa, Ala., *Intelligencer,* Dec. 5, 1835; Macon *Georgia Telegraph,* Nov. 2, 1847; Milledgeville, Ga., *Federal Union,* Jan. 17, 1854, Oct. 10, 1854, Dec. 19, 1854, Mar. 6, 1855; Charleston, S.C., *City Gazette and Daily Commercial Advertiser,* May 21, 1822; Kohn, *Internal Improvement in South Carolina,* 5, 151–52; Jacqueline Jones, *Saving Savannah: The City and the Civil War* (New York: Alfred A. Knopf, 2008), 85–86; Edward L. Ayers, *Vengeance and Justice: Crime and Punishment in the 19th-Century American South* (New York: Oxford University Press, 1984), 110.

16. *The* (New Orleans) *Daily Picayune,* July 3, 1839.

17. Kohn, *Internal Improvement in South Carolina,* 36–37.

18. Macon *Georgia Telegraph,* May 2, 1839.

19. Kohn, *Internal Improvement in South Carolina,* 28–29.

20. Gustave de Beaumont and Alexis de Tocqueville, *On the Penitentiary System in the United States and Its Application in France,* trans. Francis Lieber (Philadelphia: Carey, Lea & Blanchard, 1833), 13.

21. Hindus, *Prison and Plantation,* 146–47; Ayers, *Vengeance and Justice,* 102; Walker, *Trial and Imprisonment,* 69; Don F. Fehrenbacher, *The Slaveholding Republic: An Account of the United States Government's Relations to Slavery* (New York: Oxford University Press, 2001), 65; Karl Bernhard, *Travels through North America during the Years, 1825 and 1826,* 2 vols. (Philadelphia: Carey, Lea, and Carey, 1828), 2:8–10; Francis Colburn Adams, *Manuel Pereira, or, Sovereign Rule of South Carolina with Views of Southern Laws, Life, and Hospitality* (Washington, D.C.: Burell & Blanchard, 1853), 129–30; *Augusta* (Georgia) *Chronicle,* June 14, 1826.

22. Emily Burke, *Pleasure and Pain: Reminiscences of Georgia in the 1840s* (Savannah, Ga.: Beehive Press, 1978), 13–15.

23. William Banks Taylor, *Brokered Justice: Race, Politics, and Mississippi Prisons, 1798–1992* (Columbus: Ohio State University Press, 1993), 7; *Augusta Chronicle*

& Georgia Advertiser, June 14, 1826. Starting in 1818, Louisiana occasionally sentenced enslaved felons to prison "as an alternative to hanging," and for a period following a revision to state law in 1845, Maryland sent slaves to the penitentiary before transporting them out of state.

24. Robert Everest, *A Journey through the United States and Part of Canada* (London: John Chapman, 1855), 108. On the changing complexion of those confined to the South's county and community jails, see Ayers, *Vengeance and Justice,* 61, 101, 295; Fehrenbacher, *Slaveholding Republic,* 70; Macon *Georgia Telegraph,* Dec. 5, 1832.

25. Fehrenbacher, *Slaveholding Republic,* 70; Steven Deyle, *Carry Me Back: The Domestic Slave Trade in American Life* (New York: Oxford University Press, 2005), 99, 107.

26. Tyre Glen to Isaac Jarratt, Nov. 9, 1833, Jarratt-Puryear Family Papers, Manuscripts Department, Duke University Library.

27. "Marie to the District Court, West Baton Rouge Parish, Louisiana, 1848," in *The Southern Debate over Slavery,* vol. 2, *Petitions to Southern County Courts, 1775–1867,* ed. Loren Schweninger (Urbana: University of Illinois Press, 2008), 249–51.

28. A[lexander] Farnsley to Mary E. E. Thurman, Oct. 12, 1860, Alexander Farnsley Papers, Filson Historical Society, Louisville, Kentucky.

29. *State v. Isaac,* Dec. 1828, North Carolina Supreme Court, manuscript case file 1667, *Slavery, Abolition and Social Justice, 1490–2007: A Portal for Slavery Studies* (Adam Matthew Digital), http://www.amdigital.co.uk, accessed July 30, 2009; N. Wolfe to [Governor Lazarus W. Powell], Sept. 13, 1851, Governor's Official Correspondence File: Petitions for Pardon, Kentucky Department for Libraries and Archives, Frankfort, Kentucky; Walker, *Trial and Imprisonment,* 26; see also, Burke, *Pleasure and Pain,* 13.

30. "Peregrine Hendrickson to the Court of General Quarter Sessions, New Castle County, Delaware, 1826," in *Petitions to Southern County Courts,* 130–32.

31. *The* (New Orleans) *Sunday Delta,* Nov. 7, 1858.

32. Petitions of Morgan Roland to Hon. John I. Guion, Feb. 21, 1838, ser. 2, reel 15, Race and Slavery Petitions Project, accession no. 21083802; David C. Rogers to the Honorable John Guion Judge of the Criminal Court in & for the County of Warren, Jan. 27, 1838, ser. 2, reel 15, Race and Slavery Petitions Project, accession no. 21083801.

33. John Hope Franklin and Loren Schweninger, *Runaway Slaves: Rebels on the Plantation* (New York: Oxford University Press, 1999), 150–51.

34. Huntsville, Ala., *Southern Advocate,* June 25, 1847.

35. Ibid., June 17, 1848.

36. Statement of F. W. Davis, Jan. 1856, in petition of J. H. Griswold to the Hon. Stephen A. Brown Judge of Probate, July 7, 1854, ser. 2, reel 18, Race and Slavery Petitions Project, accession no. 21085413.

37. Milledgeville, Georgia, *Federal Union*, Oct. 30, 1849.

38. Petition of John S. Burch to Hon. James B. Clark, May 6, 1859, ser. 2, reel 13, Race and Slavery Petitions Project, accession no. 20185901.

39. Fredrika Bremer, *The Homes of the New World*, trans. Mary Howitt, 2 vols. (New York: Harper & Brothers, 1853), 2:210–11.

40. Peter Linebaugh and Marcus Rediker, *The Many-Headed Hydra: Sailors, Slaves, Commoners, and the Hidden History of the Revolutionary Atlantic* (Boston: Beacon Press, 2000), 60–61.

41. Milledgeville, Ga., *Federal Union*, Jan. 9, 1830, Feb. 6, 1830; Taylor, *Brokered Justice*, 4, 8.

42. Thompson, *Prison Life and Reflections*, 317.

43. Henry Bibb, *Narrative of the Life and Adventures of Henry Bibb, an American Slave, Written by Himself* (New York: Author, 1849), 92.

44. Phillip Troutman, "Grapevine in the Slave Market: African American Geopolitical Literacy and the 1841 *Creole* Revolt," in *The Chattel Principle: Internal Slave Trades in the Americas*, ed. Walter Johnson (New Haven, Conn.: Yale University Press, 2004), 203–33; Walter Johnson, *Soul by Soul: Life Inside the Antebellum Slave Market* (Cambridge, Mass.: Harvard University Press, 1999), 63–77; Susan Eva O'Donovan, "The Politics of Slaves: Mobility, Messages, and Power in Antebellum America," working paper; Wm. Capers to Charles Manigault, Sept. 23, 1859, box 27, folder 254, Ulrich B. Phillips Collection, MS397, Yale University Library.

45. Walker, *Trial and Imprisonment*, 50–51.

46. Jacobs, *Incidents in the Life of a Slave Girl*, 161.

47. Bibb, *Life and Adventures*, 94–95.

48. Israel Campbell, *An Autobiography. Bond and Free: or, Yearnings for Freedom, from My Green Brier House. Being the Story of My Life in Bondage, and My Life in Freedom* (Philadelphia: Published by the Author, 1861), 47–50, http://docsouth.unc.edu/neh/campbell/campbell.html, accessed May 20, 2011.

49. *State v. Jefferson* (a slave), June 1846, North Carolina Supreme Court, manuscript case file 3699, North Carolina State Archives, *Slavery, Abolition and Social Justice*.

50. David N. Livingston, *Putting Science in Its Place: Geographies of Scientific Knowledge* (Chicago: University of Chicago Press, 2003); Bruno Latour, *Reassembling the Social: An Introduction to Actor-Network Theory* (New York: Oxford University Press, 2005); John Law, *After Method: Mess in Social Science Research* (New York: Routledge, 2004).

51. E. A. Andrews, *Slavery and the Domestic Slave-Trade in the United States* (Boston: Light & Stearns, 1836), 136–42; Deyle, *Carry Me Back*, 113–19.

52. Charles Emery Stevens, *Anthony Burns: A History* (Boston: John P. Jewitt, 1856), 186–92, http://docsouth.unc.edu/neh/stevens/stevens.html#steve181, accessed May 20, 2011; Janette Thomas Greenwood, *First Fruits of Freedom: The*

Migration of Former Slaves and Their Search for Equality in Worcester, Massachusetts, 1862–1900 (Chapel Hill: University of North Carolina Press, 2009), 17.

53. Stokely Carmichael, *Ready for Revolution: The Life and Struggles of Stokely Carmichael* (New York: Scribner, 2003), 194.

54. Thompson, *Prison Life and Reflection*, 13–14; Walker, *Trial and Imprisonment*, 63.

55. Thompson, *Prison Life and Reflection*, 89, 161, 317, 322, 345, 366.

56. John P. Parker, *His Promised Land: The Autobiography of John P. Parker, Former Slave and Conductor on the Underground Railroad*, ed. Stuart Seely Sprague (New York: W. W. Norton, 1996), 60–61; Bibb, *Life and Adventures*, 95.

57. Troutman, "Grapevine in the Slave Market," 203–33.

58. *Macon* (Georgia) *Telegraph*, July 23, 1839.

59. Milledgeville, Georgia, *Federal Union*, Mar. 6, 1855.

60. Ibid., April 3, 1855.

61. Bibb, *Life and Adventures*, 89.

62. Petition of Rebecca Crouch to the Honorable George Coalter Judge of the first Judicial District of the state of Mississippi, Aug. 16, 1841, ser. 2, reel 15, Race and Slavery Petitions Project, accession no. 21084108.

63. *The* (New Orleans) *Daily Picayune*, Dec. 27, 1856.

64. Petition of John Pedro to the Honorable John I. Guion Judge of the Criminal Court of the State, Sept. 25, 1837, ser. 2, reel 15, Race and Slavery Petitions Project, accession no. 21083707; Petition of Richard, or Dick, Coleman to the Honorable John I. Guion Judge &c. of the Criminal Court of the State of Mississippi, Jan. 30, 1837, ser. 1, reel 15, Race and Slavery Petitions Project, accession no. 21083705.

65. Charles Ball, *Fifty Years in Chains, or, The Life of an American Slave* (New York: H. Dayton, 1859), 271; John Brown, *Slave Life in Georgia: A Narrative of the Life, Sufferings, and Escape of John Brown, a Fugitive Slave, Now in England* (London: L. A. Chamerovzow, 1855), 31. http://docsouth.unc.edu/neh/jbrown/jbrown .html, accessed Apr. 28, 2007; for extended discussions of the importance nonliterate people attached to words that were heard, see Walter J. Ong, *Orality and Literacy*, 2nd ed. (New York: Routledge, 2002); and Jack Goody, *The Domestication of the Savage Mind* (Cambridge, U.K.: Cambridge University Press, 1977).

66. Richard Newman, ed., *Narrative of the Life of Henry Box Brown written by Himself* (New York: Oxford University Press, 2002), 20–21.

67. For examples of Moses's travels, see Hamilton Limosin [&] Parnell to Richard Russell, Feb. 24, 1822, Hamilton Limosin [&] Parmill to Richard Russell, Apr. 13, 1822, Hamilton Limosin [&] Parnell to Richard Russell, May 10, 1822, and Hamilton Limosin [&] Parnell to Richard Russell, May 25, 1822, all in ser. 1.1, folder January–May 1822, Hawkins Family Papers, MS 322, Southern Historical Collection, University of North Carolina, Chapel Hill, in *Slaves in Antebellum Southern Industry*, ed. Charles B. Dew (Bethesda, Md.:

University Publications of America, 1993), ser. B., reel 9 (hereafter: SASI, ser. B, reel 9); Wm. Parmill to Richard Russell, Dec. 14, 1824, ser. 1.1, folder August–December 1824, Hawkins Family Papers, SASI, ser. B, reel 9; S. M. McDowell to Dear Uncle & Aunt & Cousins, Feb. 21, 1853, William G. Dickinson Papers, SASI, ser. B, reel 4; Milledgeville, Georgia, *Federal Union*, Dec. 21, 1852.

68. W. C. Berry, Slave Manifest, 1860, Vertical History File, folder 15, Georgia State Archives; J. R. Schenk, Slave Manifest, Aug. 4, 1860, Vertical History File, folder 15, Georgia State Archives; M. S. Woodhull, Slave Manifest, Aug. 11, 1860, Vertical History File, folder 15, Georgia State Archives; Toby, Slave Manifest, May 9, 1818, Records from the Department of the Treasury, Customs Service, Collection District of Philadelphia, Office of the Collector of Customs, Record Group 36: Records of the U.S. Customs Service, NARA Mid Atlantic Region, Philadelphia.

69. James Pennington, *A Narrative of Events of the Life of J. H. Banks, an Escaped Slave, from the Cotton State, Alabama, in America* (Liverpool, U.K.: M. Rourke, Printer, 1861), 71–72; Richard F. Lyon to Joseph E. Brown, Aug. 9, 1862, Governor's Incoming Correspondence, Georgia State Archives.

70. Bibb, *Life and Adventures*, 88–89; Brown, *Slave Life in Georgia*, 121–22.

71. R. J. M. Blackett, "Dispossessing Massa: Fugitive Slaves and the Politics of Slavery after 1850," *American Nineteenth Century History* 10 (June 2009): 119–36; James Oakes, "The Political Significance of Slave Resistance," *History Workshop* 22, Special American Issue (Autumn 1986): 89–107.

72. Steven Hahn, *A Nation under Our Feet: Black Political Struggles in the Rural South from Slavery to the Great Migration* (Cambridge, Mass.: Belknap Press of Harvard University Press, 2003), 7.

73. Bibb, *Life and Adventures*, 194.

PART TWO

Writing the
Carceral Experience

Reading Prisoners on the Scaffold

Literacy in an Era of Disciplinary Spectacle

JODI SCHORB

MALCOLM X'S ANIMATED RECOLLECTION of his time spent copying an entire dictionary by hand and voraciously devouring books in the prison library provides one of the most famous accounts of the transformative effects of literary acquisition, a recurrent theme in American prison writing. In eighteenth-century colonial American jailhouse writing, scenes in which prisoners encounter texts and mediate their incarceration experience through reading and writing are less visible and, consequently, less emphasized in scholarship. Histories of incarceration, from the colonial American jail to the early modern penitentiary, have been largely silent about the relationship of reading, writing, literacy acquisition, and literacy instruction to the regimes of punishment, discipline, and reform that define their development. As a result, literacy as a subject of inquiry has held a minor place in current scholarship on the early American prison.[1]

The colonial American prison remains an unlikely site to study the role and function of literacy acquisition. First and foremost, early jails were designed neither for education nor for reform. Colonial-era correction was swift and relied primarily on fines and public punishment through stocks, pillories, whipping posts, and scaffolds. The colonial jail served largely as a holding cell, detaining men and women awaiting trial, debtors, prisoners of war, and convicts awaiting execution.[2] As a result, keepers and magistrates had sparse inclination and little motivation to provide inmates with books or instruction.

The limited utility and miserable conditions of colonial jails endured until the second half of the eighteenth century, when citizens eager to demonstrate their cosmopolitan sensibility began to emphasize the plight of prisoners in urban jails. Nevertheless, prisoner education remained a minor refrain in the emergent eighteenth-century discourses of prison reform. Relief society volunteers monitored conditions in jails, visited prisoners, donated blankets and clothing, and lobbied against the "undue and illegal sufferings" wrought by imprisonment.[3] Even as a penitentiary system took shape between the 1780s and 1840s, new theories of prison design, prisoner discipline, and reform emphasized systems of separation and classification and regimes of labor, diet, and hygiene over comprehensive educational programming. In fact, from the birth of the penitentiary to its expansion in the 1840s, the literate prisoner remained an ambivalent figure: better prepared for penitence and reform, the literate prisoner was also a potential discipline problem, especially as these institutions worked increasingly to limit all contact between prisoners and restrict their communication with the outside world.

Accounts of the early prison's development have traditionally overemphasized the educational possibilities inside the early American penitentiary while undertheorizing the role of literacy during the era of colonial discipline and punishment. This essay seeks to destabilize this familiar yet misleading narrative. Centering attention on the forms and functions of literacy among colonial-era prisoners, I argue that prisoner literacy was fundamental to the rituals of spectacular punishment in early eighteenth-century America and that literate prisoners were figures of intense interest in colonial execution narratives. On the scaffold, the elaborate performances of public justice were inscribed, explained, transfigured, and disseminated by texts intimately shaped by the literacy performances of prisoners. As Daniel E. Williams and Daniel Cohen have argued, gallows literature constituted a popular and widespread part of eighteenth-century print culture. Accounts published prior to the 1750s were particularly attentive to "reading prisoners"—a term I use to signal both the prisoner who reads and the act of interpreting the prisoner who reads. To understand this fascination, gallows literature from the colonial period must be read alongside and in dialogue with the history of literacy instruction in the colonies. Bringing these two traditions together, this essay examines the role that prisoners' literacy performances played in rituals of colonial-era corrections. "Reading prisoners" were not only central to the pedagogical function of the execution ritual, but they also helped to stage the possibilities of and anxieties over expanded print literacy and missionary education programs in the colonies.

Prison Writing and the Eighteenth-Century Communications Circuit

Prior to the development of the modern penitentiary, Foucault famously argued, visual display—the "spectacle of the scaffold"—defined regimes of public punishment. Following Foucault, Michael Meranze begins his impressive study of Philadelphia penal history with a section entitled "Display" that situates use of the whip, the pillory, and the scaffold as part of a "larger penal system geared toward the public display and seizure of the body." Public execution in particular, Meranze argues, was a system "predicated on display—display of the condemned, display of the penalty, display of violence."[4] In these and other recent treatments of early punishment, the tropes of theater and visual performance dominate analyses of the tools of social control.

Histories of American punishment, however, too often neglect the role of print in this complex interplay between actors and audiences.[5] Nevertheless, from its earliest inception, the visual theatrics of discipline and punishment were mediated by texts. An early example of what cultural historian Louis P. Masur and others have called the "theater of execution" illustrates this dynamic. Directing reader attention to two prisoners condemned to die for murder in 1693, Cotton Mather invoked a moment of visual display, where material bodies transformed into textual "commentaries," thus forming an elaborate visual pedagogy:

> Behold a very doleful Commentary! You have before your *Eyes*, a Couple of
> Malefactors, whose Murderous *Unclean-ness*, has now in their *Youth* brought
> upon them, a most miserable *Death*. May your *Hearts* now give a profitable
> Attention unto the *Use* that should be made of such a dismal Spectacle.

Foregrounding the relationship between visual display ("before your
Eyes") and affective response ("May your *Hearts*"), Mather maximized
the pedagogical significance of the colonial execution ritual, using the
written warning of one of the condemned as his prompt: "Give Ear unto
the Dying Speeches of the young Woman, whose Execution you are to
see this Afternoon. She has put into *my* Hand, and sign'd with *her own*,
these Dying Expressions of her Distressed Soul; which it will not be unprofitable, for me to publish this Day among you."[6] Emphasizing the
prisoner's authorizing signature and her placing the signed text into
his hands, Mather highlighted the textual exchange that legitimated a
prisoner's public confession.

Not content to "publish" from the pulpit alone, Mather assembled
the prisoner's "Dying Expressions" together with two sermons penned
for the occasion into a pamphlet, *Warnings from the Dead*, and put into
print circulation one of colonial America's first prisoner narratives. In
his *Diary*, Mather reflected upon audience hunger for this new genre
with satisfaction, noting that *Warnings* "was immediately printed . . . and
it was greedily bought up," and adding, "T'was afterwards reprinted at
London."[7] Thus the "Dying Expression" of an otherwise unremarkable
prisoner circulated from oral confession to public pamphlet, and in the
process gained the "profitable attention" of a transatlantic audience.

Criminal narratives—including sermons and prisoners' last words, dying warnings, final confessions, and religious conversion accounts—were
advertised in newspapers and pamphlets, priced cheaply, and distributed
by numerous booksellers. Mather was an early innovator in harnessing
the power of prisoner testimonials as a means to profit from public justice. He advertised prisoner narratives and execution sermons in notices
placed at the end of other printed sermons; for example, *Pillars of Salt*
(1699), an early compilation of prisoner confessions, promised access
to the "Dying Speeches" of criminals on the title page, and contained
an advertisement for Increase Mather's execution sermon, *The Folly of
Sinning* (1699). Mather distributed hundreds of pamphlets in any given
year to booksellers, ship captains and officers, and potential readers in
England.[8]

Intent on guiding prisoners through the expectations of genre and sentiment that would shape and generate their own future writing, Mather also gave copies directly to inmates. When he offered condemned pirate William Fly a copy of his 1724 sermon *The Converted Sinner* (containing a conference with two pirates prior to their execution), Fly informed his benefactor, "I read that Book before ever I was brought hither!"[9] Fly's retort revealed that prisoner confessions circulated among a diverse reading public, while suggesting their inability to halt crime. (Circulating confessions could also have unintended results; as late as 1853, a murderer claimed he was "stimulated to murder by reading the biographies of criminals, whose feats he desired to emulate."[10])

As others imitated Mather's practice of giving prisoners published execution sermons and criminal confessions, some printers began soliciting prisoner testimony independently of ministers. For example, before Rebekah Chamblit was executed in 1733, a Boston printer solicited her narrative, publishing it with the inscription: "Taken from her own mouth, and carefully drawn up as near as possible in her own words, by me, Samuel Kneeland, Printer," and adding that the prisoner signed it "with an express and solemn desire that it might be Publish'd to the World."[11] By the 1750s, upstart printers like Benjamin Franklin published longer biographical "lives" of prisoners alongside the increasingly familiar "dying speeches." Some dispensed with sermons altogether, foregrounding first-person accounts and occasionally illustrating prisoners' confinement in woodcuts (see figure 13).[12] These changes ensured that a steady stream of gallows literature entered the eighteenth-century print marketplace.

Together, this diverse genre of sermons, prisoner-penned narratives, as-told-to accounts, and third-party biographies facilitated what Robert Darnton has elsewhere theorized as an eighteenth-century "communications circuit" that linked together authors, printers, suppliers of ink and paper, booksellers, readers—and future writers.[13] For example, in 1772, a Boston bookseller used an execution sermon to publicize not only Bibles and testaments but also spelling books, writing-paper, quills, and ink powder, highlighting how publishers envisioned an audience of not only readers but writers (see figure 14). In E. Russell's ad and elsewhere, publishers used prisoners' accounts to market the emerging tools and technology of colonial literacy.

When viewed as part of the eighteenth-century communications circuit, the early rituals of public punishment emerge as "literacy events,"

FIGURE 13.
Anon., *Account
of the Robberies
Committed by
John Morrison*
(Philadelphia:
Anthony
Armbruster,
1750/1751).
Courtesy of
the Rosenbach
Museum &
Library.

those observable episodes and activities of daily life in which literacy plays an active role.[14] Despite the central role of spectacle, execution was nonetheless an important literacy event, for the reading of a public confession was itself dependent on other literate practices—from scriptural interpretation to familiarity with the conventions of confession. According to Darnton, authors "form notions of genre and style" by familiarity with texts and writers, which helps the communications circuit "run full cycle."[15] Prison reading facilitated this cycle directly, as one prisoner recounted reading *The Declaration and Confession of Esther Rodgers* from his cell in 1726, and another recollected the "many Malefactors

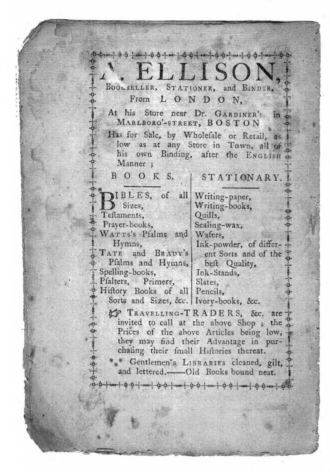

FIGURE 14.
Bookseller's
advertisement
for spellers and
testaments in
Samuel Stillman,
*Two Sermons . . .
Delivered . . . before
the Execution of
Levi Ames*, 4th
ed. (Boston: E.
Russell, 1773).
Courtesy of
the American
Antiquarian
Society.

that I had read . . . out of Dr. *Cotton Mather's* Church History." Moreover, the publication of prisoner confessions promoted the literacy practices of inmates while reflecting the literacy norms of the era, merging the prisoner narrative with the "ordinary Road" of colonial literacy instruction.[16]

Daniel Cohen has argued that the widespread circulation of these (albeit highly mediated) prisoner narratives requires us to reevaluate Michael Warner's contention that the emergent public sphere excluded the voices of women and minorities. According to Cohen, attention to the early American confession genre reveals that "condemned criminals were actively integrated into an ongoing public discourse, not only as readers but also as authoritative speakers and even as posthumous authors. There is every indication that the criminals seized upon that discursive opportunity with passion and courage and spiritual conviction, recognizing that the printed word could provide them with both comfort and strength during their last days on earth."[17] Cohen's argument is compelling, yet might be made without such a universalizing claim about prisoners' motives. As the next section will show, prisoners actively participated in this textual proliferation, whether incited by sincere eagerness, coercion, accommodation, or resistance.

Reading Prisoners

Most commonly, prisoners' literacy practices entered the genre as indicators of the prisoners' spiritual readiness for death, with the reading prisoner serving as a pedagogical example to the reader. Sudden interest in reading the Bible, revived attention to passages of scripture, or intense meditation on a religious pamphlet as execution day approached — all warranted inclusion and emphasis in early criminal confession accounts. In 1738, for instance, an observer noted approvingly how Patience Boston sat on her execution cart and read her Bible with "such composure" while a minister delivered "a Paper, at her desire, taken from her Mouth" (34). The drama of her encroaching death enacted with more intensity and immediacy the reckoning many readers may have imagined themselves facing. Alternately, "bad" reading signaled a failure of proper education or preparation. Esther Rodgers began her 1701 "Declaration" by noting, "I was born at *Kittery* . . . was taught to Read, Learned Mr. *Cottons* Catechism, and had frequent opportunities of going to Publick Meetings, but was a careless Observer of Sabbaths, and Hearer of Sermons; no Word that ever I heard or read making any Impression upon my Heart."[18] Rodgers's lack of affective response to "the Word" served to demonstrate her lack of discipline and her unregenerate spiritual state, and thus, by extrapolation, her later descent into vice and crime. Bryan Sheehan, a convicted and condemned rapist, confessed that he "confined his reading . . . to history and books of diversion," evidence of his delinquent character.[19] The ministers who attended upon these prisoners encouraged disciplined reading practices that could stir spiritual awakening, prompt reform, and testify to the direct "imprint" of God on the heart. They hoped that by soliciting, recording, and circulating accounts of the strained yet often powerfully transformative reading practices of prisoners, they could encourage similar spiritual renewal in readers.

While accounts of prisoners' reading practices appeared sporadically in the earliest execution sermons, they became far more visible between 1700 and 1750, when the literary marketplace experienced a surge of demand for personal tales of piety under duress consistent with the evangelical revivalism that culminated in the first Great Awakening.[20] During this period, argues Daniel E. Williams, ministers sought to awaken "personal, evangelical piety," and their execution sermons became "less concerned with the excitement of terror and more concerned with the process of conversion."[21] This meant that the inward, reflective process of feeling one's sin entailed a parallel outward process of "verbalizing sin," so ministers and publishers willingly solicited prisoner accounts that dramatized scenes of spiritual struggle. As this theme of "miraculous conversion" came to dominate early-eighteenth-century criminal narratives, prisoners' reading practices became particularly crucial. Consequently, prisoner accounts published between 1700 and 1750 are filled with testimony of prisoners' literacy practices while awaiting execution, most often during jail visits by a spiritual adviser. Visitors monitored prisoners' interpretation skills (such as their ability to locate and apply scripture to their situation), the industry that prisoners devoted to reading (amount of hours spent, number of texts read or reread), and the prisoners' emotional responses to their reading. For example, Samuel Moody noted in 1726 how spectators were "much affected, perhaps almost beyond Example" by Joseph Quasson, and offered a detailed account of his literacy practices, praising Quasson's

> natural Love to Reading, from first to last, and by his great Diligence therein whilst a Prisoner; together with personal Instructions by a good number of Visitants; who also furnished him with Variety of the most suitable Books, lesser and larger; all or most of which he deliberately read over; and some of them not once only nor twice; *Fox* of Time and the End of Time, and Mr. *Stoddard's* Guide to Christ; with *Charnock* of Man's Enmity against God . . . Examples also, peculiarly that of [murderer and jailhouse convert] *Esther Rogers* [*sic*] . . . were of special Use to him. (27, 9–10)

Intense attention to prisoners' reading practice was central to the drama of death and potential salvation in the execution genre at mid-century.

Yet, reading was not merely a measure of sin or salvation. These accounts reflected the popular literacy pedagogy of the colonies. David D. Hall identifies the dominant characteristics of "traditional literacy" in the seventeenth and eighteenth centuries: a higher valuation of reading literacy over writing literacy, reading instruction based heavily on memorizing devotional texts, and contact with a small range of texts (a Bible, a psalm book, a "steady seller," and a yearly almanac) comprising the "ordinary road" of literacy instruction in New England and many mid-Atlantic colonies.[22] The narratives reiterated widespread proscriptions against "idle" reading across the eighteenth century and encouraged a reading process marked by diligence, attentiveness, and reflexivity. "Properly performed, the practices of reading and hearing became spiritual exercises that abetted the ever-necessary, ever-continuing process of self-examination," Hall notes.[23] Writing, on the other hand, "was not necessary for salvation . . . and did not have the social cachet it would acquire later," and was not mandatory for someone to be considered "literate."[24] Understanding the contours of colonial literacy helps us to read prisoners' fraught encounters with reading materials not merely as religious preparation, but as encounters with early American literacy pedagogy.

Although ministers and magistrates emphasized examples of reading that successfully mobilized penitence and conversion, prisoner accounts demonstrated a range of literacy practices. After feeling the "power of the Word" at a Sabbath service, Esther Rodgers returned to her cell and became a focused reader who "set her self to search the Scriptures diligently, out of which she collected many Texts, that encouraged her to hope for mercy and pardon." Rodgers read with a purpose: to exonerate herself. Similar accounts reveal the innovative ways that prisoners used literacy acquisition for other ends. When Reverend Eliphalet Adams praised local ministers for putting "good Books" into Indian servant Katherine Garret's hands, he interpreted her enthusiasm for the texts as evidence of her receptivity to their devotional content. However, in the narrative penned "under her own hand" prior to her execution, Garret gave thanks for "other good Books I have been favoured with, by peoples giving and lending them to me, which has been blessed to me."[25] Throughout her account, Garret represented reading as an opportunity for interpersonal exchange rather than an exercise in solitary contemplation: when she accepted books, she mentioned them consistently in the context of receiving visitors and holding discussions in her jail cell. For Garret, a text's value lay predominantly in the social exchange of giving, lending, and visiting, often as an antidote to the isolation of prison, rather than in a book's particular contents.

Moreover, confessions featuring detailed accounts of prisoners' literacy practices often illuminated the difference between sanctioned forms of reading and more subversive literacy practices. While many prisoners used their "last words" to testify to the justice of their punishment and even to express gratitude for being imprisoned, others, like Patience Boston and Katherine Garret, used scriptures to articulate their social dislocation. Boston, for example, prefaced her account of extreme violence and abjection by recounting, "I read in my Testament how cruelly *Christ* was buffetted[,] scourged and spit upon," and later invoked God's "Long Suffering Patience," a phrase that served as both a plea and a self-referential articulation of her own pain (2, 6). Likewise, Joseph Quasson used his newfound facility with reading to quickly reach for books in his cell during visits with spiritual counselors, identify relevant passages, and enter into debates over scriptural interpretation (22–23). Owen Sullivan forged bills from inside prison, and "for want of a Rolling Press, struck [the currency] off by Hand, sign'd it in Goal [*sic*] and gave it out by Quantities to my Accomplices."[26] Still others wrote to proclaim their innocence, including Abraham Johnstone (1797), a manumitted slave later executed for murder, who addressed his narrative "to the people of colour" and condemned "the keen shafts of prejudice" against "those of our colour."[27] While such displays of outright rebellion were rare in early-eighteenth-century narratives, execution accounts still served as flashpoints for debate over the interpretation and significance of prisoner literacy.

The Color of Literacy

Fascination with the reading habits of the condemned was not solely the product of enduring Protestant expectations about the spiritual preparations required to face death. As an analysis of the narratives of Joseph Hanno and Joseph Quasson reveals, the "reading prisoner" became an important figure in debates over literacy education of blacks and Native Americans in the colonies.

Joseph Hanno was an African-born ex-slave who had received some limited literacy education from his New England master before attaining his freedom. Convicted in 1721 for murdering his wife (after which he confessed his guilt), he was incarcerated in Boston's Queen Street jail. There he was visited by Cotton Mather, who, consistent with his innovations in the genre, appended a "Conference between a Minister and the Prisoner" to Hanno's execution sermon, *Tremenda* (1721).

By the minister's account of their encounter, the two men engaged in a fraught battle over the meaning and uses of prisoner reading practices. Mather seized upon Hanno's reading habits to make the case that the condemned man lacked the proper humility and composure to submit to eternal judgment, while Hanno, on the other hand, expressed particular pride in reading as a form of self-fashioning. "You have been many Months in the Prison. I pray, how have you spent your Time hitherto? I hope, they have not all been *Months of Vanity*," Mather queried. Hanno replied, "In Reading and Praying, Sir." "In *Reading!*" his interlocutor exclaimed, noting that Hanno had no Bible in his cell. Provoked by Hanno's perceived insolence, Mather called him a "Great pretender," someone who covered for his secondhand scriptural knowledge by "always vain gloriously *Quoting* of Sentences from them wherever you came." Hanno gave no ground and when Mather later inquired of him, "Do you understand what I say to you?" Hanno responded, "Yes, Sir. I have a Great deal of Knowledge. No body of my Colour, in Old *England* or New, has so much." "I wish you were less *Puffed up* with it," Mather retorted.[28]

If a good prisoner demonstrated proper self-composure through reading practice, Hanno's "puffed" sense of self conflicted with Mather's conception of a prostrate penitent. Hanno's confidence also threatened Mather's investment in black submission. Mather hoped reading would make Hanno a positive example, a "Pattern of all Goodness unto other *Ethiopians*."[29] But Hanno interpreted his abilities quite differently, fashioning himself as a literate, and thus exceptional, man of color.[30] Abandoning his hopes of transforming Hanno's educated exuberance into Christian submission, Mather chastised the "Wretched *Ethiopian*," warning that "the Sins of your more Ignorant Country-men, have not such Aggravations as yours."[31]

By wishing for Hanno to be a "Pattern of all Goodness" to other blacks, Mather foresaw the benefit of using prisoners to advocate for colonial missionary projects. Here, and in numerous other narratives dating from the early eighteenth century, the prisoner's account of his literacy education revealed the imprint of colonial policies toward racial others. Reading and religion were so deeply intertwined in the colonies that, in the words of E. Jennifer Monaghan and Ross Beales, "the history of African-American literacy [was] also one of philanthropic agencies undertaking to introduce slaves and free blacks to Christianity, and putting catechisms, spelling books, the *Book of Common*

Prayer, and Bibles in their hands as part of this program."[32] These missionary projects galvanized in the eighteenth century through organized efforts by the Church of England, particularly the Society for Propagating the Gospel in Foreign Parts (S.P.G., founded in 1701). The S.P.G. boasted an accessible curriculum, while emphasizing a paternalistic doctrine of subordination whose "watchwords were obedience and deference, fidelity and dependence."[33] After 1701, blacks, Indians, and the poor thus became objects of sustained educational interest.

Seen in this light, Joseph Hanno's literacy became a measure of not merely his conversion but the potential of all blacks to learn proper doctrines of submission. In fact, Cotton Mather used Hanno's execution to develop his arguments on the relationship between black education and black servitude. In *The Negro Christianized* (1706), Mather had argued on behalf of missionary efforts among Africans and blacks in the American colonies, criticized the "*Bruitish* insinuation" that blacks lacked souls, and advanced the Calvinist argument that the "elect" might be anywhere, including among Africans.[34] Consistent with these beliefs, he arranged for his own slave Onesimus to learn to read.[35] In 1717, Mather even erected a children's charity school "for the Instruction of poor Negro's, and Indians" that provided reading instruction in scriptures and catechism, but offered no writing instruction.[36] The school was short-lived, closing in 1721, the year he encountered Hanno. Mark S. Weiner draws the conclusion: "Joseph Hanno's crime opened a rift in Mather's complex views about race, slavery, and Christianity: it put them in tension. On one hand, Joseph Hanno was the product of precisely the kind of spiritual inclusiveness that Mather advocated [being well versed in Christian principles]. . . . And yet Hanno's knowledge of Christ clearly had not made this particular African more law abiding, as Mather promised whites it would."[37]

As Weiner astutely observes, Mather was in a compromised position: he needed to account for Hanno's crime, but in doing so "[deflect] the criticism that Christian education was somehow at fault in the case and thus inappropriate for blacks."[38] Mather's solution was to reject Hanno's claims of textual and spiritual literacy. The problem, then, became not black education per se but Hanno's misguided, solitary process. Accusing him of having no Bible, of misquoting, of lying about his knowledge, Mather undermined Hanno's claims to religious and textual authority.

If Mather's encounter with Joseph Hanno revealed the limitations of using prisoners to promote missionary education projects, Joseph Quasson's experience proved a far more successful example. Quasson, a Native American originally from Monomoy on Cape Cod, shot a fellow soldier and "kinsman" in August 1725, while volunteering with an English militia in Maine. For almost a year, he languished in York's Old Gaol until his execution in June 1726. During this time, he was visited frequently by Samuel Moody, York's well-respected Congregationalist minister, who solicited Quasson's confession and published it after his death. The forty-page narrative blends Moody's observations, Quasson's first-person account, and a lengthy interview between Quasson and an anonymous Visitant (probably Moody), typical of the composite structure of many prisoner confession accounts. The Moody/Quasson narrative invoked Quasson's reading practice as a sign of his diligence, spiritual readiness, and likely salvation, and also as an illustration of the painful process of true conversion. Structured like a typical conversion narrative, the text sketches Quasson's childhood, his descent into crime, and his subsequent imprisonment.

Tellingly, however, much of this familiar story is told by tracing Quasson's text-centered spiritual struggle while incarcerated in York's Old Gaol. Moody took careful note of how the prisoner's "extraordinary Agitations" had transformed to calm resignation by the Sabbath prior to his execution, as Quasson meditated upon a verse from Isaiah: "For my thoughts are not your thoughts, neither are your ways my ways, saith the Lord" (20). Insisting on the unbridgeable gap between two worlds ("my thoughts are not your thoughts"), the line evocatively, perhaps unintentionally, gave voice to the dislocation, isolation, and adjustment that Quasson experienced as both Indian convert and colonial prisoner facing his ensuing death.

Like Mather's account of Joseph Hanno's literary life, Quasson's literacy narrative originated in colonial missionary endeavors. New England and New York had a long tradition of Indian education projects, and his literacy practices were deeply embedded in this history. Quasson was born in 1698 in Monomoy, Cape Cod, where he lived with his parents until he was six years old. In 1698, the Monomoyick Indians (a small tribe considered part of the Eastern branch of the Wampanoag) had a recognized tradition of Native Christian education and religious instruction, including their own Indian preacher and schoolmaster, John Cosens.[39] A quarter-century earlier, a missionary reported that of the 71 "praying Indians" at Monomoyick, 20 could read in their own language, 15 could write, and one could read English.[40]

For Quasson, as with many other Indian prisoners, learning to read English was accompanied by scenes of communal and family disintegration, dislocation, and loss. According to the narrative, when Quasson turned six, his father fell into debt and bound him out as a servant to Samuel Sturges of Yarmouth, who taught him his catechism. The economic stress on Quasson's father propelled young Quasson from the small, tight-knit Native Christian community into English servitude, where he was kept under "strict and regular Government Night and Day" and taught his catechism, a traditional stage of reading acquisition as well as spiritual education. Years later, Quasson stopped attending the English church and attempted to return to the "Indian Meeting," but he reported that, after such a long separation, "I understood nothing" (3–4).[41]

Quasson further emphasized his vulnerability and sense of dislocation as he described how he ended up condemned to die. After enlisting as a volunteer in an English militia during Dummer's War, Quasson was sent to Maine. During an argument in August 1725, he shot John Peter, a fellow militia member and Indian from Barnstable; much to Quasson's dismay, John Peter died days later. Alone and highly conscious of his precarious and unsympathetic position, Quasson sought out the assistance of the local minister, "because I thought, being a poor *Indian* and in a strange Place, especially in a Time of War, People would be little concerned about me. However I thought there was a Minister in the Town, and if he were a good Man he would have Compassion on my Soul: I sent for him." Soon afterward, under the care of Samuel Moody, Quasson embarked on a course of diligent reading and prayer, noting that "I read more or less, every Day, the whole Time of my Confinement, and for the most part of several Hours in a Day" (6–7).

In jail, Quasson reclaimed a literacy that helped him articulate his struggles. Consisting of just two dungeon rooms in an eighteen-by-thirty-foot building close to the meeting house, the jail was small yet porous.[42] While Quasson complained about the continuous singing and swearing of a cellmate, he was allowed to leave the jail to attend church services, and he recounted experiences with numerous visitors, including several ministers and a "good Woman" who visited him frequently before his execution. Indeed, these visits proved to be instrumental. During this woman's visit, Quasson took out his Bible, with its "Scores of Leaves turned down," and read to her those passages that resonated with his personal struggle. His chosen verse was from *Psalms*: "*I am a stranger in the Earth, hide not thy Commandments from me.*" The blend of confinement and social exchange in York's Old Gaol thus turned Quasson into a model penitent, a transformation made possible through a reading process marked by estrangement, grief, and doubt (6–7, 14).

As in Hanno's text, the narrative crisis centers on Quasson's reading practices. Earlier in his account, Quasson had lamented, "I have had many Books and have read much — but I don't see that I'm a lot the better." The statement captures the ambivalent labor of colonial-era bibliotherapy: Quasson reads, but fails to feel better, instead suffering doubt, futility, and fear of failure. Crucially, Quasson's assertion that he "read much" but was no better off threatened Moody's entire project. Rather than interpret the prisoner's assertion as a repudiation of literacy, Moody sensed a moment of opportunity and redoubled his efforts to supply texts and monitor the prisoner's response to his readings. Shortly thereafter, Moody reported, the prisoner evinced a "remarkable Alteration" after much diligent reading and interaction with visitors. Now marked by a "natural Love to Reading," Quasson read voraciously, experienced "Awakening, Conviction," and shortly thereafter, died a model penitent (12, 20, 9–10).

Following Quasson's eventual execution, Moody moved quickly to assemble his forty-page account of the deceased's life and death; it would be the first prisoner conversion narrative ever published as a stand-alone work. He chose as the publisher Samuel Gerrish, a Bostonian with a reputation for "aggressively marketing works of popular piety and adventure."[43] The selection was telling: for readers, Quasson's story was both a piety and an adventure tale — a harrowing journey through sin and redemption, marked by doubt and struggle.

Reading Denominational Difference

The prisoner's private drama of crime and conversion also transformed into a public battle over how literacy was taught in the colonies. While several scholars of prisoner writing have correctly linked the popularity of the genre to a broad outpouring of interest in evangelicalism in the first half of the eighteenth century, "miraculous conversion" narratives should also be understood as deliberately shaded expressions of denominational competition over literacy instruction and religious education.

During the 1720s, Congregationalists fretted over the success of their missionary efforts among Indians. In 1724, for example, just prior to Quasson's narrative (and years after his own charity school for "poor Negro's, and Indians" had met its demise), Cotton Mather wrote a dejected letter to the new governor of the Boston commissioners. In the letter, he expressed his "Despondencies" about the "Gospelizing of our Indians" and articulated his hopes that new leadership would "procure something more Effectual" and "inspire a New Vigour into all our Motions."[44]

While Mather mourned the lack of vitality and lack of success of Congregationalist efforts, the S.P.G. was funding a massive effort to place hundreds of Anglican clergymen and dozens of schoolmasters in colonies from Maine to Georgia to convert and to educate underserved rural, black, and Indian communities. Despite widespread hostility toward Anglicanism in the northern colonies, between 1714 and 1763, 65 Anglican schoolteachers established themselves, including 37 in New York, 6 each in New Jersey and Pennsylvania, and 11 in Congregationalist strongholds in New England.[45] Additionally, Anglicans enjoyed a "great coup" in 1722, when Yale's president, two of the college's tutors, and four additional clergymen announced their conversion to Anglicanism, establishing the Church of England as a "serious intellectual rival in New England."[46]

Against this backdrop, the efforts of Congregationalists like Moody and Mather to gather and publish narratives of black and Native American prisoners attempt to demonstrate their influence as missionary educators, even as Anglicans gained ground through their missionary work and free charity schools. Moody himself actively promoted Quasson's case during an annual gathering of Congregationalist ministers in New England, noting the special "Providence" that enabled him to have the "Anniversary Convention of Ministers" pray for Quasson and to bring the condemned prisoner's "Desires of Prayer to more than an hundred—the Ministers of four Colonies" (29). Thus, Quasson's designation as a "Prisoner of Hope" contained multiple resonances; the phrase suggested not only Quasson's personal struggle to maintain hope against crippling feelings of resignation, loss, and despair, but also the process by which a "poor *Indian* and Malefactor" embodied the hopes of New England Congregationalists for the success of their endangered missionary projects (24, 41).

Sensitivity to the differences between Anglican and Congregationalist reading practice sheds additional light on their shared fascination with the literacy of Christian converts. Like the Congregationalists, Anglicans were committed to literacy instruction as the basis for spiritual instruction; however, unlike Congregationalists, the S.P.G. preached a more accessible path to faith and conversion: "Theologically far less demanding than the Congregationalists and far more confident that salvation could be won by faith, decent behavior, and steady church attendance," E. Jennifer Monaghan argues, "the Anglicans brought a new vision of what literacy was to accomplish." On the other hand, Congregationalists placed far more emphasis than Anglicans on painstaking reading and interpretation as a means to spiritual growth and conversion. Thus, in practice, S.P.G. literacy missions among Native Americans and enslaved and free African Americans were less educationally ambitious, guiding students toward facility with the *Book of Common Prayer,* a less demanding reading curriculum than the Testaments or Bible-reading demanded by Congregationalists.[47]

Thus, a narrative like Quasson's not only fed the era's interest in tales of piety but also ostensibly demonstrated the superiority of Congregationalist literacy curricula. Obtaining a "Variety of the most suitable Books, lesser and larger; all or most of which he deliberately read over; and some of them not once only nor twice," Quasson demonstrated the more rigorous practices advocated by Congregationalists; by association, the Quasson/Moody narrative attributed such enhanced literacy practices to his successful spiritual reformation.

Prisoner confession accounts by Joseph Quasson and Joseph Hanno demonstrate the illuminating and complex "literacy effects" of colonial-era imprisonment. By studying the criminal confession genre alongside the history of literacy education and competing missionary projects in the Americas, we gain a better understanding of not only how colonial prisoners learned to read but what was significant about how and what they read. Their narratives highlight the wide-ranging investment and fascination with the "literate" prisoner in early colonial accounts.

Moody reserved his final appeal to the "good Reader," urging audiences to remember Quasson's struggles. This phrase provocatively served as both an appeal and a challenge. The narrative demonstrated that being a "good Reader" takes immense discipline, and that transformation does not occur in solitude. By highlighting Quasson's jailhouse network of visitors, the narrative captured the way that the "labor" of colonial-era prison literacy was mobilized by face-to-face encounters and mediated by the exchange of texts and ideas. This belief in the inherent value of reading's "labor" would be debated and challenged as the colonial prison transformed into the modern penitentiary.

From the Scaffold to the Penitentiary

In colonial jails, reading was not leisure, but labor, and "public labor" at that. It was visible, regimented, monitored, and explicitly emphasized in written accounts to promote, by example and counterexample, the sort of reformed spiritual practice that "good Readers" might themselves adopt. The public nature of colonial punishment, with its large crowds and corresponding networks of print, kept narratives by and about prisoners consistently in the public eye.

All this was to change beginning in the 1780s, as support for public executions began to erode. Arguing that capital punishment was barbaric and inhumane, prison reformers also began to worry about the contact between prisoners and audiences generated by the rituals of public execution. Benjamin Rush, the tireless reformer who helped pioneer the Pennsylvania model of prison reform, structured his argument against public execution largely as an attack on the affective exchange facilitated by the public nature of criminal confession. Rush disapproved of the "uncommon pains . . . taken to prepare criminals for death, by the conversation and instructions of the clergy. After this, they are conducted to the place of execution with uncommon pomp and solemnity. The criminals, under these circumstances, suffer death with meekness—piety—and sometimes with dignity."[48] For Rush, the lure of such lavish attention encouraged prisoners to make false confessions. Besides fortifying and even valorizing the prisoner, the ritual, Rush repeatedly argued, mismanaged spectators' sympathies: "By an immutable law of our nature, distress of all kinds, when *seen*, produces sympathy, and a disposition to relieve it." His solution: not to relieve the prisoners' distress, but to render it invisible. "While we pity," Rush noted, "we secretly condemn the law which inflicts the punishment: hence, arises . . . a more feeble union of the great ties of government." By removing the prisoner from the public eye, Rush hoped the "great ties" of citizenship might again flow properly and restore the public's sentimental attachment to the state.[49]

Rush joined a transatlantic chorus advocating the shift from public to private punishment.[50] One goal was to silence prisoners, or more precisely, to make silence an integrated part of their daily regime. "Speech was devalued in the new penal system," argues Michael Meranze. In place of spectacular punishments conducted in the midst of crowds, reformers imagined a new carceral system, one that would punish prisoners privately, in seclusion from the public gaze. Moreover, the new carceral system would protect prisoners from each other. Communication among prisoners and between prisoners and the outside world would now be intensely regulated and largely forbidden. Criminologist J. L. Gillin synthesized in 1926 the merits of this new carceral arrangement, as touted by early Republican reformers:

1. Experience in the Walnut Street Jail, Philadelphia; Newgate, New York; Charlestown, Massachusetts, and other prisons, had shown that communication in any way contributed to the contamination of the less hardened by the vicious, gave place to all kinds of plots, and marked the man upon his return to society.

2. Solitary confinement without the opportunity of communication with fellow prisoners will stop all contamination.

3. Shut away from all his fellows, except those who are interested in his reformation, the opportunities for bringing him into a different state of mind are greater. . . .

4. Living in silence day and night, he will inevitably reflect upon his sins and resolve never more to return.[51]

As reformers in Pennsylvania, New York, and elsewhere tried to turn these rationales into reality, prisoner writing and confessional literature were quickly sidelined. Publication of "last speeches" and "Dying Warnings" declined abruptly after the 1790s, and execution sermons waned by 1825.[52]

Moreover, while the advent of modern prison theory provided a rich surge of new ideas about the value of hygiene, labor, routine, and the role that prison architecture could play in facilitating the reform of criminals, the new body of prison discourse had little to say about the role of education in relation to reform. Reading instruction was rarely a central component of the new regimes of reformative labor that assumed center stage after the Revolution. Instead, reformers figured reading as a diversion from labor, or more generously, a reward after a long day's work, to pass time in solitude. To the extent that reading "good books" could help prompt reflection and repentance, defenders of the penitentiary supported making some books and reading materials available. But education and literacy instruction were not central components of early penitentiary design and management. On the contrary, some defenders of the penitentiary system actively opposed educational attempts: for example, in 1824, Auburn prison warden Elam Lynds, fearing the "increased danger to society of the educated convict," blocked efforts to teach prisoners to read and write.[53]

There were, to be sure, some important exceptions: a short-lived school attended by some inmates of Walnut Street Prison in 1798; efforts by the Philadelphia Society for Alleviating the Miseries of Public Prisons to stock a library at Walnut Street Prison in the 1790s and, later, at Eastern State Penitentiary; and a Sabbath School at Auburn in 1826 that had 160 inmates by 1830, later replicated in 1828 at the Massachusetts State Prison.[54] Yet, it was not until 1847 that education became legally articulated as a desirable element of American prison management.[55] Even then, the problems that plagued prisons during the second half of the nineteenth century, such as overcrowding, gangs, drugs, and corrupt staff, quickly undermined administrations' attempts to construct a progressive narrative about the central "educational mission" of the modern penitentiary. In fact, according to a recent article in the *Prison Journal*, nineteenth-century prison academic schools remained "substandard and underfunded into the mid-twentieth century, many relying entirely on inmate teachers and with no special provision any longer for teaching illiterate inmates."[56]

An engraving from an 1836 prisoner account figuratively captures the uncertain place of the literate prisoner after the shift toward private reformative incarceration (see figure 15). The engraving depicts a familiar scene: the transfer of a text between a convicted criminal and a visiting minister. Yet, while early-eighteenth-century exchanges of "dying words" had taken place in highly public settings, before thousands of spectators gathered at the foot of a scaffold, in the 1836 illustration, the prisoner's complete isolation is intensely rendered. The interaction appears hasty: the visitor wears a coat, extends his hand to receive the inmate-authored text, and looks poised for a hasty exit. Though a quill is visible on the

FIGURE 15.
"Rev. E. T. Taylor
Receiving Crockett's
Confession," in Anon.,
*A Voice from Leverett
Street Prison* (Boston:
Suffolk County
Temperance Society,
1836). Courtesy of the
American Antiquarian
Society.

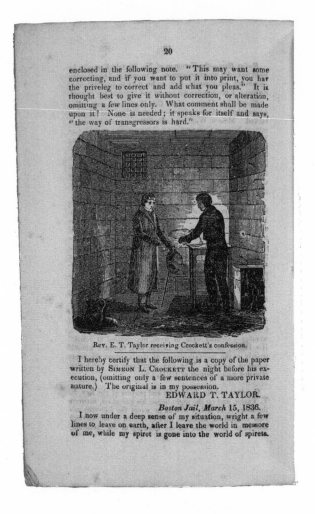

20

enclosed in the following note. "This may want some
correcting, and if you want to put it into print, you hav
the priveleg to correct and add what you pleas." It is
thought best to give it without correction, or alteration,
omitting a few lines only. What comment shall be made
upon it! None is needed; it speaks for itself and says,
"the way of transgressors is hard."

Rev. E. T. Taylor receiving Crockett's confession.

I hereby certify that the following is a copy of the paper
written by SIMEON L. CROCKETT the night before his execution, (omitting only a few sentences of a more private
nature.) The original is in my possession.
EDWARD T. TAYLOR.

Boston Jail, March 15, 1836.
I now under a deep sense of my situation, wright a few
lines to leave on earth, after I leave the world in memore
of me, while my spiret is gone into the world of spirets.

inmate's work table, the contents and future of the prisoner's written
narrative remain shrouded in mystery, its darkened pages left to the
imagination.

As punishment was privatized, shrouding the experiences of prisoners from the view of most ordinary citizens, that growing silence opened
"new forms of imaginary identifications" as those on the outside imagined the experiences of those inside, a process defined by Caleb Smith
as "the poetics of the penitentiary."[57] Out of this space, a new wave of
prison writing would emerge, but it would take a new era for prisoners
to gain access to the public sphere as they had in the eighteenth century.

NOTES

1. Following the work of Cathy N. Davidson, E. Jennifer Monaghan, and David D. Hall, I define literacy as a social practice rather than a quantifiable skill that one either "has" or "lacks." For a definition of literacy, see Hall, "Some Contexts and Questions," in *A History of the Book in America*, vol. 1, *The Colonial Book in the Atlantic World*, ed. Hugh Amory and David D. Hall (Chapel Hill: University of North Carolina Press, 2007), 10; see also Monaghan, *Learning to Read and Write in Colonial America* (Amherst: University of Massachusetts Press, 2005), 1–8; and Davidson, ed., *Reading in America: Literature and Social History* (Baltimore: Johns Hopkins University Press, 1989).

2. David J. Rothman, *The Discovery of the Asylum: Social Order and Disorder in the New Republic* (Boston: Little, Brown, 1971), 45–56.

3. "Preamble" to the Philadelphia Society for Alleviating the Miseries of Public Prisons, quoted in Negley K. Teeters, "The Philadelphia Society for the Relief of Distressed Persons, 1776–1777," *Prison Journal* 24, no. 4 (1944): 452. On the emergent culture of sentiment and mid-century reform, see Jennifer Janofsky, "'There Is No Hope for Me': Eastern State Penitentiary, 1829–1856," PhD diss., Temple University, 2004, 31, 43–46.

4. Michel Foucault, *Discipline and Punish: The Birth of the Prison*, 2nd ed., trans. Alan Sheridan (New York: Vintage Books, 1995), 32–72; Michael Meranze, *Laboratories of Virtue: Punishment, Revolution, and Authority in Philadelphia, 1760–1835* (Chapel Hill: University of North Carolina Press, 1996), 22, 3, 19–127.

5. Notable exceptions include Daniel E. Williams, Daniel Cohen, and Louis P. Masur, who analyze the cultural work of New England execution rituals and sermons and trace the development of the criminal confession genre across the long eighteenth century. See Williams, ed., *Pillars of Salt: An Anthology of Early American Criminal Narratives* (Madison, Wis.: Madison House, 1993); Cohen, *Pillars of Salt, Monuments of Grace: New England Crime Literature and the Origins of American Popular Culture, 1674–1860* (New York: Oxford University Press, 1993); and Masur, *Rites of Execution: Capital Punishment and the Transformation of American Culture, 1776–1865* (New York: Oxford University Press, 1989).

6. Cotton Mather, *Warnings from the Dead* (Boston: Bartholomew Green, 1693), 35, 69.

7. Cotton Mather, *Diary of Cotton Mather, 1681–1709* (New York: Frederick Ungar, 1957), 1:165.

8. Cohen, *Pillars*, 4–5.

9. Cotton Mather, *A Vial Poured Out upon the Sea* (Boston: T. Fleet, 1726), 16–17.

10. Quoted in David Paul Nord, *Faith in Reading: Religious Publishing and the Birth of Mass Media in America* (New York: Oxford University Press, 2004), 115.

11. Kneeland published Chamblit's declaration as a supplement to Thomas Foxcroft's execution sermon, *Lessons of Caution to Young Sinners* (Boston: S. Kneeland and T. Green, 1733), 72. On publishers' increased role, see Cohen, *Pillars*, 79–80.

12. For example, in *The Last Speech and Confession of Henry Halbert* (Philadelphia: Anthony Armbruster, 1765), Halbert gives his confession "from my own Mouth" to jailkeeper William Crisp and includes a letter to the father of the man he killed. For a more detailed discussion of the changes in these narratives, see Williams, *Pillars of Salt*, 13–19.

13. Robert Darnton, "What Is the History of Books," in *Reading in America: Literature and Social History*, ed. Cathy N. Davidson (Baltimore: Johns Hopkins University Press, 1989), 30–31.

14. The term "literacy event" was coined by Shirley Heath, and has been widely adopted in the field of New Literacy Studies, particularly because of the way "event" emphasizes the specific, situated, social context of literacy. On the influence of this term, see David Barton and Mary Hamilton, eds., *Situated Literacies: Reading and Writing in Context* (London: Routledge, 2000), 8.

15. Darnton, "What Is the History of Books," 30–31.

16. Samuel Moodey [Moody], *Summary Account of the Life and Death of Joseph Quasson, Indian* (Boston: S. Gerrish, 1726), 10; Patience Boston, *A Faithful Narrative* (Boston: S. Kneeland and T. Green, 1738), 18. Subsequent references to both of these works cited parenthetically in the text.

17. Cohen, *Pillars*, 79.

18. Esther Rodgers, "Declaration and Confession," in John Rogers, *Death the Certain Wages of Sin to the Impenitent* (Boston: B. Green and J. Allen, 1701), 121–22.

19. James Diman, *A Sermon, Preached at Salem* (Salem, Mass.: Samuel and Ebenezer Hall, 1772), 23.

20. On "miraculous conversion" narratives during the Great Awakening, see Daniel E. Williams, "'Behold a Tragic Scene Strangely Changed into a Theater of Mercy': The Structure and Significance of Criminal Conversion Narratives in Early New England," *American Quarterly* 38, no. 5 (1986): 827–47; Cohen, *Pillars*, 66–72. On the Great Awakening's effects on print culture in the middle colonies, see James Green, "English Books and Printing in the Age of Franklin," in Amory and Hall, *History of the Book*, 259–61.

21. Williams, "Behold," 830–31.

22. David D. Hall, *Cultures of Print: Essay in the History of the Book* (Amherst: University of Massachusetts Press, 1996), 163–64. On New England reading practice, see ibid., 57; and Hall, "Readers and Writers in Early New England," in Amory and Hall, *History of the Book*, 123. On the "ordinary Road," a term coined in 1693 by John Locke, see Monaghan, *Learning*, 13, 81.

23. Hall, "Readers and Writers," 122.

24. Monaghan, *Learning*, 37. Instead, writing instruction focused largely on penmanship and bookkeeping and was primarily intended for men entering commercial trades. On the increased professionalism of writing instruction, see Monaghan, *Learning*, 273–93.

25. Rogers, *Death*, 128; Eliphalet Adams, *A Sermon Preached [at] . . . the Execution of Katherine Garret* (New London: T. Green, 1738), 39, 43.

26. Owen Syllavan [Sullivan], *A Short Account of the Life* (Boston: Green & Russell, 1756), 9.

27. Abraham Johnstone, *The Address . . . to the People of Color* (Philadelphia: Printed for the Purchasers, 1797), 7.

28. Cotton Mather, *Tremenda* (Boston: B. Green, 1721), 32–33, 38.

29. Ibid., 23.

30. On early black Atlantic authors self-fashioning through literacy, including John Marrant, who constructs himself as a "literate black man from another world," see *Pioneers of the Black Atlantic: Five Slave Narratives of the Enlightenment 1772–1815*, ed. Henry Louis Gates and William Andrews (Washington, D.C.: Basic Books, 1998), xi, 4, 12.

31. Mather, *Tremenda*, 23, 38.

32. E. Jennifer Monaghan and Ross Beales, "Literacy in Schoolbooks," in Amory and Hall, *History of the Book*, 382.

33. Monaghan, *Learning*, 144.

34. Mark S. Weiner, "This 'Miserable African': Race, Crime, and Disease in Colonial Boston," *Common-place* 4, no. 3 (2004), <http://www.historycooperative.org/journals/cp/vol-04/no-03/weiner/>, accessed May 14, 2011.

35. Mather, *Diary*, 1:579; ibid., 2:442.

36. Monaghan, *Learning*, 244.

37. Weiner, "This 'Miserable African.'"

38. Ibid.

39. *Collections of the Massachusetts Historical Society*, vol. 10, 1809 (Boston: T. R. Marvin, 1857), 133; Enoch Pratt, *A Comprehensive History, Ecclesiastical and Civil . . .* (Yarmouth: W. S. Fisher, 1844), 39.

40. From a 1674 letter to Daniel Gookin from Richard Bourne, who surveyed the Cape tribes and reported on their literacy rates in detail; reprinted in Jill Lepore, "Literacy and Reading in Puritan New England," in *Perspectives on American Book History: Artifacts and Commentary*, ed. Scott E. Casper, Joanne D. Chaison, and Jeffrey D. Groves (Amherst: University of Massachusetts Press, 2002), 23–24. On early Indian education, see Margaret Szasz, *Indian Education in the American Colonies, 1607–1783* (Albuquerque: University of New Mexico Press, 1988; Omaha: University of Nebraska Press, 2007), 101–28; Monaghan, *Learning*, 46–80, 166–90.

41. For a similar merging of dislocation, family breakup, and English Christian reeducation, see Boston, *Faithful Narrative*, 1; and Adams, *Sermon Preached*, 38.

42. *Province and Court Records of Maine* (Portland: Maine Historical Society, 1928), xxxii.

43. Cohen, *Pillars*, 71.

44. Quoted in Szasz, *Indian Education*, 192.

45. Monaghan, *Learning*, 144.

46. Jeremy Bonner with Anthony George, "The Church of England in New England," in *New England: The Greenwood Encyclopedia of American Regional Cultures*, ed. Michael Sletcher and William Ferris (Westport, Conn.: Greenwood, 2004), 370.

47. Monaghan, *Learning*, 143.

48. Benjamin Rush, *Essays, Literary, Moral, and Philosophical*, 2nd ed. (Philadelphia: Thomas and William Bradford, 1806), 140.

49. Ibid., 141, 143.

50. On the movement away from public punishment, see Meranze, *Laboratories of Virtue*, 68–78; Paul Kahan, *Eastern State Penitentiary: A History* (Charlestown, S.C.: History Press, 2008), 12–28.

51. Meranze, *Laboratories of Virtue*, 90; Negley K. Teeters, *They Were in Prison: A History of the Pennsylvania Prison Society, 1787–1937* (Chicago: John Winston, 1937), 45.

52. On the decline of execution genres, see Cohen, *Pillars*, 25–26. Cohen argues three main genres replaced these forms: newspaper accounts, sensational criminal biographies and autobiographies, and trial reports.

53. Orlando Lewis, *Development of American Prisons and Prison Customs, 1776–1845* (New York: Prison Association of New York, 1922), 95.

54. See Rex Skidmore, "An American Prison School in the Eighteenth Century," *Journal of Criminal Law, Criminology, and Police Science* 46, no. 2 (1955): 212–13; W. David Lewis, *From Newgate to Dannemora: The Rise of the Penitentiary in New York, 1796–1848* (Ithaca, N.Y.: Cornell University Press, 1965), 106; Philip F. Gura, ed., *Buried from the World* (Boston: Massachusetts Historical Society, 2001), xxvii–xxix.

55. According to Edwin Sutherland, the New York legislature provided the "first legal recognition of academic education as desirable in penal or reformatory institutions" in 1847, when they provided two teachers for each of its state prisons; after this, prisons in other states gradually began adopting similar provisions. See *Principles of Criminology*, 11th ed. (Lanham, Md.: General Hall, 1992), 512.

56. Norman Johnston, "Evolving Function: The Use of Imprisonment as Punishment," *Prison Journal* 89, no. 1 (March 2009): 28s.

57. Meranze, *Laboratories of Virtue*, 135; Caleb Smith, *The Prison and the American Imagination* (New Haven: Yale University Press, 2009), 6.

Floating Prisons

Dispossession, Ordering, and Colonial Atlantic "States," 1776–1783

JUDITH I. MADERA

BRITAIN'S GREAT OPEN-WATER WARSHIPS of the late eighteenth century were among the age's most vital instruments for carving out pathways of transatlantic commerce and communication. They controlled the flows of shipping and conducted convoys of trade. As international captives and eighteenth-century slaves knew from wrenching experience, they were also powerful mainstays in the business of human traffic. Following the 1776 Battle of Long Island and the British capture of Fort Washington in New York City, British sea-ships would enter into the late-colonial American consciousness in yet another way: they were the deadliest prisons in early America.

The experience of Revolutionary-era American captives aboard prison ships in New York City's Wallabout Bay is not easily extractable from broader geopolitical developments in an epoch of British sea power and competitive mercantilist colonization. Prison-ship stories might be grafted onto a variety of volatile environmental histories, from the privateering coastal escapades of Jack Tar, the late-eighteenth-century colonial merchant marine (and object of British impressment gangs), to struggles within postcolonial New York, a populous harbor city without the geographical interior depth of other rebel holds.[1] Prisoners' stories could also be fitted to basic Royal Navy interests: the desperate need of recruits for its French, Spanish, and Dutch sea wars in the final decade of the First British Empire.[2] For American sailors imprisoned aboard a naval flotilla anchored in the still, coastal channels of New York City, however, the histories they recorded were those of the interior — beneath the decks of prison ships.[3]

As early as 1776, British prison ships such as the *Whitby* took anchor in Wallabout Bay, an East River water channel encircling northwestern Brooklyn. But it was not until 1780, ignited by fears that the presence of such ships in New York Harbor might spread pestilence into the city, that the British ordered the demasted hulks of the *Jersey*, *Hope*, and *Falmouth* to the more secluded Wallabout.[4] The largest and most infamous of these ships was the *Jersey*, a rudderless floating prison, stripped of spar and rigging. Its sealed gunports blocked air and light. Seventeen years old at the time of his capture, prisoner Thomas Andros described the blackened ship *Jersey* as a kind of floating sarcophagus of which "nothing remained but an old, unsightly rotten hulk." "Her dark and filthy external appearance," he wrote, "perfectly corresponded with the death and despair that reigned within."[5] Operating at maximum capacity almost immediately upon its conversion to prison hulk, the ship held up to 1,200 prisoners at any given point — more than three times its intended transport load.

There was little incentive for the British to reduce overcrowding or improve sanitation below decks. Prison ships were not intended as vehicles for reform or even for punishment per se. Their purpose was to detain prisoners and remove them from the war effort. Indeed, amid epidemics of typhus, smallpox, dysentery, and yellow fever (compounded by the general absence of Continental commissary provisions), fewer than half the privateers onboard would survive their internment.[6] For an imprisoned and able-bodied sailor, the only sure way to make it off the ship alive was by enlisting in the Royal Navy, effectively volunteering to serve aboard a British man-of-war or for garrison duty in the West Indies. Most patriot seamen flatly refused. As a result, vastly more Americans died on the prison ships of Wallabout Bay than in all the battles of the Revolutionary War.[7] Approximately twelve thousand prisoners perished on prison ships during the war. Thomas Andros recorded that "it was known that it was next to certain death to confine a prisoner here" (8).

Publication Politics

Produced by subjects at the nexus of British imperial conscription and American nationalist enterprise, prison-ship print narratives are striking for their extensive deployment of the body as a form of testament—a form for deliberating positionality. Indeed, through the wide-ranging ravages of disease and starvation that swept the prison ships, the body's materiality was what was at stake. Inside the lethal prisons of Wallabout Bay, the corporeal body functioned as a placeholder for what captives insisted was a Revolutionary ethos, a refusal to be coerced into colonial service. As the rhetoric of prison-ship authors such as Thomas Andros, Andrew Sherburne, Thomas Dring, and Ebenezer Fox demonstrates, the body itself functioned as a site for both negotiating and unsettling codes of governance. Narratives reflect the ways prisoners politicized their incarceration. They attributed their psychological torments and physical torture to the machinations of imperial dispossession, and they insisted on the validity of self-constituted forms of order. While overland correspondences between Continental and British authorities debated prisoner exchanges and the abatement of prisoner sufferings, Wallabout narratives give readers a window into another struggle: they reveal prisoners' attempts to come to terms with their physical superfluity to the Revolutionary project. Prisoner accounts lend insight into the somatics of imprisonment—into the body's mediation of the very environments that underwrite prison-ship discourses.[8]

These accounts reflect efforts to make meaning of their incarceration, outside the official custody of any clear state. Yet, with the exception of Philip Freneau's 1780 narrative poem, "The British Prison Ship" (first printed during a period of heavy Revolutionary fighting in the Carolinas), the accounts were largely transcribed years after the experience. Prison-ship authors wrote at various removes from their internment, in various political climates.

Although deposition excerpts and prisoner statements (some anonymous) attesting to the conditions aboard the British prison ships began appearing in port-city newspapers as early as 1780, the richly descriptive, expressive accounts by such prisoners as Silas Talbot (1803) and

Alexander Coffin (1807) did not reach print until almost two decades after the end of the war.[9] The bulk of narratives, though, came even later. It was a full fifty years after the American victory at Yorktown that the last wave of recollections reached print. Their authors, old Revolutionary War heroes, were in the final years of their lives.

Reverend Andrew Sherburne's *Memoirs*, released in 1828, was the first in this succession; Thomas Andros's account was published in 1833, and Ebenezer Fox's in 1838. Two important narrative accounts were actually released posthumously: Thomas Dring's personal history (heavily edited by the literary antiquarian Albert G. Greene) was published in 1829, one year after Dring's death and one year after Sherburne's testimony; and John Van Dyke's vivid "Narrative of Confinement in the *Jersey* Prison Ship" only appeared in print long after its narrator had passed. It was published in 1863.

Each of the authors almost certainly knew Freneau's poem well. "The British Prison Ship" was perhaps the most popular piece of writing by early America's best-known lyric poet. It was a poem full of declamation and righteous fury. Its conceit was massive (and timely). Freneau used scenes of prison-ship incarceration to pit lovers of freedom, young sailors of fortune, and American privateers against a baneful regime of imperial oppression. His poem directly accused "ungenerous Britons" of conspiracy to murder and declared them "foes to the rights of freedom and of men."[10]

As a political poet, Freneau knew how to get the attention of his readers. "The British Prison Ship" was first released in pamphlet form in 1781 by Ethan Allen's same publisher Robert Bell.[11] Though it was written, at least initially, from the perspective of a vitriolic anti-Loyalist during the Revolution, Freneau's own sympathies would quickly migrate to the postwar print bastions of mid-Atlantic republicanism. "The British Prison Ship" itself underwent multiple (and aggrandizing) rewritings; it was revised six times between 1780 and 1809.[12] Within this time frame, Freneau emerged as a staunch anti-Federalist and advocate of international republicanism. He even served as editor of the anti-Hamiltonian *National Gazette* newspaper from 1791 to 1793.

Alexander Coffin's narrative release also appears well calibrated to an early-nineteenth-century political contest that played out along Democratic-Republican and Federalist lines. Coffin's shocking report of conditions on the *Jersey* was published as an open letter to the Republican politician, popular health crusader, and congressional Wallabout memorial supporter, Doctor Samuel Latham Mitchill, in 1807.[13] Coffin's narrative also appeared at the height of tensions between Jefferson and the Royal Navy in the years leading up to the War of 1812. (That same year, Britain had fired on the American ship *Chesapeake*, and Jefferson enforced a deeply unpopular embargo of American seaports.) In describing the political climate of this period, Edwin G. Burrows, Robert E. Cray, and others have vividly portrayed the scenes of acrimony between Federalists, intent on establishing a statue of George Washington in New York City, and the archly Republican interests of the city's Tammany Society.[14] Rather than commemorate a Federalist icon, the Tammany Society instead insisted on a monument and depository where the bones of the Wallabout dead might be reinterred. For Republican politicians and local veterans alike, prisoner narratives could help advance a useful goal: they were the voices of the espoused, and they attested to the worthiness of commemorative efforts.[15]

The extent to which former prisoners served as anything close to Democratic-Republican mouthpieces is, however, quite limited. Although he published his history during the height of Tammany tensions, Silas Talbot was actually Federalist in his affiliation. He commanded a privateering vessel during the war but only due to the severe lack of Continental funds. He viewed himself as a bona fide Navy captain who was personally appointed to his post by George Washington.[16] In 1800, he was defended by none other than Alexander Hamilton in circuit court and represented by Federalist congressman James Bayard in Supreme Court in a maritime law case.[17] His son with wife Anna Richmond was named George Washington. A dedicated Federalist until his death as a gentleman farmer and speculator, his aims for publishing his history cannot be easily interposed with any clear Republican inducements.

Even further removed in time from the goals or means of Tammany Republican politicking are the bulk of prison ship narratives. By 1838, the year Ebenezer Fox's narrative came to print, New York Republican commemorative drives, marked by funeral processions and pageantry, had long ceased in obvious form. No Wallabout memorial had been built and, until 1873, the collected bones of the prisoners of war lay in a privately owned lot in an aging vault near Brooklyn's Navy Yard.[18] Within this last wave of publications, it is difficult to cite any overt Republican political motivation. As the following pages will demonstrate, narrators as a whole were uncritical of Federalist policy and exonerative of

Washington. They placed their stories on a different register—one that was, for the most part, politically nonpartisan. Instead, they asked questions about human dispensability, exchange, and the meaning of order in stale flotillas of decay.

Paradoxical Positionings: Washington and Prisoners on Water

When in June of 1782 prisoners aboard the *Jersey* came together as legal subjects to petition George Washington for relief, the impasse in agency between their situation and the official Continental apparatus was made explicit.[19] Although facilitated in their efforts by the British Rear Admiral Robert Digby, who actually paroled two prisoners to deliver their "memorial," the prisoners' plea was not received with any great enthusiasm by Washington.[20]

In his response to Admiral Digby on June 5, 1782, the general was quick to stress that prisoners aboard the *Jersey* were outside of his purview: "As I have no agency in naval matters, this application to me is made on mistaken grounds."[21] Continental Commissary Abraham Skinner on June 24, 1782, gave this same response, quoting Washington in his emphasis that he was not "invested with any power of interference respecting the exchange of naval prisoners." Their petition, he suggested, should be directed somewhere, elsewhere, and down the line of command. "This business," he wrote, "was formerly under the direction of the Board of Admiralty, that upon annihilation of that Board Congress had committed it to the Financier (who has in charge all our naval prisoners) and he to the Secretary at War."[22] Washington's naval prisoner policy, stated most archly by Secretary of War Benjamin Lincoln, was "to reconcile them as much as possible to the miseries of a loathsome confinement until they can be exchanged—and to prevent them—from an idea that they are neglected, engaging in the service of Britain."[23] Washington believed that exchanging the likes of prison ship Tars for rank-and-file British or Hessian soldiers would give "the enemy a great and permanent strength for which we could receive no compensation, or at best but a partial and temporary one."[24] Thus, he explicitly instructed the commissary-general of prisoners "to reject every overture of exchanging" those privateers and civilians who were not "proper subjects of military capture."[25]

It is interesting that prisoner narratives cast Washington in a very different light. In prisoner records citing the Washington petition, the warring general is quickly exculpated as unhappily powerless in effecting prisoner trades. Far from the compound accusations of social engineering and authoritative antirepublicanism that were to hound the president—even prior to his 1797 departure from office—the Washington of John Van Dyke, Thomas Dring, and Ebenezer Fox's narratives is ascribed a mostly narrow frame of military venture. He is announced to be removed from congressional politics, "the General Government," and naval affairs altogether. Written in hindsight of an American war victory, and in the interest of attaching a prisoner martyrdom to that victory, narrators such as Thomas Dring and Ebenezer Fox placed responsibility for the terminal condition of captured seamen on the vagaries of process. Dring's narrative, for instance, quoted a detailed response (attributed to Washington, but more likely the reconstructed composition of editor Albert G. Greene). It attempts to lay bare the crux of Washington's political dilemma:

> That, in the first place, but little exertion was made on the part of our countrymen to secure and detain their British prisoners for the sake of exchange, many of the British seamen being captured by privateers, on board which, he understood, it was a common practice for them to enter as seamen; and that when this was not the case, they were usually set at liberty as soon as the privateers arrived in port; as neither the owners, nor the town or State where they were landed, would be at the expense of their confinement and maintenance; and that the officers of the General Government only took charge of those seamen who were captured by the vessels in public service. All which circumstances combined to render the number of prisoners, at all times, by far too small for a regular and equal exchange.[26]

Ebenezer Fox, who clearly worked out the details of his own narrative with a copy text of Dring's own, also glossed the content of Washington's 1782 reply to the prisoner memorial:

> Permission was obtained, and the memorial was sent. In a few days, an answer was received from Gen. Washington, containing expressions full of interest and sympathy, but declaring his inability to do anything for our relief by way of exchange, as his authority did not extend to the marine department of the service, and that soldiers could not consistently be exchanged for sailors. He declared his intention, however, to lay our memorial before Congress, and that no exertion should be spared by him to mitigate our sufferings.[27]

Records show that Washington was convincingly constrained on multiple fronts. Prisoner commissaries competed with scarce suppliers for troops and allied forces. Prisoners understood this. But privateers, on the frontlines of trade interception and seaport labor agitation, were also unlikely to believe that some unsurpassable command vacuum existed between the general and the navy. The professed disconnect between the Continental war machine and revenue streams from captured British cargo, gunpowder stores, and intercepted Atlantic trade goods was, in all actuality, artificial. In the leanest of war years, there was ultimately little financial or military gain in effecting the rescue of privateers. Within this stagnant infrastructure, Wallabout testimonies read as testimonies of neglect by writ of *not* being officially politicized subjects. With the exception of Silas Talbot, who was effectively only part-privateer, prisoners were beyond the protection of both the Continental Army and Navy; they were not officially politicized subjects.[28]

Through his description of the *Jersey*'s external appearance, Thomas Andros suggested an analogy between prison-ship form and prisoner function. He compared the converted ship's missing prow ornament to the paradoxical position of the captives aboard. As mostly privateers who preyed on British commerce for prize and adventure, naval prisoners had operated with open license and encouragement to depredate British shipping. But they were also without protection or representation in the event of British capture. Though in the words of Andros, privateering was widely "considered as a national act" (9), the failure of their efforts to secure aid from George Washington reminded them that they were indeed without a real aegis of protection. They lacked a figurehead. They did not belong to what Andros characterized as the proper body of a national "civil government" (9). Nor, "in the view of the English," should they be accorded the treatment "expected by prisoners taken in a war with a foreign nation" (12).

So while the treatment of said foreign prisoners hardly appears enviable (something other prisoner accounts make clear), Andros's point speaks to a distinctive sense of loss. For American prisoners in New York Harbor hulks, incarceration meant both civil and corporeal death. Proud patriots were reduced to mere "rebels and traitors," having "risen against the mother-country in an unjust and wanton war" (12). They performed the actual work of a national navy, to a far greater extent than the ad hoc Continental Navy ever managed. They successfully raided British commerce and supply chains. Their gains were the country's. But their losses were their own. With neither commission nor protection of an official figurehead, there was little recourse for their claims of service. Effectively, their bodies existed in a negative relation to the same Continental Congress to which they espoused loyalty.[29]

Destruction and Construction in the "Republic of Misery"

As they strove to reconcile their domestic exile, the authors of Wallabout prisons contributed to the work of making a political corpus. They generated representations of a Revolutionary-styled body through a number of what might be called participatory tropes. In this usage, "tropes" are ways to elaborate a *tropos*, a shift and redirection. Such tropes are not quite styles of discourse as much as figurative turns, which can be extracted from various records of experience. They may be thought of as participatory insofar as they contain a directive *tropos* that fashions collective, representative claims from more particularized, synchronic experience. In the case of the prison-ship narratives, where collectivity is a generic feature of mass imprisonment, participatory tropes are particularly interesting because they produce political forms from testimonial representations.

Calling such devices "tropes" might appear to overdub prison-ship narratives with a conspicuously literary idiom. Indeed, Freneau's poem, as has been more recently documented, was more likely the work of sympathetic art than of experience.[30] Thomas Andros's classically framed extension of Virgil's *Aeneid* in the First Letter of *The Old Jersey Captive* (as commentary on the role of recollected experience) was also more anomalous in its craft. Ebenezer Fox borrowed extensively from Thomas Dring's account, which was, in turn, shaped into a sixty-page folio by his editor, Albert G. Greene. Greene prefaced the narrative chapters of Dring's folio with referential stanzas from Freneau's "The British Prison Ship."

But for the most part, prisoners insisted that their aim was transparency—substance over style. Andrew Sherburne announced at the outset of the 1829 edition of his *Memoirs* that although "solicited by gentlemen of literature and taste, to give his narrative to the public," it was a formidable undertaking. His "limited education, diffidence of his own abilities to write, and in a word his poverty and shattered constitution, rendered the thought so appalling, that he shrank from the task."[31] Editor Albert G. Greene effectually highlighted his own role in making form from Thomas Dring's professed fact, stating in the preface that "while containing a great number of interesting facts," Dring's manuscript was "thrown together, without much regard to style or to chronological order."[32] These editorial aims are somewhat notable in that they appear to be at odds with Dring's own stated purpose for writing his memoirs: that "few statements have been given to the world in authentic form" (18–19). More circumspect is the narrative of Ebenezer Fox, which, despite its original depictions of several prisoner escape capers and Tory-rousing antics, takes its cues from Dring's narrative in detail, descriptions, and overall narrative sequencing.[33]

Viewed collectively, the narratives encompass a variety of modes—religious, affective, romantic, ironic, factual. Nonetheless, underlying this generic diversity are two tropes that emerge in nearly all the extant accounts: dispossession and ordering. These tropes are participatory because they signal the way political participation is enacted through endured performance as prisoners. From within the prison container, these modes signified a collective experience and, to a certain extent, the grounds for a collective identification. By representing illness, overcrowding, and inadequate sanitation as the result of imperial dispossession, narrators mobilized their experiences into print tropes. Disease, malnourishment, and containment became political expression—a claim to republican subjecthood, and to what one prisoner even called a "vindication of the rights of man."[34]

A second print "turn" mobilizes in a similar fashion; it is an arena for collective experience. It shapes prisoner memories of what was more likely a collective despondency into something that reads as an embattled but sturdy appeal to principle. It gives meaning to the notion of representational politics aboard the *Jersey*. This second arena for collective experience might be thought of simply as "ordering." Ordering practices, as the narratives demonstrate, are at once internal and associative. Tropes of order cover acts of self-management and containment; they are expressions of discipline and self-resolve but can also extend to modes of community-fashioning onboard the ship. Built on the body's negotiation of order and physical deprivation, these combined tropes inscribe a sort of political corpus in scenes of death and rapid physical deterioration.[35]

On Dispossession

For prisoners, the experience of deprivation was foremost physiological, felt most acutely through the manipulation of human thirst. On board the *Jersey*, captives were allowed one pint of water below deck, an amount that when considered alongside the high demand for water for communal use, massive dysentery, and fever-inducing typhus, was woefully insufficient. For the poet Philip Freneau, whose (affective and affected) six-week imprisonment aboard the *Scorpion* and the prison hospital ship the *Hunter* inspired his poem "The British Prison Ship" (1781), the theme of thirst dominates the greater part of Canto II. Describing the scorched underground quarters, "where cruel thirst the parching throat invades," Freneau wrote:

> No waters laded from the bubbling spring
> To these dire ships these little tyrants bring—
> By plank and ponderous beams completely walled
> In vain for water, still in vain we called.
> No drop was granted to the midnight prayer. (29)

In heroic couplets the poem contrasts the image of fresh, abundant water to the prisoners' dry invocations of thirst, a contrast that foregrounds the strategies of dispossession exercised by colonial captors. For Freneau, suffering is an anguish always connected to an agent, a colonial foe, "pick'd from the British or the Irish bands, / Some slave from Hesse, some hangman's son" (30). It could not be depersonalized as a state of affairs or a condition. The neoclassically fashioned burlesque that dominates his representation of every identifiable agent of British colonial authority, especially in Canto III, ensures that action is attributed.

To *Jersey* captives, the dispossession of water was most tantalizing because unlike the limited resources of food, clothing, firewood, or building materials, fresh water was not a scarce commodity in occupied New York, coastal New Jersey, or Connecticut. Subsequently, the unfulfilled need for water was a collective experience various prisoners recognized as an imperial strategy for making their vital life functions contingent on the exercise of colonial power. Prisoners described being trapped below the deck with the gratings closed through long nights of fever; they were without manageable access to drinking water. Thomas Andros wrote, "While so many were sick with raging fever, there was a loud cry for water; but none could be had, except on the upper deck, and but one allowed to ascend at a time. The suffering, then, from the rage of thirst during the night was very great" (11). He further described the rituals of regulation: "Nor was it at all times safe to attempt to go up. Provoked by the continual cry for leave to ascend, when there was already one on deck, the sentry would push them back with his bayonet" (11–12). Andrew Sherburne, captured first at age eighteen and twice a prisoner aboard the *Jersey* after a gangrenous hospital ship internment, described having "given three days [food] allowance to have a tin cup of water brought me" (115). He wrote, "I was under the necessity of using the strictest economy with my cup of water; restricting myself to drink such a number of swallows at a time, and make them very small: my thirst was so extreme that I would sometimes overrun my number" (115).

For Sherburne, the experience of thirst left marks other than those of the bayonet. Dispossession, he claimed, conditioned the prisoners: "I became so habituated to number my swallows, that for years afterwards I continued the habit, and even to this day, I frequently involuntarily number my swallows" (116). Drawing upon Michel Foucault's concept of biopower, a form of power exercised on the collective body of whole populations through regimes of "governmentality," Michael Hardt and Antonio Negri have argued that the kind of power that regulates life from the interior exceeds disciplinary power in its ability to rewrite or reprogram its subjects.[36] Sherburne's experience demonstrates the ways survival is about the mediation of biological impulse and personal economy—an economy which, in turn, could be manipulated by colonial parsimony. By limiting water distribution, the British regime and its underpaid agents about the ship could tighten control over a group of prisoners who at all times outnumbered them. Authority thus appears to be grounded in that very deprivation—the tension between biological survival and sovereign power.

Dispossession, not surprisingly, extended to food distribution in the waters of Wallabout Bay. Prisoners all wrote that they were deprived of basic nutrition. Virtually all suffered through stages of malnourishment and scurvy. Plagued by the general absence of a Continental commissary (a troubling point, which notably goes unsaid in a number of the narratives), their dietary mainstay was food rejected for consumption or sale by the British Navy.[37] Captives were officially given two-thirds the ration accorded to British sailors. But because of misappropriation and the due negligence of individuals such as Joshua Loring, general commissary of army prisons, and David Sproat, naval prison commissary, they frequently received far less. "All the prisoners," wrote Thomas Dring, "were obliged to fast on the first day of their arrival, and seldom on the second could they obtain any food in season for cooking it" (154–55). Following his May 1780 capture aboard the frigate, *Hancock*, John Van Dyke recalled that he and the crew were kept aboard his ship "without anything to eat for 46 hours." After this two-day interval, the food finally allotted to his mess, a group of six men, was meager: "I received the allowance of my mess, and behold! Brown water, and fifteen floating peas — no peas on the bottom of my drawer, and this for six men's allowance for 24 hours."[38] Alexander Coffin, who was approximately seventeen years old at the time of his first capture in 1782, claimed a similar fare: "They frequently gave us pea-soup, that is pea-water, for the peas and the soup, all but about a gallon or two, were taken for the ship's company, and the coppers filled up with water, and brought down to us in a strap-tub" (185). Another captured seventeen-year-old, Roswell Palmer of Stonington, Connecticut, described spoiled food and sea biscuits "so worm-eaten that a slight pressure of the hand reduced them to dust, which rose up in little clouds of insubstantial aliment, as if in mockery of the half famished expectants."[39] According to Andrew Sherburne, "The bread had been so eaten by weevils, that one might easily crush it in the hand and blow it away" (111). Ebenezer Fox recalled an even more grotesque experience with rations: "The bread was mouldy and filled with worms. It required considerable rapping upon the deck before the worms could be dislodged from their lurking places in the biscuits" (102).

By constructing their experiences as the design of colonial dispossession, prison narrators examined strategies of reduction that took them in distinct directions: to yield in one direction was to act out a brute animal existence; the other motioned toward bodily dispossession, to a state of obsolescent ghostliness. In "The British Prison Ship," Freneau's lines raged back at the mean primitivism instilled in prisoners by colonial authorities. He wrote: "Here, doom'd to starve, like famish'd dogs we tore / The scant allowance, that our tyrants bore" (27), connecting the exercise of food distribution to his captors' efforts to vitiate republican life to the terms of animal drive. Alexander Coffin, who in addition to being on the *Jersey*, spent time aboard the *John*, a narrow transport ship receiving the overflow of *Jersey* captures, reported that prisoners were offered mostly raw, uncooked food: "All the time I was on board this ship, not a prisoner eat [*sic*] his allowance, bad as it was, cooked, more than three or four times; but eat it raw as it came out of the barrel" (188). To prisoner John Van Dyke, this daily spectacle of subordination and human corralling on the ship was a sort of animal dramaturgy. He wrote, "At sunset the prisoners were ordered by the sentinels on deck, hallooing, below, and if the prisoners were not brisk in moving," Van Dyke recalled, "they had the point of the bayonet in them. And ever since that time, when I see a flock of sheep going through a pair of bars, one tumbling over others, I think of the old Jersey Prison Ship" (149).

Equally desperate, but in a distinctly different way, were the accounts of retreat from animal subjection into spectral forms. "Utter derangement was a common symptom of yellow fever," Thomas Andros wrote of his experience aboard the *Jersey*, "and to increase the horror of the darkness that shrouded us (for we were allowed no light betwixt decks) the voices of warning would be heard 'Take heed to yourselves. There is a madman stalking through the ship with a knife in hand.' I sometimes found the man a corpse in the morning, by whose side I laid myself down at night" (10). In crowded septic chambers, fever quickly did the work of war. It destroyed Patriot bodies and blighted physical forms of resistance. Andros maintained that beneath decks, the strongest and most energetic were pestilence's earliest conquests: "The most healthy and vigorous were first seized with the fever and died in a few hours. For them there seemed to be no mercy" (42). By contrast, the less robust tarried longer. He wrote, "My constitution was less muscular and plethoric, and I escaped the fever longer . . . and the first onset was less violent" (11).

While Freneau's poem burns with bombast and fury, a number of symptomatic lines indicate the inevitability of depletion under the hold of imperial dispossession. In such moments: "A pallid hue o'er every face was spread" and "meager and wan" men walk the ship listlessly (29). "We looked like ghosts," reads the poem, "pallid forms" of "infernal night" (31). Dring's narrative virtually echoes Freneau's phraseology in its description of prisoner forms on the *Jersey* when first perceived above deck by the light of day: "Pale and meager the throng came upon deck; to view, for a few moments, the morning sun and then to descend again, to pass another day of misery and wretchedness" (16).

Through the trope of dispossession, illness could be attributed to an agent, an "infernal agent," in words echoing Freneau. Describing the crowded conditions of the *Jersey* where more than a thousand bodies were said to lay confined together, Thomas Andros wrote, "All the most deadly diseases were pressed into the service of the King of Terrors, but his prime ministers were dysentery, small pox and yellow fever" (10). For Freneau's narrator, his near-fatal fever from typhus is the specific result of colonial water deprivation: "deign'd that healthy juice to lade" (31). The tropes of dispossession emphasize the tableau of the body in resistance against animal life and effete vitiation. Moreover, the denial of the very food and water material that sustained life further infuses testimonies with a telos constructed against the closeness of death—a condition Freneau called "the shades" (29). For Andros, no skirmish or battle loss could compare with his epic fight through derangement and fever. It was a fight to contain the life spirit in what he called its "tenement of clay" (42).

Epidemiologies of Air

In considering the subjugation of bodies through dispossession, it is important to address the ways the prison ships gained their frightful hold over prisoners' imaginations through wartime strategies of containment. Eighteenth-century prisons were popularly recognized as breeding grounds for diseases. In his 1774 treatise on maintaining health within the Royal Navy, physician James Lind commented, "As prisons are the chief source of contagion, these first claim our attention."[40] From the Hippocratic Corpus until well into the nineteenth century, diseases were believed to be primarily infestations of air. "A free air," Lind wrote, "is the first article of importance," even illustrating at length "the most effectual means of procuring a general circulation of air throughout the whole prison" by a device called the "wind-sail" (331–33). That pestilence was affixed to air was a belief shared by the College of Physicians of Philadelphia in 1798, who described elaborate air purification rituals involving smoke made from layered fires.[41]

In an open letter to the popular physician and career House Republican, Dr. Samuel Latham Mitchill, Alexander Coffin made particular mention of the quality of air aboard the *Jersey* overflow prison transfer ship, the *John*. His 1807 letter was printed under the sweeping title, "The Destructive Operation of Foul Air, Tainted Provisions, Bad Water, and Personal Filthiness, Upon Human Constitutions, Exemplified in the Unparalleled Cruelty of the British to the American Captives at New

York during the Revolutionary War, on Board Their Prison and Hospital Ships." Coffin's account described the nighttime conditions beneath the closed hatchways: "The effluvia arising from these, together with the already contaminated air," Coffin wrote, "occasioned by the breath of so many people so pent up together, was enough to destroy men of the most healthy and robust conditions" (188). His representations of the *John* also applied to the nearby *Jersey*. Forced to spend long nights with dead bodies below deck—bodies not yet deposited into the riverbank silt for burial—prisoners endured what eighteenth-century physicians believed were the polluting and even fatal emanations of decomposing corpses.[42]

Silas Talbot, who was confined on board the *Jersey* from the fall of 1780 until December 1781, recorded: "All her port holes were closed. There were about 1,100 prisoners on board. There were no berths or seats, to lie down on, not a bench to sit on. Many were almost without clothes. The dysentery, fever, phrenzy and despair prevailed among them, and filled the place with filth, disgust and horror."[43] John Van Dyke, taken prisoner in May 1780, recalled upon boarding the *Jersey*: "This ship had been a hospital ship. When I came on board her stench was so great, and my breathing this putrid air—I thought it would kill me, but after being on board some days I got used to it, and as though all was a common smell" (249). Seventeen-year-old Ebenezer Fox recounted "visages pallid with disease . . . shriveled by a scanty and unwholesome diet, ghastly with inhaling an impure atmosphere, exposed to contagion" (252). And Thomas Dring described his first impression upon entering the *Jersey* in a hauled station boat that pulled up alongside the ship's side airport:

> From this aperture proceeded a strong current of foul vapor of a kind to which I had been before accustomed while confined on board the *Good Hope*, the peculiar disgusting smell of which I then recollected, after a lapse of three years. This was, however, far more foul and loathsome than anything which I had ever met with on board that ship, and it produced a sensation of nausea far beyond my powers of description. (199)

Thomas Andros claimed that the *Jersey*'s pestilence was too potent to be eradicated by cleaning. Rather, it was said to seep into the fibers of the ship; "the whole ship, from her keel to the tafferel [taffrail] was equally affected, and contained pestilence sufficient to desolate a world; disease and death were wrought into her very timbers" (68).[44] Freneau wrote on the daily ritual of descent: "Hail, dark abode! What can with thee compare? / Heat, sickness, famine, death, and stagnant air" (28). Far from the "breezy" free air that billowed sails with "favouring gales," characteristic of the free ship's enterprise in Canto I, the floating prisons were stagnant. The prison ship was paradoxical. It was a vehicle for movement and a space of detention and impermeability.

Further, its impermeability meant physical contamination. It meant death. In putrid, airless holds, disease was rendered as a kind of politics, a method of control and application of power exercised on the body. In the narratives, the prison ship becomes a vessel for cultivating disease, something that is modeled by the coercive state. The trope of dispossession made pestilence the tool of the imperial state. It grounded political resistance in the process of survival. Yet, at the same time, the most acute experiences of suffering became the revolutionary property of the body who passed the threshold between life and death — between decks of the British prison ship.

Reflecting on the display of *Jersey* dead, whose uninterred bodies now lined the shore of Long Island, prisoner Silas Talbot would recognize these half-buried subjects as true Revolutionary bodies, a spectacle that he claimed "manifestly demonstrates that the Jersey prison ship had been as destructive as a field of battle."[45] Andrew Sherburne's narrative even included a July 4, 1800, oratorical extract from a Jonathan Russell Esq., delivered in the Baptist Meeting House of Providence, Rhode Island. Russell's transcribed speech attributes a recognizable, glorious martyrdom to the fallen on the War for Independence battlegrounds. The sunken interiors of prison ships, however, yielded no quick life sacrifices to a Patriot ideal of glorious freedom. These were instead the amorphous spaces of interiority, the shrouded but virulently real spaces where imperialism took its numberless victims. He wrote:

But, it was not in the ardent conflict of the field only that our countrymen fell. It was not the ordinary chances of war, alone, which they had to encounter. . . . Happy those other gallant spirits, who fell with glory in the heat of battle; distinguished by their country, and covered with her applause. Every soul sensible to honor, envies rather than compassionates their fate. It was in the dungeons of our inhuman invaders! it was in their loathsome and pestiferous prison-ships, that the wretchedness of our countrymen still makes the heart bleed.[46]

Measure for Measure: Regulating Print Bodies

Beyond the critical resistance that was raw survival, ex-prisoners aboard the *Jersey* relayed yet another story of collective experience, a story constructed through an appeal to order. In the narratives, an ideal of order emerged as a principal way to reclaim Patriot will (if not agency) from the seeming deadlock of imperial dispossession. If prisoners could not escape the hold, they could, in certain specific ways, keep their captors from becoming totalizing masters. Order adhered within the practices of exchange and the forms of personal containment that constituted prisoner expression. As the narratives detail, prisoner-imposed order was elaborate and disciplinary. It extended to nearly all arenas of life aboard the prison ship. Prisoners structured their behavior according to codes of exchange concerning conduct, sharing of food and supplies, and quartering. They devised rules that dictated death to any inmate who revealed a secret to a guard. "Another rule," Thomas Andros wrote, was that "no giant-like man should be allowed to tyrannize over or abuse another who was in no way his equal in strength" (13). Thomas Dring noted that "no prisoner when liberated could remove his chest," something captives frequently put to communal use (129). Organization was pivotal in efforts at escape. Prisoners organized in a variety of fashions in often ingenious (but always desperate) efforts to reach the shore.[47] Through their own organization, they could detect lapses in colonial security. Ebenezer Fox noted a weakness: "Although we were guarded with vigilance yet there did not appear much system in the management of the prisoner" (115).

Within the trope of order were possibilities for both self-imposed and collective action. Prisoners organized into parties to self-inoculate against smallpox with live virus shortly after arrival, an inexact science that for Thomas Dring's crew would cost them the youngest of their party, a twelve-year-old waiter. But such organization was nonetheless an effort at preservation. An appropriation of order further ensured that individuals were fed. Ebenezer Fox wrote that upon his arrival at the *Jersey*, "The first thing we found it necessary to do after our capture was to form ourselves into small parties called messes, consisting of six" (100). Messes constituted the feeding system for efficient food apportionment from the commissary to naval prisons.

Order circulated underneath basic acts of colonial dispensation, such as the practices of cooking prison food. Prisoners aboard the

Jersey described the "Great Copper" under the forecastle, a large copper boiler enclosed in an eight-foot-square brickwork, where prisoners designated their food portions with tallies fastened to string.[48] Yet, in ensuring they were fed from the pot, prisoners were also slowly poisoned from the copper verdigris–salt water compound they consumed.[49] According to Thomas Dring, "This side of the boiler was filled with salt water from alongside the ship; by which means, the copper became soon corroded, and consequently poisonous: the fatal consequences of which are so obvious, that I need not enlarge upon the subject" (29). However, organizing beneath the processes of general distribution, a number of messes obtained permission to cook their own food, apart from the general group. (Dring's mess cooked in a suspended tin kettle with splinters of wood they secured from vendors with land access, or fished out of the water.) Why the British allowed this was unclear. It was perhaps believed to lessen the burden of care, and the consumption of the green chestnut fuel that fired the copper. Dring attributed his own survival to the fact that during "the whole period of my confinement I never partook of any food which had been prepared in the Great Copper. It is to this fact that I have always attributed, under Divine Providence, the degree of health which I preserved on board" (34).

Additionally, by cooking their own food, the prisoners were able to acquire fire from the ship's cook, which they in turn circulated between themselves, something widely believed to purify the poisonous air below decks. Dring wrote, "After one had thus procured fire, the rest were also soon supplied, and our pipes were all in full operation in the course of a few minutes. The smoke which rose around us appeared to purify the pestilential air by which we were surrounded; and I attributed the preservation of my health in a great degree to the exercise of this habit" (87). Indeed, Dring's beliefs were supported by contemporary public health paradigms. The College of Physicians of Philadelphia in 1798 described elaborate fumigation rituals involving alternate layers of charcoal, brimstone, and bark kindling for forty-eight hours, something they maintained to be "very beneficial in destroying contagion in sick rooms" (21–22). Physician James Lind had earlier pronounced in 1774, "it now gives me the highest satisfaction to affirm that I seldom or never knew of a proper application of fire and smoke to be unsuccessful in producing the happy consequence of effectually purifying all tainted places, materials, and substances." He concluded, "I have never heard of any ship, which, after having been carefully and properly *smoked*, did not immediately become healthy" (227).

Self-Management: Interior Republics

Prisoners adhered to a system of by-laws, framed and circulated throughout the *Jersey*, which covered such topics as sanitation, guarding information, and punishments for violations. According to Andrew Sherburne, "notwithstanding they were located within the absolution dominions of his Britannic majesty," prisoners "adventured to form themselves into a republic, framed a constitution and enacted wholesome laws, with suitable penalties" (81). By Dring's account, these by-laws effectively became the religion of the ship. This was no better personified than through the figure of a young man from Virginia, identified only as "Cooper" in Dring's narrative, whose Sunday morning speeches, mounted upon the spar-deck, commanded the attention of his audience. His stated purpose, according to Dring, "was not to preach to us . . . he wished to read us our By-laws, a copy of which he held in his hand:"

> He enforced the necessity of our unremitting attention to personal cleanliness, and to the duties of morality; he dwelt upon the degradation and sin of drunkenness; described the meanness and atrocity of theft; and the high degree of caution against temptation necessary for men who were perhaps standing on the very brink of the grave; and added that, in his opinion, even sailors might as well refrain from profane language, while they were actually suffering in Purgatory. (90, 91–92)

On the other hand, prisoners such as Thomas Andros seemed to view order as an exercise in interiority. Andros claimed that general despondency ran deep, and that organizational power and appetite restraints were not exercised coevally for the benefit of all. He noted that "prisoners were furnished with buckets and brushes to clean the ship, and with vinegar to sprinkle her inside; but their indolence and despair were such that they would not use them, or but rarely" (12). Andros understood the desire for order as something less communally associative than internal. It was, if anything, more a sense of commissioning one's individual, privately reflective life to a viable source and future. It also meant the rejection of actions centered on the social tides of exploit-privateering and adventure.

In effect, redemptive order was not to be found in a return to lives pre-imprisonment. (Andros would himself find his vocation as pastor of the Congregational Church of Berkley, Massachusetts, from 1788 to 1845.)[50] Constructing his story at the end of his life, he recollected, "but as every man had almost the certain prospect of death before him, no doubt there were more or less who, in their own mind, like myself, had some serious thoughts of their accountability—of a future state and of a judgment to come" (13). While recognizing the disciplinary functions of order on the ship in relation to issues of personal property, Andros's claims remain at odds with the model of an encapsulated republic represented in narratives by Fox and Dring. They appear more reasonably fitted to an also-pervasive mode of democratic self-regulation in early national print discourse described recently by Christopher Castiglia as the equation of self-examination and self-scrutiny with self-management and a democratic accession to order.[51]

Ultimately, prisoner accounts were divided over the extent to which they located political resistance in the subnational potential of order. Regardless, order was treated as valuable (no less so by Thomas Andros), precisely because it was a mediating structure between brute life, reduced life, and the imperial state. An inscription of order gave narratives a formative sense of agency. It allowed prisoners to retain the vestige of a national body (perhaps a fiction) rather than subsisting as the undifferentiated subject of imperial law and the unrecognized subject of Continental support.

As the accounts clearly demonstrate, imprisonment was a leveler. To American prize-masters, officers, and captains aboard the ship *Jersey*, it added to the humiliating experience of delegitimized enterprise, an embarrassed sense of rank. As prisoners would repeatedly claim, their captors appeared to take at least some satisfaction from debasing Continental measures of status: "Whether taken on the land or on the ocean, in arms, or from our own firesides, it was the same to them. No matter in what rank or capacity a prisoner might have been known before his capture, no distinction was here made; we were 'all Rebels,'" wrote Thomas Dring (24). In *Forgotten Patriots*, Edwin G. Burrows quotes an incredulous Hessian as remarking, "Among the prisoners are many so-called colonels, lieutenant colonels, majors, and other officers, who however, are nothing but mechanics, tailors, shoemakers, wigmakers, barbers, etc."[52] The impudence of such individuals apparently galled their captors: "Some of them were soundly beaten by our people, who would by no means let such persons pass for officers."[53] Thomas Dring detailed the contemptuous relationship between prisoners and local Tories, known by captives as Royalists and Refugees. He commented on a typical exchange when prisoners' hostile comments toward their guards (from afar) were not returned: "They never answered any of our remarks respecting them, but would merely point to their uniforms, as if saying, We are clothed by our Sovereign, while you are naked" (70).

Yet, prisoners insisted on their own measures of status, something reflected most clearly in the quartering arrangements they made. Within the depersonalized bulk holds between decks, they imposed ideas of order. They organized compartments below the deck with tiers of chests, arranged into lines, and a large partition for general halls.[54] They also kept rank. A twenty-five-year-old officer at the time of his capture, Thomas Dring was among those officers who described his "place of abode being in the Gunroom," between decks with other captured officers. It was less crowded and its occupants supposedly more innovative and organized in rationing their firewood and water (25). Ebenezer Fox claimed the same: "The only distinction known among us was made by the prisoners themselves, which was shown in allowing those who had been officers previous to their captivity, to congregate in the extreme afterpart of the ship, and to keep it exclusively to themselves as their place of abode" (101).

The separation of captains and officers from the general population of prisoners actually favored British efforts at enlisting able-bodied men into service, and thus did not function in tandem with the practical aims of the Continental Congress. Indeed, while prisoner quartering reflected an effort to establish meaning beyond the reach of imperial authorities, it was no less a practice circumscribed by imperial expectation. As might be evinced from the *Jersey* narratives, self-management and sovereignty existed in an uneasy relationship within the locking middle and lower orlop decks of the prison ships. Staged hierarchies of order among prisoners, based on external identities prior to capture, still appeared to ensure some forms of entitlement. Yet, they were ultimately forms that protected personal interests, not those of any clear external cause such as the nationalist anticolonial struggle that was emblematized by the figure of Washington as these narratives came to print in the early nineteenth century.

By fighting against reduction, captives aboard the *Jersey* and the even deadlier prison hospital ships such as the *Hunter* and *Scorpion* fought the idea that they were already lost lives—that they were the expendable bodies of republicanism.[55] They made the structures of human partici-pation the discourses for living. Practices of order were a kind of route, or path, between the disembodied political subject with the politically disassociated, physical body. Condemned to disease and starvation, and denied the status of political prisoners, these inmates of prison ships militated against dispossession. Their own elaboration of order, in a sense, flattened the hierarchy of subjugation. They operated according to prisoner-formulated constraints. In losing freedom on one level (fur-ther constraining selves within a recognizable colonial death grip), they gained it on another.

NOTES

1. An occupied New York City, not Canada, was actually the center for British Navy recruitment in the New World. New York was also an interception net for Irish and Scottish immigrant ships arriving in port, many of whose male oc-cupants were enlisted even before touching land. See William Bell Clark and William James Morgan, eds., *Naval Documents of the American Revolution*, vol. 1 (Washington, D.C.: U.S. Government Printing Office, 1964), 911–13.

2. Shortly on the heels of the American War for Independence, France de-clared war on England in 1778, followed by Spain's declaration of war in 1779; subsequently, the Dutch United Provinces, longtime and nearby rivals for the commercial empire, went to war with England for the fourth time in 1780. The attenuation of the British Royal Navy in European conflicts created intolerable service conditions, resulting in high desertion rates. Commenting on the cycles of desertion and conscription, Admiral Robert Digby claimed in a letter to Lord Shelburne in May 1782 that were it not for impressed American privateers, it would be impossible to keep the ships "Mann'd." See Philip Ranlet, "British Recruitment of Americans in New York during the American Revolution," *Military Affairs* 48, no. 1 (January 1984): 27; Letter, Digby to Shelburne (May 10, 1782), CO 5/186/1–4, Library of Congress transcript.

3. For psychologically inflected approaches to interiority and ideological con-flict beyond the deeply grooved divides of republican and liberal value indexes, see Elizabeth Barnes, *States of Sympathy: Seduction and Democracy in the American Novel* (New York: Columbia University Press, 1997); Julia A. Stern, *The Plight of Feeling: Sympathy and Dissent in the Early American Novel* (Chicago: University of Chicago Press, 1997); and Christopher Castiglia, *Interior States: Institutional Consciousness and the Inner Life of Democracy in the Antebellum United States* (Durham, N.C.: Duke University Press, 2008).

4. See Henry R. Stiles, *A History of the City of Brooklyn*, 2 vols. (Brooklyn, N.Y.: published by subscription, 1867), 1:333 for ordering, traffic, and prisoner volume of ships, beginning with the *Whitby's* October 1776 arrival.

5. Thomas Andros, *The Old Jersey Captive* (Boston: William Pierce, 1833), 7–8. Subsequent references cited parenthetically in the text.

6. Feb. 20, March 4, April 3, 5, 1781, Adm 51/4228. Lemisch, "Listening to the 'Inarticulate': William Widger's Dream and the Loyalties of American Revolutionary Seamen in British Prisons," *Journal of Social History* 3 (1969): 10.

7. The most quoted eighteenth-century figure, first circulated on April 17, 1783 in Boston's *Continental Journal*, stated that 11,644 Americans perished "by inhuman, cruel, savage and barbarous usage on board the filthy and malignant British Prison Ship called the *Jersey*." (Notice by "An American," *Continental Journal* [Boston], April 17, 1783.) Philip Ranlet cites a figure supported by a deposition given to Thomas Jefferson in 1786 from Richard Riddy, a former prisoner in New York in 1783, who claimed that the general commissary for prisoners, David Sproat, maintained records listing the deaths of more than 11,000 American prisoners. Philip Ranlet, "Tory David Sproat of Pennsylvania and the Death of American Prisoners of War," *Pennsylvania History* 61 (1994): 185–205. For the magnitude of prisoner losses, see Edwin G. Burrows, *Forgotten Patriots, The Untold Story of American Prisoners during the Revolutionary War* (New York: Basic Books, 2008), 197–204. Pertaining to the casualties aboard the *Jersey* ship itself, the early-twentieth-century compiler of histories Danske Dandridge noted that the English War Records of prisoners on board the *Jersey* lists about 8,000, although this was an incomplete list. Dandridge, *American Prisoners of the Revolution* (Charlottesville, S.C.: Michie Company Printers, 1911), 149.

8. The term "somatics" here is influenced by Jay Fliegelman's idea of a public created through shared discourses of affective experience in *Declaring Independence: Jefferson, Natural Language and the Culture of Performance* (Stanford, Calif.: Stanford University Press, 1993). It is also influenced by Christopher Looby's construction of nationalist longing as something that experienced "quasi-somatically" in contrast to a depersonalized rhetoric of the civic self. Christopher Looby, *Voicing America: Language, Literary Form, and the Origins of the United States* (Chicago: University of Chicago Press, 1995), 5.

9. One deposition taken from *Jersey* prisoner George Batterman of Massachusetts reached Washington in 1780. He, in turn, sent it to British Admiral Marriot Arbuthnot. It testified to the crowded conditions, brutality, and starvation diet endured by captured seamen. See George Washington to Arbuthnot, Jan. 25, 1781, in *The Writings of George Washington from the Original Manuscript Sources, 1732–1799*, ed. John C. Fitzpatrick (Washington, D.C.: U.S. Government Printing Office, 1931–1944), 21:133–34.

10. *The Poems of Philip Freneau: Poet of the Revolution*, ed. Fred Lewis Pattee, 3 vols. (Princeton, N.J.: University Library, 1902), 25, 39. Subsequent references cited parenthetically in the text.

11. Eric Burns, *Infamous Scribblers: The Founding Fathers and the Rowdy Beginnings of American Journalism* (New York: Public Affairs, 2006), 277–93.

12. Freneau's source material was an anonymous prose account from the "Log Book of the Brig *Rebecca*" (Freneau Collection, Alexander Library, Rutgers University). In the best-known version of "The British Prison-Ship," from 1780, Freneau added to the amount of time said to be spent by the narrator on the prison ship *Scorpion*, claiming he was held captive for two months.

13. Alexander Coffin, "The Destructive Operation of Foul Air, Tainted Provisions, Bad Water, and Personal Filthiness, upon Human Constitutions, Exemplified in the Unparallelled Cruelty of the British to the American Captives at New York during the Revolutionary War, on Board Their Prison and Hospital Ships. By Captain Alexander Coffin, Junior, One of the Surviving Sufferers," in a Communication to Dr. Samuel L. Mitchell, dated Sept. 4, 1807. In *The Narrative of John Blatchford*, ed. Charles I. Bushnell (New York: Privately Printed, 1865), 117–27. Subsequent references cited parenthetically in the text. This letter is reprinted in Dandridge, *American Prisoners*, 184–90.

14. See Robert E. Cray Jr., "Commemorating the Prison Ship Dead: Revolutionary Memory and the Politics of Sepulture in the Early Republic, 1776–1808," *William and Mary Quarterly* 56 (July 1999): 565–90, esp. 565–68; Burrows, *Forgotten Patriots*, 211–20.

15. Nathaniel Prime, *History of Long Island* (New York: H. Ludwig, 1845), 367; Henry R. Stiles, ed., *Account of the Internment of the Remains of American Patriots, Who Perished on Board the British Prison Ships during the American Revolution* (New York: Privately Printed 1865).

16. Henry T. Tuckerman, *The Life of Silas Talbot, a Commodore in the Navy of the United States* (New York: J. C. Riker, 1850); James F. Simon, *What Kind of Nation: Thomas Jefferson, John Marshall, and the Epic Struggle to Create a United States* (New York: Simon and Schuster, 2002), 154–57.

17. See U.S. Supreme Court, The *Amelia*, 4 U.S. 34 (1800) 4 U.S. 34 (Dall.), Talbot v. The Ship *Amelia*, Seeman, Claimant. August Term, 1800.

18. Burrows, *Forgotten Patriots*, 230–31.

19. See "The Memorial to General Washington Signed by All the Prisoners and Delivered by Captain Aborn and Dr. Joseph Bowen," New York, June 5, 1782. Partially reprinted in Dandridge, *American Prisoners*, 226–28.

20. Rear Admiral Digby to Washington, New York, June 8, 1782, in *Writings of George Washington*, 24:315.

21. Washington to Rear Admiral Robert Digby, June 5, 1782, in *Writings of George Washington*, 24:315–16.

22. Letter from Commissary Skinner to Commissary Sproat, Camp Highlands, June 24, 1782. Quoted in Dandridge, *American Prisoners*, 336–47.

23. Letter from Benjamin Lincoln, Secretary at War to President of Congress. From *Papers of the Continental Congress War Office*, June 28, 1782. Reprinted in James Lenox Banks, *David Sproat and Naval Prisoners in the War of the Revolution* (New York: Knickerbocker Press, 1909), 99–100.

24. Washington to John Beatty, Aug. 19, 1779, in *Writings of George Washington*, 16:131.

25. Ibid.

26. Thomas Dring, *Recollections of the Jersey Prison Ship*, ed. and pref. Albert G. Greene (New York: P. M. Davis, 1831), 228. Subsequent references cited parenthetically in the text.

27. Ebenezer Fox, *The Adventures of Ebenezer Fox, in the Revolutionary War* (Boston: Charles Fox, 1838), 132. Subsequent references cited parenthetically in the text.

28. Talbot was appointed to the Continental Navy on September 17, 1779. However, since Congress had no ready warship to offer him, he went to sea in command of the privateer *General Washington*. See Ralph Eastman, *Some Famous Privateers of New England* (Whitefish, Mont.: Kessinger, 2004), 48–61.

29. The term "negative relation" is taken from Michael Warner's reading of the eighteenth-century post-Revolutionary public self in *The Letters of the Republic: Publication and the Public Sphere in Eighteenth-Century America* (Cambridge, Mass.: Harvard University Press, 1990).

30. The most convincing essay I have encountered that casts doubt on Freneau's actual imprisonment, following his return from the Caribbean to British-occupied Monmouth County in 1778, was written by Mary Weatherspoon Bowden: "In Search of Freneau's Prison Ships," *Early American Literature* 14 (1979): 174–92.

31. Andrew Sherburne, *Memoirs of Andrew Sherburne: A Pensioner of the Navy of the Revolution, Written by Himself*, 2nd ed. (Market Square, N.Y.: H. M. Brown, 1831), iv. Subsequent references cited parenthetically in the text.

32. See Dring, *Recollections of the Jersey Prison Ship*, iv–v.

33. For instance, Dring's narrative describing the *Jersey*'s illustration plate in the narrative preface (xiv), a logical/likely place for such a description, is echoed almost exactly by Ebenezer Fox, in the middle of *The Adventures;* see *The Adventures of Ebenezer Fox, in the Revolutionary War*, 96–97.

34. Thomas Dring quoting "the Jersey Orator," *Recollections of the Jersey Prison Ship*, 94.

35. Cray, "Commemorating the Prison Ship Dead," 3.

36. Michel Foucault in *The History of Sexuality* used the term *biopower* more or less synonymously with *biopolitics*, a complex of power (power deployments)

strategically grafted onto consensual relations. Hardt and Negri define biopower as a kind of totalizing effort to regulate and reconstitute social life from the interior. See Michael Hardt and Antonio Negri, *Empire* (Cambridge, Mass.: Harvard University Press, 2000), 23.

37. Some captives such as Captain Thomas Dring managed to secrete monies and were able to buy food supplies such as soft bread, tea, and sugar from visiting boat merchants. Many were not as fortunate (Dring, *Recollections of the Jersey Prison Ship*, 77).

38. John Van Dyke, "Narrative of Confinement in the *Jersey* Prison Ship, by John Van Dyke, Captain in Lamb's Regiment, N.Y.S.A.," *The Historical Magazine and Notes and Queries Concerning the Antiquities, History, and Biography of America* (New York: Charles B. Richardson, May 1863), 7:147–51, 148. Subsequent references cited parenthetically in the text.

39. Quoted in Dandridge, *American Prisoners*, 182.

40. James Lind, *An Essay on the Most Effectual Means of Preserving the Health of the Seamen in the Royal Navy. By James Lind, M.D. A New Edition, Much Enlarged and Improved* (London: D. Wilson and G. Nicol, 1774), 331. Subsequent references cited parenthetically in the text.

41. *Proceedings of the College of Physicians of Philadelphia, Relative to the Prevention of the Introduction and Spreading of Contagious Diseases*, College of Physicians of Philadelphia (Thomas Dobson: Philadelphia, 1798), 21–22.

42. Victor C. Vaughan and George T. Palmek, *Epidemiology and Public Health: A Text and Reference Book for Physicians, Medical Students and Health Workers*, 3 vols. (St. Louis: C. V. Mosby, 1922), 19. See also John Huxham, *Observations on the Air, and Epidemic Diseases: From the Beginning of the Year 1738, to the End of the Year 1748*, translated from the original, by his son, John Corham Huxham, A.M. (Plymouth, England: J. Hinton, 1759), 2:168–75.

43. *An Historical Sketch, to the End of the Revolutionary War, of the Life of Silas Talbot, Esq., of the State of Rhode-Island [microform] Lately Commander of the United States Frigate, the Constitution, and of an American Squadron in the West-Indies* (New York: G&R Waite, for H. Caritat, 1803), 107.

44. Contamination extended to water. See Coffin, "Destructive Operation of Foul Air," 186; Dring, *Recollections of the Jersey Prison Ship*, 73.

45. *An Historical Sketch . . . of the Life of Silas Talbot*, 109–10.

46. Quoted in Sherburne, *Memoirs of Andrew Sherburne*, 109–10.

47. See Andros, *Old Jersey Captive*, 12; Dring, *Recollections of the Jersey Prison Ship*, 107–12; Fox, *Adventures of Ebenezer Fox*, 116, 119–20.

48. One member of each mess was to oversee the boiling in the copper until ordered to remove the portion by the company cook. Dring, *Recollections of the Jersey Prison Ship*, 100; Andros, *Old Jersey Captive*, 13.

49. Fox, *The Adventures of Ebenezer Fox*, 102–6; Andros, *Old Jersey Captive*, 9.

50. Editor's Preface to Andros, *Old Jersey Captive.*

51. Castiglia, *Interior States.*

52. Quoted in Burrows, *Forgotten Patriots,* 30.

53. Ibid.

54. See Dring, *Recollections of the Jersey Prison Ship,* 36–41; on quartering and deck configuration, also see Dandridge, *American Prisoners,* 205.

55. Conditions aboard hospital ships were considered even worse than prison ships, and were even more overcrowded and unsanitary. Two men usually shared a bunk. See Dandridge, *American Prisoners,* 208.

"The Horrors of This Far-Famed Penitentiary"

Discipline, Defiance, and Death during Ann Carson's Incarcerations in Philadelphia's Walnut Street Prison

DANIEL E. WILLIAMS

BEFORE NARRATING HER FIRST REMOVAL to the solitary confinement cells of Walnut Street Prison in 1816, Ann Carson—having declared herself to be the victim of "the most unrelenting persecutions"—described her last-ditch effort to seek redress: "I wrote a letter descriptive of my wretched situation, which I threw into the street from the cell window. It was found, I presume, by some of the citizens, and returned, accompanied, as I understood, with a letter of remonstrance" (1:222, 224).[1] Although she added that her letter "produced no change in my situation," Carson must have been pleased with her act of authorship. Her words had not only reached an audience but also elicited a reaction. This small act of literally throwing her text out into the public from an unexpected and somewhat ignoble position, and hoping for a sympathetic response that would gain her some measure of revenge, prefigures Carson's appearance in print culture six years later. In 1822, when she collaborated with Mary Clarke to publish *The History of the Celebrated Mrs. Ann Carson*, she again dropped something out to the public, once again hoping not only to gather an audience of readers but also to exploit their empathetic response.[2] Feeling persecuted and oppressed, Carson used her text—and manipulated her self-characterization—as a means of making a public appeal. Rather than in the halls of justice or the cells of Walnut Street Prison, she sought vindication in the public sphere.[3]

Carson's description of what followed her letter-dropping petition is also emblematic of her authorship. In describing her imprisonment in solitary confinement, she—the narrator Ann Carson—directly appealed to the sympathies of early national readers: "To the cells then I was conducted; I started with horror as I entered these abodes of human wretchedness, that were at this period filled with miserable victims, who had given some slight offence to the sovereign lords of this *American Bastille*" (1:224). In order to dramatize her struggles in the grandiloquent rhetoric of tyranny, oppression, and persecution, Carson concluded her florid description by imploring God's help:

> God of heaven, what were . . . the agonies that rent my heart? thou alone witnessed them, and to thy vengeance I consign the author. Here, in solitude, stretched on a blanket perhaps to die, as many an unhappy prisoner had done, amidst the dregs of creation, lay the woman that had once been the idol of an affectionate family, the object of tenderest love, whose every wish had been anticipated by partial friends, and whose society had been courted by gentlemen of the first rank; now, alas! The victim of oppression. (1:225)[4]

Rather than a heavenly response from an omnipotent God, both Carson and Clarke obviously collaborated to evoke an emotional response from readers, which they must have perceived as having a greater efficacy to help them achieve their all-too-worldly goals. Using the turgid language of sentimental novels, they depicted Carson's imprisonments in the Walnut Street Prison as a series of struggles against ruthless arbitrary power, in effect as a microcosm of the Revolutionary struggle for liberty. Ironically, Carson was less interested in divine retribution than in her own; as an author, quite clearly she sought vengeance, and her 1822 emergence into print culture was a calculated effort to position readers as witnesses of her heart-rending agonies. Rather than a villain, she cast herself as a heroine.

I.

Ann Carson was the most notorious fallen woman in early America, and she became notorious years before she appeared in print culture as an author. Born in 1786, Carson was just fifteen years old when she married John Carson, a twenty-four-year-old man who had served under her father in the Navy during the 1790s.[5] The marriage was a disaster. An abusive alcoholic when he was home, John Carson was a ship's captain who was away at sea for months and sometimes years at a time. His wife, a headstrong and passionate young woman, caused considerable rumor and scandal during her husband's absences by—according to her later descriptions—innocently entertaining male admirers. But in 1816 the steady hum of gossip erupted into a deafening roar of outrage and vilification.

Four years previously, at the outset of renewed hostilities with England in 1812, John Carson had left on a voyage to Europe and had not returned. Hearing no news of him, except a vague report that he had died, Carson soon moved on and married Richard Smyth, a recently furloughed Army lieutenant. But after only "three little months of bliss," John Carson reappeared to confront the newlyweds, demanding the return of his wife and property (1:146). After a series of confrontations and scuffles, which included Carson's first husband trying to stab her second husband, Richard Smyth fired a pistol into the face of John Carson on the evening of January 20, 1816. Shortly after Carson died nine days later, Smyth was arrested for his murder, and Ann Carson was arrested as an accessory, which resulted in her first experiences behind the walls of the Walnut Street Prison.

Yet this was only the beginning of both Carson's downward spiral and her rising notoriety. Not long after Smyth was tried and condemned four months later, Carson—acquitted as an accessory but rearrested for bigamy—began conspiring with a "gang of robbers" to break her second husband out of prison (1:191). They concocted several plans either to overpower or to bribe the two night guards, but abandoned one after another until Carson and her "fraternity of desperadoes" resolved, as a last resort, to blow up the Walnut Street Prison (1:191). Coloring her resolve in the maudlin language of sentimental fiction—and in fact consciously imitating "all the terror I had once experienced in reading of banditties, in various novels I had perused"—the narrator Carson declared: "My last hope was thus o'erclouded by dark despair, and I became prey of that heart consuming fiend. Thus driven to desperation I forgot every thing but the dread of Richard's suffering an ignominious death, and I resolved to blow up the cells with gunpowder" (1:191, 195). But just when she had "sunk to the lowest gulph of human wretchedness," Carson seized on an even more daring plan. She and her cohorts decided to kidnap Simon Snyder, the governor of Pennsylvania, and force him to sign a pardon. "I sat one day being absorbed in anxious thought, when suddenly despair suggested the idea of making a prisoner of Simon Snyder, and holding him in custody till he signed Richard's pardon, and he was released from the walls that then immured him. The idea no sooner entered my mind than its brightness dazzled my imagination" (1:196). Typologically conflating herself with "heroines [of novels] whose courage had risen superior to sex," Carson and her gang left Philadelphia for Harrisburg. But they were soon betrayed, pursued, and arrested, and after a brief stay in the Harrisburg jail, she was again brought to Walnut Street Prison.

On their ignominious return, Carson and her conspirators caused an immediate sensation. Although in her later self-depiction she repeatedly labeled herself as the "heroine of the famous conspiracy," the newspapers of the day—aided by gossip in the streets—disseminated a scandalous public narrative that quickly circulated throughout the eastern states (1:215). In countless notices and reports, and in half a dozen sensational narratives related to Smyth's May trial and August execution, Carson was depicted as totally iniquitous and even infernal.[6] Refusing to accept such disparaging labeling, Carson defied her public condemnation and circulated her own lexicon. Although equally a prisoner of both Walnut Street Prison and her notoriety, she made use of writing to renarrate her life, first dropping her letter into a public street in 1816 and then in 1822 dropping her narrative into the public sphere.

As much as Carson was notorious, the Walnut Street Prison was famous.[7] Built originally in 1773 as a traditional holding facility for debtors, vagrants, and those awaiting trial, the prison was at the forefront of a wave of penal reform initiatives that took place during the post-Revolutionary years when it was expanded in 1790. Walnut Street Prison was the first penitentiary in the United States remodeled to include cells for solitary confinement. Such a harsh environment of isolation was actually perceived as a progressive advancement over previous penal practices that invariably involved public displays of physical punishment, most often whippings and hangings. While arguing that public spectacles did little to restore civil and social order, and in some ways actually encouraged the opposite, reformers like Benjamin Rush claimed that rehabilitation might be possible if criminals were isolated, forced to follow rigid schedules that most notably included hard labor, and given time to reflect upon their transgressions. Compared to previous jails that miscellaneously housed all inmates in large, open rooms, and which were often overcrowded, unsanitary, and corrupt, Walnut Street Prison was indeed a model of Enlightenment thinking. Little wonder, then, that it attracted a steady flow of visitors from throughout the United States and Europe.

Yet, as Michel Foucault insightfully demonstrated, the penal reforms of the penitentiary, intended to make the prisoners feel remorse, inflicted a different kind of torture.[8] The punishment of the body was replaced with the punishment of the mind. Rigid regulations, enforced silence, hard labor, and solitary confinement turned out to be just as punishing, and just as disfiguring, as whippings and brandings. In its first decade or so, however, Walnut Street Prison was hailed for its successes. In fact, as one of its many visitors remarked, it was designated as a "house of correction."[9] Walnut Street Prison became known as a model of what reformers discussed as the "Pennsylvania system," and soon after its 1790 expansion and reorganization, a steady stream of public reports pronounced its achievements. Caleb Lownes's 1794 "Address of the Grand Jury," published in several newspapers, commended the prison for its "humane and beneficial improvements" (*Independent Gazetteer*). Walnut Street Prison's leading advocate, Lownes declared:

> The system adopted for the treatment of those who are confined at hard labor seems as perfect as could be expected, and that the beneficial effects of it are very apparent. It must afford great satisfaction to the court and to our citizens to learn that much attention is paid to the cleanliness, health, and morals of the prisoners. (*Independent Gazetteer*)

Extolling the prison's "mild system of criminal treatment," he further noted that "the effects of this system in preventing the commission of gross crimes formerly so frequent in this city, are so strikingly obvious that no one can overlook them" (*Independent Gazetteer*).[10]

That same year Lownes also published *An Account of the Alteration and Present State of the Penal Laws of Pennsylvania*, a brief twenty-page narrative that similarly promoted Walnut Street Prison's ameliorations.[11] After describing how the "new system" rewarded good behavior with pardons and punished bad behavior with severe isolation in solitary confinement, and thus that the prisoners' "treatment would depend on their conduct," Lownes declared: "A change of conduct was early visible. They [the prisoners] were encouraged to labour, and a number were employed . . . Their good conduct was remarked. Many were pardoned, and before one year expired, their behavior was, almost without exception, decent, orderly and respectful" (11). Further on, Lownes commented that Walnut Street Prison was so successful in rehabilitating and reforming that "out of 200 persons who at different times have been recommended to, and pardoned by the governor, only four have been returned" (19). Although he added that "old offenders . . . would not long behave as honest citizens," he declared that Philadelphia was safe from such unredeemable criminals, that "they have chosen to run the risk of being hanged in other states, rather than encounter the certainty of being confined in the penitentiary cells" of Walnut Street Prison (19). Lownes then concluded his commentary with a rather rosy picture of civic tranquility in the City of Brotherly Love:

> Our streets now meet with no interruption from those characters that formerly rendered it dangerous to walk out of an evening. Our roads in the vicinity of the city, so constantly infested with robbers, are seldom disturbed by those dangerous characters . . . . Our houses, stores, and vessels, so perpetually disturbed and robbed, no longer experience those alarming evils. We lay down in peace—we sleep in security. (19)

Two years later in 1796, the French nobleman and writer, Francois Alexandre Frederic duc de La Rochefoucault Liancourt, came to the United States to visit the Walnut Street Prison, and in the account he subsequently published, *On the Prisons of Philadelphia* (1796), he similarly praised the institution's successes. Published in both French and English editions in Philadelphia, the account described the efforts of Lownes and the Philadelphia Society for Alleviating the Miseries of Public Prisons as the "respectable work of reason and humanity" (22). With its system of rewards (pardons) and punishments (solitary confinement), its rigid regulations and schedules, and its use of hard labor, Walnut Street Prison had overcome the corruptions and failures of the past; "harshness and injustice," La Rochefoucault Liancourt intoned, "have been happily banished from the goal of Philadelphia" (29). "The result of this experiment," he concluded, is "that many persons formerly lost to society are restored to it, become useful members of the community, and bring back into it those habits of labour and industry, which in every quarter of the globe are the most certain and powerful preservatives against wickedness and crimes" (30). With the help of such "able and zealous advocates" like Rush and Lownes, Walnut Street Prison had furthered "the cause of humanity" by the "almost entire abolition of the punishment of death" and by "the substitution of a system of reason and justice, to that of bonds, ill-treatment, and arbitrary punishment" (33).

An American visitor, Robert Turnbull, similarly offered an equally enthusiastic account in his narrative, *A Visit to the Philadelphia Prison* (1796):

> I declare . . . that never before did I visit a place which gave me so much satisfaction . . . in which industry and her almost inseparable companions, good order and contentment, appeared to have so firm a hold . . . in a word, the whole presenting one picturesque scene of humanity, justice, benevolence[,] and gratitude.[12]

To express his sense of admiration, Turnbull labeled Walnut Street Prison as a "WONDER of the world," likening it to Egyptian pyramids and Babylonian gardens (4).

II.

When she first came to be incarcerated in Walnut Street Prison a decade later in 1816, Carson—a reckless and defiant woman on a relentless downward spiral—complained that the prison was an altogether unpicturesque scene of inhumanity, injustice, and malevolence, and the only wonder she contemplated was the cruelty and corruption of her keepers. Yet, there was one thing that she and all penal reformers agreed on: solitary confinement was oppressive punishment. Originating in the Quaker emphasis on inner reflection, solitary confinement was justified as a means of leading prisoners to regret and self-reproach. Solitude was believed to be salutary because a prisoner so inexorably isolated would be forced to confront the indignant reproaches of his or her awakened conscience. In an inhospitable environment of total deprivation, prisoners would be compelled to recognize their iniquity; following a conventional pattern of conversion, this recognition would then lead to a desire to reform.

In describing this innovation of penal reform, La Rochefoucault Liancourt asserted: "In this situation [of extreme isolation], separated from every other individual, given up to solitude, to self-reflexion, and to remorse, he can only communicate with himself. He sees the turn-key but once a day" (10). While experiencing such "total separation from every other human being," a prisoner "may be induced to turn his thoughts sooner upon himself, and upon those transgressions, the bitter punishment of which he is undergoing" (11). In a similar observation, Turnbull commented that the effect of solitary confinement irrevocably led individuals to self-knowledge:

> There is not perhaps a physical cause, which has so powerful an influence on the moral faculty [than solitary confinement]; inasmuch as it is the only one which can give a friendly communication with the heart. We become by it gradually acquainted with a true knowledge of ourselves. (58)

Despite its supposed benefits, solitary confinement was nevertheless perceived to be severely punitive. Even the most zealous promoters of the Pennsylvania system believed that it was relentless punishment. For a nonspecific period of time, prisoners were placed in a six-by-eight-foot cell without any furniture other than a mattress, or sometimes simply a plank. They were fed only once a day in the morning, a meal of bread and water, and even this meager portion was denied them during the first two days of their solitary confinement. As Jodi Schorb's essay reminds us, prisoners were generally not allowed books other than the Bible, or any other diversions; nor were they allowed any form of communication, not even with the guards. Such harsh treatment was used not only to crush recalcitrance and promote reformation but also to punish prisoners who were disobedient or disruptive. "Solitary confinement is the only punishment known in the goal," La Rochefoucault Liancourt noted. "The goaler and turn-keys are without arms, without dogs; they are even forbidden to carry sticks, lest in a moment of passion they should strike a prisoner, and break in upon that system of tranquility and impartial justice, from which is expected so much benefit" (19). When considering the effectiveness of being isolated for extended periods of time, he also observed that prisoners reacted "with horror" at the prospect of being sent to Walnut Street's solitary cells, and he related one example when a prisoner preferred execution over isolation. He concluded that solitary confinement was "the most dreadful of all punishments" (27, 29). Lownes was equally blunt, stating that solitary confinement was far more "intolerable, than a sharp, but momentary punishment" (19). The anticipation of such unrelenting deprivation, he believed, acted as a real deterrent for the prisoners: "These cells are an object of *real terror* to them all" (19).

Ironically, when she was taken from the Harrisburg jail and sent back to Philadelphia to be incarcerated in the Walnut Street Prison in the late summer of 1816, Carson requested, even demanded, solitary confinement. At least at first, the terror of isolation seemed more preferable to her than the prospect of being housed with vagrants. Although indicative of her desire to cling to the shreds of her genteel respectability, Carson's preference for solitary confinement also suggests something of Walnut Street Prison's deteriorated conditions. In just one decade since La Rochefoucault Liancourt and Turnbull offered their glowing accounts, the prison had succumbed to the exigencies of Pennsylvania's overstrained penal system. In a remarkably short period of time, the dreams of Rush and Lownes for rehabilitating convicted criminals had been crushed under the unremitting weight of overpopulation.

Although at first allowed to remain in the sickroom, Carson was soon "ordered by one of the inspectors to remove to number seven," one of the ten twenty-by-thirty-foot open rooms in the women's west wing (1:222). In her narrative, she vividly described the scene inside: "This was a room occupied by the lowest vagrants, in which were about twenty-eight or thirty persons at that time confined, and not more than twelve feet square[,] alive with vermin" (1:222).[13] Carson refused to move, and when she was soon approached "by several of the board of inspectors," she "repeated my resolution of not going among the vagabonds" (1:223). Although the inspectors "remonstrated and urged my compliance," Carson later wrote: "I was firm in my determination not to submit, but said I would willingly go to the cells, as I would rather be alone than in such infamous company" (1:223). Even after one of the inspectors reminded her that "those apartments are places of punishment," she still obstinately persisted in her refusal. When the common cells were being locked down for the night, Carson was asked one last time if she was refusing to go to number seven: "I replied in the affirmative, observing such was my choice" (1:223).

There are several issues apparent in Carson's choice. No doubt she was trying to maintain her notions of class and social order. Number seven was not only filled with people she considered homeless transients far beneath her middle-class status, but in all probability the cell was racially mixed with whites and African Americans. Attempting to maintain her fading social position, Carson refused to mix with those she considered beneath her. Yet, the numbers must have been as overwhelming as the mixture. When he visited in 1796, La Rochefoucault Liancourt observed that "the number of female convicts is generally about five or six" (20). In the decade between his visit and Carson's incarceration, this modest number had multiplied several times over, and inevitably such overcrowding had led to breakdowns in the organization and order that were so important to prison reformers. Rather than a well-managed system of discipline and order that promoted new behavior, Walnut Street Prison had collapsed into disorder.

By the time Carson was taken to Walnut Street Prison in 1816 to await her trials, first as an accessory to murder and then more than half a year later for conspiracy to kidnap, the inmate population had exploded. In his study of Philadelphia's prisons and penal system, *Laboratories of Virtue*, Michael Meranze describes Walnut Street Prison's breakdown:

> By the late 1810s, overcrowding, combined with the prison's structural problems, helped to cause a general collapse of prison order. From 1815 onward, the inspectors' Minutes were filled with a litany of discouragement and failure. The prison order, never fully stable, dissolved. The end result was disease, violence, riot, and death. (219)[14]

Far from the "house of correction" that La Rochefoucault Liancourt had described in 1796, the prison had become, in Meranze's words, a "school of depravity, and a nursery for vice" (223).

Carson quickly discovered that solitary confinement was a poor choice. In later describing her first stay in the cells, she remarked: "I remained a close prisoner within this noisome abode for nearly two weeks." She later wrote, "When my health beginning gradually to decline, owing to the putrid atmosphere I inhaled" (1:227). Then, in a long parenthetical explanation, she added:

> (The cells being injudiciously constructed over the common sewer, from which there is flue leading to each apartment, that at once accounts for the numerous deaths and ruined constitutions of the unfortunate inhabitants of the penitentiary, who, for the most trifling fault, are hurried into these abominable receptacles for thirty, sixty, and ninety days, with one miserable blanket for their covering, and an allowance of three ounces of brown bread for twenty-four hours.) (1: 227)

Although a fair account of solitary confinement, Carson's description introduces two serious problems that she, writing later as the narrator, frequently alluded to in the narrations of her incarcerations. These were problems that the reformers had specifically wanted to eliminate: the prevalence of filth and disease and the prevalence of corruption.

Prior to the reforms of the 1790s, prisoners had not been segregated according to age and crime, and they were generally allowed to occupy themselves however they pleased, which often resulted in remarkably high rates of intoxication and dissipation. Jailers were not paid annual salaries but collected various fees from the prisoners and their families, an "injurious custom" that, according to Lownes, resulted in a "variety of evil consequences" (6). To supplement their income, jailers sold liquor to the prisoners, a practice that—as Meranze has also demonstrated—resulted in "great irregularities an[d] even outrages" (179). The penal reforms that had brought solitary confinement cells to Walnut Street had been intended not only to promote order and hygiene but also to eliminate corruption. In his 1794 "Address of the Grand Jury," Lownes noted "that the success of all punishment by hard labour and solitary confinement, must finally depend upon the wisdom of the regulations . . . and upon the prudence and attention of those to whom the management of the prisoners are committed" (*Independent Gazetteer*). Thus the success of Walnut Street Prison depended on the quality and integrity of its jailers and inspectors, who had to manifest good judgment and restraint in dealing with the prisoners. In his rhapsodic account of the prison's order, Turnbull commented:

> Under the present discipline, prisoners are not governed by beatings, irons, or any capricious constraints of the turnkeys. Convicts, vagabonds, persons accused, unruly or runaway apprentices or servants, are not now intermingled and heaped together. Lenity has superceded the abuse of power; cleanliness and comfort take the place of filth and misery. Hence [there are] not as many diseases, quarrels, or escapes. (60–61)

Had Turnbull made his visit two years later in 1798, after a devastating outbreak of yellow fever and an arson fire that destroyed much of the prison's manufactory, he might not have been so effusive in describing Walnut Street Prison's successes. Certainly Carson found considerable filth and misery in 1816, and—as a self-designated "victim of oppression"—she described constant abuses of power.

III.

In the final section of the original 1822 narrative, Carson indicted Walnut Street Prison for a continual series of abuses and corruptions. At least in part, it was her desire to seek revenge by publicly exposing those who mistreated her that led her to seek Mary Clarke's help in producing a narrative of her life.

In October 1820, Carson was arrested as an accessory to a robbery committed by her lover, Charles Mitchell. Then in January 1821, she was convicted and sentenced to two years in the Walnut Street Prison, where she spent eleven months before her sentence was reversed on January 14, 1822. According to the narrator Carson, she was innocent and unjustly convicted because of what she termed a "fatal scroll" (2:59), a note to Mitchell that she had inserted into half a pound of butter but that had been discovered by one of the prison jailers. Regardless of Carson the historical figure's innocence or guilt, Carson the narrator was particularly scathing in her indictment of her conviction and subsequent imprisonment. Satirically referring to Walnut Street Prison's renown, she introduced her final section by clearly announcing her authorial intention to indict: "I will now conclude with an account of my sufferings while I remained there [Walnut Street Prison], having gone over the persecutions I endured previous this mock trial . . . and enter on the horrors of the far-famed penitentiary of Philadelphia, to which, as a convict, I was for the first time conducted" (2:63). To emphasize the horrific nature of the prison and the satiric pretense of its fame, Carson immediately described the penitentiary as "this abode of vice, misery, and tyranny" (2:63). A couple of pages later, while commenting on "the general situation of the interior of this penitentiary," she again used obvious satire when she commented that the prison was "celebrated for its *humanity*, and the *wisdom* manifested in its regulations" (2:66). Such ironic juxtapositions and contradictions not only mark the narrator's rhetorical position as a textual adjudicator and arbiter but also her intention to expose the disparity between the prison's prominence as a "house of correction" and its actual conditions as a "school of depravity."

Knowledge of this disparity, however, was already circulating in the public sphere. A year before Carson was taken to the penitentiary, in March 1820, a riot, perhaps racially motivated, broke out in Walnut Street Prison. According to the newspaper accounts, the riot resulted in a "general insurrection," and prison officials responded by calling in the aid of armed civilians and the local militia to put down the revolt. In his evaluation of the insurrection and its aftermath, Meranze concludes that "the riot shattered the prison's public image" (219). By the time Carson was marched through the prison's doors a year later, and certainly by the time she collaborated with Clarke two years later in 1822, Philadelphians would already have had some knowledge that the prison was now no longer the "picturesque scene of humanity, justice, benevolence, and gratitude" that it was once purported to be. Carson was not so much divulging the prison's problems as she was dramatizing them. Her narrative intent was not to inform readers as it was to manipulate them by exploiting a public perception they already shared. Carson, at least the character created by the historical figure and her collaborator, played to her audience.

As a narration, Carson's description of her eleven-month imprisonment in Walnut Street Prison is structured as a series of confrontations depicted as struggles for liberty. As both a daughter and a wife of Revolutionary naval officers, she depicted herself in battles with corrupt and tyrannical jailers who were intent on denying her the most basic of human rights. Referring to the Walnut Street Prison as the "*American Bastille*" was only one of many references used to add ideological heft to the narrator's descriptions. Although incarcerated in a penal institution purposely created to deny liberty to convicted malefactors, Carson, ever bold and headstrong, nevertheless confronted her keepers and inspectors over what she considered should be her liberties while in prison and then later framed her descriptions of these skirmishes as clashes over liberty. When she first entered the west wing, Carson was overcome with the sight:

> I . . . walked into the women's hall, where the sight of fifty miserable wretches, of all colors and ages, spinning, clothed in the convict apparel, so shocked me that my fortitude evaporated . . . the idea that I too would make one of this delectable group so oppressed my heart that, had not a flood of tears relieved me, I really think it would have at that instant burst. (2:64)

This melodramatic bursting of her heart, quickly followed by a "paroxysm of rage," was only assuaged by her desire "to breathe the air of liberty." To indicate the powerful effect of this hope, she added: "this reflection soothed the stormy passion of despair, which fled before the calmness of reason" (2:65). Similarly, when reflecting back on her imprisonment, Carson stated that, "though I sometimes wept my fate, yet the tears were not embittered by severity from the inspectors or keepers, who, generally appreciating my services [as a seamstress] issued but few commands, leaving me to the impulses of my free will, generously giving me this semblance of liberty" (2:67). Like the dream of breathing the "air of liberty" that calmed the "stormy passion of despair," here the ironic guise of liberty is enough to create what the narrator described as her "comparative tranquility," allowing her to be "generally serene, and sometimes gay" (2:67–68).[15]

Yet, whenever her "semblance of liberty" collapsed under the severity of her surroundings, Carson lost not only her "comparative tranquility" but also the most basic elements of personal freedom. For her infractions and refusals, she was sent several times into solitary confinement. Although such confinement was clearly announced as punishment for violations of prison order, she carefully portrayed the scenes of her confinements in language filled with emblematic references readers would have recognized and responded to.

The first of such battles against tyranny, and the most carefully crafted, was over Carson's refusing to attend the general Sunday worship service. As she later described it, Carson refused to attend because the "smoky hall" hurt her eyes and because she preferred her own form of individual worship rather than the "social worship," which was characterized by pretension and hypocrisy. In stating her reasons, she declared that, rather than listen to the prayers and exhortations of "Mr. Manning, the tinman or tinker, with other preachers of the Methodist persuasion," she absented herself

> not from disrespect to either my Creator or his ministers, but to save myself from idle curiosity, rest from labour, and to reflect at leisure — not feeling any disposition to unite with the wretches surrounding me . . . [and] considering religion as a pure aspiration of the heart, which was as acceptable at the throne of grace rising from a cell or dungeon, as a cathedral. . . . In addition to these reasons, I was disgusted by the hypocrisy of the blacks, who formed a large majority of our female republic. (2:68)

Although her racial and class prejudices are clearly apparent — prejudices that would have been generally shared by her readers — Carson defended her absence from the mandatory worship services as an expression of her freedom of religion, one of the then most celebrated

Constitutional rights. Although bitterly sardonic, particularly in view of her reference to the "wretches" around her, the allusion she made to her "female republic" was not casual.

This notion of a republican order (in which the citizens were sovereign) was immediately shattered in the narrator's next paragraph. On a particular "sultry Sunday in July," when Carson stated she was quietly reading "a very interesting work on the divinity of Christ" in the upper hall, she was peremptorily ordered to attend the required worship service in the lower hall. Stung by the jailer's "loud imperious tone," Carson stated: "it [his command] sensibly wounded my feelings, and occasioned a momentary irritation of temper" (2:69). Searching for redress, she went looking for Mr. Palmer, one of the inspectors, who—according to the narrator—was not only revered as a "guardian spirit" but also as a "harbinger of liberty" (2:68). Instead of finding her kindhearted jailer, Carson encountered a tyrant:

> But instead of meeting the protecting spirit I was in search of, I encountered the *Nero* of the institution, of whom I inquired, did the regulations of that house enjoin all persons to attend the divine service as performed there? (I well knowing that liberty of conscience was one of the privileges our national constitution held out to its citizens, to purchase which the blood of thousands had been shed, and my own family material sufferers. (2:69)

By referring to patriotic sacrifices on both national and familial levels, Carson—if the scene is to be believed—attempted to assert "liberty of conscience" as her rightful inheritance. Moreover, by referring to her antagonist as Rome's most notorious tyrant, a man popularly known for cruel and corrupt excess, guilty even of murdering his own mother, she foreshadowed the despotic denial of this inheritance and as well her eventual martyrdom.

In describing her tyrant's dispassionate rebuff, she stated: "Instead of giving me a direct answer, he waved his hand with the haughty air of a West India planter to his slave, and in a majesterial tone answered, 'Madam, 'tis my order that *you* go'" (2:69). Depicting herself as liberty's advocate, Carson repeated her question, and again received the same imperious response, to which she rejoined: "I then observed that I had no idea of people being thus compelled to worship in a form different from the religion they were brought up too [*sic*], and walked away"

(2:70). Provoked by her comments and defiance, Carson's autocrat responded in "the most inveterate rage," exclaiming, "Away with her, put her to the cells" (2:70).

As a narrator, Carson responded to her punishment (solitary confinement) by confining this unnamed inspector in a rhetorical cell of her own rendition. This Nero of Walnut Street Prison, who had treated her with—as she described—the callous disdain of a planter to a slave, was not only castigated but also convicted and condemned in a language of hyperbole and invective. In attempting to gain retribution in the public sphere, Carson declared that

> without deviating from the truth, [he was] the principal, most malicious and inveterate tormentor and instrument of torture in this inquisition, for he was not restrained by the humanity of some of the inspectors . . . hundreds would fall victims to his diabolical propensities to torment his fellow man. (2:70)

Rich in its references, this passage places Carson's inhumane adversary both in the context of the Spanish Inquisition, a rhetorical confinement that exploited the anti-Catholic prejudices of many early national readers, and in hell itself. Inversely, by arraigning her adversary's devilish inhumanity, Carson portrayed herself as a martyr for truth and true faith.

Drawing out the scene's antithetical melodrama of good and evil, the narrator continued to utilize a rhetoric of heartless excess. In addition to condemning the inspector, Carson also was equally severe in describing the turnkey who came to take her away. Again referencing the inhumanity of her antagonists, she stated: "This pusillanimous old man has so long sacrificed humanity to interest, that he may justly be called an automaton, moved at the pleasure of the inspectors, to whom he is a fawning sycophant" (2:70). As a machine rather than a man, the jailer was without conscious thought, and certainly without conscience, and thus the perfect functionary to a devil. Mixing her metaphors, Carson also recalled a specific scene, real or imagined, when the jailer had dragged "a delicate female, but half dressed, down a flight of stairs and through a hall . . . for a frivolous offence" (2:71). After witnessing this "horrid sight," she stated that she shrank back "appalled, and fancy delineated him as a savage of the forest dragging its prey to the den to satiate its rapacious appetite" (2:71). Carson's depictions of devil, machine, and beast contradicted Walnut Street Prison's reputation as an enlightened penal institution that advanced the "cause of humanity." Rather than reason and order, the penitentiary was filled with the chaos and torments of hell.

Such a state of damnation was clearly—according to the narrator—un-American. After setting off for solitary confinement, Carson, still defiant, stated: "I trusted I should one day find redress for this oppression from the laws of my country, and equity from my fellowcitizens, [and] once more entered this noisome abode, better calculated for a Turkish prison than one in a mild republican government" (2:71). Viewing Walnut Street Prison through the distorting prism of a Turkish *bagnio*—an institution popularly depicted as a place of idolatrous brutality, where white Christians were tormented by dark-skinned Muslims—Carson's reference alluded to the irrational inconsistency between her punishment in solitary confinement and the liberal ideology of the early republic that led to the penitentiary's creation. To underscore this ironic contradiction, she focused on the prison's misplacement in a nation that privileged both political and personal freedom. After declaring that the cells—due to the presence of African American prisoners and the "effluvia from the common sewers"—were filled with "a complication of stenches sufficient to create infectious and malignant distempers," Carson stated:

> Let those who so pathetically paint the horrors of Dartmouth prison, or Algerine captivity, wander not so far from home, for trust me the cells of the Philadelphia penitentiary equals, nay, exceeds them all. I have read accounts of slavery and imprisonment, but none ever said they were left two days without food. (2:71)

Like her reference to "Turkish prisons," Carson declared that Walnut Street Prison surpassed even the most horrific places of incarceration, at least those perceived in the popular imagination. Righteously indignant, she referred to the institutional practice of withholding food from inmates in solitary confinement during the first two days to make them more compliant as a torment crueler than any endured by slaves. Here, the contrast between a slave and a citizen would again have been obvious. Moreover, most readers would have immediately seized on the disagreeable connotations her references invoked. Dartmoor Prison (mistakenly referred to in the quotation as "Dartmouth"), where captured American sailors were imprisoned during the War of 1812, and where—after the war had ended—a group of guards opened fire on American prisoners at the order of a drunken British officer, was infamous.[16] Equally notorious in the popular imagination was the capture and enslavement of Americans by Barbary Coast pirates.[17] That both England and the Barbary Coast city-states were at war with the United States heightened the irrationality of the "oppression" committed against her by her fellow citizens.

Carson's long description of this particular stay in solitary confinement culminated in a final appeal to the republican ideology of her readers. After receiving her first food following the mandatory forty-eight-hour fast, Carson "gazed on this morsel of brown bread" and—at least in the narrative—exclaimed:

> God of Heaven . . . is this the land of *liberty*, where tyranny stalks abroad unmasked and unquestioned? Is this the freedom my forefathers and husbands fought for, when daughters of Columbia perish by the hand of cruelty and oppression. . . . Oh! Suffer me but to survive this oppression . . . and I will avenge the cause of many that, perhaps, have met their fate in this mansion of horror, and unknown, unpitied, sunk to an early grave.
> (2:73)

Though disingenuous, Carson's patriotic appeal was used not only to shame readers into confronting the contradiction of denying liberty to citizens in a "land of *liberty*" but also to position herself as liberty's advocate. Similar to her first 1816 stay in solitary confinement, the narrator, while calling on God for vengeance, was clearly more interested in her own actions and advocacy. Although some readers surely would have been amused by her irreverent inattention to the continual and sensational violations that brought about her punishments, many would also have been sympathetically touched by her constant references to cruelty and slavery. To assert her heroic selflessness, and obviously to nudge readers further into sympathy, Carson concluded the scene by stating: "I divided my allowance and gave one half to a starved prisoner in the adjoining cell" (2:73).

As coauthor, Carson clearly wanted to arouse reader sympathy, and to achieve this effect she and Clarke carefully chose their words, and with equal care they crafted their narrator. Using language certain to evoke pointed and indignant reactions, the narrator draped herself in the garb of a patriotic and righteous heroine struggling to fight against injustice. With Clarke's help, Carson transcribed her eleven-month stay in 1821 as a series of uprisings that depicted the narrator/character heroically and compassionately defending not only liberty but also humanity. In addition to the long "liberty of conscience" scene, Carson narrated revolts when she surreptitiously ordered oysters to please a dying inmate's request and when she made gingerbread cookies. Describing this latter rebellion, she satirically stated: "My next offence was preparing a few short-cakes and gingerbread for suffering invalids, which heinous crime was punished by reducing our allowance of molasses and flour" (2:76).

This use of satire to emphasize the ludicrous discrepancy between the benevolence of her actions and the malevolence of her jailers' reactions was particularly apparent in her last rebellion. In order to position readers to perceive this discrepancy, she stated: "My third, last, and most unpardonable crime, was equally in favor of one of these unhappy sufferers" (2:76 [misnumbered 73; hereafter mn73]). In her capacity as nurse of the sickroom, Carson tried to help an inmate clearly addicted to opium, "which she had ever been permitted the use of until the doctor thought proper to withhold her usual allowance" (mn73). The doctor's cold-turkey refusal resulted in the inmate becoming both sick and hysterical: "she became so dangerously ill, that I feared she would expire, while her feeble voice tortured my heart by continually entreating me, for God's sake, to procure her the medicine" (mn73). Not only did the woman entreat Carson to take action in the name of God, but also on behalf of the human race: "she fell on her knees, pathetically entreating me, for humanity['s] sake, to obtain her an opiate" (mn73). In answer to the woman's pathetic supplication, Carson circumvented the doctor's denial by beseeching one of the inspectors, who indeed helped her procure "a small portion of laudanum" (mn73). According to Carson, "the apothecary inadvertently filled the phial," and she secreted half of the dose, supposedly so to keep the ailing woman from demanding the whole quantity. When the doctor returned he demanded the remaining laudanum, and—as she narrated—"I presented him with the part I intended for immediate use" (mn73). When the doctor later learned that Carson had withheld some of the opium, he immediately ordered her into solitary confinement. Using her usual melodramatic rhetoric, Carson declared:

> Thus was I, in the depth of a cold winter, removed from a warm room and comfortable bed to a damp, dreary cell, slightly warmed by a stove in the passage, the plank my bed, a blanket my covering; yet what was my crime? An act of humanity, for which a recording angel will drop a tear on many a future error of my life, and blot it from the book of fate. (mn74)

Ironically, a close reading of the Carson narrative might deconstruct the narrator's grandiloquent declaration that she acted on behalf of humanity. On at least two occasions, Carson described her own opium overindulgences, the first during the week after her second husband shot her first husband, and the second during her first stay in solitary confinement. This latter incident was an overdose serious enough to scare the Walnut Street Prison jailers into calling in a nurse to give Carson an emetic, purging her, and resulted in a rumor circulating that she had tried to commit suicide. Though not an addict, Carson certainly did not hesitate to use opium as an escape.

Yet there are deeper levels of irony in Carson's self-depiction as humanity's champion. Unquestionably, she was not fond of the humanity that surrounded her in prison. Several of her uprisings, in fact, involved her attempts to distance herself from the other inmates, particularly the African Americans toward whom she expressed the most rampant and virulent forms of racism. She described these people as being "generally the lowest grades of society, scarce one removed from Hottentots" (2:65). Although she claimed that she "undertook to civilize" her fellow inmates, she added: "Many of them hated me for the care I manifested for them" (2:66). Clutching at her lost status, Carson attempted to maintain her particular grade of society by expressing racial bigotry. Rather than identify with those around her, she struggled to distance herself from them, and in her narration she used racism as a ploy to identify with her white readers. Rather than expressing her regard for those around her, her repeated use of the catchphrase, "act of humanity," was both an appeal for reader sympathy and a means of reinforcing her self-characterization as a heroine.

Moreover, her appeal for the cleansing tears from a recording angel is equally specious, particularly when viewed as an appeal for remission from future—rather than past—errors. Carson might well have desired angelic intervention, but she—as coauthor of her own story—also worked diligently to complete a more temporal, and textual, absolution. With considerable help from Mary Clarke, Carson acted as her own recording angel, blotting out her own errors with carefully selected catchwords. In various forms and contexts, words weighted with ideological allusion—particularly words like liberty, slavery, oppression, tyranny, and humanity—were continually repeated in a relentless rhetorical chorus.

Such positioning was indeed revolutionary, not because Carson was a champion of liberty and human rights, but because she used writing to defy and subvert both criminal conviction and popular opinion. Refusing to accept the labels attached to her in court and in the street, she—with Clarke's collaborative support—disseminated her own lexicon, exploiting a linguistic legerdemain of connotations and invocations. As Bakhtin and others have argued, language is an arena of contest where individuals struggle to appropriate words for their own use; words and meanings are continually being grasped and then lost, taken, and retaken.[18] As a narrator and character, the Carson in the narrative constantly appropriated words for her own use, words that often were at ironic variance with her settings and situations. Nevertheless, Carson used them to identify herself as belonging to the community of her readers. As Bakhtin and his followers have further argued, language has a profound community-building function. Communal identities are shaped through the subtle inflections created by a mosaic of distinct social, regional, professional, and political contexts. As a narrator, Carson, though decidedly a woman of uncommon experience, appropriated language to create a common ground of perspectives and prejudices to embrace her readers. Rather than criminal acts, she urged readers to infer her various exploits as acts of heroic humanity by rhetorically manipulating their contexts with melodramatic descriptions and by portraying herself in the shape of a fictional heroine. With Clarke's collaboration, Carson—the historical figure—made use of writing and publication in the public sphere in order to secure both personal and financial equity from her fellow citizens, who generally were by no means inclined to provide either.

IV.

Was she successful in her revolution? Were readers carried away by her catchwords and catchphrases, her grandiloquent descriptions, and her indignant appeals? Yes and no. For a short time after the 1822 publication of the *History*, Carson was surprisingly successful in securing the different forms of equity she wanted from her fellow citizens. The sensational book sold quite well during the first month after its appearance, and—according to Clarke's later description—public opinion indeed began in her favor. But Carson's collaboration with Clarke immediately broke down after the *History*'s publication, and in a series of scandals and outrages Carson lost the sympathy—and indulgence—that she had gained in the public sphere. Taking 250 copies of the *History*, Carson traveled to New York City, where she sold the books to a "Mr. Wiley, a bookseller in Wall St.," and with the profits bought $1,100 in counterfeit bank notes (2:105). On returning to Philadelphia with "this valuable cargo," she and Clarke quarreled over the spurious notes, and she then absconded, taking Clarke's furniture and clothing along with her counterfeit money. Within months, Carson was arrested for passing a counterfeit five-dollar note, and after the sensational spectacle of a public trial, was returned to Walnut Street Prison in July 1823. The scandalous public narrative reignited with a vengeance, adding counterfeiter to the familiar list of popular labels: adulterer, murderer, prostitute, and thief.

Sadly, less than a year later, Carson died of complications resulting from a severe beating and typhoid fever; she was only thirty-nine years old. In a final irony, the public learned that the two women who had savagely attacked Carson were two of her former counterfeiting conspirators. While forging Stephen Girard's signature on notes drawn from his Philadelphia bank, Carson had misspelled his name, igniting the brawl that would leave her badly beaten and nearly unconscious. Delivered to the women's sickroom, Carson was—according to Clarke—intentionally placed in a bed recently vacated by an inmate who had just died of typhoid fever by another one of her former conspirators. Although she had embraced writing as a means of redemption, Carson's poor spelling paradoxically contributed to her death.[19]

Yet, in a remarkable resurrection, her story reappeared long after her demise. Sixteen years later, in need of her own equity, Clarke republished the Carson narrative under her own name as *The Memoirs of the Celebrated and Beautiful Mrs. Ann Carson . . . Whose Life Terminated in the Philadelphia Prison . . . Revised, Enlarged, and Continued Till Her Death by Mrs. M. Clarke . . . in Two Volumes* (1838).[20] Declaring that she never received her "pecuniary part resulting from the sale" of the first edition, Clarke stepped forward to stake proprietary claim of the Carson narrative with a copyright in her name, not only republishing the *History* as volume one but also adding a second volume as a metanarrative commenting on the original's publication (1:v). While offering truly unique glimpses into early antebellum print culture, the second volume also traces Carson's final misadventures, which Clarke characterized as "a career of vice and low, vulgar dissipation" (2:134).

Comparing the two volumes provides a study in contrasts. In 1822 Carson and Clarke had collaborated to create a narrative voice intended to minimize the historical figure's culpability and maximize her public equity, but when Clarke reappropriated the narrative sixteen years later for her own use, superimposing her narration over Carson's narrative voice, she accentuated the scandalous self as much, if not more, than the victimized self who had been melodramatically presented to readers in the 1822 volume as the "victim of oppression." Seeking her own profits from writing, Clarke promoted what the original edition had tried to suppress. Most of the second volume was narrated through Clarke's voice and perspective, effectively silencing Carson.

In telling her story, Carson constructed a rhetorical platform from which she could repudiate the altogether disreputable characterization of her scandalous public narrative, and though Clarke later usurped this stage, the platform remains, and Carson's voice can still be heard. Her narrative, in fact, has long outlasted Walnut Street Prison, which was closed in 1830 and later razed. In her desperation to save her condemned second husband from the gallows, Carson had plotted to blow up the penitentiary, a frantic plot she abandoned in favor of kidnapping Pennsylvania's governor. Yet, ultimately this is exactly what she did, at least textually. The publication of her narrative was an act of subversion. The historical figure not only plotted her life to mitigate her guilt but also plotted to subvert the convictions and institutions that imprisoned her. She—the narrator—acknowledged her guilt, but only in the liminal margins of her self-dramatizations as a champion of liberty and justice. Moreover, she used her text to undermine the most basic foundations of Walnut Street Prison.

Rush, Lownes, and other penal reformers all stressed the necessity of private punishment, of eliminating the carnivalesque public spectacle of whippings and hangings. In order to be most effective, punishment had to take place in a private penal space where those convicted would be most likely to feel remorse. Carson, who expressed little if any remorse, used her text to turn Walnut Street Prison inside out, taking the most private of penal spaces, the cells of solitary confinement, into the public sphere. The narrator wanted a public spectacle, and she needed the inversions of order that resulted from carnivalesque gatherings of people. She used her narrative as a scaffold not only to display her unjust punishments but also as a platform to inflict her own punishments. Using melodramatic and ideologically charged language, she installed readers as her own board of inspectors, granting them a supervisory capacity to censure cruelty and corruption within the prison's walls. By opening up Walnut Street Prison's solitary cells to public view, she contested nearly every point that Lownes and other celebrants had proudly proclaimed. In her narrative, readers perceived that the penitentiary was overcrowded, filthy, unhealthy, disorderly, corrupt, and unprofitable. Although she did not knock down its walls, Carson detonated a devastating rhetorical blast that rocked the penitentiary's partitions of privacy and isolation. Having been branded by a variety of scornful labels, she fully understood that language could imprison. Perhaps she and Clarke also understood that a compelling story would ultimately endure long after brick and mortar crumbled.

NOTES

1. All quotations will be taken from *The Memoirs of the Celebrated and Beautiful Mrs. Ann Carson* (New York: n.p., 1838). The 1838 *Memoirs* was published in two volumes, and volume 1 is essentially a republication of the original Carson/Clarke collaboration, *A History of the Celebrated Mrs. Ann Carson*, which was published in 1822. Sixteen years after the original *History*, Clarke reappropriated and extended Carson's by adding a second volume, describing their writing collaboration and Carson's subsequent criminal activities and her death in Walnut Street Prison. Carson was well acquainted with Walnut Street Prison, having been incarcerated twice in 1816—the first time for a couple of weeks after she was arrested as an accessory for murder in the death of her first husband; and then for several months during the late summer and fall while awaiting trial for conspiracy to kidnap Simon Snyder, governor of Pennsylvania. In 1821 she was again incarcerated in Walnut Street Prison for eleven months after she was convicted as an accessory in a burglary (she was released in January 1822); and finally, for nearly a year from June 1823 to April 1824, she was again incarcerated in Walnut Street Prison after being convicted for counterfeiting. Carson died in the prison. Susan Branson also notes the probability that she was held in the Prune Street apartments, the debtor's section of Walnut Street Prison, sometime between 1812 and 1815. See Susan Branson, *Dangerous to Know: Women, Crime, and Notoriety in the Early Republic* (Philadelphia: University of Pennsylvania Press, 2008), 36.

2. For the best historical information on both Carson and Clarke, and insightful information on their collaboration, see Branson, *Dangerous to Know*.

3. Originally discussed by Habermas, the public sphere has been lucidly discussed by a number of historians and cultural critics. For recent discussions, see Craig Calhoun, ed., *Habermas and the Public Sphere* (Boston: MIT Press, 1993); Joan Landes, *Women and the Public Sphere in the Age of the French Revolution* (Ithaca, N.Y.: Cornell University Press, 1988); Grantland S. Rice, *The Transformation of Authorship in America* (Chicago: University of Chicago Press, 1997); and Michael

Warner, *The Letters of the Republic: Publication and the Public Sphere in Eighteenth-Century America* (Cambridge, Mass.: Harvard University Press, 1990).

4. For the rise of sentimentality and sentimental fiction, see Michelle Burnham, *Captivity and Sentiment: Cultural Exchange in American Literature, 1682–1861* (Hanover, N.H.: University Press of New England, 1997); Cathy N. Davidson, *Revolution and the Word: The Rise of the Novel in America* (New York: Oxford University Press, 1986); Joseph Fichtelberg, *Critical Fictions: Sentiment and the American Market, 1780–1870* (Athens: University of Georgia Press, 2003); Julia A. Stern, *The Plight of Feeling: Sympathy and Dissent in the Early American Novel* (Chicago: University of Chicago Press, 1997); and Jane Tompkins, *Sensational Designs: The Cultural Work of American Fiction, 1790–1860* (New York: Oxford University Press, 1985).

5. According to Branson, marriage at the age of fifteen was unusual for the time (*Dangerous to Know*, 142). For information concerning Philadelphia's demographics, see Susan E. Klepp, *Philadelphia in Transition: A Demographic History of the City and Its Occupational Groups, 1642–1859* (New York: Garland, 1989). For information concerning the history of marriage, see Nancy F. Cott, *Public Vows: A History of Marriage and the Nation* (Cambridge, Mass.: Harvard University Press, 2000).

6. For the published accounts of the murder, trial, and execution, see *Account of the Execution of Lieutenant R. Smith for the Murder of Capt. J. Carson* (Philadelphia: n.p., 1816); *An Account of the Murder of Capt. J. Carson, by Lieut. R. Smith, Late of the United States Army* (Philadelphia: n.p., 1816); A. L., *A Biographical Sketch of the Late Captain John Carson, Who Was Shot by Richard Smith, Late a Lieutenant in the United States Army, on the 20th January, and Who Died on the 4th February, 1816* (Philadelphia: published at No. 220 Market Street, 1816); *Confession and Repentance of Lieutenant R. Smith, Who Is Under Sentence of Death for the Murder of Captain John Carson, and Will Be Executed in a Few Days, in This City* (Philadelphia: n.p., 1816); *The Horrid Murder of John Carson, Committed by Richard Smith. The Judge's Charge to the Jury* (Philadelphia: n.p., 1816); *Interesting Trial! The Commonwealth of Pennsylvania vs. Lieutenant Richard Smith, Charged with the Late Murder of Captain John Carson, at Philadelphia* (Boston: Nathaniel Coverly, 1816); and *Trials of Richard Smith . . . and Ann Carson, alias Ann Smith . . . for the Murder of Captain John Carson* (Philadelphia: Thomas Desilver, 1816). In all of these publications Carson was depicted as being culpable; several went further in their depictions and cast her as an evil agent.

7. For the best discussions of Walnut Street Prison, see Michael Meranze, *Laboratories of Virtue: Punishment, Revolution, and Authority in Philadelphia, 1760–1835* (Chapel Hill: University of North Carolina Press, 1996). Subsequent references cited parenthetically in the text. Although dated, Negley K. Teeters's work has much useful information: *The Cradle of the Penitentiary: The Walnut Street Jail at Philadelphia, 1773–1835* (Philadelphia: Pennsylvania Prison Society, 1955).

8. Michel Foucault forcefully makes this point throughout his *Discipline and Punish: The Birth of the Prison*, trans. Alan Sheridan (New York: Pantheon Books, 1977).

9. Francois Alexandre Frederic duc de La Rochefoucault Liancourt, *On the Prisons of Philadelphia* (Philadelphia: Moreau de Saint-Mery, 1796), 15. Subsequent references cited parenthetically in the text.

10. One of the leading advocates for penal reform and a member of the penitentiary's board of inspectors during the 1790s, Caleb Lownes is a central figure in Walnut Street Prison's early history. Lownes, "Address of the Grand Jury, to the Mayor, Recorder and Aldermen, of the City of Philadelphia." Lownes's piece was printed in four newspapers in 1794: *Aurora Grand Advertiser*, December 30; *Independent Gazetteer*, December 31; *Dunlap's American Daily*, December 23; and *Philadelphia Gazette*, December 22. For further information, see Meranze, *Laboratories of Virtue*, and Teeters, *Cradle of the Penitentiary*.

11. Lownes also collaborated with William Bradford's *An Enquiry How Far the Punishment of Death Is Necessary in Pennsylvania with Notes and Illustrations* (Philadelphia: T. Dobson, 1793), which included his *Account*. See Caleb Lownes, *An Account of the Alteration and Present State of the Penal Laws of Pennsylvania, Containing also an Account of the Gaol and Penitentiary House of Philadelphia, and the Interior Management Thereof* (Lexington, Pa.: J. Bradford, 1794). Subsequent references cited parenthetically in the text.

12. Robert J. Turnbull, *A Visit to the Philadelphia Prison; Being an Accurate and Particular Account of the Wise and Humane Administration Adopted in Every Part of That Building; Containing also an Account of the Gradual Reformation, and Present Improved State, of the Penal Laws of Pennsylvania; with Observations on the Impolity and Injustice of Capital Punishments. In a Letter to a Friend* (Philadelphia: Budd and Bartram, 1796),59. Subsequent references cited parenthetically in the text.

13. According to the reformers and the prison's early regulations, prisoners had to be segregated by age and crime, but runaways, vagrants, and those awaiting trial were usually thrown together.

14. Both Meranze and Teeters note that throughout this period the reports from the inspectors became increasingly vocal in their frustration and despair. See Meranze, *Laboratories of Virtue*, and Teeters, *Cradle of the Penitentiary*.

15. Not only was "liberty" one of the most popularly disseminated political concepts of the Revolutionary period, it also was undoubtedly one of the most frequently used words in political discussions. For a discussion of liberty's importance as both concept and word, see John Phillip Reid, *The Concept of Liberty in the Age of the American Revolution* (Chicago: University of Chicago Press, 1988). Certainly Carson and Clarke were aware of the word's importance.

16. The Dartmoor Prison massacre was notorious and popularly disseminated in early national print culture. On April 6, 1815, British guards at Dartmoor

opened fire on American prisoners, killing 7 and wounding 31; according to later accounts, the guards were ordered to fire by a drunken officer who mistakenly thought the Americans were trying to escape. Within a few weeks, American newspapers were filled with accounts of the "horrid massacre." A search of the APS database under "Dartmoor massacre" results in 224 hits in 1815. Also, within a short period of time, several separate publications appeared in print: *Dartmoor Massacre* (Pittsfield, Mass.: Phineahas Allen, 1815); *Horrid Massacre at Dartmoor Prison England . . .* (Boston: Nathaniel Coverly, 1815); John Melish, *A Description of Dartmoor Prison, with an Account of the Massacre of the Prisoners* (Philadelphia: Bioren, 1815); Benjamin Waterhouse, *A Journal, of a Young Man of Massachusetts, Late a Surgeon on Board an American Privateer, Who Was Captured at Sea by the British, in May, Eighteen Hundred and Thirteen, and Was Confined First, at Melville Island, Halifax, Then at Chatham, in England, and Last, at Dartmoor* (Boston: Rowe and Hooper, 1815); and Charles Andrews, *The Prisoners' Memoirs, or, Dartmoor Prison; Containing a Complete and Impartial History of the Entire Captivity of the Americans in England* (New York: n.p., 1815). Although Carson and Clarke misremembered its name, their reference to the notorious prison (where innocent Americans were massacred seven years earlier) would still have had resonance with their readers. On the War of 1812 and American prisoners, see Richard Buel, *America on the Brink: How the Political Struggle over the War of 1812 almost Destroyed the Young Republic* (New York: Palgrave Macmillan, 2006); Donald R. Hickey, *The War of 1812: A Forgotten Conflict* (Urbana: University of Illinois Press, 1989); and Reginald Horsman, *The War of 1812* (New York: Knopf, 1969).

17. Although still relatively unexamined, there has been recent discussion of American relations with the Barbary Coast and of Americans in North African captivity. For example, see Robert J. Allison, *The Crescent Obscured: The United States and the Muslim World, 1776–1815* (Chicago: University of Chicago Press, 1995); Frank Lambert, *The Barbary Wars: American Independence in the Atlantic World* (New York: Hill and Wang, 2005); and Frederick C. Leiner, *The End of Barbary Terror: America's 1815 War against the Pirates of North Africa* (New York: Oxford University Press, 2006). Like the Dartmoor reference, sensational accounts of Barbary captivity would still have been relatively fresh in the collective public memory.

18. There have been many perceptive analyses of Bakhtin's theories. Among those I have found useful are: David K. Danow, *The Thought of Mikhail Bakhtin: From Word to Culture* (New York: St. Martin's Press, 1991); Ken Hirschkopf and David Shepherd, *Bakhtin and Cultural Theory* (New York: Manchester University Press, distributed by St. Martin's Press, 1989); Michael Holquist, *Dialogism: Bakhtin and His World* (London: Routledge, 1990); Gary Saul Morson, *Bakhtin: Essays and Dialogues on His Work* (Chicago: University of Chicago Press, 1981); Michael Gardiner, *The Dialogics of Critique: M. M. Bakhtin and the Theory of Ideology* (London: Routledge, 1992); Graham Pechey, *Mikhail Bakhtin: The Word in the*

World (London: Routledge, 2007); and Sue Vice, *Introducing Bakhtin* (New York: Manchester University Press, distributed by St. Martin's Press, 1997).

19. In her recent monograph, Branson offers excellent insight into the personalities and events concerning Carson's death. See *Dangerous to Know*, 128–30.

20. Mary Clarke, *The Memoirs of the Celebrated and Beautiful Mrs. Ann Carson, Daughter of an Officer of the U.S. Navy, and Wife of Another, Whose Life Terminated in the Philadelphia Prison. In Two Volumes.* (Philadelphia: n.p., 1838).

Harry Hawser's Fate

*Eastern State Penitentiary and
the Birth of Prison Literature*

CALEB SMITH

IN THE VAST ARCHIVE OF TEXTS from the early decades of the U.S. penitentiary system—the pamphlets, treatises, open letters, architectural plans, rules and regulations, prayer books, travel narratives, records of costs and profits, medical reports, outraged protests, reasoned defenses, and myriad other, sometimes unclassifiable documents—only a few pieces offer the testimony of the inmates who lived and died in the controversial new institutions. Early American prison discourse was mainly composed by prison inspectors, reformers, and men and women of letters from the world at large. Occasionally, as Daniel E. Williams's essay in this volume shows, an extraordinary ex-prisoner like Ann Carson might describe her time behind bars in an effort to bring public shame on the institution. Elsewhere, the archive offers interviews with the incarcerated, such as those appended to Gustave de Beaumont and Alexis de Tocqueville's classic *On the Penitentiary System in the United States;* or brief, formulaic autobiographical narratives describing the convict's fall from virtue into a wretched life of crime. Such accounts, though, seem to bear the marks of careful editing by prison officials who sought to conscript inmates into the propaganda wars over the meaning and value of reform.

The authorities who oversaw the first full-scale American penitentiaries enforced a regime of solitude that depended on their control over the production and circulation of texts. Many inmates were illiterate when they entered the prison. Those who could read were provided with materials at the discretion of their keepers. Those who wrote had to submit to a severe censorship. The general rule of silence was broken, however, in 1844, with the publication of *Buds and Flowers, of Leisure Hours*, a book of poems by a Philadelphia convict using the pen name Harry Hawser.[1] Composed at Pennsylvania's renowned Eastern State Penitentiary, it is the work of a literate, articulate inmate, reflecting at length on his experience in solitary confinement, on how captivity remakes the self, and on the place of the prison in a modernizing world. In his preface to the volume, Hawser identified himself as a man addressing the public from the hidden world of the prison interior: "The author of the following pages, during a period of involuntary seclusion from society, devoted his leisure hours to reading and reflection, and the while, he composed these fugitive pieces, now offered to the reader."[2] Here, Hawser suggested, was the work of one who had lived through the reality of confinement that others had only wondered or dreamed about—a piece of authentic testimony from a zone beyond the pale. Overlooked by all but a few scholars of Pennsylvania penal history, Hawser's book might be recovered as a founding document of the genre that we have come to call "prison literature." Indeed, I will argue that some of the defining interpretive problematics and characteristic tropes of American prison literature in the age of the penitentiary were developed, in part, by the publication and reception of *Buds and Flowers*.

While its appearance was an event of note during the reform movement of the 1840s, Hawser's book has not become part of the scholarly canon of prison literature, in part because studies of the genre rarely look to the nineteenth century for sources. A brief discussion of *Buds and Flowers* by Negley K. Teeters and John D. Shearer, in their 1957 history of Eastern State, establishes the identity of the author (a sailor and convicted larcenist named George Ryno) but dismisses the poetry as "a kind of doggerel verse" unworthy of careful reading.[3] Along with this aesthetic judgment, there are also political reasons for leaving Hawser outside the tradition of prison literature. The value of this tradition, for the scholars and activists who have been shaping its canon since the

1960s, is its peculiar capacity to expose the secret, grotesque violence of the carceral interior, and to record the spiritual and social resistance devised by the men and women who have endured that violence. As Angela Davis writes in a review of recent anthologies, prison literature "comprises a literary genre whose significance resides not so much in its formal qualities, but rather in the alternative knowledges it is able to generate about the prison."[4] It records the experiences of the "imprisoned men and women [who] have managed to invent subversive spaces within which to nurture their knowledge and creativity."[5] By contrast, Hawser's 1844 book is neither an exposé of prison violence nor a memoir of subversion. Instead, its author seems to celebrate the prison system and its benevolent effects on his character. Hawser refers to his time in solitary as a period of "leisure hours"; he calls his incarceration "the happiest event of his life"; and he dedicates his book to Richard Vaux, the president of the board of inspectors at Eastern State and the chief defender of the Pennsylvania system of prison discipline. Again and again, Hawser's verses return to the ideals of repentance, sobriety, and moral and social responsibility that modern prison discipline was supposed to instill. On first reading, the entire book can seem to be a sustained utterance of blessing by the inmate upon his keepers.

On a closer reading of Hawser's poetry, however, other accents and other modes begin to emerge. Devoting a few pages to Hawser in a recent history of Eastern State's early decades, Leslie C. Patrick-Stamp notes, for example, that the poem "Our City Not a Paradise" advances a subtle critique of the criminal justice system. "Some starve, or force a livelihood by stealth," Hawser writes, "While others unconcern'd may roll in wealth" (55).[6] There is the suggestion, in such lines, that the causes of crime lie in an unjust economic order, not in the moral failings of the incarcerated; the prison is an instrument of oppression, wielded by the rich against the poor.

In my own studies of the nineteenth-century prison system, I have been haunted by another of Hawser's poems, "The Captive." Here, the poet leaves aside his characterization of the prison as a place of leisure and self-cultivation. He turns instead to the imagery of living death:

> But, fated to a living tomb,
> > For years on years in woe to brood
> Upon the past, the captive's doom,
> > Is galling chains and solitude. (70)

In "The Captive," Hawser's ordinarily pious and sentimental tone grows grim, and his usually plodding verse becomes more sophisticated. The long vowels in the final words of each line, a series of rhymes and off-rhymes, toll like solemn bells. The enjambment at the center of the quatrain extends the phrase "to brood / Upon the past," communicating the sense of a long, dismal confinement. The ghostly imagery recalls Poe's gothic tales of live burial and Dickinson's poems spoken from the grave. In both its careful composition and its cold depiction of a de-humanizing confinement, the poem belongs to the richest tradition of writing from the modern penitentiary. If the dominant mode of *Buds and Flowers* is a blessing spoken by a redeemed convict to his benefactors, "The Captive" sounds more like a curse from the lips of the living dead.

This essay is a study of Harry Hawser's *Buds and Flowers* in its historical context. Attending to the complex forms of mediation between the secluded space of the solitary cell and the public world of letters and opinion, I examine the conditions that helped to produce, circulate, and interpret this odd, self-contradictory book of poems. My approach seeks to move beyond the oversimple division between "inside" and "outside" that shapes much discussion of prison writing. I argue that the modern understanding of prison literature was born out of the encounter between a divided prison-reform movement and the mass public of the 1840s, an emergent collective entity whose social imaginary was mediated by the wide circulation of inexpensive texts. As prison authorities called on inmates like Hawser to testify before the mass public, the prisoner was endowed with new kinds of authenticity, becoming a figure whose formative experience in the prison enabled him to reveal the truth about the hidden, mysterious interior of the institution. As it happened, the rhetorical conflict between the critics and the defenders of the Pennsylvania system of prison discipline also took shape around a trope that has continued to inform prison literature for more than a century and a half—the image of the cell as a living tomb. In the end, the very circumstances that required Harry Hawser to give his blessing to the penitentiary also enabled him to pronounce his bewitching curse.

Prisons and Publics

What are the forms of contact and communication between the prison interior and the outside world? One account of the birth of the prison in the late eighteenth and early nineteenth centuries, sometimes associated with Michel Foucault's *Discipline and Punish* (1975), holds that punishment in this transformative period was withdrawn from the town square and hidden behind the imposing walls of new institutions.[7] The spectacle of bodily violence, a ritual enacted before an assembled crowd, gave way to a secret discipline conducted by experts in penal science who carefully kept and controlled the records of their experimental systems. In short, punishment disappeared.

Certainly some of the early authorities on prison discipline saw their projects in this light. In an influential and often cited essay from the early days of penal reform in Philadelphia, the physician Benjamin Rush protested the many evils of spectacular torture and executions: "public punishments," he argued, "are injurious to criminals and to society."[8] In place of the terrible scaffold, Rush called for a secluded "house of corrections" where officials would administer a punishment of justly measured pain, labor, and spiritual reflection. After a period of subjection to this invisible discipline, the reformed convict would emerge from the penal cloister like a man reborn from the darkness of the grave: "His friends and family bathe his cheeks with tears of joy; and the universal shout of the neighborhood is, 'This our brother was lost, and is found—was dead and is alive.'"[9]

For Rush, the precondition for the convict's resurrection was a near-total separation between the prison and the rest of society. The generation of reformers who followed him, and who built the first great model penitentiaries, made this ideal a part of their designs. The penal code enacted by Pennsylvania in 1829, when Eastern State received its first inmates, established it as policy: "None but the official visitors can have any communication with the convicts, nor shall any visitor whatever be permitted to deliver to or receive from any of the convicts, any letter or message whatever."[10] The prison was to be removed from the common spaces of communication and circulation.

Scholars of prison literature have generally accepted the institution's claim to have raised an almost absolute barrier between two worlds. For many commentators, prisoners' writings provide precious insights into an otherwise unknowable zone of dark miseries and struggles. Thus Tom Wicker, in his preface to a recent volume of prison writings, writes that they "disclose the nasty, brutish details of the life within—a life the authorities would rather we not know about, a life so far from conventional existence that the accounts of those who experience it exert the fascination of the unknown, sometimes the unbelievable."[11] Having spent time behind bars confers a particular kind of authority on the writers of prison literature, giving a special, revelatory force to their narratives and poems. The documentary work carried out by these writers is thus presumed to be a threat to the system that confines them; it exposes abuses and promises to mobilize readers in opposition to the prison system.

The history of the prison, however, is not simply a history of disappearance. As Foucault himself was careful to emphasize, the decline of the scaffold entailed the rise of new modes of observation and representation; indeed, the whole modern discourse of penal science took shape with the development of new prison systems around the turn of the nineteenth century. Interdisciplinary research by several scholars has explored the complex set of mediations between prisons and the societies that build them. John Bender's *Imagining the Penitentiary*, for instance, shows how certain literary innovations in the depiction of character helped to shape the Anglo-American reform movement's conceptions of "the architecture of mind."[12] Thomas L. Dumm's *Democracy and Punishment* describes the relations between modern forms of citizenship and the disciplinary subjectivity enforced in the penitentiary.[13] And Michael Meranze's major studies of the institutional and cultural history of Pennsylvania in the Revolutionary era demonstrate how carefully the reformers attended to the public display and discussion of punishment as they attempted to create a new penal system commensurate with their dream of a virtuous republic. Echoing Foucault, Meranze writes that the establishment of the "reformed system of punishment" in the penitentiary "replaced the public symbol of the body with the concealed practice of discipline"; but Meranze goes on to stress that "as punishment receded from public view, the distance between everyday life and the world of penalty was filled with mechanisms of observation, communication, and imagination."[14]

Rather than describing the penitentiary as a space of concealment, then, we might attend to the ways in which the authorities behind the institution sought to address, and to transform, a variety of publics. Indeed, the media through which they communicated included the very walls that separated prison cells from society at large. The architect John Haviland's plans for New York's "Tombs" and Philadelphia's Eastern State, among other prisons, surrounded their technologically and philosophically modern interiors with gothic facades that recalled the dungeon-tombs of the old world. In accounts circulated by reformers, the result was praised as an architecture of a "grave, severe, and awful character" that "produces on the imagination of every passing spectator . . . [a] peculiarly impressive, solemn, and instructive" impression.[15] Prison architecture placed the structures of humane correction behind imposing walls designed to menace a public which was presumed to have criminal tendencies, needing a visible reminder of the "awful" power of the law.

Prison architecture, though, had a limited audience; rather like the scaffold, it could communicate its "grave" message only to the spectator who passed within view of the scene of punishment. A wider audience could be reached through the spoken word. In his essay on the house of corrections, Rush had described how the public circulation of "tales" from the new "abode of misery" would replace the theater of the scaffold. He suggested that people who were kept ignorant of the realities of the prison interior would invent the liveliest ghost tales and horror stories. "Children," Rush wrote, "will press upon the evening fire in listening to the tales that will spread from this abode of misery. Superstition will add to its horrors: and romance will find in it ample materials for fiction, which cannot fail of increasing the terror of its punishments."[16] Rush and his followers wanted punishment out of sight, but not out of mind. Jason Haslam makes this point clear: "Although the visual spectacle of punishment might disappear from the public square, the spectacle would (and should, according to Rush) continue to exist—and have an impact on society—in publicly circulated narrative forms."[17] Public torture was too grotesque, too difficult to manage, and an American polity conceived in enlightenment should extend its humanizing embrace even to the unfortunate criminal. At the same time, authorities hoped to cultivate a salutary terror by encouraging the circulation of imaginative tales.

If reformers depended on gothic fantasies to instill a fear of punishment in potential criminals, however, they also developed other genres for other publics. In their many pamphlets, open letters, and reports, they attempted to explain the aims and practices of prison reform to an educated audience; in the process, they hoped to win the support of enlightened public opinion for their costly, controversial plans. Consider, for example, the civil tone and humble style of an open letter from Franklin Bache, the Philadelphia penitentiary physician, to the reformer Roberts Vaux, printed and circulated in 1829: "My Dear Sir, I regret very much that I have not been able, sooner, to reply to your letter . . . in which you pay me the compliment of requesting my opinion on the subject of the separate confinement of prisoners."[18] Documents like this one offered readers a glimpse, behind facades and fictions, into the hidden processes of modern prison discipline—and, no less, into the polite social world of those who managed penal policy. Here, the reformers developed the theory and grammar of their systems. They built a canon of authorities that included such founding figures as Cesare di Beccaria, John Howard, and Benjamin Rush. They explored the relations between prison discipline and mental health reform, poverty relief, temperance, and the antislavery movement. They assessed the progress of their endeavor and the obstacles it continued to face. Above all, they debated the merits of the Pennsylvania and New York systems, the two rival models of discipline that divided their movement.

The accounts of the prison interior that circulated in the late eighteenth and early nineteenth centuries, then, addressed not a single audience but multiple and divided publics. According to the reformers' conception of a stratified public sphere, lower-class audiences would be terrified by nightmarish tales from the abode of misery, while educated readers were enlightened and persuaded by reports on the methods of humane correction. For an unruly, semiliterate public of "children" and the poor, imaginative fiction would carry on a version of the ritual performances associated with the disappearing scaffold. Among the governing elites, rational, polite discussions of prison administration would inform public opinion and, in turn, influence official policies.

This distinction between ritual and reason, however, would not hold forever. By the mid-nineteenth century, the character of the public sphere was being transformed by the rise of mass literacy and the mass media. At the same time, the reading audience that knew the details of prison reform—the difference, for example, between the Pennsylvania system of near-total solitude and the New York system that permitted congregate labor—had split into antagonistic factions. It was to this expanded and divided public that the prisoner-poet Harry Hawser was called to testify in 1844. As the case of Hawser's book shows, the reform movement would create new uses for sentimental appeals and gothic terror as the mass public became fascinated by the prison interior.

Live Burial and General Circulation

Hawser's public life had begun two years earlier, in 1842, when Charles Dickens visited the Philadelphia prison and wrote the famous exposé of the institution that appeared as part of his *American Notes, for General Circulation.*[19] On his way to the United States, Dickens remarked that he wished most of all to see two world-famous sites, Niagara Falls and the Eastern State Penitentiary. Like other transatlantic voyagers including Alexis de Tocqueville and Harriet Martineau, Dickens seems to have felt that the new penitentiaries were capable of revealing certain peculiar aspects of America's social and political character. The Pennsylvania administrators obliged the famous author by opening the doors of the prison and guiding him through its corridors and into its cells. Dickens spent most of a day at Eastern State, talking with the inspectors and with several of the inmates. The long passage he wrote about the penitentiary was one of the most disturbing and controversial in his wildly popular travel book.

Although he would turn to a gothic mode in his depiction of the prison interior, Dickens recognized the penitentiary as a new development in the Anglo-American social order. Eastern State was not a dungeon lingering from ancient times. It was a novel experiment undertaken in the name of enlightenment and humanity. Dickens described the keepers as men of learning and compassion; he defined their system, as they did, against the ritualized bodily violence of the past. In the end, though, Dickens's conclusions were damning. "In its intentions," he wrote, "I am well convinced that [the Pennsylvania system] is kind, humane, and meant for reformation; but I am persuaded that those who devised this system of Prison Discipline, and those benevolent gentlemen who carry it into execution, do not know what they are doing" (90). In Dickens's judgment, the system at Eastern State was a well-meaning endeavor gone horribly, monstrously wrong: "I hold this slow and daily tampering with the mysteries of the brain to be immeasurably worse than any torture of the body" (90). The penitentiary was devised to lead convicts through mortification to reflection and redemption, but it left them lingering instead in a nightmarish living death.

In Dickens's view, isolation — the guiding principle of reform at Eastern State — was no means of rehabilitation; it was a dehumanizing violence. His account of the prison was built around several portraits of inmates, each in a state of miserable abjection. "In every little chamber that I entered," he wrote, "I seemed to see the same appalling countenance" (99). There was one convict who "look[ed] as wan and unearthly as if he had been summoned from the grave" (94); there was another "dejected, heart-broken, wretched creature" who represented the "picture of forlorn affliction and distress of mind" (93); there was the "helpless, crushed, and broken man" (95); and there were three young women, in adjoining cells, whose "looks were very sad, and might have moved the sternest visitor to tears" (95). Dickens's readers watched these figures appear like a ghostly parade, gothic others to whom the author offered his tearful sympathy.

American Notes was an international sensation. According to one study, 3,000 copies were sold in Philadelphia in the first thirty-five minutes after they became available, and more than 100,000 pirated copies would be in circulation by the end of the year.[20] Clearly, a wide American audience was eager to learn the English author's views of their culture and their institutions. Soon, his remarks on Pennsylvania's prison system would be known not only to those who bought his book but also to anyone following the news in England and the United States. The *Times* of London, for example, recommended *American Notes* for both its ethical insights and its graceful style, calling it a "powerful and masterly sketch of the painfully-depressed and despondent feelings by which the imprisoned convict is in all possibility racked, when he awakes to a full sense of the dismal monotony of his doom."[21] A more measured response in *The New World* acknowledged the "powerful language" of Dickens's portrayal of Eastern State and conceded that the novelist would have "some influence in forming public opinion in regard to the Prison Discipline of Pennsylvania."[22]

Thus the reformers who had welcomed Dickens into Eastern State, perhaps in the hope that he would support their cause, found themselves instead defending their system against his protest in the public sphere. They mobilized to answer him in print, attempting to discredit his motives and his right to judge the institution. The author of "British Critics and British Travelers," for instance, writing in the *United States Magazine and Democratic Review* in April 1844, argued that Dickens's real aim in visiting the United States had been to advocate for an international copyright law; the sentimental novelist was "utterly disqualified" to judge American society or its institutions, and it was regrettable, "in this reading age, when the circulation of books is growing every day more general" and "national curiosity has become of the greatest consequence to the peace of the civilized world," that Dickens's distorted views had gained such significant influence.[23]

In response, authorities including the British consul-general William Peter and the esteemed South Carolina Professor Francis Lieber, who had translated and introduced Beaumont and Tocqueville's study of American prisons for an Anglo-American audience, were called to Philadelphia to meet with the inmates Dickens had encountered. Peter's report would appear in the inaugural issue of the *Pennsylvania Journal of Prison Discipline and Philanthropy*, a quarterly publication launched in support of the separate system. There, Peter gave his own brief descriptions of the several inmates who had made their way into Dickens's work, including the "Poet" who, according to Peter, had been discharged from Eastern State in 1843 and was "now in respectable business, reconciled to his father, and respectably married."[24]

Lieber made his rebuttal to "Mr. Dickens's sentimental tirade against eremitic imprisonment" in an open letter to the Honorary Secretary of the Philadelphia Prison Society.[25] He paid special attention to one of the female inmates whom Dickens had portrayed with such pathos. As if to undermine the sentimentality of Dickens's description of a lovely but ghostly creature, Lieber described her as "a yellow mulatto, rather short and not ill-looking," of a "disreputable" character, who had been convicted with two others of seducing and robbing several men. Much of Lieber's letter, though, was a transcript of the inmate's own purported speech. Lieber's rhetorical strategy was not to answer Dickens in his own voice but to present this convict's testimony as evidence against Dickens's "sentimental effusion upon a subject he is absolutely ignorant of." Dickens's "tirade" thus became the occasion for Lieber's publication of a convict's own first-person testimony about the effects of solitude on the self.

According to Lieber, the inmate confessed, "I am nearly twenty-one years old, and feel very well here. They treat me with much kindness. I have learned here to read and write, and pray." She continued: "It is sometimes lonely here, but now I am accustomed to it; it lasted about six months before I got accustomed to it. I felt, then, sometimes very down." The period of loneliness and low feeling was followed, happily, by a moral reawakening: "I have been very bad: I will surely try to live like a good girl, if they will give me a chance." The inmate's words were recorded as the truth that would dispel the novelist's "ignorant" and fanciful fiction. Along the way, her testimony did not deny that incarceration at Eastern State involved a painful loneliness, but it represented this abjection as an initial phase that had prepared the inmate for her moral rebirth. The old, criminal self was mortified so that a new, redeemed self—literate, prayerful, reconciled to family and society—could be born.

On the other side of the Atlantic, the response to Dickens was taken up by Lieber's correspondent Joseph Adshead, a reformer who supported the adoption of the Pennsylvania system in English prisons. Adshead's *Prisons and Prisoners* (1845) was, according to the Dickens scholar Philip Collins, the most sustained critique to be published during the controversy and "the basis for most of the subsequent attacks on *American Notes* during Dickens's lifetime."[26] Like Lieber, Adshead insisted that Dickens was ignorant of the realities of prison discipline. The aesthetic and market demands that had informed Dickens's work were those of a popular novelist, not a serious reformer: "a book had to be written . . . ; effects must be produced; the mere dry detail of fact was not contemplated, by [Dickens], as sufficiently exciting; the regions of fiction, therefore, had to be explored, to supply what truth would not furnish."[27] *American Notes*, Adshead argued, offered no true glimpse into the secret recesses of the penitentiary; it was a work of sensational fiction.

Of course, reformers since Benjamin Rush had allowed fiction—including sensationally gothic tales—a role in mediating between punishment and a certain uninformed public. The new problem, as Adshead and his circle understood it, was that Dickens's fiction had been falsely advertised and received as the authoritative truth about the system of prison discipline in practice at Eastern State. A category mistake had been made in the public sphere of letters:

> The flights of fancy may take what altitude they please in works of fiction; the imagination may range discursively in the regions of romance; but the public ought not to be deceived by misstatements in matters of vital importance to the well-being and regulation of society; however pleasing the style, or fascinating the language, if a narrative *which should have the impress of truth* be marked by a departure from it, much as genius may be admired, it must be matter of regret that talent should thus defeat its more noble purpose. (114)

Dickens's work, Adshead argued, had violated the boundary between popular romance and the refined public opinion responsible for "the well-being and regulation of society." Adshead's collaborators in

Philadelphia followed his lead in attempting to reinforce this distinction: Richard Vaux wrote that Dickens's "delineation of character" in *American Notes* "is marked by the strong contrasts which he paints in his fictions" and dismissed his protest as so much "crude and emotional criticism."[28]

What neither Adshead nor Vaux quite acknowledged was that this problem of genre—Dickens's fiction masquerading as the truth about the Philadelphia prison—was also a problem of audience. In the ideology of reform, gothic and sentimental "tales" from the "abode of misery" were appropriate for the lower classes. Such fictions might even serve as part of the system of law and order, frightening would-be offenders and thus deterring crime. But Dickens had addressed this sensational material to readers who thought of themselves as enfranchised members of the governing order; in the process, he threatened to turn public opinion against Eastern State Penitentiary and its solitary system. The Reverend J. Field, an English chaplain whose work was cited with admiration by Richard Vaux, seems to have grasped the challenge, complaining that Dickens's "works have obtained a wider circulation than his veracity deserved."[29] The hierarchical relationship between rational discussion and gothic sensation had somehow shifted to become a conflict between two groups with competing claims to sovereignty in the "regulation of society."

The problem confronting the reformers, then, was more than an eloquent protest by a celebrated author. It was a public sphere whose character was being transformed by the emergent mass market for popular printed texts such as *American Notes*. As they had designed the relationship between the prison interior and the outside world in the late eighteenth century, Rush and his contemporaries had never reckoned with such a public. They had addressed a stratified society, where the appetites of the lower classes could be satisfied (and suppressed) with terrifying tales, while the educated readers who considered themselves the engineers of civilization could engage in refined discussions about penal policy. Rush's formulation had gone so far as to imply a distinction between the printed medium of his own "Enquiry," circulated among likeminded reformers, and the oral medium of the terrifying tale, which mutated like gossip as it traveled through the community and reached the ears of eager children. By the 1840s, the old patterns of publication that informed Rush's system were becoming obsolete. Dickens's haunting vision of the prison interior had addressed an audience that could be moved by sensations of terror and sympathy but which might also consider itself a sovereign people capable of organizing to influence state policy.

Harry Hawser's Fate

In response to this disturbing phenomenon, Adshead undertook what he imagined as a kind of surgery on the collective psyche: "We cannot . . . suffer the public mind," he wrote, "to retain the prejudicial taint with which it must necessarily be affected by the remarks of Mr. Dickens, and it shall be our study to remove it" (95–96). Adshead's rhetorical technique was to quote at length from Dickens's portraits of Philadelphia prisoners and to answer each of them with a more authoritative—less fictionalized—account, informed by his correspondence with Lieber and others who had conducted their own interviews. Of the three women whose mournful beauty had moved Dickens to tears, for example, Adshead wrote that "they were of the inferior class of low women to whom the appellative, 'beautiful,' was inappropriate and unworthy; two of them were Mulattoes, and one of them a Negress!" (115), as if this excited identification of their race would suffice to give the lie to Dickens's sentimentality.[30]

Adshead's most elaborate discussion, though, was devoted to another inmate to whom Dickens had referred in passing as "a poet, who . . . wrote verses about ships (he was by trade a mariner), and 'the maddening wine-cup,' and his friends at home" (94). Adshead would not reveal the poet's identity; the young convict, he wrote, "is tenacious of his name; and inquiry respecting it, fallen though he be, would be altogether improper" (105). The anonymity of the inmate's identity was important to the program of reform, since it ensured that rehabilitated convicts would not carry the shame of their past crimes into their future lives as responsible citizens. Calling on his sources in Philadelphia, though, Adshead purported to give a full picture of this particular inmate's life, crimes, and redemption. Dickens's "mariner" was the poet who would soon be known as Harry Hawser.

"This young man," Adshead wrote, "had been a clerk in a sailing packet, and was well educated, but being in a frolic in which several were intoxicated, he joined in taking a pocket-book, containing about seventeen dollars, from a passenger, which were spent during their state of inebriety" (105). As a consequence of this drunken spree, the "clerk" was sentenced to three years of solitary confinement at Eastern State. Prison discipline, Adshead assured his readers, had been good for the young sailor:

> It cannot fail to be pleasing to Mr. Dickens, to be informed, that this writer about "the maddening wine-cup," &c., when discharged, carried with him the respect and esteem of all the officers of the prison; he had signed the temperance pledge, and had become, in the opinion of every one who knew him, a thoroughly reformed man; and was reconciled to his father, with whom he has since been engaged in a respectable business. He married an industrious, reputable tradeswoman . . . with whom he has lived happily since. Upon application to the Governor of the State, this young man was restored to the enjoyment of his civil rights, of which his conviction as a felon had deprived him. (111–12)

Adshead's representation of the anonymous prisoner-poet followed the model laid out in Lieber's earlier letter. Against Dickens's portrayal of crushed, abject figures, the prison's apologists advanced a narrative of just conviction, severe but humane punishment, and moral reformation. Where Dickens had seen the monotonous wretchedness of living death, they saw a phase of mortification leading to rebirth.[31] Their prisoner was one who, as Benjamin Rush had imagined, "was dead and is alive."

In composing their resurrection narratives, Lieber and Adshead drew from a range of popular discourses, each of which involved some kind of personal transformation. They used the language of labor discipline and education, emphasizing the literacy and penmanship learned in prison. The once "fallen" poet, Adshead observed, "writes well in verse, his pieces are of an ethical tendency, and executed in an elegant style of calligraphy" (105). They told stories of families broken and repaired. They alluded to Protestant narratives of conversion—"I have learned to pray here," says Lieber's "yellow mulatto," "for I had forgotten since my childhood" (117)—and to the legal restoration from civil death to civil rights. And, in the case of Harry Hawser, Adshead made the passage from "inebriety" to temperance the central event in the convict's career. The once intoxicated young man, seduced into a criminal frolic, had been persuaded in prison to sign the temperance pledge, beginning a new life of sober responsibility.

As the centerpiece of his polemic against Dickens, Adshead reproduced a poem of over 120 lines, entitled "The Inebriate's Solitary Thoughts" (107–11). Adshead must have received the poem from his correspondents in Philadelphia. Introducing the five pages of verse, he noted that he was in possession of "an autograph copy by the author," which he would "give . . . entire, without further note or comment," allowing the reformed convict to speak, as it were, for himself (107). In "The Inebriate's Solitary Thoughts," Hawser adopts the persona of the reformed drunkard. He recalls the miseries his intemperance had brought to himself and his family, and he offers his apology:

> Would I could drown, in Lethe's gloomy stream,
> The memory of two and thirty years,—
> That vast amount of precious time misspent,—
> But conscience whispers, "thus it may not be!"
> Nay, in my waking hours, and when in sleep
> My eye-lids close upon life's chequer'd scene,
> Her voice is heard within this tortured breast,
> Speaking of crime. (107)

Afflicted by regret in his solitary cell, the convict recalls how his drinking and other transgressions have broken his mother's heart, estranged him from his father, and wasted his life. He looks back in sorrow on "Base Dissipation's poison-teeming bowl" and the other "wiles" that led "the artless youth / From virtue's track to that of crime and woe" (110). In the final stanzas, he prays to Christ, "who died a felon's death," to redeem his soul and restore him to virtue.

Designed to appeal to an emergent mass public, "The Inebriate's Solitary Thoughts" united three discourses of rebirth—the correction of the convict in prison discipline was linked to the reformation of the drunkard in the personal commitment of temperance and the salvation of the sinner in evangelical conversion. In the constellation of prison reform, temperance, and evangelicalism, we can begin to see why Adshead made Harry Hawser the key figure in his response to Dickens, and why he chose "The Inebriate's Solitary Thoughts" to be Hawser's testimony in support of the Philadelphia system. The poem makes the solitary misery of incarceration, the suffering that provoked Dickens's sentimental response, a precondition for the glorious reformation of the soul. At the same time, it links the invisible transformation of the convict, locked away from the world, to the forms of publicly performed conversion that readers were likely to have seen in the immensely popular evangelical revivals and temperance meetings of the age. Through several layers of mediation—the poem composed in solitude, published under a pseudonym, and quoted and framed by Adshead in his debate with Dickens—Hawser appeared to enact his own humble reformation before a transatlantic audience.

The relationship between prison reform and temperance went back at least to the first generation of post-Revolutionary reformers in Philadelphia, where the two forms of discipline had been advocated by such prominent figures as Benjamin Rush and Benjamin Franklin. The cultural historian David S. Shields describes the emergence of temperance discourse in the city in the eighteenth century, when the taverns that served as the centers of anti-Quaker society were attacked in pamphlets and newspapers as "site[s] of corruption."[32] The temperance movement that took shape in the public sphere, Shields observes, gave rise to a new mode of address that drew from both religious and political vocabularies but could speak to a variety of social problems. "As print consolidated a sense of the public distinct from state and church, particularly after the founding of newspapers in the provincial metropolis, the old objectors were supplied a new mask through which to voice their criticisms: the 'sober citizen.' The sober citizen was a figure of sufficient generality to encompass both religious and state interests."[33]

By the early 1840s, as Harry Hawser's poems began to circulate in Philadelphia and beyond, the radical, mainly working-class temperance advocates known as the Washingtonians were renovating temperance rhetoric—and stirring up new controversies—with their grotesque, sensational stories of the crimes and sufferings produced by drink. Their mass movement, claiming half a million members by the mid-1840s, involved not only crowded lectures but also the publication of enormously popular stories and novels, including best-sellers like George B. Cheever's *Deacon Gile's Distillery* and the young Walt Whitman's *Franklin Evans, or, The Inebriate*, first published in 1842, the same year as Dickens's *American Notes*. While temperance literature was generally published in cheap editions for mass audiences, its tropes and rhetorical modes found their way even into some of the canonical literary works of the antebellum period.[34]

In *Publics and Counterpublics*, Michael Warner notes that, between the late 1820s and the early 1840s, the press and American social movements "transformed each other in the context of temperance. The early national entrepreneurial press became a mass medium, and the temperance reform societies that had been popping up in every American locale became a full-scale, mass mediated social movement—that is, one that understood itself as such." Thus, Warner adds, "temperance and the mass press planted each other on the national scene."[35] Aligning Harry Hawser—and, by extension, the personal transformation enacted by prisoners in the Pennsylvania system—with the temperance movement, then, Adshead and his fellow reformers attempted to address the new kind of public that was taking shape, the audience that had been so feverishly agitated by Dickens's revelations. As they did so, they helped to invent a new subject of public address, claiming peculiar new kinds of performative force and authenticity: the anonymous convict whose verses would testify to his own conversion, in solitude, from the wretchedness of crime to a redeemed life of virtue. Through the mouthpiece of Harry Hawser, the inmate invited to speak so that his testimony could express his own reformation and exonerate the prison from Dickens's charges, the Pennsylvania system sought a way to legitimate itself in the court of public opinion. In the encounter between an embattled reform movement and an emergent mass public, the figure of the prisoner-poet was conceived.

From the Gallows Confession to the Prison Poem

Of course, Harry Hawser's prison poetry had a cultural lineage. As Patrick-Stamp observes, Hawser's verses in some ways "conform[ed] to the earliest literature by convicted American criminals in its purely confessional character."[36] Most clearly, *Buds and Flowers* evolved from the gallows confession, in which condemned felons addressed the execution day crowd, acknowledging their guilt, recognizing the justice of the legal power that had convicted them, and praying for forgiveness in the next life. These speeches had been transcribed and circulated on both sides of the Atlantic for centuries in such volumes as Cotton Mather's *Pillars of Salt*. Like the condemned men and women who were their purported authors, Harry Hawser performed an act of expiation; he confessed to his guilt and justified the powers that punished him. "Intemperance consigned [the author] to a prison," Hawser wrote in his preface. "Justice to a system of prison discipline, which has received the severe and unjust criticism of many intelligent persons, has induced him to lay before the public the results of its operation upon himself, as the best and most indisputable refutation of the criticism it has received." Such self-referential lines, as well as many of the poems themselves, suggest that Hawser's book was rehearsing some of the conventions of the gallows confession.

Yet, *Buds and Flowers* also departed from the confessional tradition in meaningful ways, evolving into a new genre of literature that would be viewed through a new set of interpretive lenses. The old gallows speech had conventionally been delivered by a known member of the community. Even readers who encountered the confession in print were invited to imagine a familiar scene of address, a man or woman speaking to his or her neighbors. The author of the confession had a proper name and a life story that proceeded from the innocence of childhood into the corruption of crime, concluding with the righteous punishment that was about to be executed. By contrast, "Harry Hawser" was a pseudonym that functioned, like many other features of the Pennsylvania prison system, to conceal the convict's identity. Even reformers such as Adshead and Vaux, who knew the author's real name, declined to reveal it.

The authenticity of the prisoner-poet's testimony, then, would have to depend not on his recognizable face or name, but on how his book was presented to the public. It required a set of framing texts, including Adshead's biographical sketch and the preface attributed to Hawser. These commentaries claimed that the poet's personal experience of solitary confinement—the system's "operation upon himself"—had enabled him to compose "the best and most indispensable refutation of the criticism [the prison] ha[d] received." Unlike the professional writer of fiction, with his wild imagination and his disposition to produce sensational best-sellers, the prisoner's concern was to tell the truth about what had happened to him in the solitary cell. Anonymity also allowed Hawser and the reformers who published him to suggest that his experience of personal transformation could be generalized. Hawser's story was presumed to stand for the reformation of many other, perhaps less articulate inmates at Eastern State. Thus, by way of the pseudonym, a special kind of authenticity was enabled: the veracity of the testimony depended on the remaking of the author's subjectivity through a system of discipline, but any number of such subjects might be created by the same prison.

As it turns out, though, the convict who was called on to answer Dickens's charges in his own voice, the reformed prisoner-poet known as Harry Hawser, was himself something of a fiction. The prison records examined by Teeters and Shearer show that George Ryno, the inmate behind *Buds and Flowers*, had been convicted of two counts of larceny and confined at Eastern State from July 1840 until July 1843. Adshead referred to Hawser as "a clerk in a sailing packet," but the official documents suggest a more weathered mariner. Ryno had been "7 or 10 years at sea," much of that time in the U.S. Navy. He was described as a "reckless and hardened man," with a "long scar" across his face and the initials "G. R." tattooed on his arm. He seemed "of a light and trifling spirit" and was "disposed to smile at the introduction of any serious topic." Upon his release, prison authorities noted in his file that he "reads and writes" and that he "drinks." He was paid thirty dollars for extra labor performed in the prison and fifty dollars for the copyright to his book.[37]

The archive reveals, then, that the convict George Ryno had little in common with the public persona known as Harry Hawser. Along the way, there are also hints that Ryno may have known a good deal about how to address the mass public for whom his book was published. His fluency in the idiom of the evangelical temperance movement, for instance, offers some insight into what he may have been reading at Eastern State. His verses also indicate other encounters with popular and didactic texts. "To a Dying Slave" uses the imagery of suffering and the sentimental affect common to antislavery writing on both sides of the Atlantic.[38] Likewise, an occasional poem on the death of William Henry Harrison indicates that the inmate was following the national news from his cell; Harrison died on April 1, 1841, several months into Ryno's sentence.

Beyond his knowledge of temperance and other national causes, Ryno may have been familiar with prison reform debates even before he entered the controversial penitentiary and talked with Dickens. The prison records mention that Ryno had a brother who died while incarcerated at Eastern State, and that his father was "a cruel and bad man" who had served as "head keeper of Trenton prison."[39] This unsavory character must have been Ephraim Ryno, the notoriously corrupt keeper who had presided over the New Jersey State Prison during the scandal of 1829–1830.[40] Under Ephraim Ryno's administration, conditions in the institution so deteriorated that the legislature commissioned a detailed report by a committee of specialists, to be supervised by the eminent Boston reformer Louis Dwight. The penal historian Harry Elmer Barnes, in his study of New Jersey prisons, refers to their report as "the most important document in the history of New Jersey penal institutions up to that time, and both an epitaph of the old system and a prophesy of a new order."[41]

The committee reported that the State Prison under Ephraim Ryno was losing money and that its accounts were poorly kept; that the outmoded construction of the building did not permit the solitude and surveillance necessary for maintaining discipline; that the subordinate officers were unruly, often consorting with the prisoners and neglecting their duties; and, above all, that the institution had a destructive influence on its inmates. A semisecret organization called the Staunch Gang organized conspiracies and escapes, threatening to murder anyone who exposed them. "They consider him a traitor, who informs on their deeds," a witness told the inspectors. "Such men are called snitch."[42] In an inept and arbitrary effort to enforce discipline, the keeper inflicted severe punishments including an "iron neck yoke," chains, and prolonged solitary confinement in an unheated cell. The inmates were wounded and debilitated, often "requir[ing] nearly as much time in the hospital . . . as they have had in the cells"; and at least ten prisoners had died "in consequence of being severely punished."[43] From the details of bookkeeping to the administration of labor and discipline, the Trenton prison was an appalling institution in the eyes of the era's leading reformers. The committee recommended "a speedy remedy" to the "evils" of the prison in the form of a new penitentiary. After some years of discussion and negotiation, including a long debate about the relative merits of the rival systems, New Jersey opened a new state prison, designed by John Haviland and operated on the Pennsylvania model, in 1836.[44]

Louis Dwight's committee had been aggressive in its attacks on the evils of the New Jersey State Prison, but it had been circumspect in the attribution of blame. In general, the reformers faulted the architecture of the institution, which made it impossible to enforce anything approaching the ideals of modern prison discipline: solitude, silence, and vigilant surveillance of the officers and the inmates. It seems clear, however, that the head keeper, Ephraim Ryno, was embarrassed by the scandal. Ryno kept the position for only one year, and the occasional mention of him in histories of Trenton and its institutions takes an apologetic tone.[45] In any case, the family history of George Ryno, the keeper's son and the poet who would call himself Harry Hawser, involved deep entanglements with the penal system and the reform movement. Nor did George Ryno's own relationship to the penitentiary end with his release in 1843. Five years later, he was again convicted of larceny and confined at Eastern State from January 1848 until February 1850.[46]

None of this, however, would be known to the public that read the work of Harry Hawser. In England and the United States, the reception of the poetry was shaped by Adshead, who had used it to refute the "fictions" of Dickens. Thus the *Manchester Guardian* praised Adshead for correcting the "mistakes and erroneous statements of Charles Dickens."[47] The *New York Herald*, reviewing Adshead's book, was "glad to see a work of this kind come from the English press."[48] An open letter on the Pennsylvania system from the English reformer William Tallack, reprinted in at least two American periodicals, quoted extensively from the preface of Hawser's book and repeated Adshead's interpretation of its meaning: "This testimony is very important, for this reformed prisoner [Hawser] thus fully refutes the jail fictions of the genial, imaginative novelist [Dickens]."[49] The peculiar new relationship between the prison interior and the mass public—the reformers' need to answer sensational fiction with an inmate's true testimony—definitively informed the rhetoric and reception of *Buds and Flowers*, making the poet's authenticity a central issue in the meaning and political force of the poetry. This new kind of authenticity, however, was paradoxically an effect of the inmate's anonymity; it depended on the reformers' capacity to obscure the life of George Ryno behind the screen of Harry Hawser.

At the same time, Hawser's book also reworked the tradition of the gallows confession in another significant way, by shifting the speaker's orientation toward death. The confession had traditionally expressed the convict's readiness to meet death, with a prayer for God's mercy. Hawser's task, instead, was to show how he had already passed through a disciplinary mortification and emerged into a new life. Very much unlike the gallows confession, the testimony of the reformed inmate had to display the author's bodily and psychic well-being. Thus the unnamed girl tells Lieber that she "feel[s] very well" in the prison; and Hawser insists that he "is neither morose, imbecile, dispirited, or deranged" (preface). His abjection in the prison had been a virtual death, but it had been absorbed into a narrative of spiritual resurrection.

This was the heart of the Philadelphia reformers' response to Dickens: where he saw the wretchedness of men and women buried alive, they sought to display a stern discipline that broke down the offender in order to nurture the awakening of a disciplined subject. As the public's fascination with the prison interior continued to grow, this fundamental opposition between the gothic nightmare of living death and the sentimental fantasy of personal rebirth would inform the tropes and modes of popular representation. In order to defend the prison system, Hawser had to communicate the blessings it had conferred on him. Line by line and page by page, his poems were supposed to manifest his earthly redemption.

In the years following the publication of *Buds and Flowers*, the connection between prison discipline and other forms of personal transformation, especially temperance, would be fortified. By 1852, the reformer Joseph Edward Turner had applied to the New York legislature for the incorporation of the first state-run asylum devoted to reforming drunkards. Chartered in 1854 and finally opened in 1864, the New York State Inebriate Asylum was a central institution in the formation of modern addiction treatment. Its practices included temperance lectures, group meetings, and a "literary and social support club" known as the Ollapod Club.[50] Meanwhile, the rival to the Philadelphia system, the "congregate" system in place in the penitentiaries of New York and Massachusetts, began to circulate its own examples of prison literature in such publications as *The Prisoner's Friend*, a monthly magazine founded in Boston in 1845. The editors would later claim to have issued "probably four hundred thousand copies" of the magazine in its first four years.[51] *The Prisoner's Friend* published essays and reports by reformers as well as original works by convicts. An 1846 poem by Charles Meadows, for example, concluded with this celebration of the temperance pledge:

> We, who now pace the prison cell,
> We who have drained the cup and fell,
> Oh, is there naught for us to do,
> Yes, *take the pledge*, and keep it too,
> Look up and breathe an earnest prayer,
> And hope will bid us not despair,
> But cheer us with its warmest ray,
> And show a future brighter day.[52]

By way of such poems, the advocates of the congregate system suggested that their institutions, no less than the solitary prison in Philadelphia, could lead the inmate through "despair" to "a future brighter day"—through the darkness of abjection to the awakening of a new life. (It was in the pages of *The Prisoner's Friend* that, after an absence of six years, Harry Hawser returned to the world of letters in 1850 with the publication of "Youth's Hopes," a mournful poem of unfulfilled promises. Amid the conventional, trite phrases—"airy dreams," "pathways green"—is one remarkable command to the reader, "Peruse my life," which faintly gestures toward the textual, even fictional character of the author.[53])

Those who wished to attack the prison in the public sphere, meanwhile, would cast doubt on its promise of resurrection by insisting that its secluded interior was a dungeon-tomb of living death. Karen Halttunen has identified a whole subgenre of mid-nineteenth-century popular fiction that used a gothic literary mode to protest the abuses suffered by inmates. These "gothic exposés of asylum life," Halttunen argues, revealed the gap between enlightened theory and violent practice, between humane intentions and cruel realities.[54] Such exposés both influenced and were influenced in turn by the most famous of such works, the depiction of Eastern State in Dickens's *American Notes*, with its memorable passages on the living entombment of the prison interior:

> Over the head and face of every prisoner who comes into this melancholy house a black hood is drawn; and in this dark shroud, an emblem of the curtain dropped between him and the living world, he is led to the cell from which he never again comes forth until his whole term of imprisonment has expired. He never hears of wife or children; home or friends; the life or death of any single creature. He sees the prison officers, but, with that exception, he never looks upon a human countenance, or hears a human voice. He is a man buried alive; to be dug out in the slow round of years; and in the meantime dead to everything but torturing anxieties and horrible despair. (91)

Returning, by way of conclusion, to Hawser's "The Captive," the poem of "living doom" that first drew me to *Buds and Flowers*, its haunting power now seems to arise from its resonance with Dickens's narrative, the very text it was published to refute, and with a whole tradition of imaginative prison literature that has developed the imagery of the penitentiary as a dungeon of civil death, bodily violence, and psychic dissolution. "The Captive" abandons the idiom of personal reformation and, calling incarceration a "doom," interrupts its blessing with a curse. Yet, this is not exactly, or not only, the subversive power of an incarcerated artist exposing the dehumanizing force of an institution he had been required to justify. Rather, the curse of "the captive's doom," the subversive potential of prison literature, is the menacing counterpart created alongside a genre whose official purpose was to bless or legitimate the modern regime of punishment. *Buds and Flowers* is animated by the deep contradictions—between authenticity and sensationalism, between subversion and complicity—in the very concept of prison literature that it communicated to the emergent mass public and its collective imagination.

NOTES

1. Harry Hawser was the name of a character in Samuel James Arnold's comic opera *The Shipwreck, or The Female Sailor,* performed in Boston and elsewhere in the United States in the early nineteenth century. For the text, see Arnold, *The Shipwreck, or The Female Sailor* (London: W. Simpkin and R. Marshall, Printers, 1820).

2. Harry Hawser, *Buds and Flowers, of Leisure Hours* (Philadelphia: Geo. W. Loammi Johnson, for the author, 1844), preface (n.p.). Subsequent references cited parenthetically in the text.

3. Negley K. Teeters and John D. Shearer, *The Prison at Philadelphia, Cherry Hill: The Separate System of Prison Discipline, 1829–1913* (New York: published for Temple University Publications by Columbia University Press, 1957).

4. Angela Davis, "Writing on the Wall: Prisoners on Punishment," *Punishment and Society* 3, no. 3 (2001): 428.

5. Ibid., 427.

6. See Leslie C. Patrick-Stamp, "George Ryno: Prisoner-Poet, 1840–1850," in Eastern State Penitentiary Task Force of the Preservation Commission of Greater Philadelphia, *Eastern State Penitentiary: Historic Structures Report* (Philadelphia: Philadelphia Historical Commission, 1994), 140–42.

7. Michel Foucault, *Discipline and Punish,* trans. Alan Sheridan (New York: Vintage, 1977).

8. Benjamin Rush, "An Enquiry into the Effects of Public Punishments upon Criminals and upon Society" (1787), in *Essays: Literary, Moral and Philosophical,* ed. Michael Meranze (Schenectady, N.Y.: Union College Press, 1988), 89.

9. Ibid., 91.

10. Quoted in Richard Vaux, *Brief Sketch of the Origins and History of the State Penitentiary for the Eastern District of Pennsylvania at Philadelphia* (Philadelphia: McLaughlin Brothers, Printers, 1872), 48.

11. Tom Wicker, preface to *Prison Writing in Twentieth-Century America,* ed. H. Bruce Franklin (New York: Penguin, 1998), xi.

12. John Bender, *Imagining the Penitentiary: Fiction and the Architecture of Mind in Eighteenth-Century England* (Chicago: University of Chicago Press, 1987).

13. Thomas L. Dumm, *Democracy and Punishment: Disciplinary Origins of the United States* (Madison: University of Wisconsin Press, 1987).

14. Michael Meranze, *Laboratories of Virtue: Punishment, Revolution, and*

Authority in Philadelphia, 1760–1835 (Chapel Hill: University of North Carolina Press for the Institute of Early American History and Culture, 1996), 173, 174. See also Meranze's "A Criminal Is Being Beaten: The Politics of Punishment and the History of the Body," in *Possible Pasts: Becoming Colonial in Early America,* ed. Robert Blair St. George (Ithaca, N.Y.: Cornell University Press, 2000); Jason Haslam, "Pits, Pendulums, and Penitentiaries: Reframing the Detained Subject," *Texas Studies in Literature and Language* 50, no. 3 (September 2008): 268–84; and my book, *The Prison and the American Imagination* (New Haven: Yale University Press, 2009).

15. Thomas M'Elwee and George W. Smith, quoted and reproduced in Vaux, *Brief Sketch,* 56–61.

16. Rush, "Enquiry," 88.

17. Haslam, "Pits, Pendulums, and Penitentiaries," 269.

18. Franklin Bache, "On the Penitentiary System: A Letter from Franklin Bache, M.D., to Roberts Vaux" (Philadelphia: Jesper Harding, Printer, 1829), 3.

19. Charles Dickens, *American Notes, for General Circulation* (1842; reprint, New York: St. Martin's, 1985). Subsequent references cited parenthetically in the text.

20. James M. Volo and Dorothy Denneen Volo, *The Antebellum Period* (New York: Greenwood, 2004), 220. On the many pirated editions of Dickens's texts in America, especially *American Notes,* see Meredith McGill, *American Literature and the Culture of Reprinting, 1834–1853* (Philadelphia: University of Pennsylvania Press, 2007).

21. *Times* (London), quoted in Philip Collins, *Dickens and Crime,* 3rd ed. (New York: St. Martin's Press, 1994), 130.

22. J. J. Telkampf, "Remarks on Prison Discipline in the United States, Suggested by the Chapter on Philadelphia and Its Solitary Prison in the 'American Notes' of Charles Dickens," *New World* 6, no. 3 (January 21, 1843): 67.

23. "British Critics and British Travelers," *United States Magazine and Democratic Review* 14, no. 70 (April 1844): 335–44.

24. William Peter, "Mr. Dickens' Report of His Visit to the Eastern Penitentiary," *Pennsylvania Journal of Prison Discipline and Philanthropy* 1, no. 1 (January 1845): 85–88. Quotation is from 87.

25. Francis Lieber, Letter to Mr. Barclay, Honorary Secretary of the Philadelphia Prison Society, September 18, 1843, reprinted in Joseph Adshead, *Prisons and Prisoners* (London: Longman, Brown, Green, and Longman, 1845), 115–17. All quotations are from these three pages.

26. Collins, *Dickens and Crime,* 118.

27. Adshead, *Prisons and Prisoners,* 99. Subsequent references cited parenthetically in the text.

28. Vaux, *Brief Sketch,* 112–13.

29. J. Field, *Prison Discipline* (1846; 2nd ed. 1848), quoted in Collins, *Dickens and Crime*, 119.

30. Commenting on Dickens's treatment of the female prisoners, Philip Collins notes that "the bitterly hostile reception which *American Notes* received in the United States was caused by many other features of the book than its penology, . . . and the vigour of the counter-attacks in defence of Philadelphia doubtless owed something to the general indignation which his sympathy for negroes excited" (*Dickens and Crime*, 127).

31. My use of the term "mortification" follows Erving Goffman, *Asylums: Essays on the Social Situation of Mental Patients and Other Inmates* (New York: Anchor, 1961).

32. David S. Shields, "The Demonization of the Tavern," in *The Serpent in the Cup: Temperance in American Literature,* ed. David S. Reynolds and Debra J. Rosenthal (Amherst: University of Massachusetts Press, 1997), 10.

33. Ibid., 15.

34. On the Washingtonians, the varieties of temperance rhetoric, and literature, see David S. Reynolds, "Black Cats and Delirium Tremens: Temperance and the American Renaissance," in Reynolds and Rosenthal, *Serpent in the Cup*. On Whitman and temperance, see also Michael Warner, "Whitman Drunk," in his *Publics and Counterpublics* (New York: Zone Books, 2005).

35. Warner, *Publics and Counterpublics*, 270. On the transformation of the economics and technology of print in early national Philadelphia, see Rosalind Remer, *Printers and Men of Capital: Philadelphia Book Publishers in the New Republic* (Philadelphia: University of Pennsylvania Press, 1996). On the formation of wider, national and international book markets in the antebellum period, see Ronald J. Zboray, *A Fictive People: Antebellum Economic Development and the American Reading Public* (New York: Oxford University Press, 1993).

36. Patrick-Stamp, "George Ryno," 140.

37. Teeters and Shearer, *Cherry Hill,* 126–27.

38. On the transatlantic tradition and popularity of the dying slave genre, see Brycchan Carey, *British Abolitionism and the Rhetoric of Sensibility* (Basingstoke, U.K.: Palgrave Macmillan, 2005); and Russ Castronovo, *Necro-Citizenship: Death, Eroticism, and the Public Sphere in the Nineteenth-Century United States* (Durham, N.C.: Duke University Press, 2001).

39. Teeters and Shearer, *Cherry Hill,* 127.

40. Ephraim Ryno is named as the keeper of the state prison in 1829 in the records of the New Jersey state legislature and in John O. Raum, *History of the City of Trenton, New Jersey* (Trenton, N.J.: W. T. Nicholson, Printers, 1871), 262.

41. Harry Elmer Barnes, *A History of the Penal, Reformatory and Correctional Institutions of the State of New Jersey: Analytical and Documentary* (1918) (reprint ed., New York: Arno Press, 1974), 73.

42. New Jersey Legislative Committee on Prison Discipline, "Report to the Legislature" (1830) (reprinted in Barnes, *History of the Penal, Reformatory and Correctional Institutions*, 396–423), 405.

43. New Jersey Legislative Committee, "Report," 411.

44. Barnes, *History of the Penal, Reformatory and Correctional Institutions*, 81–118.

45. See Raum, *History of the City of Trenton*, 262: "Ephraim Ryno, being a member of the board [of inspectors], succeeded in getting the appointment by having a majority of the board in his favor, and this, with his own vote, bestowed the appointment of keeper upon himself. He held it for one year only."

46. Teeters and Shearer, *Cherry Hill*, 127.

47. "Varieties," *Manchester Guardian*, October 22, 1845, 5.

48. "Literary Notices," *New York Herald*, January 40, 1846, 2.

49. William Tallack, "Charles Dickens's Prison Fictions," *Journal of Prison Discipline and Philanthropy* (January 1, 1895): 33. Tallack's essay was excerpted and reprinted in *The Friend: A Religious and Literary Journal* 68, no. 29 (February 9, 1895): 226.

50. See John W. Crowley and William L. White, *Drunkard's Refuge: The Lessons of the New York State Inebriate Asylum* (Amherst: University of Massachusetts Press, 2004). On the Ollapods, see 67–68.

51. "History of *The Prisoner's Friend*," *Prisoner's Friend* (September 1848): 3.

52. Charles Meadows, "Poem by Charles Meadows, a Convict," *Prisoner's Friend* (December 9, 1846): 193.

53. Harry Hawser, "Youth's Hopes," *Prisoner's Friend* 2, no. 12 (August 1, 1850): 544. Thanks to Ryan Carr for calling my attention to this source.

54. Karen Halttunen, "Gothic Mystery and the Birth of the Asylum: The Cultural Construction of Deviance in Early-Nineteenth-Century America," in *Moral Problems in American Life: New Perspectives on Cultural History*, ed. Karen Halttunen and Lewis Perry (Ithaca, N.Y.: Cornell University Press, 1998), 42.

"The Floor Was Stained with the Blood of a Slave"

Crime and Punishment in the Old South

MATTHEW J. CLAVIN

ON JULY 18, 1844, UNITED STATES DEPUTY MARSHAL James Gonzalez escorted a notorious criminal through a crowd of curious onlookers to the small brick jail in Pensacola, Florida, an exotic and bustling southern frontier town on the northern coast of the Gulf of Mexico. The prisoner, loaded in heavy iron chains, was Jonathan Walker, a well-known sailor, shipwright, and railroad superintendent. Local residents regarded the New England transplant as an honest and hard-working man, yet his views on the region's "peculiar institution" meant that he would always be considered an outsider. Indeed, Walker's hatred of both slavery and white supremacy had led to his captivity and confinement. Four weeks earlier, several bondsmen employed in the city and at the United States Navy Yard asked the former ship captain to help them escape from Pensacola to the Bahamas, a British colony off the coast of East Florida where slavery had recently been outlawed. Walker agreed, and under the cover of darkness, the seven runaways quietly boarded Walker's small

259

green whaleboat, drifted into the warm waters of the Gulf of Mexico, and set sail for the British West Indies and for freedom.

The journey was a disaster from the outset. Walker fell ill from heatstroke, while the fugitives quickly exhausted their supplies. Nevertheless, two weeks into their 700-mile journey, the vessel rounded the southern tip of the Florida peninsula and came within a day's journey of reaching its destination. A chance encounter with the eighty-eight-ton wrecking sloop *Eliza Catherine* ended the voyage when a suspicious captain directed members of his crew to board Walker's boat and take the fugitives into custody. The eight men then began the long trip back to Pensacola, where their lives would take very different turns. Upon their arrival, the fugitive slaves were quickly turned over to their owners, but not before four of them were delivered to the city jailer and brutally beaten.

The radical white abolitionist who had become their ally faced a different fate. A local court found him guilty of stealing slaves and ordered severe chastisement. Authorities placed Walker in a pillory on the courthouse lawn for an hour. They then brought him back inside, where Ebenezer Dorr, the United States Marshal for the Western District of Florida, pressed a red-hot branding iron into the palm of his hand, permanently scarring the flesh with the letters "ss" for "Slave Stealer." Unable to pay the numerous fines and penalties levied against him, Walker spent nearly a year chained to the floor of a small cell in the Pensacola city jail. It was a tremendous price to pay for attempting to deliver enslaved people from the house of bondage, but the sacrifice was not in vain.

During his captivity, Walker became a *cause célèbre* of the transatlantic abolitionist movement. His branded appendage in particular had become an important abolition icon, the subject of songs, poems, and widely distributed illustrations, including an early black-and-white daguerreotype. Abolitionists printed icons of the branded hand on large broadsheets "to be put up in offices, shops, &c." and also on abolitionist letterhead as "a mode of circulating very convenient and useful."[1] In January 1845, the *Liberator* announced the publication of *The Branded Hand*, a newspaper dedicated to "noble anti-slavery martyrs" like Walker. Its editors intended to distribute all profits from the sale of the monthly tract to Walker and other abolitionists held in captivity throughout the South.[2]

Walker's notoriety brought powerful allies to his defense. Titans of American and British abolitionism, including Wendell Phillips, Frederick

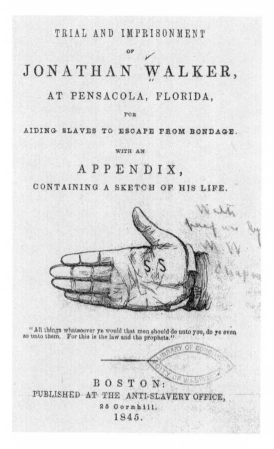

TRIAL AND IMPRISONMENT

OF

JONATHAN WALKER,

AT PENSACOLA, FLORIDA,

FOR

AIDING SLAVES TO ESCAPE FROM BONDAGE.

WITH AN

APPENDIX,

CONTAINING A SKETCH OF HIS LIFE.

"All things whatsoever ye would that men should do unto you, do ye even so unto them. For this is the law and the prophets."

BOSTON:
PUBLISHED AT THE ANTI-SLAVERY OFFICE,
25 Cornhill.
1845.

FIGURE 16. Jonathan Walker, *Trial and Imprisonment of Jonathan Walker, at Pensacola, Florida, for Aiding Slaves to Escape from Bondage* (Boston: Anti-Slavery Office, 1845). This frontispiece illustration of the one-of-a-kind hand would become a resonant icon of the abolitionist movement. Courtesy of the Library of Congress.

Douglass, and Thomas Clarkson, joined the campaign to raise money to both pay his legal fees and court fines and provide sustenance for his wife and children while he remained in jail. These and other prominent abolitionists sponsored meetings, passed resolutions, and delivered speeches. On May 20, 1845, they delivered to the U.S. Marshal who had branded Walker the more than one thousand dollars necessary to secure Walker's release.[3] Twenty-seven days later, he was free.

Within a matter of months, abolitionist journals advertised the sale of a manuscript Walker had written behind bars and revised subsequently. Published for the first time in 1845, the book found a wide audience, going through four editions in five years and appearing in various formats in numerous abolitionist publications. In addition to offering a rare eyewitness account of slavery on the Florida frontier, *Trial and Imprisonment of Jonathan Walker, at Pensacola, Florida, for Aiding Slaves to Escape from Bondage* provides one of the most extensive published descriptions of slave imprisonment and punishment in early America. Based on a daily log Walker kept during his imprisonment, the book describes the corporal punishment of black prisoners over an eleven-month period, occurring at the same time the territory of Florida was acquiring statehood (see figure 16). Told from the perspective of a southern conductor on the Underground Railroad, it overflows with textual and visual depictions of the routine jailhouse tortures inflicted on the bodies of enslaved Floridians. When viewed alongside contemporary accounts of slave incarceration, the narrative reveals that from the day the United States first acquired Florida in 1819, Pensacola's evolution from a colonial Spanish village to a southern American city was neither automatic nor accidental. Throughout the difficult transitional period, slaveowners had a powerful weapon at their disposal.

The public jail located on the outskirts of this "Rogue's Paradise" provided a number of important services.[4] The building served as a part-time residence of many of the roughneck sailors and scoundrels who drank, gambled, and fought in excess. It was also the temporary home of more serious offenders—thieves, robbers, rapists, and murderers—who awaited trial or, in rare cases, execution. But it functioned primarily as a house of horrors for bondspeople, a public institution where at the behest of a small but powerful group of slaveowners, law enforcement officials daily employed violence to discipline intractable black men and women. An examination of the history of the Pensacola jail in the four decades before the Civil War illuminates the role of institutionalized corporal punishment in securing the expansion of slavery to the periphery of the United States. It reveals further that at the same time the belief in the rehabilitative potential of incarceration spread throughout much of the new republic, such philosophical change never occurred in Pensacola or, for that matter, wherever the incarceration of enslaved people continued.[5] While prisoner punishments moved behind fences and doors in the South—as it did elsewhere—its purpose remained retributive and became increasingly racial.

The Receptacle of Filth

Jonathan Walker's incarceration in Pensacola's jail was not the first time the old calaboose was at the center of a major international incident. In

1821, as a result of the Adams-Onís Treaty, which ceded Spain's expansive Florida territory to the United States two years earlier, the American war hero and newly appointed territorial governor Andrew Jackson arrested the former Spanish governor of Pensacola, José Callava, "at the point of a bayonet" for failing to turn over public documents. He then locked him behind bars until the documents materialized.[6] The brash act chafed Spanish residents and officials at the same time it reinforced the idea among both groups that there was a new governor in town. Callava's captivity was short-lived, lasting less than twenty-four hours; however, the United States' control of the region was only beginning. In the coming decades, Florida embarked on a period of transition from a neglected colony on the periphery of a declining European empire to a full and equal member of the United States of America. The territory also embarked on becoming a part of the South, a transition that would prove equally as challenging.

Of the many obstacles that stood in the way of Florida acquiring southernness, none proved as daunting as the issue of slavery. Florida's unique history regarding bondage is well known. Primarily a Spanish outpost since the permanent establishment of the settlement of St. Augustine on the Atlantic coast in 1565, the region offered a degree of racial tolerance and at times a relatively benign system of slavery that granted enslaved people certain rights and privileges that were unthinkable in most parts of the English-speaking Atlantic world.[7] In this context, Florida could never be a typical southern state.

As an urban center on the edge of the Atlantic world, Pensacola was particularly ill-suited to adopt southern ways and mores due to its geography, climate, and demographics. Subtropical heat, hurricanes, and sandy soil spelled the doom of any large-scale cotton enterprise. Consequently, residents searched in vain for alternative cash crops. While the production of timber, textiles, and assorted other industries met with varying degrees of success, it was the decision of the United States government to build a Navy Yard and a series of defensive forts around the city and along the Gulf Coast that put Pensacola's economy on the path to long-term viability.[8] Regarding demographics, Pensacola's multiracial and multiethnic Creole community, which derived from the region's African, French, and Spanish populations, ensured continued resistance to the political, social, and economic ascendancy of a single white race.

The United States' acquisition of Florida in 1819 spelled the end of Creole rule in Pensacola. It failed, however, to end black resistance, which continued unabated in the decades that followed. For example, the city's diverse population and its proximity to the Gulf of Mexico and the greater Atlantic world, along with the number of urban and maritime industries that employed both free and enslaved black men, made the city a refuge for runaway slaves from throughout the Deep South. Consequently, in the advertisements for fugitive slaves that filled local papers in the decades before the Civil War, slaveowners frequently noted that escaped bondspeople were "endeavoring to get to Pensacola," "will make for Pensacola," and "will no doubt try to get to Pensacola."[9]

It was clear after the United States gained possession of Florida territory that American slaveowners would need help in controlling Pensacola's unruly black population. Almost immediately, a powerful institutional ally emerged in the city jail. There were, in fact, two places for incarceration in Pensacola in the early nineteenth century. Located on the northeast corner of the city's residential grid, the structures occupied the same location, southwest of a large Catholic cemetery. Little is known of the first jail, though one traveler recording his impressions of the city's public buildings in 1820 described "a very conveniently situated calaboose, and neighboring gallows, pillory, whipping post and stocks."[10] Built by the British in the late eighteenth century and then inherited by the Spanish after the American Revolution, this "Calabozo" was, according to one visitor, a "receptacle of filth" that "assailed the organ of smell."[11] Another observer described it as a small, low, and narrow brick building that resembled a stable more than a jail. It was "as forlorn, dirty and uncomfortable an edifice as can be imagined."[12] Decades of disrepair and countless prisoner escapes led to public outcry for a replacement.[13]

It was the same throughout the antebellum South. As historian Edward Ayers has shown, while in the northern United States citizens embraced the idea of a centralized system of state penitentiaries where prisoners served lengthy sentences, the forces of honor and slavery led some in the South to launch "the most sustained opposition the penitentiary has ever confronted."[14] Consequently, incarceration remained a local responsibility, and the southern jail was a demonstrably inadequate partner in any effort to modernize southern law enforcement. Frequent prisoner escapes were a clear indication of the failure of the institution to exact justice, as a cursory glance at antebellum southern newspapers demonstrates. "It was," in the words of one peripatetic southern lawyer, "a matter of free election for the culprit in a desperate case, whether he would remain in jail or not, and it is astonishing how few exercised their privilege in favor of staying."[15] At the periphery of the American republic, the situation was even worse, leaving the citizens of one East Florida community to complain of the local lockup that "no prisoner can be detained within its walls against his will."[16]

In spite of the magnitude of the problem, Floridians exhibited no desire to provide the resources necessary to build and maintain a prison. Indeed, in the decades before the Civil War, Florida was one of only three southern states that resisted the national trend toward erecting a penitentiary. Consequently, the expansive region developed into a haven for "outlaw gangs, lynch mobs, and regulators," according to historian James M. Denham, becoming a dangerous and violent frontier society where guns and knives were the only recourse to justice.[17] This was the case in Pensacola as late as 1857, when the capture of two suspected murderers led one frustrated resident to vent, "We ought to have a penitentiary!"[18]

The unlikelihood of federal or state officials constructing a penitentiary in Florida led to calls for a secure and reliable local jail in Pensacola. The requests began immediately upon Florida's achieving territorial status. In a letter to Secretary of State John Quincy Adams in 1822, a local district attorney pleaded for a new jail, insisting the existing structure was "in such a state of dilapidation as to be wholly unfit for the confinement of offenders." This was alarming in a place so often frequented by a class of lawless men who required "the *strongest* edifice for their accommodation or security."[19] The jail's shortcomings were made apparent several years later when a notorious highway robber, arrested for the attempted murder of a mail carrier, escaped four times and ultimately remained at large. In 1835, fortuitous economic circumstances convinced the well-respected editor of the *Pensacola Gazette* to beg the city's residents to construct "a cheap and substantial building which would serve all the necessary purposes for the city, the Territory and the United States."[20] They listened, and a year later built a new facility where the old calaboose had stood.[21]

Jonathan Walker's 1845 narrative provides the best surviving description of the new jail. It was a rectangular two-story brick building, roughly eighteen by thirty-six feet (see figure 17). There were two rooms on each floor. Prisoners occupied the lower floor, while the jailer's family resided

FIGURE 17. Rembert Wallace Patrick, *Florida under Five Flags* (Gainesville: University of Florida Press, 1945). A sketch of the jail where Jonathan Walker spent eleven months and daily witnessed the brutal punishment of bondspeople. Courtesy of the Special & Area Studies Collections, George A. Smathers Library, University of Florida.

on the upper floor. The jail cells were approximately fifteen square feet, fronted with double doors and containing two small grated windows that rose six to eight feet from the floor. Above the cells was a single-board floor, "which but little obstructs the noise of the upper part from being distinctly heard below, and *vice versa*."[22] Though unusual today, the presence of inmates in the same building that housed the jailer and his family was common throughout the eighteenth and nineteenth centuries; the indistinguishable architecture of both jails and contemporary houses likewise had a long tradition.[23] Immediately after his incarceration, Walker wrote matter-of-factly that he was committed to a jail, "or rather to the house in which the constable lived." The man Walker referred to was Francis Touart, the jailer "more commonly designated by the title of city marshal."[24]

Walker described the misery of jailhouse life in detail and, to communicate the agony of incarceration more clearly, begged readers to imagine themselves in the same situation. Doing so was necessary if they were
going to comprehend the "misery and suffering of imprisonment" in a
southern jail from the safe comfort of their distant northern dwellings.
Walker was an ill man upon his arrival at the jail, suffering from both
heat exhaustion and malnutrition, in no condition to be caged "like
some rabid, dangerous animal." Things only worsened: "I was chained to
the sleeper of a solitary cell, rolling from side to side, and shifting from
one position to another on the floor to relieve my aching bones, which
were covered with little more than the skin wrapped over them." Placed
alone in a cell, Walker was secured by a "ring-bolt by a large size log-
chain, and a shackle of round iron, weighing about five pounds, round
the ankle." His feet and legs quickly swelled because of the restraints,
which "were partly buried in the flesh, but after some weeks' entreaty
they were taken off and replaced by others larger."[25]

There were few of the appurtenances of everyday life, even for a common laborer and seaman. "The floor was my bed, seat, and table," Walker
explained, "and it was nearly a month before I could procure anything
to lie upon, other than a few clothes which I had with me." He nevertheless obtained a chair and table, along with some straw, from which he
fashioned a bed on the floor. In spite of the spartan accommodations,
adapting to jailhouse fare proved more trying. "One of my first objects
after I was incarcerated," Walker wrote, "was to procure such nourish-
ment as would not quarrel with nature, and this I found rather difficult
at first; a part of the jail feed I could not relish, and if I attempted to
eat it, it would sicken and distress me." Walker could barely stomach the
bread, soup, and fish provided by the jailer, and at times went "two or
three weeks" without receiving any sustenance. Relief for his appetite
came eventually in the form of a sympathetic immigrant grocer who
supplemented his diet throughout the duration of his confinement.[26]

Another disadvantage of incarceration in a small city jail was the lack
of mobility. Heavy shackles forced Walker to always sit or lie down. "If
I could walk the room it would afford me great relief," he complained
shortly after taking up residence in the jail.[27] Months later, little had
changed. "The want of exercise is a great privation, and serves materi-
ally to impair both the physical and mental faculties," Walker elucidated.
"Having always been in the habit of laborious exercise, the entire deprivation of it is more sensibly felt. I would much rather be incarcerated in

a State prison, a penitentiary, where I could be allowed to labor. Out of two hundred and fifty-six days solitary confinement in this place, I have been one hundred and seventy-three days in heavy irons."[28]

Walker's reference to the state penitentiary was strategic, underscoring an important sectional contrast. By the 1840s, as a part of the humanitarian effort to rehabilitate prisoners, private and public yards for recreation and exercise had become commonplace in the North's most prominent penitentiaries. Consequently, Walker's highlighting of the distinction played perfectly into his abolitionist argument.[29] In calling attention to the antiquated nature of one of the South's important peculiar institutions, Walker undermined the justification for all of them, slavery especially.

At least one reader of Walker's account denied the existence of any inherent defect in southern incarceration. He saw in Walker's treatment the elements of a system of incarceration that was both fair and firm. According to the local editorialist, Walker's imprisonment "was no further rigorous than was necessary to prevent his escape." Though Walker complained of inadequate sleeping arrangements, this was easily explained: "A bed was offered him and he declined accepting it, supposing, probably, that it would be charged to him, and paid for out of a small fund which was found on him and taken from him, when he was taken into custody." Regarding meals, the prisoner received standard "fair, to which we understand several benevolent ladies of the neighborhood of the prison, added some little comforts, nearly every day, until W. recovered his health, which, when he landed here, was very bad." There was no denial of any "enjoyment compatible with his safekeeping." Walker had a chair, table, writing materials, and books and newspapers for reading. Such benevolent treatment was extraordinary, given the prisoner was a "thriftless, indolent, useless member of society, a sort of transcendentalist" whose treatment at the hands of white southerners was of no cause for concern among northern abolitionists. That Walker exaggerated his suffering was evidenced by the fact "that he went into jail in bad health, and came out as fat as a pig."[30]

The partisan editorial exaggerated Walker's benevolent treatment in an attempt to demean northern abolitionists and defend southern culture. It is significant, nevertheless, indicating the special handling Walker's race accorded him. Though Walker faced a truly terrible situation, there is no mention in his narrative (or any of the other publications or correspondence of his that survives) of his being flogged.

Though pilloried and branded in a series of sensational public displays soon after his capture, once behind bars Pensacola's jailer never laid a hand on him. Quite the contrary, Walker noted the preferential handling he received from the jailer and the jailer's wife, writing, "It may be asked what treatment I received at their hands? I answer, that for the most part of the time, it was better than that which fell to the lot of the other prisoners."[31]

As a matter of fact, not one white burglar, brawler, or bandit lodged inside the jail received corporal punishment during Walker's long imprisonment. A review of newspapers and court records reveals no evidence of any white prisoner being punished corporally anywhere in Pensacola after the 1820s. The same cannot be said of the long procession of black men and women who passed through the doors of the city jail. While slaveowners and law enforcement officers in the South ostensibly shared northerners' aversion to bodily punishment, they in reality reserved whips and other instruments of torture exclusively for enslaved people, whom they accused of committing various crimes, including truancy and theft, drunkenness, insubordination, and, in the case of one bondswoman, "attempting to defend herself when about to be whipped by her mistress."[32]

"Where cowhide, paddle, chains, and slavery does prevail"

Unlike Walker, whose complexion mitigated his punishment, several of the runaways who sailed with him toward the British West Indies learned quickly of the severe jailhouse thrashing that awaited intractable black people. Naval Officer Robert C. Caldwell claimed ownership of three of the runaways—Moses Johnson and the brothers Silas and Henry Scott—and took the men into his custody shortly after their return to Pensacola. The owners of Anthony Catlett and Moses Johnson's three younger brothers, Charles, Philip, and Leonard, took a different approach. Perhaps because of logistical reasons, or more likely in an effort to draw the jailer further into the slaveholder's orbit, they left their bondsmen in the jail for several days. Walker noted their arrival in the cell opposite his, and a week later reported that the men were "whipped fifty blows each, with a paddle." Shortly thereafter, they hobbled from the jail and into the custody of their owners. Walker watched as they left the building, noting in his journal, they "with much difficulty could walk, being very sore."[33] The scene belies the words of a writer who defended the treatment of the incarcerated bondsmen, writing in the *Pensacola Gazette*, "the slaves returned most gladly to their masters."[34]

Walker's description is the first of his many mentions of the vicious mode of slave punishment known as paddling, a subject he returned to throughout his text. Though placed in a private cell throughout most of his stay, Walker made a mockery of the southern mode of solitary confinement by recording the paddling of roughly half of the approximately forty black prisoners he encountered. Shocked by what he saw and heard, Walker endeavored to exploit the humanitarian sensibilities of his predominately northern middle-class reading audience. His graphic description of the paddling of black men and women situates his narrative squarely in an emerging antislavery literary genre that eagerly exploited slave suffering to, in the words of historian Elizabeth B. Clark, "provoke a sympathetic response from right-thinking Christians."[35]

To impart the viciousness of "paddle-whipping," Walker employed the violent language found in some of the most popular abolitionist tracts of the antebellum era, including Theodore Dwight Weld's *American Slavery as It Is* and Frederick Douglass's *Narrative of the Life of Frederick Douglass: An American Slave*.[36] The paddles were made of pinewood, nearly twenty inches long and up to an inch-and-a-quarter thick. Beyond a narrow round handle was a wide flat surface punctuated with anywhere from ten to fifteen holes, "the size of a large nail gimblet." The black captives were tied at the wrists and then forced to the ground. In a sitting position, they bent their legs and pushed their knees through the opening between their arms, at which point the jailer inserted either a stick or broom handle behind the knees and over the arms, leaving them "in a doubled and helpless condition." What followed constituted physical and sexual assault. After properly restraining the victims, the jailer stripped them of their clothing from the waist down and rolled them on to their sides, exposing their posteriors. He then applied the paddle forcefully to their backsides, "stopping at short intervals to allow the sufferer to answer such questions as are asked, or make such promises as it thought best to exhort; and to give the numbness which has been excited by repeated blows, time to subside, which renders the next blows more acute and painful."[37]

Every blow that found its target cemented the bond between slaveowners and the state, Walker explained. The jailer delivered as many as fifty strikes with the paddle, "as the master or mistress" dictated, and then applied the "raw-hide switch" to the "bruised and blistered parts,

FIGURE 18. Jonathan Walker, *Trial and Imprisonment of Jonathan Walker, at Pensacola, Florida, for Aiding Slaves to Escape from Bondage* (Boston: Anti-Slavery Office, 1845). This engraving illuminates both the sexualized nature of paddling and the alliance such flogging forged between the jailer and the enslaved woman's owners. Courtesy of the Library of Congress.

with as many or more blows laid on." Finally, the victim was released and "suffered to get over it the best way they can." There was, Walker concluded, "no precise rule to be observed in regard to punishment, but the masters and mistresses are the sole judges as to method and quantity; and whenever the paddle is brought in requisition, it means that the rawhide (more commonly called cow-hide) is not equal to the offence."[38]

Though bodily punishments had fallen into disrepute in the North, two illustrations included in different editions of Walker's publication confirmed this was not the case in the South. Here, support for the corporal punishment of slaves showed no signs of abating.[39] In the words of one of the leading scholars of southern criminal justice, "most white Southerners simply did not perceive whipping to be a particularly cruel or even harsh punishment for blacks."[40]

The first engraving, published in Boston in 1845, depicts a nearly naked black woman lying on the ground with her feet and buttocks exposed (see figure 18). A long stick inserted behind her knees and through her arms forces her into the fetal position. The constable's power over the prisoner—both physical and sexual—is apparent, as he suspends the paddle high in the air and prepares to bring it down with great force on the defenseless body beneath him. The exposure of the enslaved woman's private parts underscores the extraordinary moral depravity of southern white men; for readers familiar with tales of sexual violence in the slave South, the image carried great resonance.

The second image, published a year later in a slightly revised edition of the narrative, reverses the vantage point of the viewer, making the bondswoman's face both visible and impossible to ignore (see figure 19). Her hair, which stands on end, amplifies the terror she is experiencing; the fear is palpable. The look of horror on her face, as well as the cowering and crying black child in the background, suggests the psychological toll that such beatings took on black mothers and their children, the latter of whom were undoubtedly apt pupils in this peculiar institution of higher learning.

FIGURE 19. Jonathan Walker, *Trial and Imprisonment of Jonathan Walker, at Pensacola, Florida, for Aiding Slaves to Escape from Bondage* (Boston: Anti-Slavery Office, 1846). This engraving from a later edition of Walker's narrative illuminates the powerlessness of the victim and her child, as well as the power of the slaveowners who supervise nearby. Courtesy of the Library of Congress.

One similarity of the two illustrations worth noting is the conspicuous presence of two white bystanders, likely slaveowners, who take more than a passing interest in the beating. Depicted as voyeurs, their male posture and gaze underscore the sexualized nature of the punishment. As we have seen, men such as these directed the horrifying scenes that played out behind the jail's walls, something their spectatorship conveys. Both images encapsulate the utilitarian as opposed to humanitarian nature of slave incarceration in the Old South. Instead of serving the public's interest, Pensacola's jail and its employees served the interest of the city's slaveowners, a select group that proved remarkably successful at bending public institutions like the jail to their will.

To awaken northerners to the horrors of slave imprisonment made possible by slaveowners' unmitigated power, Walker took readers on a vicarious journey, confident the experience would assault their senses — as it did his. Walker described some of the sounds that emanated from the jail, writing, "I was often pained in being compelled to hear the blows of the whip and the paddle."[41] What he heard recalled Frederick Douglass's famous observation of the corrupting influence of slavery on slaves, slave masters, and slave mistresses.[42] Referring to the jailer's wife, Walker continued, she "whipped the cook severely with a broomstick; scolds tremendously; gives unlimited scope to passion, and tapers off by crying herself."[43]

Walker's explicit testimony of the cook's floggings, which he watched from his small cell window, made voyeurs out of the readers of his narrative. He described the kitchen as a doorless wooden building about twenty feet from the jail, with wooden window shutters that swung and crashed in the wind. "I had a pretty fair view of what was transacted there from the only window which I could look out of, and from which I was often compelled to turn away, for the scene was too disgusting to look upon." What Walker witnessed on a daily basis sickened him: a woman and her children at the mercy of two sadists, both the jailer and his wife. The actions of the latter were particularly revolting. While Walker had met the jailer briefly before his incarceration, he was unfamiliar with his spouse. "But I soon found that what St. Paul called the weaker vessel was the stronger vessel, for none could carry so great a press of sail as my hostess. Her colors were nailed at mast-head, and all about the premises were to be controlled by her undisputed sway." Walker labeled the jail a "woman whipping-shop," for during his confinement Touart or his wife flogged the cook nearly fifty times. "Whenever the cook was whipped,"

Walker explained, "it was done, with a few exceptions, with a raw-hide switch, about three feet in length, generally from twenty to fifty strokes at a time." This and other similar "exhibitions" stirred the reluctant eyewitness to wax lyrical about the jail, borrowing several lines from a well-known antislavery poem:

> "Hate's quivering lip, the fix'd, the starting eye,
> The grin of vengeance, and the forehead pale,
> The deep drawn breath, the short hyena cry,
> All in connection tell the dreadful tale"
> Where cowhide, paddle, chains, and slavery does prevail.[44]

An Engine of Discipline

The routine assault on the cook by one of Pensacola's few municipal employees was part of a larger regional culture in which white slaveowners and their collaborators marked and mutilated the bodies of black people. At the same time northerners were losing faith in the ability of bodily punishments to modify behavior, runaway slave advertisements published in Pensacola's newspapers confirmed the widespread and unchanging belief among white southerners that, in the words of one proslavery theorist, the slave "can be reached only through his body."[45] In January 1828, Richard Legon of Mount Meigs, Alabama, offered $600 for the return of six bondsmen whose bodies testified to the brutality of bondage. Among them was Buckner, with "a scar between the nose and the upper lip"; Mason, with "a scar projecting from the upper lip to the right cheek"; and Moses, who had "several large gashes on the head." The anomalous nature of Toby's back drew the following observation: "smooth, and clear of scars."[46] The lash took an incredible toll on its victims. James T. De Jarnett offered an astounding $500 for the return of Celia, whom he described as both intelligent and beautiful, adding, "I do not recollect any visible marks, except she has holes in her ears, and on examining has a scar, I think on her left arm, about the elbow, which has the appearance of having been burnt or scalded." Stretched across her left shoulder blade were thick scars "caused by the whip, and about the size of a man's thumb nail which rises above the level of the skin."[47]

Whips were only one weapon used to punish and intimidate. Eli Townsend of Pike County, Alabama, sought the return of Ben, his wife Fillis, and their six-month-old son. In addition to the "large scars on his back and hips," Ben bore additional distinctive marks: "he has a scar on his right hand his thumb and fore finger being injured by being shot last fall, a part of the bones came out of his finger and thumb and has caused his thumb more particularly to shrink."[48] While some bondspeople were identifiable for missing fingers and ears, others bore invisible scars. George Willis, a prominent Pensacola businessman, offered $30 for the return of Smart, a serial runaway whom he described as a "short mulatto fellow, lame in the left leg, having had his thigh broken."[49] The use of passive voice left little doubt as to the probable cause of the traumatic injury.

That a man enslaved by George Willis suffered extremely was anticipated, given the owner's reputation as a cruel and ruthless slaveholder. Walker knew Willis well. In addition to owning three of the men who ran away from Pensacola with Walker, Willis had thrown rotten eggs at Walker's face during his pillorying in front of the Pensacola courthouse. Walker never forgot the egging, but his extreme dislike of one of Pensacola's most powerful men was not entirely personal. According to Walker, Willis was a haughty, overbearing, and cruel man who associated with very few individuals. He nevertheless claimed a high rank in society. He owned considerable property, including a large number of bondspeople whom he treated with great severity. Worst of all, he had earlier used public office to extend his power over the city's black population. Walker wrote of Willis, "He was marshal of the west district of Florida, two or three years, whilst I lived in Pensacola; during which time he had the honor of hanging three or four colored men."[50]

Given the unlimited power of local law enforcement, the threat of punishment in the Pensacola jail or any jail in the antebellum South must have terrified bondspeople. According to the renowned abolitionist and native South Carolinian Angelina Grimké, the sight of the enormous city jail and adjacent workhouse in her hometown even caused whites to tremble. As a teenager, Grimké was attending a seminar in Charleston when she interviewed black women who were brutalized in the workhouse and white women who were sickened by the cries that emanated from behind its walls—walls that, according to historian Douglas R. Egerton, workers packed with sand to "muffle the screams of inmates."[51] Grimké never forgot walking past the "house of blood," writing years later that "I felt as if I was passing the precincts of hell." The mere sight of the building "smote me with such horror that my limbs could hardly sustain me."[52]

Fear of a jailhouse battering would explain the motivation behind a ghastly incident that occurred in the jail cell opposite Walker's in September 1844. The *Pensacola Gazette* reported that a bondsman and suspected thief had committed suicide by slashing his throat and slicing his stomach open with a razor. "He was about 36 years of age and bore the character of a trust-worthy, respectful and obedient servant in the Navy Yard, where he has been steadily employed for a number of years." Walker recorded the aftermath of the gruesome event in his journal:

> On the 4th September I was moved to the adjoining room. . . . On one side of the room, much of the floor was stained with the blood of a slave, who had three days before committed suicide by cutting open his belly and throat with a razor; he had been committed that morning, charged with stealing, but it was subsequently ascertained that the article which he was accused of stealing had only been removed by some other person to another place, and nothing had the appearance of dishonesty in the case.

The paper blamed the man's suicide on "conjugal infidelity on the part of his wife," though Walker believed that the prospect of a jailhouse beating provided the real motivation: "I have no doubt but his miserable condition as a slave to a severe master, and the expectation of undergoing severe punishment for the alleged offense, was the cause of his putting an end to his degraded existence."[53]

Dismayed by what he experienced, Walker revealed the inner workings of the Pensacola jail. The building was city property, and the jailer won his post in an annual election. In return for his services, he received a monthly salary. As the city's highest-ranking and at times only police officer, his responsibilities were several. Upon taking up residency in the top floor of the jail, he spent most of his time admitting and releasing drunks, gamblers, and other petty criminals. Providing these prisoners with food and drink earned him thirty-seven-and-a-half cents per day. As was the case throughout the South, slave catching was often the primary responsibility of the jailer, for, as historian Sally E. Hadden has demonstrated, jails served frequently as the institutional center of the southern slave patrol.[54] By ringing the city bell every evening at eight o'clock in the winter and nine o'clock in the summer, the jailer further assisted slaveowners and patrollers in their effort to control the movement of bondspeople.

In addition to incarcerating slaves who were on the streets after the ringing of the bell or who failed in their attempts to abscond, the jailer also disciplined bondspeople sent to him by their owners for various infractions. The service entitled the jailer "to extra pay" from the slave-owner who employed him. Unsure of the exact price, Walker estimated the jailer received 70 cents per beating or flogging, noting further, "I know not whether he is under any official obligation to perform this task, or whether custom has made it a rule." The cost of public punishment would help explain why some slaveowners had their slaves incarcerated and others did not. There was, according to Walker, another reason why some slaveowners failed to avail themselves of the use of jail. "By a few minutes' exertion of their own muscular powers," they could "feed their rapacious revenge upon their helpless slaves."[55]

Walker's account suggests how little northerners understood the symbiotic relationship that existed between the public jail and southern slaveowners, something his narrative intended to correct. His description is largely consistent with the historical record. While Pensacola's jailers left no descriptions of their day-to-day activities, the testimony of a Norfolk, Virginia, constable in 1851 confirms Walker's observation:

> It was part of my business to arrest all slaves and free persons of color, who were collected in crowds at night, and lock them up. . . . The punishment is flogging. I am one of the men who flog them. They get not exceeding thirty-nine lashes. I am paid fifty cents for every negro I flog. The price used to be sixty-two and half cents. I am paid fifty cents for every negro I arrest, and fifty cents more if I flog him. I have flogged hundreds. I am often employed by private persons to pursue fugitive slaves. I have been employed since 1833. I never refuse a good job of that kind.[56]

The underfunding of public facilities helps explain the economic incentive behind slave incarceration that developed at Pensacola's jail. However, city employees were not alone in reaping the economic benefits of slave imprisonment. In June 1839, a Pensacola newspaper announced the successful public auction of three fugitive slaves, after their incarceration in the jail for more than a year. The newspaper expressed great pleasure that the three men earned the county almost two thousand dollars, because the entire community would benefit. Fortunately, the profits from the sale of the three black men were to be set aside for an essential public improvement, "the object of building a substantial jail."[57]

Though slave imprisonment was a lucrative business in Pensacola, its central function throughout the antebellum period remained assisting slaveowners in their effort to dominate a resistant black population. One case in particular illuminates the jail's primary function as "an engine of discipline."[58] In the winter of 1845, Walker noted the imprisonment of an older bondsman three separate times during a three-month period. During each stint behind bars, the jailer flogged the prisoner with both the paddle and the cowhide. The beatings, which occurred under the watchful eyes of the slaveowner's wife and at her command, left the bondsman sick for days. Walker explained the circumstances of the man's frequent confinement. The bondsman with his owner's permission visited his family on a neighboring plantation at Christmas, but was late in returning. The transgression landed him behind bars for sixteen days. Upon his release, he was moved to New Orleans for sale. "But being too old to meet with a ready sale in that market, he was returned again the 1st of April, and lodged in jail until the 12th, when his mistress came there in a rage, under the influence of liquor, and caused him to be flogged." Throughout the "performance," the woman "stood by and gave directions to the operator, yelping all the while at the mangled victim of her anger." In spite of the concerted efforts of both this inebriated mistress and the jailer, incarceration and violent retribution failed to have the desired effect on this bondsman. To the contrary, both seemed to steel his resolve. For shortly after his third stint in the jail, he escaped from his "tormentors" and, Walker noted with satisfaction, was never heard from again.[59]

The war inside Pensacola's jail between slaves and slaveowners raged continually throughout the many months of Walker's incarceration. However, at least one significant change had taken place beyond the building's walls and fences. The territory of Florida joined the United States of America as the twenty-seventh state and fourteenth slave state on March 3, 1845. In many respects, the transformation of the former Spanish colony to an important constituent of both the new republic and the Old South had already been completed. Walker made no mention of the historic event in his narrative; instead, in the days surrounding the occasion, he documented the torture of black men and women just a few blocks from where raucous public celebrations ensued. His daily log survives as a testament to how Pensacola's slaveowners and their publicly elected collaborators terrorized black men and women throughout the early nineteenth century.

The effort embedded slavery and white supremacy deeper into the region's culture and secured slaveowners' power additionally. Yet it was, in the final analysis, only partially successful. While the city jail and its jailers frightened and intimidated the region's bondspeople—to which extent, we can only imagine—they failed collectively to affect the behavior of those who continued to resist their enslavement variously, including walking, running, and sailing away from their homes, shops, and plantations in search of freedom. And when sectional discord over slavery culminated in a terrible civil war, Pensacola again became a refuge for free and enslaved African Americans as it had been so many years before.

NOTES

1. "The Branded Hand," *Boston Emancipator and Weekly Chronicle*, August 13, 1845.

2. "The Branded Hand," *Liberator*, January 10, 1845.

3. Jonathan Walker, *Trial and Imprisonment of Jonathan Walker, at Pensacola, Florida, for Aiding Slaves to Escape from Bondage. With an Appendix, Containing a Sketch of His Life* (Boston: Anti-Slavery Office, 1845), 98–100; "Devilish Democracy," *Liberator*, August 29, 1845.

4. "Our Character Abroad," *Pensacola Gazette*, May 2, 1828.

5. Lawrence M. Friedman, *Crime and Punishment in American History* (New York: Basic Books, 1993), 74; Adam J. Hirsch, *The Rise of the Penitentiary: Prisons and Punishment in Early America* (New Haven: Yale University Press, 1992); Mark E. Kann, *Punishment, Prisons, and Patriarchy: Liberty and Power in the Early American Republic* (New York: New York University Press, 2005); David J. Rothman, *The Discovery of the Asylum: Social Order and Disorder in the New Republic* (New York: Aldine de Gruyter, 2002); Michael Meranze, *Laboratories of Virtue: Punishment, Revolution, and Authority in Philadelphia, 1760–1835* (Chapel Hill: University of North Carolina Press, 1996).

6. "Florida—and the 'Floridian,'" *Richmond Enquirer*, December 13, 1821.

7. Jane Landers, *Black Society in Spanish Florida* (Urbana: University of Illinois Press, 1999).

8. Ernest F. Dibble, *Ante-bellum Pensacola and the Military Presence* (Pensacola: Pensacola News-Journal, 1974).

9. *Pensacola Gazette*, August 7, 1822, August 11, 1829, October 13, 1838.

10. "Pensacola," *Louisiana Advertiser*, August 16, 1820.

11. "Extract of a Letter Dated Pensacola, May 14th," *Connecticut Mirror*, June 21, 1824.

12. James Parton, *Life of Andrew Jackson*, vol. 2 (Boston: Houghton, Mifflin, 1888), 632.

13. Leonora Sutton, "Pensacola Jails, 1776–1920," Sutton Manuscript Collection, Pensacola Historical Society.

14. Edward L. Ayers, *Vengeance and Justice: Crime and Punishment in the 19th-Century American South* (New York: Oxford University Press, 1984), 35.

15. Joseph G. Baldwin, *Flush Times of Alabama and Mississippi: A Series of Sketches* (San Francisco: Bancroft-Whitney, 1901), 59.

16. James M. Denham, *"A Rogue's Paradise": Crime and Punishment in Antebellum Florida, 1821–1861* (Tuscaloosa: University of Alabama Press, 1997), 182.

17. Ibid., 185.

18. "A Bigamous Scoundrel," *West Florida Times*, March 17, 1857.

19. William F. Steele to the Secretary of State, Clarence Edwin Carter, May 22, 1822, in *The Territorial Papers of the United States*, vol. 22 (Washington, D.C.: U.S. Government Printing Office, 1934), 447–48.

20. "Pensacola," *Pensacola Gazette*, October 24, 1835.

21. Brian Rucker, "Hutto the Highwayman," *Pensacola History Illustrated* 4, no. 3 (Spring 1995): 13–19.

22. Walker, *Trial and Imprisonment*, 18.

23. David J. Rothman noted that since the eighteenth century, "jails in fact closely resembled the house-hold in structure and routine." *Discovery of the Asylum*, 55.

24. Walker, *Trial and Imprisonment*, 14–15.

25. Ibid., 16, 19–21, 23–24.

26. Ibid., 16–17, 20–23.

27. "Pensacola, July 29, 1844," *Boston Emancipator and Weekly Chronicle*, August 28, 1844.

28. "Letter from Jonathan Walker," *Boston Emancipator and Weekly Chronicle*, May 21, 1845.

29. Rothman, *Discovery of the Asylum*, 85–86, 97–98.

30. "Jonathan Walker," *Pensacola Gazette*, September 6, 1845.

31. Walker, *Trial and Imprisonment*, 70.

32. Ibid., 46.

33. Ibid., 25.

34. "Jonathan Walker."

35. Elizabeth B. Clark, "The Sacred Rights of the Weak: Pain, Sympathy, and the Culture of Individual Rights in Antebellum America," *Journal of American History* 82, no. 2 (September 1885): 465.

36. Theodore Dwight Weld, *American Slavery as It Is: Testimony of a Thousand Witnesses* (New York: American Anti-Slavery Society, 1839); Frederick Douglass, *Narrative of the Life of Frederick Douglass: An American Slave* (Boston: Anti-Slavery Office, 1845).

37. Walker, *Trial and Imprisonment*, 26–27.

38. Ibid.

39. Friedman, *Crime and Punishment in American History*, 74.

40. Ayers, *Vengeance and Justice*, 102.

41. Walker, *A Picture of Slavery, for Youth* (Boston: J. Walker and W. R. Bliss, 1846), 14.

42. Douglass, *Narrative of the Life of Frederick Douglass*, 32–33.

43. Jonathan Walker, *Trial and Imprisonment*, 32.

44. Ibid., 18, 24, 47, 69–70; Walker copied the quoted material from Dugald Moore's "The African," in *The African, a Tale; and Other Poems*, 2nd ed. (Glasgow: Robertson & Atkinson, 1833), 12.

45. Ayers, *Vengeance and Justice*, 61.

46. "$600 Reward," *Pensacola Gazette*, January 18, 1828.

47. "$1000 Reward," *Pensacola Gazette*, August 25, 1838.

48. "Ranaway," *Pensacola Gazette*, July 22, 1837.

49. "$30 Reward," *Pensacola Gazette*, April 15, 1837.

50. Walker, *Trial and Imprisonment*, 66.

51. Douglas R. Egerton, *Death or Liberty: African Americans and Revolutionary America* (New York: Oxford University Press, 2009), 157–58.

52. Weld, *American Slavery as It Is*, 54–55.

53. Walker closed his brief discussion of the suicide with a remark that tantalizes as much as it confounds: "This was one of the seven slaves whom I had vainly endeavored to save from bondage, and on whose account I was now imprisoned." Walker claimed to have known the suicide victim, and the newspaper confirms that the owner of the bondsman was a servant of George Willis's father, Colonel Byrd C. Willis, who claimed ownership of Anthony Catlett—one of the men who absconded with Walker. Yet, estate records reveal that Catlett was both very much alive and still enslaved by the Willis family years later. Inexplicably, Walker seems to have mistaken the bondsman's identity. "Suicide," *Pensacola Gazette*, September 7, 1844; Walker, *Trial and Imprisonment*, 21.

54. Sally E. Hadden, *Slave Patrols: Law and Violence in Virginia and the Carolinas* (Cambridge, Mass.: Harvard University Press, 2001).

55. Walker, *Trial and Imprisonment*, 68–69.

56. George Teamoh, *God Made Man, Man Made the Slave: The Autobiography of George Teamoh*, ed. Nash Boney, Rafia Zafar, and Richard Hume (Macon, Ga.: Mercer University Press, 1990), 175–76.

57. "Pensacola," *Pensacola Gazette*, June 15, 1839.

58. "Pensacola," *Pensacola Gazette*, June 24, 1848.

59. Walker, *Trial and Imprisonment*, 45–46, 50–51.

Afterword

LESLIE PATRICK

THE VOICES OF THE POOR AND THE PUNISHED can be hard to hear. Inmates confined to the jails, almshouses, prison ships, and penitentiaries of early America have long struggled to be heard over the clamor of voices belonging to the administrators, reformers, and politicians whose accounts of the expansion of penal power and definitions of the incarcerated dominate the historical record. The essays gathered here argue that the voices of the poor and punished deserve a hearing. Close attention to the words, actions, and injuries of those confined behind bars is essential if we are to understand the nature of carceral institutions, the power that they wield, and the role that they have played in shaping the modern state. Societies reveal themselves through how they define deviance and how they punish it.

The authors of *Buried Lives* reject an older, celebratory scholarship that paid little attention to the negative effects of incarceration upon their subjects and took the claims made about both the institutions and their inmates at face value. Rather, by giving subalterns their due, these scholars challenge us to look critically at what American "enlightenment" and "revolution" meant to the people who did not enjoy their putative benefits.

Serious difficulties have stood in the way of such a seemingly obvious enterprise. The history of carceral institutions has, until fairly recently

282

and with some important exceptions, assumed the perspective of those in authority.[1] Inmates' voices often survive in the historical record only in muted and highly mediated forms. Scholars must thus read past the rhetoric and against the grain to recover the vicissitudes of penal practices, bearing in mind that the voices of the incarcerated did not speak in unison. Their expressions were as varied as their experiences. This collection demonstrates both the inherent richness of the material available and how we might ask new questions of existing sources.

Furthermore, with few exceptions, carceral institutions have generally been examined in isolation from one another, thus making even cursory comparisons of the inmate experience difficult to accomplish. Almshouses and penitentiaries have their own histories and historians, as do the institutions of slavery and the military. On one level, they were enclosed worlds of their own. Yet, on another level, historiographical separation obscures both the commonalities of incarceration and the larger social and political purposes that confinement served.

Buried Lives points the way forward. The incarcerated individuals who populate this volume constitute but a fraction of the tens of thousands of men and women who lived on or near the margins of poverty and transgression. Narratives of investigation and incarceration can tell us much about the circumstances of the lower sorts and, especially, about how they were defined and dealt with by the authorities. Inmates were at the mercy of the authorities just as the enslaved were at the mercy of masters, and they had few means with which to defend themselves. Yet, they were not passive. The ways in which they sought to improve their circumstances and contest their repression by persons in authority raises the question of a counternarrative, a history of penal practices from within and below.

However, scholars must also step back and consider the wider context in which these people encountered authority that punished the poor, jailed the enslaved, tortured military captives, and did little or nothing to rehabilitate prisoners. These practices were aimed at changing the individual, not the conditions that gave rise to their alleged transgressions. Contextualization raises a number of further points. One addresses the purpose of incarceration. Officially, incarceration was designed to reform as well as to confine; from the perspective of inmates, however, these institutions revealed the capriciousness of authority and their own vulnerability. Reform was another manifestation of the power to define the reality of others. Another examines the definition of transgression and the ways in which it was embedded in relations of power. Transgression might, however, have different meanings, depending on one's vantage point. To what extent did inmates' self-presentation challenge or conform to the categorization imposed upon them? Were inmates able to make use of both the institutions themselves and the way in which they were viewed for their own ends? Consideration of these wider issues links incarceration to its context and at the same time further problematizes it in ways that promise to be fruitful for the study not only of carceral institutions themselves but also of the formation of American society, for the power to punish was central to the nation's development.

Indeed, putting the experiences of inmates at the center allows us to see beneath the self-interested pieties of reform and nationhood to the heavy toll that confinement exacted on the minds and bodies of its subjects. This does not imply that we should substitute a celebration of the oppressed for that of the oppressor. What is required is the scholarly fortitude to move beyond imagination and to confront and convey the reality for so many of America's lower sorts. As Richard J. Evans observes in his study of crime and punishment: "It is important to remember that what we are dealing with here is real bodily violation, real suffering, real violence, real death."[2]

Buried Lives signals a welcome beginning. By keeping the focus on the voices of inmates, it opens up new perspectives on the social, not just the institutional, history of punishment. Furthermore, by including studies of a variety of different carceral institutions, it suggests connections among them within the wider context of the continuous drive for social control that so characterized the English colonies that became the new republic.

NOTES

1. Historical scholarship critical of penal institutions began with Georg Rusche and Otto Kirchheimer, *Punishment and Social Structure* (New York: Columbia University Press, 1939).

2. Richard J. Evans, *Rituals of Retribution: Capital Punishment in Germany, 1600–1987* (Oxford: Oxford University Press, 1996), xiii.

CONTRIBUTORS

RICHARD BELL is assistant professor of history at the University of Maryland, College Park. He is the author of *We Shall Be No More: Suicide and Self-Government in the Newly United States* (2012) as well as several articles examining the cultural politics of violence in early America.

JACQUELINE CAHIF is a research associate at the University of Cambridge. She is at work on a medical history project, funded by the Wellcome Trust, that examines the relationship between venereal disease and fertility. She received her PhD from the University of Glasgow in 2010; her dissertation is titled "'She Supposes Herself Cured': Almshouse Venereal Women in Late Eighteenth and Early Nineteenth Century Philadelphia."

MATTHEW J. CLAVIN is associate professor of history at the University of Houston. He is the author of *Toussaint Louverture and the American Civil War: The Promise and Peril of a Second Haitian Revolution* (2009) and numerous articles on race, slavery, and memory in the United States and Atlantic world.

JENNIFER LAWRENCE JANOFSKY is a lecturer in American history at Villanova University, where she teaches classes in the History of Philadelphia and Public History. She has worked as a historical consultant at the Eastern State Penitentiary Historic Site for the past thirteen years, helping to research and design exhibits documenting the penitentiary's past.

JUDITH I. MADERA is assistant professor of English at Wake Forest University. She studies constructions of race, colonization, and environment in American literature and letters before 1900. Her recent scholarship has appeared in *Radical History Review, Discourse, Journal of American History,* and *Nineteenth-Century Prose.*

MICHAEL MERANZE is professor of history at the University of California, Los Angeles. He is the author of *Laboratories of Virtue: Punishment, Revolution, and Authority in Philadelphia, 1760–1835* (1996) and the co-editor (with David Garland and Randall McGowen) of *America's Death Penalty: Between Past and Present* (2011).

SIMON P. NEWMAN is the Sir Denis Brogan Professor of American History at the University of Glasgow. He is the author of *Parades and the Politics of the Street* (1997) and *Embodied History: The Lives of the Poor in Early Philadelphia* (2003).

SUSAN EVA O'DONOVAN is associate professor of history at the University of Memphis. She is a former member of the Freedmen & Southern Society Project; coeditor of the documentary history, *Land and Labor, 1865* (2008); and author of *Becoming Free in the Cotton South* (2007). She is also a recipient of the James A. Rawley Prize from the Organization of American Historians.

LESLIE PATRICK is associate professor of history at Bucknell University. She writes on race and penal practices in the colonial and early republic, most notably on the Walnut Street Prison ("Numbers That Are Not New: African Americans in the Country's First Prison, 1790–1835," *PMHB* [1995]) and Eastern State Penitentiary (*Historic Structures Report,* 1994).

JODI SCHORB is assistant professor of English at the University of Florida. She has published articles in *Legacy, Tulsa Studies in Women's Literature,* and *Early Native Literacies in New England: A Documentary and Critical Anthology* (2008). She is writing a book on prisoner writing and literacy instruction in the long eighteenth century.

JASON T. SHARPLES is assistant professor of history at the Catholic University of America. He is working on a book project called *Mastering Fear: Imagination, Rebellion, and Race in Early America and the Atlantic World, 1640–1800*.

BILLY G. SMITH is professor of history and Distinguished Professor of Letters and Science at Montana State University. His primary research interests focus on issues of class, race, gender, geography, and disease in early America and the Atlantic world. His *Ship of Death: The Voyage That Changed the Atlantic World* is forthcoming from National Geographic books.

CALEB SMITH is associate professor of English and American studies at Yale University. He is the author of *The Prison and the American Imagination* (2009), and he edits the website Imagined Prisons (*www. imaginedprisons.org*).

MICHELE LISE TARTER is associate professor of English at The College of New Jersey. She has published articles on eighteenth-century Quaker women's writing, and is coeditor of *"A Centre of Wonders": The Body in Early America* (2001). She teaches a memoir-writing program for inmates in New Jersey's only maximum-security prison for women.

DANIEL E. WILLIAMS is professor of English and director of TCU Press at Texas Christian University. His area of focus is American print culture from the Revolution to the antebellum era, and he has specialized in narratives of crime and captivity. He is the author and editor of *Pillars of Salt* (2002) and *Liberty's Captives* (2006), as well as numerous articles.

INDEX

Note: Italicized locators indicate illustrations. A locator followed by *t* indicates a table.

abolitionists: incarcerated with slaves, 24, 125–27, 136–37; as transatlantic movement, 260–61, 268–70, 275–76

Account of the Alteration and Present State of the Penal Laws of Pennsylvania, An (Lownes), 207–8, 210–11, 213, 228n10

"Address of the Grand Jury" (Lownes), 207

Adshead, Joseph, *Prisons and Prisoners,* 242–52

Africans/African Americans: as almshouse residents, 66, 72, 75; in antebellum Florida, 263–79; Antigua conspiracy panic, 35–59; education of, 159–64; migration to Philadelphia of, 61–62, 67; militancy of, 62; racism against, 212, 219, 222, 257n30, 261–62, 269, 279; restricted emplyment op-

portunities, 66, 69–70; in Walnut Street Prison, 211–12, 219. *See also* race/class distinctions

alcohol: in almshouses and jails, 70–71, 74, 213; in treatment of venereal disease, 88

Allen, Stephen, *Reports on the Stepping or Discipline Mill, 16*

almshouses: admission system for, 89–91, 98–99; applicants to, 65, 77, 85–86, 95–96; children in, 65, 70–71, 80; contrasted with jails, 70–72; escape from, 66, 71–73, 78, 85, 92–96, 103n24; financial difficulties of, 78–79; inmates of, 63–70, 63*t*; for moral reform, 70–72, 74, 86; as precursor to hospitals, 100; and prostitutes, 66–68, 69*t*, 86–100, 101n4, 102nn10–11, 103n17; slaves in, 66, 72, 75–76; and social offenders, 11, 15, 60–62; as winter refuge, 74–75, 79–80, 82n27, 95; and workhouses, 64, 70–72. *See also* venereal wards

charivari. *See* riots/violence

Charlestown (Mass.), prisoner uprising, 17

children in almshouses, 65, 70–71, 80

Church of England, literacy education efforts, 161, 164–67

Clark, Elizabeth B., 270

Clarke, Mary, 204, 214, 220, 222–25

clergy, 1–3, 9, 151–54, 167

Cobb, R. R., 130

Coffey, W. A., *Inside Out . . . by One Who Knows*, 20, 21

Coffin, Alexander, "The Destructive Operation of Foul Air . . . ," 178–79, 187–90

Cohen, Daniel, 151, 155–56, 174n52

Collins, Philip, 242, 257n30

communication: and Antigua conspiracies, 35–42; of Eastern State inmates, 109–12, 119–21; of enslaved inmates, 24, 44–45, 53–54, 125–38; of inmates and passersby, 126; politics of talk, 138–40; restricted by prison reformers, 17–18, 150, 168–69, 210, 234–36. *See also* isolation; solitary confinement

communications circuit, 151–56

congregate-labor model. *See* Auburn (New York) system

Congregationalists, 165–67, 195

conspiracies: Ann Carson gang, 205–6, 225–26; Antigua slave rebellion, 23, 35–59; arson plots, 39–40; averted plots, 55n2; British Navy accused of, 178; investigation of, 40–46, 50, 53–54, 58n27; New Providence island, 39; New York,

58n27; and social connections, 53–54; Staunch Gang, 251

The Converted Sinner (Mather), 153

copyright: Dickens's advocacy of, 240; held by Ann Carson, 224; purchased by Eastern State from Ryno, 250

corporal punishment: at Auburn and Sing Sing, 110; ideal vs. reality, at Eastern State, 110; as race-based, 269–74; reformers' view of, 18; of slaves, 271, 21, 24, 129, 262, 269

Creole (slave ship), 137

Creoles, of Florida, 263–64

crime: capital, in eighteenth century, 9–10, 12; conspiracy as, 53–54; poverty as, 60–62, 79–80; public punishment for, 10–11; reevaluation of penalties, 12–15; vagrancy as, 60–62, 67, 69*t*; of vagrants, 69*t*. *See also* death penalty

Cummings, John, 85, 89, 96–100, 105n51

Darby, Philip, 44

Darlington District, S.C., jail, 129

Darnton, Robert, 154

Dartmoor Prison massacre, 219, 228n16

Davis, Angela, 233

death: civil *vs.* social, 26; in fetid jails, 129; incarceration as, 182–84, 190–91, 233, 239, 245, 252, 254; prisoners' spiritual readiness for, 1, 3, 156–57, 159–64, 167; on prison ships, 176–77, 198n7; from torture or flogging, 42, 261–63, 269–79, 271, 272; from venereal disease, 100